THE

LITTLE

BIG

NUMBER

THE

LITTLE
BIG
NUMBER

HOW GDP CAME TO RULE THE WORLD
AND WHAT TO DO ABOUT IT

DIRK PHILIPSEN

Princeton University Press
Princeton and Oxford

Copyright © 2015 by Princeton University Press

Published by Princeton University Press, 41 William Street, Princeton, New Jersey 08540

In the United Kingdom: Princeton University Press, 6 Oxford Street, Woodstock, Oxfordshire OX20 1TW

press.princeton.edu

Jacket background image: Detail of Stanford's General Map of the world on Mercator's projection. London: Edward Stanford, 1922.

All Rights Reserved

Library of Congress Cataloging-in-Publication Data

Philipsen, Dirk, 1959–

    The little big number : how GDP came to rule the world and what to do about it / Dirk Philipsen.

        pages cm

    Includes bibliographical references and index.

    ISBN 978-0-691-16652-0 (hardback) — ISBN 0-691-16652-8 (hardcover)   1. Gross domestic product.   I. Title.

    HC79.I5P515 2015

    339.3'1—dc23

                              2014044458

British Library Cataloging-in-Publication Data is available

This book has been composed in Minion Pro and Gill Sans

Printed on acid-free paper. ∞

Printed in the United States of America

10 9 8 7 6 5 4 3 2 1

CONTENTS

ACKNOWLEDGMENTS

This book was a long time coming. Without an enormous amount of input and support of lots of people, its very conception would not have been possible. Its core ideas rest on a rich intellectual tradition of excellent scholarship that is radical in its attempts to decipher the roots of cultural and social organizing principles. I owe much debt to those mentioned in footnotes and the bibliography, and there are many more.

Over the course of seven years, the manuscript went through dozens of drafts, more or less useful experiments, and new starts. Several ideas I considered downright priceless at one point or another ended up in the trash bin. Many words put down with great effort proved superfluous or worse in the way of clear expression.

Every idea has a history. And for it to get developed and brought to light requires an environment that inspires and prods and supports and pushes back and contributes meaning. Above all people. People who both build context and are the product of it. People who struggle, design, construct, and deconstruct. People who, in the process of interacting, create this endlessly rich tapestry of experiences that can never be reduced to a simple measure.

A number of wonderful friends helped me throughout this process—listening, reading, debating, probing, responding, and, without exception, providing invaluable suggestions. Sections of drafts throughout the years were read by Peter Wood, John Srygley, Chris Caldwell, Susanne Freytag, Klaus Philipsen, Larry Goodwyn, Thad Williamson, John Wagner, Niklas Philipsen, Randall Kramer, Veit Hannemann, Tom Levinson, Tom Nechyba, Bill Chameides, and students of my "History of Capitalism" course. Thanks so much to all of you.

In the spring of 2013, I finished the last chapter—finally a full manuscript. But then relocation of family, new appointment, and illness prevented completion. A vital—and very creative—push to pass the last hurdle was initiated by my colleague Walter Sinnott-Armstrong. He offered his support (not to mention his house) to bring together a group of readers who would spend one full Saturday discussing the manuscript. Grateful yet also somewhat frightened by the prospect of twelve people taking apart my work, the result was one of the most intellectually enhancing experiences I've ever had. It was also a day of spirited community among a diverse group of people.

For their time and effort to read the whole manuscript, and for the wide range of thoughtful, probing, and creative responses, my deep thanks to Walter Sinnott-Armstrong, Renée Hill, John Srygley, Michaeline Crichlow, Michael Hardt, Shana Starobin, Bill Greider, Norman Wirzba, Alexa Dilworth, Mac McCorkle III, Tony Hughes, and Wesley Hogan-Philipsen. Our discussions lasted deep into the night; my apologies for tired flights home the next day.

Good work requires material support—time, of course, but also money to pay the bills, allow for research trips, or provide release from classes to teach or yet another committee meeting to attend. Critical material support for the research behind this book came from the Mellon Foundation, Duke University's John Hope Franklin Center, and the National Endowment for the Humanities. I am deeply grateful for their confidence in this project. Particular thanks goes to Srinivas Aravamudan, who did much to afford me a fantastic sabbatical experience.

Without the expert advice of archivists who pointed me in the right direction at the National Archives, the Harvard Archives, and the Library of Congress, I would have missed many a lead. Patiently and kindly, they guided me through a labyrinth of sources. I can't thank them enough.

I am very grateful to my editors at Princeton. Special thanks to Seth Ditchik for adopting and believing in this project; Karen Fortgang and Samantha Nader for shepherding a large manuscript through the production process with authority and grace; Dimitri Karetnikov for an excellent job with images and graphs; and Linda Truilo, whose thorough copyediting job I could always trust to catch those many little errors in style and formatting that creep into a manuscript.

Over the years, I consulted with countless experts and scholars here and abroad. Some might distance themselves from several of the arguments made in this book. I learned much from those conversations, yet responsibility for conclusions drawn lies entirely with me.

Toward the end of the project, a random medical emergency almost pushed me off the cliff. Pulling me back to safety with two complicated surgeries, I have the kind of special gratitude for Dr. Mark Shapiro, Dr. Michael Barfield, and their excellent team at Duke University Hospital usually reserved for mothers—I owe my life to them.

Special thanks also to my friends and colleagues and students at the Kenan Institute for Ethics at Duke University. Collectively they have created an environment in which exploration and creative exchange of ideas is both cherished and supported. I am very grateful for that.

My heart-felt appreciation to Leff and Jenny Lefferts, who, with indomitable spirit and hospitality, opened their beautiful home in San Francisco to me for the last round of frantic edits.

Words don't always suffice. She listened to me, asked questions, prodded me to clarify—from the beginning to end of this project. She helped me find sources and navigate archives. Over and over, she kindly but persistently suggested cuts to my long-winded Germanic prose. Despite her own full-time job, she held down the home and was there for our children when I was away on sabbatical. With all the research in place, she gave me another priceless gift: a year of WLAMF (Write Like a Mother$*%@#). It came with a certificate, a mug, a reprieve from household chores, and a deadline: one year later, have a completed first draft.

After she was appointed to a demanding academic leadership position, she spent a large part of her first three months on the new job working long hours before coming to the hospital, finding what little rest there was to be had on an uncomfortable recliner, lending support and comfort. Her kindness, curiosity, and open mind continue to inspire me. Her high standards and relentless intelligence make me strive, every day, to be a better person. My best friend, my comrade in struggle, my wife: Wesley Hogan-Philipsen. In deep appreciation and love, I aspire to be for her what she has been to me.

As the manuscript suggests, I believe that future generations have rights equal to our own. Conscious or not, the world currently operates under an organizing principle that fundamentally violates the rights of the young, the poor, the voiceless, and the as yet unborn. It is to all those, including my four children Niklas, Shamus, Sven, and Chloë, that I dedicate this book.

THE
LITTLE
BIG
NUMBER

INTRODUCTION

We Become What We Measure

The significant problems we face cannot be solved by
the same level of thinking that created them.

—*Albert Einstein*

This book tells the story of an invention—an invention that grew, in one single lifetime, from narrow tool to global rule. Today, this invention provides the underlying rationale for much of what we do, even if we strongly dislike some of its results. People and governments around the world follow its logic, independent of ideology or creed. The story itself is broadly seen as providing hope for a better future. Success and prosperity, it is said, depend on it. In the end, it effectively dictates the direction of our lives.

It is an invention that stands alone. Few, if any, can match its reach.

Its greatest power, however, may lie in its virtual invisibility. Deeply internalized, the story behind the invention is discussed only on the margins of political debate. Indeed, questioning the logic of the invention one risks losing cultural sanction.

Few inventions have ever possessed more cultural authority. It comes as somewhat of a surprise that the invention is actually quite new, its current definition newer still. Or that almost no one knows where it came from—why it was developed, and for what purpose.

From a distance, one could capture the invention in three words: growth is good. The idea is so widely sanctioned that its premise is rarely discussed. It has become an article of faith: growth gives rise to progress and prosperity; lack of growth leads to depression and misery. People and governments across the globe believe in it, and do whatever they can to support it. National economies and world systems are organized around it. Our collective compass of success is calibrated by it. Growth, in the words of two skeptical economists, represents "the beckoning buoy toward which all humanity must sail."[1]

But if our standards of living depend on continued growth, how to make sense of the fact that many of us experience a loss of purpose and foresee declining prospects for our children as we push the planet to its limits? What does it mean, in short, when people from political left to right have deeply internalized faith in growth, yet the regime of growth not only fails to deliver on its promise, but also leads us down a path of mounting dangers?

My exploration of this question began in a classroom. A graduate student in my "History of Capitalism" course asked, "How do we measure success? How do we know we're on the right track?" It was an excellent question, but one that caught me off guard. As an economic historian, I was familiar with standard answers. I told her about economic performance indicators that generally drive decision-making, small and large. By far the most important is something called "Gross Domestic Product" (GDP). One little number with enormous power. In fact, most other economic measures directly derive from it; few aspects of our lives escape it. Yet I realized that this number, however big its impact, was not much of an answer for my student.

Trying to clarify, I later ran this by her: "Imagine a pill-dependent smoker who, on the way to his divorce lawyer, crashes his oversized car into a school bus because he is texting about an impending derivatives trade. Then suppose he survives, pays his many legal and medical bills, and continues to consume expensive gas, harmful cigarettes, and addictive pharmaceuticals. Contrary to common sense, he fits the profile of a modern economic hero—someone who purchases a lot of goods and requires a lot of services, including fossil fuel, gadgets, medical care, lawyers' fees, and financial advice." My point was this: according to standard accounting, his path, however reckless it may be, would significantly boost "economic growth." According to governing assumptions, it therefore increases our standard of living and contributes to our collective "well-being." After all, he has added more than his share to the GDP.

Surely, this example of excessive living was short of a complete answer. For one, it did not yet say anything about the structural imperatives that sponsor such conduct, or what purposes mindless growth might serve, why the logic that more is better remains strangely invisible, much less why we continue to follow the promise of endless growth despite growing awareness of its many flaws. Yet the story began to illuminate a central dilemma. Our measures frequently fail to reflect what we want.

What does GDP measure? In essence, the totality of goods and services produced.[2]

This led straight back to the initial question: Is GDP a good indicator for success? Is it really something we should pursue? Put differently: how did it happen that the compass we collectively follow is so narrow and in many cases actually points us in a direction opposite to what we, as citizens and family members, value and believe? Can this be explained in ways that make any sense?

Big questions to which I had no good answers. A few weeks earlier, I had watched a documentary on the consequences of climate change with my oldest son. Though rather technical, the dire predictions underlying the film's central message clearly caught this 14-year-old's attention. When it was over, he looked straight into my eyes and somberly inquired, "Dad, what're you going to do about this?" First tempted to reassure him with something like "it'll all be fine," I proceeded to tell him about recycling, buying a smaller car, and turning down the thermostat. Not very good answers either. My responses barely scratched the surface of the problem.

Perhaps a better way to think about it should have been obvious all along. The two questions—how to measure real success, and how to respond to bad measures, particularly when they dominate our lives and lead to tragic results—are intimately related. From Amsterdam to Beijing and Rio to Washington, economies and cultures have hitched their hopes and aspirations to growth. Success and well-being is largely defined by growth. Growth, in turn, is defined by GDP.[3] And GDP is a blind meter: it counts only output; it ignores costs and losses.

The logic is deceptively persuasive: more is better. Until we realize the measure never asks "more of what?" It's like saying, as business owners or teachers or parents, "we want more activity," without ever specifying what kind of activity.

But the failure goes beyond a lack of direction and purpose. The logic of GDP foresees no end to growth. Our collective performance can receive an A+ even if large numbers of people are out of work, a sense of community and purpose is disappearing, inequality is rising, resources are depleted, and nature is turned into parking lots. Endless growth on a finite planet simply does not add up.

Bad measures inevitably lead to bad results.[4]

Both my student and my son deserved a better answer. The basic questions remained. First and foremost, what is the purpose or objective of our economy? Has there ever been a deliberate and public conversation around this question? And once a goal can be identified, what indicators do we have for our success?

"An economy is a mode of social cooperation based on a system of rewards and incentives."[5] In today's economies, this essentially means we do what we get paid for. Modern economies rely on a complex system of rules that define markets and taxes and income to provide incentives and to determine rewards. In essence, they decide what we do and don't get paid for.

Our most important performance measure says nothing about whether quality of life is improving, or even if our activities are viable. It only tells us about how much stuff was produced, and how much money has exchanged hands.[6] As a result, cultures around the world promote, quite literally, blind and mindless growth—and increasingly dangerous growth. And they do so largely independent of what they subjectively want.

We can recognize this dynamic in our own lives. Measures like grades or degrees or income provide easy and convenient placeholders for a complex reality. They also represent a target that substitutes for the purpose of our actions. They tend to replace deliberation and reflection. A goal of acquiring more money, say, can effectively replace questions about meaning or consequence of what's needed to achieve it. Meaningful work may be the initial purpose. The measuring rod of income may be a very poor indicator; when the indicator becomes the goal, the purpose is effectively lost.

The target of GDP growth, of course, can be pursued in a variety of ways. Richer and more developed countries, for instance, can afford to pay more attention to things like family-leave, environmental protection, or alternative energy sources. Some political cultures may deliberately support family businesses while others reject, say, the use of nuclear energy. But no economy of scale has yet said "no" to the imperatives of GDP growth. Indeed, many political initiatives with broad popular support—from serious carbon emissions reductions to living wage campaigns—have faltered once they were perceived to threaten the preeminent goal of GDP growth. Despite all cultural differences, today's world pursues a common goal, tracked by a common measure.

And what we measure matters. Leading up to the French Revolution, peasants realized that, since landlords controlled the scales measuring the peasants' yields, peasants would not be assured a fair price. Landlords consistently fudged and cheated. Peasants routinely faced poverty and starvation. A central demand of the revolution thus became "one king, one law, one weight, one measure!" For their own good, they needed to know what got measured, and rely on *how* it got measured.

Clearly defining the units of measures did not quite solve the problem, however. Despite general agreement on units, sharecroppers in the American South could not trust plantation owners to measure crop yields fairly any more than citizens today can trust oil companies to calibrate their own gas pumps or meat producers to write and enforce meat safety regulations or athletes to self-monitor their drug tests. Simply put, clearly defined measures require transparent implementation and reliable enforcement.

Soviet workers discovered that if the rigid goals of the "five-year plan" determined success and rewards, people in charge of the books would simply resort to massive deception. In the end, no one knew in the Soviet Union how much was produced. Quality was abandoned and production crawled along with a staggering degree of inefficiency and waste.

Following bad metrics was not a problem unique to communism. At the very centers of high capitalism, the twenty-first century started out with financial speculators massively cooking the books with deceptive measures until they almost sank the entire world economy.

Bad measures can have devastating consequences.[7]

Choices about what to count, and how to count it, define many of our core values. In the case of an entire national economy, what we measure takes on additional significance, for it routinely defines what we think and do.[8] We thus need to know what we measure, and *why*.

Perhaps it's true to say without measures we would be adrift in a sea of unorganized thoughts and purposeless activity.[9] It is certainly true that with bad measures we fall captive to misguided activity following the illusion of organized thought.[10]

How does GDP stack up? As a measure of social well-being, GDP is akin to a personal calorie intake meter, tied to the notion that food is essential, ergo the more calories we consume, the better off we are. Hungry at first, we appreciate the focus on calories. Once sated, we soon find ourselves falling ill, overfed yet in the midst of a culture that keeps cajoling and pushing us toward more.[11]

This is not an indictment of all growth. Many kinds of growth are vital for an overall improvement in quality of life. But to GDP, which largely follows the logic of "converting nature into cash, and commons into commodities," quality is merely incidental.[12] This does not need to be so. There is nothing about growth that makes it inherently blind and indiscriminate. "Value is what we ascribe. Prosperity is what we make it to be."[13]

As I explore in detail in this book, GDP follows a deceptive logic.[14] It counts everything the economy produces, even if it leaves behind, in the words of an insightful early critic, "great furrows of wreckage."[15] It counts output without any distinction between the good and bad we put out.

Historically, there is little doubt that growth initially helped create unprecedented opportunities—for human expression, for learning, and for freedom itself. Yet the more central GDP has become, the more wreckage it has produced: depletion of resources, climate change, erosion of communities, social decay, rapid decline of biodiversity, a stark divide between haves and have-nots—and resulting endless conflict. Not surprisingly, the literature on the various shortcomings of GDP has ballooned in recent years.[16]

While this book builds on such critiques, its main objective is very different, something both bigger and more specific. It traces how and why a measure constructed in times of dire need, and with legitimate yet limited purpose, rose to global predominance. Why did cultures across the globe—

Americans, Europeans, even former communists in China and Russia—buy into this model and its logic, and do so lock, stock, and barrel? How did something constructed with the narrow purpose of *describing* a crisis subsequently turn into something *prescribing* what we do, effectively serving as a substitute for democratic deliberation and political ideals? How did a narrow tool turn into the measure of our lives? Above all, what happens to individuals and communities when they tie their hopes to the "bottom line?" In the end, how can we generate a much better set of tools that actually represent our collective aspirations?

Purpose, goals, indicators. What gets measured, how it gets measured, on which track we find ourselves—all are related; all define each other. In physics as in economics, the measures influence the outcomes.

This brings up another challenge. Deeply ingrained patterns of thinking tend to be hard to break. For several generations, economic growth (as defined by GDP) has been the dominant story, the logic of our culture. Most people alive today cannot remember a time when the performance of economies was not yet measured by GDP. It doesn't matter whether we call it our dominant paradigm, our hegemonic ideology, or our collective fishbowl. By representing both measure and goal, GDP defines what we do and why we do it. And who we are. Much like other familiar measures, "it is a language that is picked up automatically and spoken without conscious thought."[17] Yet unlike other familiar measures such as "yards to go" or "speed of sound," GDP defines not only a snapshot of a state but also implies a desirable direction.

It should give us pause when critics and defenders of capitalist economies alike have built their hopes and objectives on continued GDP growth. What are the underlying assumptions behind such global faith? What are its consequences?

It is simpler to perceive the crucial significance of measures in other's lives. We can grasp why peasants in Britain, for instance, used to measure land area not by size or prize, but by how many people it could sustain; or why some native Americans judged their actions not by wealth creation but by what impact it had on the seventh generation after them. Both confronted scarcity and survival on a very immediate level, in direct interaction with nature. Different times, different cultures: relatively easy to put under the microscope.

Ironically, the further removed from our own experiences, the better we tend to see.

Figuring out our own values and assumptions, on the other hand, is hard work. Trying to understand why we do what we do runs into many barriers, not least among them habit, fear, and self-interest. Sociologists are probably right when they say, "You have to step outside the line in order to see the line." As an American audience, for instance, try this experiment with an all-too-familiar social measure: imagine a culture without race. Sure, we can show that race did not always exist. We can trace its origins, analyze the reasons behind its invention, and explore its many manifestations over time. But can we envision life without it?

Much the same is true when it comes to the logic of GDP. As a human invention less than half as old as race, its tentacles are nevertheless deeply embedded in our thinking and doing. In critical areas of our lives, it is the air we breathe, represents the language we speak. National power is ranked by GDP. The state of the economy is determined by GDP. Corporations are evaluated by their contributions to GDP. The quality of education is judged by its role in growing GDP. The work (and only recently acquired prominence) of economists is tailored around GDP. Political fortunes depend on GDP. Progress itself, we are told, is a function of GDP. Not least of all, the development of cultures around the world from "tinkerers and producers" to societies of consumers, inhabiting a growing state of "disconnect from . . . modern existence," is a direct result of GDP growth.[18]

We tend to take it for granted and move on, continuing to follow the logic that well-being equals growth of GDP, blithely assuming that jobs and a decent standard of living for growing numbers of people depend on it. We need to know how all that happened, and why, because the course of the future depends on what economic signposts we follow. "He who holds the power to define is our master," reminds the cultural critic Neil Postman, but "he who holds in mind an alternative definition can never quite be his slave."[19]

Deeply ingrained thinking comes with authority—and dangers. As Easter Islanders realized some five hundred years ago, too late, cutting trees in the pursuit of earthly wealth and spiritual salvation was fraught with peril.

Running into inevitable lumber shortages on their confined plot of land, they heightened their resolve to fell trees.[20] Eventually left on a barren island bereft of lumber for their fishing boats or firewood for their stoves, the remaining islanders died from cannibalism and starvation.[21]

Rather than trust our presumed superiority to the Easter Islanders, it is my hope that, instead, we collectively start a serious conversation about what path we want to follow. What outcomes do we desire? And what measures can actually tell us whether we're moving toward those outcomes?

CASTING A SPELL

Before a conversation about goals can turn into a practical effort, however, we need to grapple with how it is possible that cultures and peoples around the world fell under the spell of a little opaque number? Why do they subscribe to far-reaching assumptions that cannot withstand basic tests of logic and experience? Here, we need to take a brief journey into the past—a past preceding the prevailing acceptance of a narrow worldview; a not-so-distant past in which GDP did not yet exist.

As well-worn truism has it, momentous events can change the course of history. In the United States, most people's thinking about what is normal and right, for instance, was likely altered in the aftermath of the bombing of Pearl Harbor or the attacks of 9/11.[22] Collective frames of reference moved. Values shifted. The course of history changed. How to evaluate success and failure transformed with it.

But then there are seismic developments that never appear on anyone's collective radar screen. Few are aware anything happened, much less realize how important it was. Consequently, we don't recognize any shift, even if something has effectively put our lives on a different track.

This book is about one such development. The story has multiple woven strands, but it is fitting to begin with a brief account of one man behind the creation. Parts of this story have been told before, but crucial elements have remained unexplored.

In the 1930s, the nation found itself in the midst of the deepest economic downturn of its history. Millions lost their jobs. Investments seemed to stall. Breadlines grew as long as despair grew deep. Yet no one in America possessed any reliable information on productivity, on income, on employment. The 261-page report that now lay in front of the meticulous scholar was, he knew, an astonishing accomplishment. He had labored, sometimes day and night, to put together basic tables on "national income"—or what he briefly defined as "that part of the economy's end product that results from the efforts of the individuals who comprise a nation."[23] On a shoestring budget, he and a small staff of six assistants had struggled to respond to a U.S. Senate request to provide basic and up-to-date information on the entire national economy.

Simon Kuznets officially submitted his report Thursday morning, 4 January 1934. As an economist and statistician wary of economic theories unmoored from solid data, Kuznets had been engaged in studies of national income ever since he joined the National Bureau of Economic Research (NBER) in 1929.[24]

Later scholars would argue the time was ripe for Kuznets's game-changing work.[25] Since national economies had reached unprecedented dimensions by the late 1920s, they generated unparalleled calamities when they ran into crises. The Great Depression was such a blow—deep, wide, international. Yet governments could intervene and provide a helping hand only if they had reliable economic data, if they knew on a national level what was going on with basic things like income and investment, with productivity and employment. Kuznets's Senate report provided such data for the first time.

In hindsight it is not too much to say that his work contributed to liberating the United States from the tyranny of economic ignorance.[26]

Kuznets, a Russian Jew, was born in 1901. His family was forced out of the country five years after the Bolsheviks took power in October 1917. Though personally familiar with revolution and upheaval, he did not anticipate the consequences of his own work.

His "national income" first provided the necessary foundation to implement and assess New Deal policies intended to lift America's economy out of the Depression. It subsequently supplied data essential to jumpstart military production, proving critical to American victory (as well as British and Soviet survival) in World War II. Then, in the changed post-1945 world, it resulted in a greatly expanded role of government in market economies around the world.

After the war, the "national income and product" calculation became known as Gross National Product, or GNP, a quarterly figure that quickly became shorthand for economic success in capitalist countries.[27] Since then, GDP accounts have provided the essential groundwork for policy tools that have led to unparalleled periods of economic growth and a remarkable reduction in the length, frequency, and duration of economic downturns in post–World War II capitalist economies.[28]

What's the difference between "GDP" and "GNP"? In essence, GDP is a measure of production within a country's borders (including by foreigners), whereas GNP measures production by a country's nationals (including those working in other countries). In short: goods produced in, say, a GM factory in Mexico would be included in U.S. accounts if we followed the GNP model, but would be part of Mexico's accounts if we followed the GDP model. In most industrialized countries the difference between the two is very small (though in some developing countries it can be as much as 50 percent). Since both GDP and GNP display the same characteristics discussed here, they can be used interchangeably for the purposes of this exploration.

By the early 1950s, GDP had become the coin of the realm for international trade and finance among all nations outside the Soviet and Chinese orbits. To get loans or trade with others, the world's nations had to implement GDP accounting processes.[29] For noncommunist nation-states, financial transactions and economic policy decisions were subsequently defined by the rules informing GDP. Following the 1978 economic reform policies in China, and the 1991 collapse of the Soviet Union, national income and product accounts virtually identical to the U.S. / UN template conquered the rest of the globe.

There is a GDP equivalent in every country.[30] In Germany it is *BIP (Bruttoinlandsprodukt)*, and in France *PIB (Produit Intérieur Brut)*. With virtually identical names in their respective languages, China has one, Russia has one, Brazil has one. All measure the same things, promote the same choices, and allow for simple comparisons across time and national boundaries. Because of its prominence, GDP has been celebrated as the most important and useful economic invention of the twentieth century.[31]

Some eighty years after its invention, it is hard to imagine a time in which national economies were not measured by GDP. Today, the tyranny of ignorance that characterized modern economies into the 1930s and helped bring about the Great Depression has been replaced by another kind of tyranny, that of a single metric.[32]

In fairness, dissenting voices existed from the beginning. A few have decried the GDP regime as promoting an economy where humans "steal from the future, sell it in the present, and call the process 'growth.'" A tiny minority goes as far as calling the GDP concept "primitive in the extreme and certainly useless for any adequate expression of growth."[33]

While the chorus of critics has grown over time, policymakers across the world and across the political spectrum still stand virtually unanimous: the most pressing task is robust GDP growth.

It begs the question: what's behind the official definition of "totality of goods and services produced?"[34] At first glance, it seems sheer common sense—GDP attempts to count the economic contributions of people, as well as the income they make from their contributions. Simple enough. Hidden below the overall intention, however, lurk choices and decisions invisible in our day-to-day lives. What are goods and services? How are they defined? Whose contributions count? What, in the end, are we growing?

Definitions are based on a still-evolving, cumbersome system of criteria. What is counted as investment or income or expenditure, and how to define the difference between "final" and "intermediate" consumption follows a logic that often eludes even accountants.[35]

To use economic growth as the barometer of success is a historically novel idea. To use GDP as the ultimate measure of economic performance is of even more recent vintage. This book explores the fundamental shift in thinking and the revolution in social relations that made GDP possible and, in turn, were later sanctified by GDP accounts. Values that had developed over thousands of years in many different cultural contexts were largely abandoned within a generation. In a process that started with industrialization and came to full fruition after World War II, value itself came to be defined in ways that challenged core global traditions, from the nature of work to the meaning of human existence.

Quality of life itself, or what the American tradition more precisely frames as the quality of *life, liberty, and the pursuit of happiness,* has no defined space in the pursuit of growth—it is not recognized as a category in our national and international economic ledgers. As such, our economic goals are fundamentally out of sync with our political and cultural achievements.[36]

EXPLORING A PATH

It ain't what you don't know that gets you into trouble.
It's what you know for sure that just ain't so.
—*Mark Twain*

Stepping out of the darkness cast by mysterious GDP rules it becomes possible to shed light on the underlying question: what are smart economic goals? It is a question, it turns out, that lies buried beneath layers of bad history, misleading measures, and deeply ingrained yet faulty cultural assumptions.

In every century there are sorcerers—clever individuals or groups who seem to hold magical powers of explanation and foresight that can be used for good or evil. Since the Great Depression, this mantle has often been worn by economists.[37] Many marvel at their arcane skills and seemingly predictive powers over chaotic forces, while others jeer and recoil at their alchemy and its debatable results. This book is the story of their most consequential creation: put together by well-intentioned practitioners, GDP has mutated from useful *descriptive* tool to *prescriptive* be-all and end-all, a collective goal at once momentous and nearly invisible.

The chapters that follow describe in some detail how GDP accounting informed responses to the Great Depression; helped win World War II; determined the amount and focus of Marshall Plan Aid to war-torn countries in Europe; helped decide the size of military budgets during the Cold War (and continues to be used as a measure for what is deemed necessary military expenditures);[38] unleashed a torrent of financial bail-out and stimulus packages and the printing of money (what the Federal Reserve calls "quantitative easing") during the Great Recession; and, in the end, has come to define the aspirations of every mainstream political ideology in the world, defining the lives of businesses, consumers, and politicians alike.

Yet the 2007–9 Great Recession revealed once again the stark limits of economists' powers and the bankruptcy of GDP as prescriptive tool.[39] Behind the activities promoting GDP growth, a profound crisis of purpose and direction flared. People began to realize that we had no indicators reliably tracing the nature of our predicament. Above all, the data that informed political interventions failed to portray the crisis in terms that adequately reflect the human experiences of regular citizens—not just in terms of jobs and housing or education, but also in terms of purpose, community, and dignity. The bottom line: What matters to people's lives matters less and less to the official accounts of the economy under GDP rule.[40]

The crisis shook the foundation of the larger system. Even strident defenders of the presumed underlying rationale of markets, like former Chairman of the U.S. Federal Reserve Board, Alan Greenspan, were forced to admit "a flaw in the model . . . that defines how the world works."[41]

But it is more than a flaw. Following the GDP logic is a self-inflicted problem. It is not a reflection of human nature or an inevitable result of the profit motive, nor is it necessary to run modern economies. Instead, its particular logic is directly traceable to a series of responses to 1930s disaster and war. The problem is that policymakers are using a 1930s tool for twenty-first century problems.

Around the globe, the primary purpose of governments today boils down to the need to avoid recessions (as exclusively measured by GDP). Trapped in this logic, governments rack up debt, manipulate markets, ignore rising inequality and social discontent, and turn into progenitors of various versions of disaster capitalism. They do so based on the faith that what matters above all is GDP growth. The consequences are at once curious and frightening. Former Secretary of the Treasury Tim Geithner, for instance, explained his coddling of big capital after the financial meltdown of 2008 thus: when growth rates are at risk "we have to do the opposite of what seems intuitive and fair." To which his interviewer replied, "You're essentially rationalizing an extortion scheme." It is the logic of the age of GDP.[42]

The story told in these pages will start with an exploration of how we got to this point. To evaluate the uniqueness of GDP as a historical phenomenon, chapter 1 explores the historical roots of evaluating economic success with such narrow focus, and, in chapter 2, traces the emergence of growth defined in monetary terms as the primary goal of economic activity. The journey will take us to the origin of GDP creation, the focus of chapter 3. It was in the midst of the Great Depression that policymakers, desperate for tools that would allow them to slow down the runaway train of economic disaster, asked for what eventually became "GDP."

Chapter 4 picks up the story after the initial creation of national accounts—what they looked like and how they were used. It is not until the Depression was supplanted by the dire needs of World War II that the first version of GDP was fully developed. Here the forerunner of today's GDP proved its worth, becoming central to the American and Allied victory. This is the story of chapter 5.

After World War II, with depression and crisis once again threatening, GDP became the yardstick for success even during times of peace. Chapter 6 traces the process by which GDP first became the leading economic indicator in the United States and Great Britain, then in astonishingly quick succession all capitalist nations, and finally all major economies around the world.

What is the world's leading measure of success? Chapter 7 explores in detail what GDP represents today—how it is defined, how it is used, and what exactly it measures. Chapter 8 shows the impact of GDP on our political and economic lives, and summarizes the work of many of its critics. Chapter 9 investigates the results of living under the spell of GDP. The crises and opportunities this presents for the future are surveyed in Chapter 10. Finally, chapter 11 explores a series of possible alternatives. The outline is informed by the criticism that the "father of GDP," Simon Kuznets, leveled against the eventual outcome of his own labors.

Books, not unlike fields of study, have traditionally been separated into genres and disciplines. They sprout their own languages, associations, and ways of doing things, including the need for clear demarcations within and between fields and disciplines. This never made much sense to me. It undermines the promise of full inquiry and violates the spirit of good science. A great deal of exceptional work—from Karl Polanyi's masterpiece on historical transformations to Rachel Carson's wakeup call about unintentional environmental impact or Thomas Piketty's recent opus on inequality—is done by thinkers who started with a problem or question, and then proceeded to learn and synthesize from whatever fields or disciplines pertinent to the subject at hand.[43]

I make no such expansive claims. But this book is the result of a deliberate attempt to be two things not usually found between the same two covers: sound original history and a call to action. Since the topic inevitably touches on some of the big questions of history, including humanity's ability to govern itself consciously, my attempt was to bridge a wide range of audiences. The narrative includes historical explorations based on original research as well as personal anecdotes, illuminating metaphors, and a good dose of clarifying analytical reflections.

I've spent seven years exploring how and why the modern world ended up following economic goals both largely invisible and by now dangerously anachronistic. What could be learned from the past to steer us toward a more deliberate, more democratic, and, above all, more sustainable course? By necessity, this drew me beyond historical thinking to investigations into economics, sociology, philosophy, anthropology, public policy, and environmental studies. Specialists in each field will undoubtedly feel that their discipline has not received appropriate coverage.[44]

Given the sheer scale of the question, there are also a lot of things this book is not. While I provide an informed overview of international developments, my detailed exploration is based on the countries where GDP originated. I hope scholars who follow might tackle detailed explorations of how the GDP logic spread into other societies such as India or China, as well as tease out diverse cultural responses to the same logic. There are significant differences between, say, Denmark, Japan, Nigeria, and the United States, yet all operate within the same GDP paradigm.

Poor countries in particular have suffered greatly under policies requiring austerity in order to create a stable environment for GDP growth. This was not a focus of this book, but represents an important field of research. There is also a related need for detailed studies tracing the correlation between the success/failure of particular policies and their perceived impact on GDP. Politics around the world has become a handmaiden to the imperatives of GDP. In the case of the United States, to my knowledge no single large-scale policy initiative since World War II—however meritorious—succeeded if it threatened GDP growth.

In the end, my goal was not to provide pat answers, but to explore paths and intersections necessary for a viable roadmap toward responses and initiatives that will, by necessity, continue to evolve. And such a map can be useful only if based on a clear understanding of decisions made in the past. How and why did we end up at this particular point?

Debate must continue. But the distance between reality and what humanity is able to accomplish, here and now, is wider, it seems to me, than it has ever been before. The most formidable obstacles toward a smarter future are likely not any of the rationalizations routinely marshaled to excuse inaction or laziness of thought—other people; political parties; government; entrenched power; narrow cultures; human nature. The greatest obstacle might well be lack of imagination—or, more precisely, historically informed imagination. I invite the reader to follow the explorations of traps we've created for ourselves historically—both structural and ideological—and then, no doubt, to quarrel or disagree with some conclusions drawn. Above all, however, I would like to promote a much more expansive conversation about possibilities.

Both our natural and our social environment provide mounting evidence that we are witnessing the inevitable end of the GDP growth era. By choice or by force, we soon will embark on another pivotal transformation in history. The confusion between promise and reality has become untenable; increasingly, throughout modern societies, people are becoming disenchanted, yearning for new guideposts that actually reflect values that affirm life and smart development. Yet a focus on the here and now obscures choices and opportunities we have. It ignores the treasure chest of available historical insights and is blind to openings the future inevitably provides. Above all, the quality of the new course we are going to chart will greatly depend on our ability to articulate better goals and design more deliberate performance measures. For that to happen we must first find out how we got to this place.

Throughout we can follow Simon Kuznets and ask, "What are we growing? And why?"[45]

Chapter 1

MORE, BETTER, FASTER

The Beginnings

*The paths to the future are not found, but made, and
the activity of making them changes both the maker
and the destination.*

—John Schaar

A measure logically requires something to be in place that can be measured. It also requires some ideas about how to define it. What is generally considered an "economy" today—some process by which goods and services are produced, sold, and bought—is an idea of very recent vintage. Indeed, it represents a concept that required many things to be in place before it could move from idea into reality. One crucial precondition was a nation-state able to articulate and enforce laws and regulations.

Given the many different purposes one could imagine for economic activities, as well as the many different ways in which goods and services could be defined, it seems odd indeed that today's modern economies all follow essentially the same goal. Marching to the same drummer, despite a multitude of cultural differences, one could even suspect, as Karl Polanyi put it, that people from the southernmost regions of South America to Greenland and everywhere in between are following a kind of "unconscious growth."[1]

In their personal and communal lives, individuals and groups around the world pursue a wide range of different goals. This may span from spiritual salvation to rational enlightenment, from helping others to seeking wealth. How, then, did these different people succumb to one overarching economic goal? How did this globally collective "we" allow our respective economies to strive exclusively for the growth of an abstract number, often without knowledge of what it represents?

A story of many roots and several offshoots, a brief history needs to explore productivity as an essential precondition for choices, investigate theories about growth, and examine the complicated question of how to measure our collective activities.

PRODUCTIVITY, GROWTH, AND SUCCESS

The purely economic man is . . . close to being
a social moron.
—*Amartya Sen*

For those of us who had an ample breakfast and can safely assume to have a plentiful dinner, it is easy to forget that we represent, historically, a minority. Even today, nearly one out of seven people in the world suffer from chronic undernourishment.[2] And though modern earthlings may nurture many unfounded, and routinely condescending, preconceptions about so-called primitive cultures of the past, it is safe to say that our ancestors, for some 200,000 years prior to the agricultural revolution, engaged in labor only to the very extent to which it helped them survive.

While subsistence depended on many factors, ranging from climate to skills to natural enemies, work essentially consisted of securing food and shelter. Survival ordinarily involved some variety of hunting, gathering, growing, building, and, not infrequently, a battle for one's life. The goal for thousands of years, and across cultures and continents, was living, not having. For self, family, and community, the basic measure of success was to carve out an existence in direct daily interaction with nature.[3]

Even as agricultural societies formed some ten to twelve thousand years ago, only a tiny fraction of people ever had more than the essentials. Most could not even count on those. While scholars continue to debate whether it is correct to argue "all of human history entailed an unending struggle with starvation," we do know that safety or abundance beyond one's immediate needs remained largely out of reach.[4] This state of affairs persisted for much of human history. Prior to the late eighteenth century, "everyone on earth lived nearly the same way—moving only as fast as a horse, pulling only as much as an ox, and preparing food, shelter, and clothing by hand."[5] To capture this reality with our modern fixation on the accumulation of things by saying that people were poor would represent a fundamental misread—understanding the past with the narrow lenses of today. What we can say, by our standards, is that life was generally slow and simple.

All this forever changed, first with the advent of global trade and then, enabled by it, with the industrial revolution. New inventions and new forms of production made possible a wholly new concept in human affairs: growth. Growth of production and output became possible through use and exploitation of resources and people. And growth in productivity allowed an increasing number of people—only capital-owning elites at first, but later majorities of entire nations—to think about life goals in material terms.[6]

Not until growth became possible—and vastly expanded the previous confinements of biology, physics, and knowledge—did conventional forms of social interaction break apart for good. Until then, the goals people strove for followed custom and, particularly in the cultural forerunners to capitalist economies, yielded a life "of monotony and toil."

Whether in Africa, Asia, or Europe, customs and traditions remained remarkably consistent for thousands of years. Kids did what their parents had done, whether or not they spent their existence "on the edge of hunger."[7] A closer look at what brought about this relative stability reveals causes in both material conditions and cultural norms. Together they created a kind of permanence that defies many of our deeply ingrained modern beliefs about how economic life is supposed to function.

Take work, for instance. From the cabinet-maker in the Scottish highlands to the Native American hunter to the East African fisherman, people worked in order to assure survival for themselves and their families. People did not work in order to accumulate wealth or power. With the exception of a very small elite of people who lived off of the labor of others—clergy, lords, masters—people lived directly from the products of their own labor, whether they were hunters, gatherers, farmers, or craftsmen. Communities generally supported their members. Unemployment was a concept that still awaited invention. Everybody had a role to play, defined by custom and tradition.

Wage labor—the idea that a person can freely sell her or his labor power to the highest bidder—did not become a common phenomenon until the emergence of industrial capitalism. Indeed, the need for people to sell their labor power in order to survive required another fundamental shift: the enclosure of the commons, as well as the invention of private property and the ability of property owners to exclude others from its use. Thus stripped of the capacity to make an independent living, those without property were forced into service of others, because the one and only thing over which they still possessed a measure of control was their ability to work.[8] Today, this describes the condition of the vast majority of people, from the most unskilled laborer to the most highly trained executive.

Perhaps the most consequential transition, however, did not concern where people worked, for whom they worked, or the knowledge and technology they used in accomplishing their work. It was a much less visible, though fundamentally life-altering transition: the separation of work from its immediate purpose.

For all of human history people worked for clear and tangible goals—survival, most fundamentally, but also the physical enrichment of lords and kings, the subsistence of religious leaders, or the splendor of sacred edifices. This work was done in direct interaction with nature. By and large, people controlled the product of their labor, even if they eventually had to give up large parts of it. It seems reasonable to assume that they had a clear sense of what they were doing, and who or what they were doing it for, whether they were shepherds or hunters, small farmers or artisans.

All this changed with what we may refer to as the emerging regime of capital, and its rapid spread of markets and money. As soon as wealth became untethered from its usual physical manifestations, such as acreage of land, size of buildings, number of people in service, the floodgates of growth burst open. Wealth as expressed in money became the new coin of the realm. And once everything—labor, goods, services of all kinds—could be expressed and exchanged with money, there no longer was a limit to the amount of wealth one could theoretically own.

Unlike all traditional forms of wealth, money had no physical boundaries. While lord or king may have been satisfied with certain sizes of estates or amounts of trinkets, wealth as money was insatiable. The more was up for sale—goods, services, science, labor, land—the more the expansion of wealth also translated into control of others and power over nature.

Having stuff, in short, was no longer good enough. Using stuff, along with labor and knowledge, to create ever more stuff became the new invisible law of economic activity. Sold on rapidly growing markets, stuff was forever turned back into money, before starting yet another cycle of production in search of more money.[9]

In its most basic form, it is this escalating cycle—using money to spawn production in order to generate more money—that launched the unprecedented growth of wealth associated with the advent of industrialization and capitalism.

But whether one was worker or capitalist—owner of little else than one's ability to work, or owner of great fortunes—the purpose of work and production was no longer clear and direct. On the contrary, people began to work for an abstraction: money. Money that could then be used to satisfy basic needs, as in the case of most wage laborers, or for starting a new cycle of acquisitions, control, and production in order to make more money.

The point was no longer to grow potatoes to satisfy one's hunger or to build a house to live in. Rather, the new goal was to obtain a means that theoretically gave one access to unlimited potatoes or houses or anything, really. Including the accumulation of unlimited wealth.

The separation of work from purpose had, and continues to have, deep and wide-ranging effects. For one, what working people experienced—and fervently resisted at first—was that the value of their skills, and the contributions of their work, could now be reduced to a cold number: whatever monetary value the market might yield.[10] Suddenly whoever made more money was deemed more worthy; work that generated more money was seen as more important; and only goods that fetched a price on the marketplace were perceived as having any value at all. It uprooted and destroyed traditions worth thousands of years. For many, it questioned the very meaning of life.

Throughout this process, money turned into both purpose and goal. It became the expression of hopes and aspirations alike. At least in the realm of economics, it effectively obliterated other considerations about values. The object of commerce could suddenly be reduced to a simple number.

For emerging political entities—city-states, fiefdoms, and later nation-states—money understandably mattered a great deal from the beginning. Money provided rulers with an efficient means to extract surplus wealth from their underlings. What remained much less clear was this: how much money, how much wealth was actually out there?

It is here that we come to the very first impetus to possess some form of national income accounting—aggregate product, the wealth that political elites were after, expressed in money. All political entities require money to operate. All traditional functions of government—defense, security, war, public welfare—depend on people outside of government to generate the wealth.[11]

Whether the government is a city-state or kingdom or a republic or a dictatorship, revenue comes from a common set of sources: conquest, resource exploitation, rents, taxes, or tariffs. All ultimately fill the coffers with the kind of wealth that can readily be exchanged, commonly in the form of gold or money.

One of the American founding fathers, Alexander Hamilton, provided a succinct definition of the role of government in 1791 by stating that the "power to raise money is plenary and indefinite, and the objects to which it may be appropriated are no less comprehensive than the payment of the public debt, and the providing for the common defense and general welfare."[12] Government, in short, needed to be able to raise the money necessary for whatever functions it deemed necessary. Until the heyday of the industrial revolution, governments primarily needed revenue to maintain or expand power. War, conquest, and suppression of dissent cost money—lots of it.

It is thus not surprising to find that governments, time and again, began to seek ways to count their riches when they were in need of additional revenue. Only with data on national income could they effectively collect taxes and fees, impose customs duties or tariffs, or confiscate wealth. The better the data, the easier to get the cash.[13]

The first such attempt in Western national accounting histories appear to be Sir William Petty's 1664 estimates of national income. Paul Studenski, author of the only large-scale history of national income accounts, refers to Petty, a physician and economist, as "the true originator of the concept of national income."[14] Recent studies consider him to be among the most important economic writers in the "formative period of classical economics." One of these calls Petty "one of the most ingenious and practical thinkers before the days of Adam Smith."[15]

Most accounts about Petty's conceptual contributions, however, miss what is historically most instructive about him: his use of accounting for the explicit purpose of exploitation and oppression. Briefly told, Petty was a wealthy British merchant and sometime army surgeon who accompanied Oliver Cromwell's army on its final campaign to suppress and colonize the Irish in 1652. Petty's primary task was to survey land confiscated from Irish owners. Some of the land was to be used as compensation for British troops. Most of it, however, was to go toward the enrichment of British elites such as himself.

The basic idea of the campaign was to establish a permanent British occupation of Ireland, and to remove large portions of the Irish population, Catholics in particular. The immediate result was striking: some twenty thousand Irish were slaughtered during the invasion, an estimated fifty thousand fled or were sent off to Spain and France, and another ten to twenty thousand were shipped as slaves to British-owned Caribbean sugar plantations. The aftermath, according to Petty's own conservative estimates, was even more striking: robbed of land and livelihood, more than half of the remaining Irish population died of starvation and disease.[16]

Petty, in the meantime, became the richest commoner in the kingdom. Tasked by Cromwell to create a land inventory, he subsequently took ownership, as Irish Land Commissioner, of some six thousand acres of rich land he had, in his previous role as surveyor, labeled as "marginal" in value. Returning from his Irish exploits, Petty gained noble status at home. Apparently, in addition to his mathematical skills as assessor of national wealth, now Sir William Petty had an eye for opportunity. By the time Petty was appointed Surveyor-General by King Charles II in 1660, his Irish landholdings had so dramatically increased that they covered large parts of County Kerry, or some astonishing one million acres.[17]

Petty's work on Irish capital stock was squarely focused on occupation, confiscation, and exploitation. It had nothing to do with advancing Irish wealth, much less Irish well-being. As one sympathetic biographer of Petty observed, in the sterile language of well-mannered academic description, "political priorities determined both the extent and the kind of quantitative knowledge he sought."[18] Put differently, his considerable accounting skills were developed and employed in the service of imperial expansion. As such they perhaps represented the earliest case of what two admirers of Petty's accounting acumen, the economic philosophers Karl Marx and Friedrich Engels, later termed "the icy water of egotistical calculation."[19]

A leading historian of the formation of nation-states called this the "extractive and repressive" side of government.[20] It was true from the beginning: surveys of national income were conducted when governments needed money. Especially when they mobilized for war and conquest. It may thus be doubted that Petty was indeed the first to make such attempts, though he may well have been the first to couch his estimates in terms recognizable to modern economists.

It is probably safe to assume that Petty's perspective on the whole enterprise would have been quite different if members of his family had been forced off their land and turned into landless paupers. Indeed, viewpoints on purpose and goal of what we today call "economic activity" always depended on whether one lived off of one's own products of labor, or off of someone else's product. Petty assessed available wealth on behalf of a conquering empire. Irish farmers valued land based on their ability to make a living.

This much is apparent: how we define and measure "success" depends on our perspective, and historical struggles hinge on these contrasting definitions. What was success to the English was defeat and failure to the Irish. What separated Petty from Irish farmers, of course, was not only a different set of goals and purposes. Petty's ideas won the day because they consisted of data backed by raw power.[21]

On a most fundamental level, thus, success was always defined as survival. Yet combined with power and an expansion in wealth, definitions of success could suddenly take on a wide variety of forms—control and domination as much as liberation and enlightenment.

One does not have to be a materialist to recognize that almost all conceivable forms of success have a material foundation: they require wealth and development beyond simple survival. It's difficult to strive for, say, education or meaningful political participation when there is not enough food or work to go around.

As Sir William Petty was keenly aware, where we find ourselves in the hierarchy of the social order largely defines not only our goals, but with it the standards we apply when measuring success and progress.[22] What Petty measured boiled down to the very foundation of power and wealth he and his kind enjoyed. Control of the land translated into control of people and access to wealth. For the Irish, loss of land translated into poverty, dependence, and, all too often, slavery, disease, and death.

GOALS AND MEASURES

Though central in the history of measures, land is not the only criteria for wealth or success. What to measure, and how to measure it, essentially depended on time, place, and occupation. On a personal level, a sixteenth-century Arabian herder busy maintaining goats as a source of milk and meat, and saving dung as fertilizer, obviously used a very different gauge of success than, say, a twenty-first-century New York financial advisor whose interest boils down to increasing his bottom line. If nothing else, the first is practical, based on nature, and relates directly to the herder's welfare. The other is symbolic, indirect, and dependent upon an elaborate system of finance.

The importance of measures increases dramatically with size—not only size of the political entity but also volume of trade, degree of division of labor, level of wealth creation. Size generates another result: need for a fictional, abstract means of exchange and the embodiment of wealth—money as the expression of labor and prosperity; eventually, money as the manifestation of what really counts.

As we have seen, the goals we articulate are inevitably reflected in the measures we use—acres of land expropriated, harvest necessary to feed family, quantity of stock trades, number of people nourished. Accordingly, when we establish new goals, or change old ones, we routinely create new gauges. Larger sums of dollars, as either goal or measure, means as little to the goat herder as a larger drum of raw goat milk means to the financial advisor. But if, for some strange reason, the herder suddenly decided his real goal should consist of making more money, his previous measure of success would have to change dramatically, and with it, most likely, the organization of his entire life.

The measures we employ to define success—as persons, businesses, or nations—are, in turn, of great consequence: do we count the number of billionaires or do we gauge the welfare of our elders? Do we measure output or do we emphasize outcome? Is our metric money or welfare or happiness, or perhaps something altogether different?

How "normal" would our metrics of success have seemed in the past? We have already noted the surprising commonality among the majority of working peoples of various preindustrial cultures: they ordinarily did not work more than necessary to satisfy survival needs. Concepts pervasive today, like working for wealth or status, were limited to royalty or clergy. And even there they bumped up against narrow physical limits.

And cultural norms for defining success have also changed. Prior to the modern era, customs, laws, and religious beliefs from around the world testify to the fact that greed—the attempt to gain a competitive advantage over others—was at best frowned upon. Aristotle considered "getting funds of money" and being focused on "exchanging commodities," as simply "unnatural."[23] Across cultures and across centuries, it was described as sin, an indication of a sick and deranged character, often punishable by death—except, of course, when pursued by the ruler.

R. H. Tawney, the renowned historian of capitalism, tells us that during the Middle Ages,

> [society] condemned as a sin precisely that effort to achieve a continuous and unlimited increase in material wealth which modern societies applaud. . . . "He who has enough to satisfy his want," wrote a Schoolman of the fourteenth century, "and nevertheless ceaselessly labors to acquire riches, either in order to

obtain a higher social position, or that subsequently he may have enough to live without labor, or that his sons may become men of wealth and importance—all such are incited by a damnable avarice, sensuality, or pride."[24]

Of course, we can't always clearly distinguish between lofty values promoted by philosophers, and those actually lived down in the town square. What is evident, however, is that neither organization of societies nor dominant cultural values had ever been hospitable to the pursuit of economic growth. On the individual and communal level, available historical evidence strongly suggests that thinking about life as volume of economic output, or wealth measured by money, or labor productivity per unit, would have struck our forebears as most bizarre.

Whatever the cause, one result was this: economic output prior to the industrial revolution remained virtually stagnant. With the measures available today—fraught with all the conceptual shortcomings discussed throughout this book—growth of output and income can be traced over long periods of time (see table 1–1).

Table 1–1. Economic Growth over the Long-Run

Year	Population (in millions)	GDP per capita (in year-2000 international dollars)
5000 BCE	5	$130
1000 BCE	50	$160
1	170	$135
1000	265	$165
1500	425	$175
1800	900	$250
1900	1625	$850
1950	2515	$2030
1975	4080	$4640
2000	6120	$8175
2010	6896	$9037

Sources: J. Bradford De Long and Martha L. Olney, *Macroeconomics*, chap. 5, "The Reality of Economic Growth: History and Prospect" (2009); UN population estimates; CIA World Factbook.

To wit: until about 1500, available records suggest that there had been virtually no growth in output. As late as 1800, the average world inhabitant was still only a little less than twice as productive as his counterpart seven thousand years earlier. With the help of science and resource exploitation and efficient organization, many of today's citizens are thousands of times more productive.

What did this look like in the United States? In constant dollars, output (GDP) at the end of the twentieth century was nearly ten times what it was at the beginning of World War II, a hundred times larger than at the end of the Civil War, and over a thousand times larger than after ratification of the American Constitution. Until then, very little growth in output had taken place—in the American colonies or elsewhere.[25]

It is difficult to know what came first: Did lack of technology and know-how lead to cultural values rejecting growth prior to industrialization? Or did an emphasis on spiritual and communal goals translate into practices that did not include growth? In all likelihood, reality played out within a complex cultural interplay of these and other factors.[26]

For our purposes, however, we don't need to nail down the exact origins and causes of economic growth. We know industrialization brought with it growth in unprecedented scale, and it inevitably raised a new set of fundamental questions. Who or what defined the goal(s) behind all this growth? What was growing, and why? All such questions could only be answered with concepts that clearly defined the components of growth, and that provided standards for measures necessary to evaluate its performance. Growth in capital required different measures than growth in the welfare of the workers or growth in educational achievement.

But before we get ahead of ourselves, it is time to pause and take note of three observations that the reviewed historical record thus far strongly indicates. All are important to keep in mind when we further trace origins and direction of economic measures that eventually led to the now predominant GDP.

1. Most human activities take place within the realm we now call "the economy"—the place where we carve out an existence through work and, true for growing numbers of people after industrialization, where we consume, invest, and trade.

2. Significantly, most of people's personal needs, wants, and desires tend *not* to be economic, but rather social and personal. Though increasingly dominant in the modern era, the realm of the economy still only provides a means for the satisfaction of needs, wants, and desires.

3. Across cultures and historical epochs, we can find evidence that people long for things like love, security, meaning, knowledge, community, or a feeling of self-worth. Economic models, however, generally pay little attention to human wants outside of the economic realm—instead, they routinely turn the world upside down: human beings satisfying the needs of the economy, rather than the economy satisfying the needs of human beings (based on the curious assumption that satisfying economic wants roughly equals satisfying human wants).

Let's for the moment focus on the fact that most of what people want—and have wanted—out of life is not economic. As the philosopher and economist Karl Polanyi put it after decades of studying human economies, "The human passions, good or bad, are merely directed towards noneconomic ends."[27] Moreover, basic noneconomic needs of human beings such as survival or social interaction or community are common to all peoples and times.

It would seem to follow that neither growth nor wealth inevitably or logically increase human well-being. At a minimum, one would have to ask, "What kind of growth, how is it produced, and how are the spoils distributed?" If, hypothetically, all growth flowed to the top 1 percent, the bottom 99 percent would not see any benefits from growth. Or if growth undermined the obtainment of social goals—say, security and happiness—it might require mental acrobatics to see it as contributing to human well-being.

Today, economics textbooks portray humans as forever rationally striving for *utility maximization*, or what one maverick economist derided as "the crude economic utilitarianism that underlies equilibrium economics."[28] Of course, in most real-world circumstances this simplistic concept turns out to be quite naive: people act irrationally; or, more precisely, they follow rationales different from economic models, they routinely don't possess sufficient information and are often not aware of, or don't actually possess, real choices.[29]

The modern economists' simplistic concept of human nature, however, merely reflects a much larger phenomenon: the dramatic transformation of life itself. What makes societies "modern" is that they have moved from the rule of traditional authority to the rule of the market. From virtually no change to exponentially accelerating change. From very slow pace to frantic pace. From work that sustains life to work and markets that determine lifestyle.

Within two centuries, thousands of years of cultural accomplishments and values were effectively turned upside down. The consequences go beyond the visible changes in today's societies. On the most basic level, what we believe motivates people, what we think is possible for the future, and how we think about ourselves has fundamentally shifted.

More and more, our lives, while still aimed at goals that are largely not economic, are circumscribed and defined by economic values. Increasingly, modern economic values are becoming the language through which we express noneconomic goals. What is the cost of helping my neighbor? How do I get the biggest bang for my buck? What education will help me get ahead? And, of course, what is the health of our country? The logic of growth-economics has become the measuring rod for the good life.[30]

VALUES AND MEASURES

What were the ideas behind this massive transformation? Did our early economic thinkers merely follow and describe, or did they help set in motion the journey toward growth and commodification?

To answer this question, we need to investigate how such thinkers thought about purpose and function of productive activity. How did they define things like value and labor? Even more fundamentally: what did they think about growth?

The first official economics professor in the Western world, Thomas R. Malthus, leaned toward a materialist analysis. Essential work took place on the land; the fountain of growth would thus depend on farming. Yet he was pessimistic: in the 1790s he argued that population growth, even if made possible by improvements in knowledge and technology, would ultimately be kept in check by hunger, disease, and poverty. His conclusion seemed inevitable: growing populations would preclude progress and rising standards of living.[31]

Agriculture—people making a living off the land—was the natural focus of all early economists. Some European theorists, known as physiocrats, believed agriculture represented the only productive activity in society. It made sense: farmers represented the majority of people during the eighteenth century, and what they produced constituted the most essential thing to life itself. No food, no life. All other activities—the carpenter building the barn, the vet birthing the calf, the advocate drafting the deed for the land—were seen as "unproductive," or, more precisely, as merely providing the necessary preconditions for the functioning of agricultural production.[32] Thus assigning centrality to farming, physiocrats consequently scorned urban life, where only things of secondary importance took place. They were also fierce defenders of private property. The farmers most secure in their land holdings were seen as the most productive.

The man widely noted as the father of classical economics, Adam Smith, studied the physiocrats and sympathized with many of their views. Attending urban universities during the middle of the eighteenth century, however, he could not help but notice the rapidly growing significance of manufacturing. England was the first country to industrialize. By the time Smith published his ground-breaking economic treatise, *The Wealth of Nations* (1776), rebels in the American colonies were drafting radical demands for freedom and independence. More importantly for Smith, growing numbers of English workers were finding employment in small proto-factories, producing unprecedented amounts of wealth by having their labor organized in ways that generated rapidly improving efficiency.

Breaking from the physiocrats, Smith thus concluded that what created wealth was the "production of commodities," regardless of whether they were farmed or manufactured. Importantly, this commodity production would lead to economic growth only if entrepreneurs made a profit, and then employed this profit to further contribute to productive labor in a process that Smith called "the great wheel of circulation."[33]

Smith, in short, made economic growth—rising output that leads to increased wealth and the eventual spread of opulence to all—a central feature of his theory. Beyond identifying preconditions of growth (growth in labor force and stock of capital, increased division of labor, increased foreign trade), however, Smith remained exceedingly vague. Aside from "productive powers" that allowed for generating profit, Smith remained largely silent on the question of what to grow and why.[34]

Thinking about the nature of growth led to another important insight by a later scholar, John Stuart Mill. He wrote that economic growth essentially has two different sources: increasing the elements of production, namely "labour, capital, and land," or increasing the "productiveness" of these elements. The first simply meant increasing number of workers or fields plowed and capital invested, or what economists today would call "extensive growth." The latter denoted a very new phenomenon: increases in productivity. Smith, for his part, had written about the astonishing increases in productivity as a consequence of the utilization of division of labor—the same worker producing more, the same land yielding more, due to increased use of science and technology and efficient organization, or, in short, increased knowledge. This is today known as "intensive growth." It should be noted that "intensive growth" has been the primary cause for exponential growth during industrialization, and the reason why Malthus's prediction that increased population would thwart growth proved wrong.[35]

With the full onset of industrialization, and the resulting steep increase in output, the question of productivity became an urgent concern. What contributed to productivity? What factors led to the creation of wealth? Early economists, even if they understood the importance of knowledge and technology, continued to contemplate only "labour, capital, and land" as sources of wealth. This matters because later economists stuck with this conceptualization.

Other sources of wealth such as social, human, cultural, or ecological capital were either ignored or collapsed into the three big pillars "labor, capital, and land." It was a way of thinking that would severely limit the economics profession for a long time to come.[36] Business, and the economy at large, according to this view, is strangely unaffected by anything other than labor, capital, and land. Knowledge, creativity, social cohesion, freedom, or the many free services of the ecosystem—none received any sustained attention as pillars of wealth creation in the minds of the early European theorists of economic development. Before revisiting the implications of such limitations, however, we need once more to return to Adam Smith.

The ideas that made Smith famous—unrestrained self-interest working like an "invisible hand" through the free market to achieve the greatest good for all—are grounded in his own experiences with English commerce in the mid- to late eigtheenth century, and have been widely misinterpreted since.[37] Important for our purposes, Smith followed the physiocrats in his claim that value was produced only when "realized in some subject or vendible commodity"—or tangible good for sale, in today's terminology.[38] While there continues to be some debate as to what exactly he meant by that, it is quite clear that many "service sector" jobs—including lawyers, doctors, bankers, accountants—in most of their functions do not, according to Smith, contribute "productive labor." The reason, as he succinctly concluded, was that what they do "adds to the value of nothing."[39]

The only use of many services is to *enable* productive work in agriculture, trades, and manufacturing. For Smith it thus followed that to maximize economic growth, "unproductive" labor, which is siphoning off part of the national income, needed to be reduced to a minimum. After all, many people who provided services received what Smith called "unearned income." It is worth noting that this basic categorization of labor was adopted, with slight variations, by most major Western philosophers and economists of the new era, ranging from David Ricardo and John Stuart Mill to Karl Marx.

Underlying Smith's separation between productive and unproductive labor is another idea that goes back to Aristotle, who insisted over 2,000 years ago on the necessary distinction between production for use versus production for gain. Given the role of finance and money in today's market economies, it was a prescient distinction between efforts geared toward the actual satisfaction of the needs of the "household" versus those merely geared toward wealth creation. Only the former made up the essence of what the Greeks called *oeconomia*, while the latter was viewed as "not natural to man."

Along the same lines, Adam Smith maintained that wealth is exclusively created through productive labor, and not through activities such as trading, or mining precious metals, or speculation, or collecting interest. What Aristotle and Smith appeared to have had in common was that both were no friends of people whose sole or primary purpose was to amass great amounts of wealth based on the productive labor of others, whether they were estate owners, manufacturers, or bankers. Those people, Smith argued, distorted, or even destroyed, the market's "natural ability" to establish a price that provides a fair return on land, labor, and capital.

The person now commonly portrayed as the "father of capitalism," in short, considered a free market of small independent producers pursuing their own economic interest as the ideal framework to satisfy the needs of the greatest number of people. The whole point of the economy, in his words, was to be able "to feed, clothe, lodge, maintain and employ the people."[40] Both Aristotle and Smith perceived what is now called "profit maximization," when it became the central goal, as something unnatural and, in any case, not desirable for the welfare of the community. "Wherever there is great property there is great inequality," Smith stated, for "the affluence of the few supposes the indigence of the many."[41]

For Smith, quite simply, purpose and goal of a national economy was to satisfy the needs of its members—all members. He was quite explicit. His chapter on the "Political Economy" begins by explaining the two "distinct objects" of an economy. The first is "to provide a plentiful revenue or subsistence for the people, or more properly, to enable them to provide such a revenue or subsistence for themselves." The second object, Smith noted, was "to supply the state or commonwealth with a revenue sufficient for the publick services."[42] In the end, as Karl Polanyi noted, Adam Smith considered wealth as merely "an aspect of the life of the community, to the purposes of which it remained subordinate."[43]

It is worth a mention that Smith, writing a full century after Petty, never addressed how to measure success of an economy. "I have no great faith in political arithmetic," he wrote in *The Wealth of Nations*.[44] The idea of capturing either goals or performance of the larger political economy with statistics and mathematical models apparently did not instill a lot of confidence in Smith.[45]

By the time Smith died in Edinburgh in 1790, of course, what we now call "industrialization" had just begun in England. As far as the rest of the world was concerned, nothing much had changed in centuries. Life and its production still largely happened on the land. Of all the cities in the Western world, only London had a population of more than five hundred thousand. In America, more than three-quarters of people still engaged in agricultural endeavors, whether as tenant farmers, slaves, or landowners. Science and technology had barely begun to leave a mark on daily life, with the possible exception of the dispossessed men, women, and children who provided cheap and expendable labor to the early manufacturers. Governments were tiny in comparison to their counterparts today. Income taxes had not yet been invented, any more than industrial corporations or a system of welfare. Transportation was difficult and communication was slow—the first steam locomotive, for instance, was not built until 1804, and trains did not become significant means for moving goods in England until well into the nineteenth century.

From today's perspective, life some two hundred years ago would have seemed astonishingly slow, methodical, narrow, and traditional. There were few economic choices, and few surprises.

Adam Smith may thus be excused for not foreseeing the floodgates of change about to burst. At an accelerating pace, the combined forces of a market-driven industrialization swept away anything and everything standing in their way—traditions of work and family as much as forms of government or values concerning the common good.

Not surprisingly, Smith's thinking about "productive labor" was soon superseded by a much more expansive vision of the income-generating economy. Alfred Marshall, son of a bank cashier and himself a gifted mathematician, became professor of political economy at Cambridge a little less than a century after Smith published *The Wealth of Nations*. Marshall suggested a broader definition of "national income" by proclaiming that "labour and capital, acting on its natural resources," produce a "net aggregate of commodities, material and immaterial, including services of all kinds."[46] This is the theory followed by most economists to this day: the value of a commodity (what economists call "marginal utility") is determined by what someone is willing to pay for it.

Marshall's view avoided all complicated questions about the origins of value or the distinction between productive and unproductive labor. Quite simply, his theory stated that value is determined by price realized. Of course this seeming simplicity created new problems, notably not discussed by Marshall, two of which need to be highlighted in this context. For one, the greatest good of all became a function of wealth: the rich have a lot more money to pay for things than the poor. It was as if we disseminated votes in an election in proportion to wealth. Who would have the most votes? And how well would that represent either will or welfare of the commons?

Secondly, Marshall's idea of value exploded the meaning of commodity, the resulting fallout continuing to blur our vision to this day. Originally, and logically, a commodity was something produced for exchange—goods and services. Marshall's theory allowed for a radical extension of this definition: a commodity became everything that catches a price on the market—including human beings and nature.

With people and land and resources thrown into the mix, there was suddenly no limit anymore as to what could be subordinated to the logic of the profit-driven market. The value of a person? Whatever someone was willing to pay for his or her labor power. The value of land? Whatever supply and demand of the market dictates. The value of air? Nothing, since it's abundantly available. Of course, if one could find ways to get people to pay for things like water or safety or sex, all the merrier: "the great wheel of circulation" just got bigger. The humanist Karl Polanyi, in his masterful study of this "great transformation," called this definition of commodity a "crude fiction." Unless we effectively protect ourselves against the resulting "ravages of this satanic mill," he mused, society "cannot survive."[47]

The great economists closely reflected their own times: from the physiocratic understanding that land was the fountain of all wealth, to Mill's assertion that wealth was a product of "labour, capital, and land," to Marshall's claim that "labour and capital" (acting on its natural resources) produced wealth. Their understandings changed with the realities of industrialization and its unprecedented accumulation of material and monetary wealth, specifically through drastic increases in the production and sale of goods and services. Increasingly, their focus moved away from land or resources, or what we would more broadly call the ecosystem today, and instead concentrated on the actions and contributions of human beings.[48]

Marshall, today described as the father of neoclassical economics, laid the essential groundwork for a shift in Western economic thought toward defining national income as an indiscriminate total of net services and commodities produced and consumed.[49] Productivity, in turn, became defined by the sheer volume of what was exchangeable on the market for money, no matter how it was produced or what possible "use-value" it may or may not have. Money turned into the expression of both—value (of goods and services expressed in price), and goal (of production expressed in profit). This was the new bottom line: if it's sellable on the market, it has value; if it can be made and sold with a profit, it's worth producing.

Part of this shift from classical economics had profound consequences. Smith, Ricardo, Mill, Marx, Baudrillart—virtually all the classics made a distinction between production activities and nonproduction activities. After Marshall, however, the classical notion was replaced with the idea that all "socially necessary" activities result in a product. Henceforth any number of pursuits—including the work of lawyers, speculators, traders, or salespeople—were included in "productive activities." Even bureaucrats, the police, the courts, and the military were no longer seen as providing merely a means to an end, a service allowing productive work to take place, or what is commonly called an "intermediate" service today.

Everything counted that could be counted as transaction in the marketplace. Price became the exclusive criteria. No longer was it necessary—or even possible—to distinguish between goods and bads, between use value and exchange value, or to figure out whether a "service" provided a service or a disservice. No longer was there a clear conceptual attempt to distinguish between means and ends, between what facilitates reaching the goal, and the goal or end product itself. Simply enough, price determined value. Modern society had a new secular god in the marketplace of historical ideologies.[50]

The foundation was laid. It is worth noting that none of those theorists conceptualized, much less introduced, a gauge to measure economic performance.

Chapter 2

THE ORIGINS OF BLING

The Spirit of Economic Growth

A thatched roof once covered free men; under marble
and gold dwells slavery.

—*Lucius Annaeus Seneca*

There may not yet have been a workable measure of economic performance as industrialization was getting under way. But as the nineteenth century came to a close, the world of dominant ideas was now populated with the "invisible hand of the market" (Adam Smith) in search of "the greatest good" (Jeremy Bentham) of all those striving to maximize "utility" (John Stuart Mill) in an ever more unrestrained economy that counted all goods and services exchanged (Alfred Marshall). The one thing that held it all together was value expressed in money. It did not matter what it was, or what utility it provided.

It seemed like a brilliant breakthrough: a clearly defined common denominator with which to measure a limitless number of different kinds of utilities.[1] What was captured, in short, was not merely output of traditional goods. The tool itself spawned an explosive expansion of the tentacles of the economy, the market logic of value reaching into ever more spheres of life. It was the logic of economic growth pushed to its furthest extremes. Life itself was to become a reflection of the economy.

In short order, Bentham's famous advice to a young girl in 1830 to "create all the happiness you are able to create; remove all the misery you are able to remove," became largely restricted to the realm of the personal. In the marketplace, the new canon was this: make all the money you are able to make; remove all idealized notions about life beyond "stuff" you are able to remove. The new logic translated into a fundamental separation between the values of the commons—family, community, neighborhood—and the rules of the market, the place where we work, invest, sell, consume. There, the wisdom of generations made way for the presumed rationality of indiscriminate growth.

Anything that could not be turned into a commodity, to be sold at a profit, became a cultural orphan, precariously living on the outskirts of the market. Economic goals that lay outside of the logic of accumulation—independence, say, or an end to poverty—were effectively sidelined.[2] Like railroad tracks in old southern towns, voracious economic growth demarcated an essential line of segregation: on the neglected side, life in its full social and cultural variety; on the rich and expanding side, life with a singular focus on the marketplace. It also split people into two distinct roles: in their personal roles as mothers, sons, brothers, friends, citizens—people who strove for things like morality, meaning, acceptance, love; and people in their narrow economic roles as managers of commodities, either their own labor power, or the products of other people's labor. More often than not, the two proved incompatible.

The marketplace never rested in its attempts to commercialize and commodify the side of the personal and communal. There was always a killing to be made, a life or a human expression turned into a marketable good. Even the essential components of personal relationships did not remain impervious. Advice, companionship, even love, it turns out, could be bought and sold at a profit. Of course, as British economist Tim Jackson has pointed out, "Care and concern of one human being for another is a peculiar 'commodity.' It can't be stockpiled. It becomes degraded through trade. It isn't delivered by machines. Its quality rests entirely on the attention paid by one person to another."[3] None of it mattered, it turned out, as long as there was money to be made with it.

Today, we are familiar with the chief result: the culturally dominant notion that human beings are best served when relentlessly following their self-interest. It was not an idea that spread easily. In America, for instance, it took well over two hundred years of struggle before citizens began to accept, and then embrace, their roles as producers, wage earners, and, above all, as consumers.[4] Initially, the view from the "bottom up" on self-interest was, to put it mildly, unsympathetic. In all dominant cultures and religions around the world, the desire to have more, or what was referred to as "acquisitiveness" in the Anglo-Saxon world, was as culturally detested as it was officially unsanctioned.

Herman Husband, a farmer and preacher during the American Revolution, gave voice to a widespread sentiment at the founding of the republic when he denounced men who wanted to live in "idleness and luxury . . . upon [the] labour" of others. Those, he said, "our Lord called vipers."

As historian Terry Bouton's exploration of Revolutionary-era Pennsylvania reveals, "Before 1776, elite and ordinary folk united behind the belief that only an equal distribution of wealth would protect freedom and keep democracy healthy. Many of the state's most genteel leaders pushed for progressive taxation, easy access to currency and low-cost credit through a government-run land bank, and bans on for-profit corporations."[5] What we see here is work and wealth clearly subordinated to the larger goal of creating a better life, and a free and democratic republic.

Of course, there were always those who accumulated wealth. In the United States as around the world, organized religious institutions did so, as did political rulers and, increasingly, merchants and bankers. Moreover, this wealth accumulation was pursued on the backs of the working poor, most of whom never had a choice in the matter.

But here is where the great transformation took place: not until wealth became wealth in capital (economists call it a "factor in production") did it turn into the insatiable appetite trying to devour ever more aspects of life. No longer confined to physical goods—land, gold, estates—growth in capital grew up to be limitless. The more there was for sale, the more those who pursued wealth as capital could own—at first, to be sure, also labor, land, and resources, but then access to development itself and economic growth in every form conceivable. An early theorist defined capital as "that amount of wealth which is used in making profits," and, important for our story, that "which enters into [double-entry bookkeeping] accounts."[6] Increasingly, there was no longer a limit to the amount of profit to be made, to the scale of numbers to be put into double-entry accounts.

To review: The majority of Americans made a living on the land at the time of the American Revolution. Money played a secondary role, used for little more than direct trade and investment. Very few people were what we today call "wage earners." Instead, we find a range of bonded, free, and independent labor, such as tenant and yeoman farmers, slaves, and artisans. Many of the goods and services people produced were for immediate consumption, not for exchange—think of the family farmer growing corn for family and livestock, or the artisan building his own home. Barter was still common. Capital consisted primarily of physical wealth, above all land and equipment.

Contrast today: The vast majority of Americans are wage earners; a small minority can sustain an independent living.[7] Virtually all goods and services, including labor, are now part of a market exchange. Above all, money has become by far the largest form of capital (and the financial sector the largest and most profitable of modern economies): we are close to living in a global economy in which financial assets outpace the total global output (world GDP) by a factor of 10, totaling some staggering $900 trillion.[8] Money does not only make the world go around. Money, as the simultaneous embodiment of labor, land, and resources, confers to its owners control over human, social, and physical capital. It is only a slight exaggeration to say that whoever controls money controls the world.[9] And $900 trillion buys a lot of control.

In terms of both size and character of wealth production, ours is a world unlike anything that has come before. The range and intensity of controversies about what it all means have predictably grown in proportion to the wealth produced. Theories about how and why this explosion of productivity happened the way it did continue to be debated.

Adam Smith believed that land, labor, and capital in free interaction with each other would, through the market, generate growth and eventual "universal opulence." His ideological counterpart, Karl Marx, writing a little less than a century later, detected the origins of this explosion in a "bourgeois" revolution that simultaneously "freed" people from bondage *and* from all possessions, allowing for an ever-expanding system of exploitation that would eventually "nestle everywhere, settle everywhere, establish connections everywhere" until "all that is solid melts into air, all that is holy is profaned."[10]

Another generation later, Max Weber, looking for the precise elements behind the rise of capitalism and growth, listed calculable law, technology and mechanization, free labor, and the commercialization of economic life along-side the rational accounting of capital. Calling it the "spirit of capitalism," he saw those elements, together with the "Protestant ethic," bringing forth exponential growth.[11] Yet another generation later, the historian of the "great trans-formation" from industrialization to modern capitalism, Karl Polanyi, wrote that the root cause for the voracious expansion of modern market societies lay in turning not just goods and services, but also labor, land, and money, into commodities.[12]

And the debates have continued. In a recent study, two authors posit that the emergence of nation-states and big governments provided necessary regulation and protection of the market system—"capitalism could not have developed and expanded" without states; "states became increasingly dependent upon capital accumulation." The growth of capitalism and big government went hand in hand, each requiring the other.[13]

But whatever the precise elements behind the explosion and monetization of growth: most ordinary people faced this reality as being increasingly pushed into "rational calculations" about how to function as a commodity. Forced off the land by the millions, the challenge boiled down to how best to sell one's labor power. No job, no income, no survival.

More and more, human activity itself was noted only when it fetched a price on the market—after all, what good did it do to have skills or experiences one could not sell? According to the new rationale of the market, human endeavors became reduced to their labor power and their purchasing power—both mattered to the extent to which they contributed to the realization of profit.[14] In the realm of the economy, neither good nor service, neither person nor skill, neither land nor resource, had value unless and until it was finan-cialized in the market.

An ever-expanding market system fueled the process, driven primarily by competition and the prospect of profit on a scale previously unimaginable. It impacted everyone and everything—owners small and large, workers, com-munities, and nature itself.

Mounting wealth, rising material standards of living for many, and more choices in consumer goods represent the familiar upside of market-driven growth. Mounting inequality, persistent poverty, privatization of land and resources, and the looting of the ecosystem represent the equally pervasive downsides.

Life over the past century in the American Great Plains provides an instructive example of some of the core dilemmas posed by growth-driven economies.

Initially, the Great Plains represented the "symbol of our country's expansionist ambitions, flush with homesteaders drawn to the promise of 160 acres of free land in the nineteenth century, and a blank page on which to rewrite their lives." Economic reality has since turned dreams into dust. More people and more productivity led to overdevelopment. Rapidly expanding consumption habits depleted the massive underground water reserves of an area roughly one-fifth the size of the lower 48 states. Drought blanketed the region in the 1930s, and again in the early twenty-first century. Prairies turned into dustbowls. Banks and corporations moved in for the take. Hundreds of thousands of farmers lost their livelihoods.

Two of the few holdout farmers who have neither gone bankrupt nor sold out to mega-sized agribusinesses recently reflected on the massive changes they have witnessed. Jack Geiger, a rancher struggling to survive, reflected, "It used to be, when one family was struggling, all the other families would help them out." No more. "Now, if somebody's in trouble, everybody else is looking to see if they can buy their land." Donn Teske, a fifth-generation family farmer, agreed: "These days, you've got to grow to survive," he said. "It changes how people relate."[15] Growth in volume did not only deplete resources, it also reduced people to the cold calculations of callous competition.

Greed and selfishness have likely existed throughout human history. Prior to the advent of modern capitalism, however, they were never formalized as a systemic goal, and thereby turned into cultural norm. Henceforth, the quest for moral conduct—whether informed by religious doctrine or rational enlightenment thought—was essentially banned from the marketplace, replaced by the "pursuit of self-interest." The more aspects of life were subordinated to the laws of the market, of course, the more self-interest became dominant. The search for moral and intellectual enlightenment was quite effectively transformed into the pursuit of profit, utility, and competitive advantage—all part of a larger cost-benefit analysis. The "commons"—the idea of communal stewardship of people, land, and resources—largely disappeared, both as idea and as reality.[16]

The newly emergent dictum was simple: more money supposedly translated into more success and more happiness—and presumably less misery. Indeed, the very definition of happiness and misery was increasingly reduced to a cost-benefit analysis. As one famous student of the emergence of profit-driven markets observed, the average person moved "from a spiritual being, who, in order to survive, must devote a reasonable attention to economic interest . . . to become an economic animal." In less than two hundred years, R. H. Tawney argued, industrializing societies such as England, and, later, the United States, Germany, and France, tilted from the values of divine providence and natural law to the value of utility: the idea that "the attainment of material riches is the supreme object of human endeavor."[17]

The pursuit of happiness shriveled into the pursuit of purchasing power. The many flavors of life vanishing behind the stench of greed.

Commenting on the historical fact that "there is scarcely a practice commonly seen in one part of the world that is not shunned in another," the part-time economist George Brockway humorously debunked the notion of self-interest as a universal motivator. Using the father of the self-interest doctrine as a point of reference, Brockway commented on Adam Smith's rather provincial life and wrote, "Even in Smith's day enough was known of the customs of the Chinese and the American Indians and, nearer at hand, some sadly disreputable Frenchmen, to understand that their behavior differed from that of a Scottish scholar who lived much of his life with his mother."[18] Speculating on universal human motives based on one's own narrow experiences, or particular academic lens, is akin to studying the universe based on the assumption that earth represents its center. It allows for many interesting theories. All predictably carry the distinction of being wrong.

If nothing else, level of development both limits and shapes how we think about work and life goals and incentives. It was neither possible, nor would it have made any sense, for the goat herder three hundred years ago to think about the possibilities of globalization in his personal ambition to maximize profit. For today's financial advisor in New York it might be theoretically possible to think about life outside of cutthroat competition, pursuing goals other than financial gain. Most likely, however, his thinking is shaped in ways that will preclude him from having any broader visions—or, even if he has them, to see them as mere personal dreams, somehow completely unrealistic and thus relegated to the sidelines.

It can be stated, simply enough, that time, place, and circumstances fundamentally shape the way we think about the economy, and our position in it. It follows that the more economic life in general, and specific economic goals in particular, dominate our lives, the more we are prone to "naturalize" characteristics that allow us to be successful. If greed is culturally dominant, and we see, beginning in early childhood, that it leads people to what our culture considers success, we are likely to emulate it as a model for ourselves. This does not make greed any more "natural" to humankind than, say, generosity. It merely makes it culturally predominant.

A community of American farmers in the 1770s did not measure its wealth by money accumulated but rather by the richness and size of land they farmed, the yield of their harvest, the quality of their neighbors, and the level of independence they managed to accomplish. A highly trained machinist replaced by a robot in 2014 does not just suffer a collapse in income, but also a painful loss of respect and status in a world that increasingly makes her knowledge obsolete.

Having puzzled for many years over the seeming proclivity of people to detect only one single overarching motive behind human activity (at the exclusion of many other possibilities), Polanyi concluded the following:

> Single out whatever motive you please, and organize production in such a manner as to make that motive the individual's incentive to produce, and you will have induced a picture of man as altogether absorbed by that particular motive. Let that motive be religious, political, or aesthetic; let it be pride, prejudice, love, or envy; and man will appear as essentially religious, political, aesthetic, proud, prejudiced, engrossed in love or envy. Other motives, in contrast, will appear distant and shadowy since they cannot be relied upon to operate in the vital business of production. The particular motive selected will represent "real"

man. As a matter of fact, human beings will labor for a large variety of reasons as long as things are arranged accordingly.[19]

The big dilemma seems to be that, again and again, we create ideas and goals and systems that subsequently turn into our masters.

True enough. But this insight does not yet account for who is creating such ideas, and in the service of what, or whom? In capitalist market economies, theorists and commentators began talking about the birth of "economic man," whose motive was reduced to self-interest—the rational pursuit of utility maximization and growth. Not surprisingly, today people "appear as essentially" driven by economic self-interest and the restless pursuit of more, for things are clearly "arranged accordingly."[20]

As we have seen, none of this was a result of some kind of natural, much less inevitable or smooth, process. On the contrary, the transition generally did not sit well with received cultures and traditions. And people resisted. The march forward of the logic of private market-driven growth was always accompanied by people rebelling and organizing against it. The primary benefits always accrued only to a select few, usually the ones most adamantly pushing for the change.

The largest working-class movement in American history, for instance, is still poorly understood as a direct challenge to the economic values of the relentlessly expanding "market" of the 1880s and 1890s. Based primarily in the agrarian South, the Populists fought back against the rising power of industrialists and bankers, and the predominance of narrow economic goals of efficiency, output, and profit. Ultimately, they rejected a growth-centered definition of progress itself.

Stubbornly resisting the centralized power of corporate money, Populists took Jefferson's ideas of democracy to their logical conclusion. They wanted to democratize the monetary system. Make low-interest credit available through the government, not banks. Allow all people to have a seat at the table. Don't just give people a political vote, give them an economic voice. Allow them to make a living without total dependence on those with wealth and capital. As Jefferson had eloquently pointed out a century earlier, political rights quickly turn hollow without people having a secure plot of economic ground to stand on: "dependence begets subservience and venality, [and] suffocates the germ of virtue."[21] Or as British historian Peter Linebaugh has shown in cases around the world, "political and legal rights can exist only on an economic foundation."[22]

The fact that Populist efforts were eventually crushed by banks, with the consequence that millions lost their independent livelihoods, in no way diminishes the magnitude of their democratic aspirations. They remain a powerful reminder that people did not quietly accept the narrow logic of profit-centered economic growth as society's primary, or even exclusive, goal.[23]

Indeed, the global historical record teems with people resisting the logic of economic growth as goal of society. Resisters span from the political right to the left, alternately nurtured by longings for values of a lost past such as faith, family, or integrity, or by expansive visions for a better future of equality, sustainability, and harmony. As further explored in chapters 7 and 8, all such values are forced underground by the logic of GDP growth. Some movements have been political, some religious, but all have in common that they refused a definition of success reduced to the cold cash nexus.[24]

Ironically, the more time passes, the less we tend to understand such movements. A powerful reason suggested by the preeminent historian of Populism, Lawrence Goodwyn, is that the "reigning assumption" guiding our experiences is progress, the comfortable faith that the present is better than the past, and the future will be better still. "This reassuring belief," writes Goodwyn, "rests securely on statistical charts and tables certifying the steady and upward tilt in economic production."[25]

Progress. It serves as a powerful belief system. Implying that things essentially "work," and, more importantly, that they are always getting better, it is an article of faith that inevitably limits our imagination and stunts our ability to learn from the past. Believing in progress—today is better than yesterday—may well be psychologically uplifting. But in today's economies it blinds us to the realization that social goals and purposes could be defined—and in fact have been defined throughout most of history—as something infinitely richer than volume of output. It also blinds us to what is lost.

More is not enough. Often, it's not even better. Sometimes it's decidedly worse. As one scholar of progress put it, "An inquiry into the history of the idea of progress shows how unusual it is to think about the economy as we do—as an independent realm to be evaluated in terms of the magnitude of its output rather than in terms of its contributions to a larger vision of life."[26] Reducing our central benchmark for success to "more stuff" is quite new. Life measured a dollar or Yuan or Euro at a time, if nothing else, represents a seriously stunted understanding of progress.

Divorced from the totality of lived reality, the economy has taken on a life of its own. On any day, we can open a newspaper or blog dedicated to economic matters, and find the economy "expanding" or "contracting" or "losing steam." As if it were a person in blood and flesh, the economy is depicted as "strong" or "resilient" or simply "healthy." We are led to believe that the economy is "a thing that behaves independently of anyone's will," something out there, something "with which we are forced to live."[27] Separate from us yet also, in a strange twist of logic, presumably best expressing our needs and wants, the economy becomes both alien and dominant in our lives. As summed up by Bill Clinton's campaign staffers in 1992, everything can be reduced to the phrase: "It's the economy, stupid."

Theoretically, all this is largely arbitrary, of course. Content and direction of an economy could be organized any number of ways. As we will see later on, even growth could be defined in various ways. Above all, however, the economy is nothing without people—people producing, selling, negotiating, marketing, bartering, maneuvering, scheming, struggling, making up rules and regulations as they go. We tend to forget: it makes no sense to say, "People and nature are part of the economy." In reality, the exact opposite is true: the economy is a subordinate part of nature and people.

Essential for how we think about the economy, and how we define economic success, are the rules and regulations that we, the people, establish for how to count and measure what takes place in the market—for without counting and measuring, there is no economy. "We only have an economy once these transactions are recorded, abstracted from everyday experience, quantified, and then reassembled into a whole that seems to have a life of its own." Strangely, thus, it is economists who invented the economy as something separate and divorced from the toils and aspirations of human beings. Until the revolution of economic statistics that are the focus of this book, no economic theorist would have thought of the economy as "performing." The idea of performance requires a gauge. The primary gauge today is GDP.[28]

The new calculus of "economic success" allowed for mathematical models of human conduct—from the personal to the national and international. Reduced to a single monetary figure, this success was relatively easy to define, it was quantifiable, it was convenient. It could also be communicated with an aura of objectivity, for how could the correct tabulation of numbers lie?[29]

Most importantly, providing a convenient performance measure—one central gauge—effectively redirected the conversation away from difficult questions about human welfare, from quality of life. Persistent problems with employment, poverty, inequality, and subsequent challenges with depletion and decay moved into the background or fell off the stage entirely. People began to confuse the measure with the goal in a downward spiral of circular logic. The goal became to increase the measure. When the measure had increased, the culturally sanctioned assumption became that we had moved closer to our goals. The car set on accelerating speed, in the meantime, was beginning to spin out of control.

To summarize: with self-interest and expansion as the presumed primary motive behind the conduct of players in the marketplace, growth became the goal. The question of purpose was largely forgotten. Social problems were ignored or sidestepped.

Yet even within this increasingly narrow logic, one big question remained unresolved: How exactly to measure growth? It was a question fraught with inherent problems. Who or what determined substance and direction of growth? What, in the end, was growing? And what measures might accurately capture contributions to the world of economics?

Throughout the modern era, people tried to measure what was happening in the larger economy. Those with connections, like Petty, did so for the purposes of enlarging the coffers of government and elites. A recent history of national accounts finds the origins of most attempts to measure national economies either in taxation or in the need for governments to know how they stacked up against other nations, particularly in preparation for war.[30]

But governments were not the only ones interested in economic measures. In many countries—England, France, the United States, Russia, the Netherlands, and Germany—the bulk of efforts prior to World War I actually originated with individual scholars, people concerned with issues such as employment, equality, or scarcity of resources.[31]

Rightly, economic measures were seen as providing vital information, no matter whether the purpose was war, greed, control, or the pursuit of social justice.

THE WORLD OF GROWTH: REFINING THE MEASURE

One highly instructive example of an individual effort can be found in early twentieth-century America. It highlights a development with far-reaching consequences: regardless of specific reasons behind an account of the national economy, the criteria began to follow the logic of neoclassical economics.

Willford King, a little-known American statistician from the University of Wisconsin, published the country's first comprehensive survey on wealth and income in 1915.[32] King was interested in distribution: how was income and wealth shared in American society? He noted that while many assumed wealth had increased, nobody could say with any degree of certainty by how much, or the extent to which different sectors of society might have benefited. To get to the bottom of this, he asked a troubling question: "If there has been an increase in the riches of the nation as a whole, has the increase been distributed to all classes of the population, or have the benefits been monopolized by the favored few?"[33]

To his dismay, he found significant inequality: according to his calculations, the top 1 percent accrued about 15 percent of the nation's income.[34] Worse still, while the wealth of a small minority had greatly increased, "real welfare" of the majority of the population "had been decidedly diminished."[35] King, a man of traditional views, concluded that enormous inequality in wealth was not only irrational and immoral; it was also bad for the common good:

It is easy to find a man in almost any line of employment who is **twice** as efficient as another employee but it is very rare to find one who is **ten times** as efficient. It is common, however, to see one man possessing not **ten** times but a **thousand** times the wealth of his neighbor. This discrepancy represents ability of only one type—the faculty of taking advantage of existing laws and circumstances to acquire property rights—and these rights are too frequently obtained by flagrant violations of the spirit if not the letter of the law.[36]

If nothing else, King's point represents a profound conceptual challenge to rationalizations of vast inequality in income and wealth—then and now. By providing an ethical framework to think about inequality, moreover, his 1914 examination went a step beyond the far more detailed, substantive, and famous 2014 analysis of Thomas Piketty. Both King and Piketty documented widening inequality, and both lamented its corrosive effects on freedom and democracy. But only King took the stance of calling it morally indefensible.[37]

Behind the question of equality, however, lurked a larger development in the way King went about his investigation. What King had in common with all pioneers of national income accounting, in places like Britain and Germany and Russia, was a particular understanding of how to measure the prosperity of a nation. They did not look at reserves of gold or deposits of diamonds. Neither did they study literacy rates, quality of buildings, untapped resources like oil or rivers or forests, or happiness among citizens. And they did not concern themselves with the concept of sustainability.

Though they differed, sometimes intensely, in interest and background, all early national accounting efforts were alike in that their measure was confined to monetary income. Following the logic of neoclassical economists like Alfred Marshall, their general assumption was growth of income equaled an increase in welfare. With decline in income, personally and collectively, they saw crisis and depression on the horizon. Whatever terminology they used—utility or satisfaction or welfare—the goal came to be identified with income as measured by money.[38]

The importance of this development can scarcely be overestimated. As we have seen, the scope of political economics, originally addressing values, goals, and equity, came to be confined to one singular focus: growth. Now national income accountants followed that lead—they simply *did not address* questions outside the narrow realm of growth as expressed in monetary terms. Rather, they began to define the economy as a system that turns out goods and services in order to satisfy *demand*—and demand, of course, was always as big or as small "as a person's pocketbook": little income could generate only little demand; no income could generate no demand.[39]

The idea that growth in demand correlated with well-being, in the meantime, grew from conjecture to an article of faith—among both economists and accountants. In reality, the connection was difficult to document, always tenuous, and in many cases utterly unsupported.[40] A point not lost on people who professionally deal with faith, then or now. As Pope Francis declared in 2013, the assumption that "economic growth . . . will inevitably succeed in bringing about greater justice and inclusiveness in the world . . . has never been confirmed by the facts," but rather "expresses a crude and naïve trust in the goodness of those wielding economic power and in the sacralized workings of the prevailing economic system."[41]

We reach here a problem that goes to the heart of both goal and measure, of both economic thought and accounting: there is no logical connection between market price and utility. Price is a function of supply and demand. Utility is a function of benefit.

Few things provide a greater benefit—urgent, immediate, and existential—than breathing air. As long as it is abundant and free, it costs nothing. Great utility, huge benefit, no price. Also, having breathed a lot yesterday does not make it any less valuable today—there are no diminishing returns. We can see this disconnect between benefit and price everywhere: just because I can skype for free today makes it no less valuable to be in touch with my aging parents. Just because housing prices skyrocket does not mean I will sell the house that I have updated to my family's personal preferences, since the benefit (utility) of the house may override its market value. Examples are endless, the result the same: "no equivalence holds between price paid and marginal benefit."[42]

But here is where it gets tricky. If we define value by price fetched in the marketplace—as economists do, and accountants emulate—we have not necessarily said anything about utility or benefit or use-value. Indeed, by such strange standards, it becomes obvious that something like our ecosystem or our freedom has no value, even though it may be of more benefit to us than any number of gold barrels or smartphones.

The underlying problem is that "value" is never defined clearly. It becomes a stand-in for whatever one wants it to be. Mainstream economics blithely solves this thorny problem by getting caught in yet another form of circular reasoning: "the amount someone is willing to pay for something correlates with its 'utility' if 'utility' is measured in terms of the amount he or she is willing to pay for it."[43] Price, in short, is not a useful measure for benefit.

But it gets stranger, for "income," the central category for national accounts, is essentially a function of price. It's the aggregate amount of prices one was able to fetch in the marketplace. Price defines income, and income, in turn, defines growth: more income, more growth. Yet growth in income logically tells us no more about benefit or utility or well-being than does price. As discussed throughout the book, the connection between growth and well-being can be positive, nonexistent, or negative—just don't look for national income accounting to provide any insight.

It is thus curious to find that *more*—which ordinarily means more economic growth—has become so thoroughly wedded to *better*. It's historically quite new, yet true across nations and cultures as much as across ideologies and classes. Whether in capitalist, socialist, or mixed economies, national goals and dreams are built on the premise of forever *more*. Growth provides the foundation, the rationale, and the direction. Over the past couple of centuries, growth served a wide range of purposes: growth filled the coffers of elites, growth paid for conquering armies, growth helped buy silence and social harmony, and growth facilitated scientific and technological development. Much of this remains true today.

But ongoing economic growth is not logical, much less inevitable. It was also not anticipated by the great theorists of modern economic thought.

From Adam Smith to David Ricardo to John Stuart Mill to Karl Marx and John Maynard Keynes, it is true that without exception all considered economic growth vital to a better future. Significantly, however, and much less known, is that these worldly philosophers did not anticipate growth to go on for long. In fact, all of them longed for a future that no longer required growth. People as far apart in time and ideological outlook as Smith, Marx, Keynes, and Schumpeter all explicitly discussed the end of growth—not at some distant point in time, but in their foreseeable future.[44]

As economic historian Robert Heilbroner noted, "It may come as something of a surprise to learn that all the great economists have pictured capitalism as tending finally toward a kind of stagnant, stationary condition."[45] All anticipated a historical moment in which continued growth was no longer necessary, no longer possible, no longer desirable. Whether they foresaw a market society that had accumulated all the capital it needed (Smith), or whether they actively argued for a revolutionary transition in which the "realm of freedom" replaces "necessity and mundane considerations" (Marx), they all foresaw an end to growth. Human development could take its place. Keynes went as far as predicting, by the beginning of the twenty-first century, a fifteen-hour workweek—plenty of time to pursue the good life.[46]

More important than whether these men stood on common ground when it came to growth, however, is that they, more than anyone, represent the intellectual parentage of subsequent economic thought, in both its capitalist and socialist varieties. And despite their collective vision of an end to growth, all subsequent economic developments came to be premised on the need for growth—ongoing, relentless, without limits, and essential for the survival of the system. The "fathers" of the right as much as those of the left, it is thus safe to argue, would have disavowed their children.

Whether the historical arc of growth-based economies is going to be long or short, we do not yet know. We do know that it bends toward turning everything into a commodity—bought, sold, traded, lost, and discarded. "The idea of gain . . . was to become so firmly rooted that men would soon vigorously affirm that it was an eternal and omnipresent part of human nature."[47] It was the reduced, simplified, truncated, processed, and easy-to-package result of neoclassical economic thought.

And as a simple tidy package, it was also an easy sell. Both economists and accountants embraced it. Who would oppose things like *wealth*, or more *goods* and *services*? A complicated reality remained well hidden behind the sparkling promise of growth: "more" and "better" soon began to part ways.

BUSINESS ACCOUNTING GOES NATIONAL

Initially, the idea of gain was restricted to the marketplace, to the world of business. How it spread beyond traditional goods and services to other spheres of life was primarily driven by a desire to maximize profits. As we have seen, the more that could be sold, the more opportunity there was to make money. The historical grand master of creative rip-offs may well be turning free tap water into a multibillion-dollar plastic-bottled water industry. It may also be a clear case of profit without utility.

In order to succeed, the process of commodification—turning ever more things into marketable items—first required a method of business accounting. What would be counted? And how? Each business needed a "bottom line": what was expenditure, what were the proceeds, how much was left over for profit? For a time, such accounting on a business-to-business basis seemed quite sufficient. But with both businesses and national economies rapidly growing, the parts (businesses) became elements of an ever more interconnected system. And sickness of one caused ripple effects throughout the entire system.

Select observers began to notice that without some form of national accounting, there was no reliable system—no oversight, no regulation, no clear knowledge of parts and aggregates of the national economy.[48] Without national accounts no one possessed any reliable information about distribution of incomes—about social stratification, about employment, about opportunities. Without national accounts government possessed no tools for effective intervention. And without national accounts there was no way to organize distribution and use of resources and capital in an efficient manner. All that one was left with was the presumed magic of the market.

Accounts of individual entrepreneurs provided a good sense of costs, expenses, and profits in their own business. Until the 1930s, no one—not corporate leaders, not even presidents of leading nations—had access to any of this information for the entire national economy.[49]

It was a state of affairs that had had multiple historical causes. Except in times of war, government activities around the world were tiny in comparison to their contemporary counterparts.[50] Above all, classical and neoclassical economic ideologies assumed that government should remain small—and play little or no role in regulating the economy. And, without centralized data-gathering, economic statistics beyond census and tax records remained beyond reach.[51] Scholars like King thus struggled with severe limitations in their efforts to generate meaningful data on national income.

As a result, until quite recently, no national indicators existed. For more than a century of capitalist development in the United Kingdom and the United States, and then, in short order, in countries such as Germany, Japan, and France, no one possessed a full, up-to-date grasp of growth of the overall economy.[52] This was like a body governed by a nervous system that was missing its head. No one could see how all elements were part of a larger body, or that all parts were interacting with each other. No one could diagnose an illness in one part that could lead to the collapse of the entire body.

And so disasters came with brutal regularity. Every few years there were recessions and depressions: 1865–67, 1869–70, the Panic of 1873 and the five long years of depression that followed. Again recessions occurred in 1882–85, 1887–88, 1890–91, followed by another great crash in 1893. And so on down the line. Indeed, until the end of World War II, the American economy had been in crisis almost as often as not. Since the 1853 recession, growth had never lasted for more than three years before the next decline caused unemployment, bankruptcies, and widespread misery.

As discussed earlier, at first the motives for national accounting were largely external—defense, security, and war. With mounting economic crises, affecting ever more people and businesses, the need for national accounting became dire and internal: again and again, the economy seemed to have declared war on itself.

In each panic and recession, the needs of businesses and the needs of society ran into direct conflict with each other. What made short-term economic sense for one did not make sense for the other. When demand was in decline, businesses scaled back and laid off people. People who got laid off, aside from being in dire straits, had no income, thus contributing to even less demand, which in turn created problems for more businesses, and so forth. What economists call "boom and bust cycles"—as if there was some kind of natural law at work—each time created enormous hardships for which the market had no answers.

Without knowledge, or even awareness, of size or makeup of the national economy, practical ideas about how to counteract economic downturns—among captains of industry, politics, or academia—were predictably in very short supply.[53]

For the purposes of understanding different concepts behind measuring economic performance, a key development in the United States emerged in one such crisis—the aftermath of World War I. It is a story of impressive accomplishments and boundless idealism.

A series of events with long-ranging consequences was initiated when two very different men encountered each other during a hearing of the New York State Factory Committee in 1915.[54] Most of Europe had been at war for a year, though the conflict had not yet earned the label "World War." America had been battered by successive crises—ten recessions in little more than thirty years.[55]

The two men were Malcolm C. Rorty, an engineer and statistician working for the American Telephone and Telegraph Company, and Nahum I. Stone, an economist who frequently served as a consultant for the U.S. government on labor disputes. During the hearing in 1915, Stone argued in favor of a minimum wage law for workers, while Rorty rejected the idea as an undue infringement on contractual freedom and counterproductive to the welfare of workers. In terms of their sympathies and ideological viewpoints, the two men could hardly have been more different. Opposed to each other on most issues, their stances were quite typical of the range of viewpoints found in American society at the time.[56]

What matters for the story of the GDP, however, is their commonality: both believed that debates should be grounded in solid evidence. People had a right to diverse perspectives and opinions, but they did not have a right to their own facts. Arguments were only as valid as the evidence supporting them. Rorty and Stone quickly developed a deep respect for each other's faith in verifiable data.

When it came to the American economy, however, they concluded separately that good and useful data were unavailable. Without it, plans to respond to specific economic crises remained useless blueprints. More specifically, both agreed that national income, the total product of the economy, was of vital interest to every American. Yet its makeup as well as its volume was very poorly understood. As Rorty put it in a conversation with Stone, "here we are considering a most important question which deeply affects every man, woman, and child in this country, [but] there is no agreement on the purely arithmetic question of what part of the national income goes to each element of society."[57] Their initial question, in short, was similar to what had motivated King to investigate national accounts. Who was getting how much?

Rorty and Stone developed a big idea that was as logical as it was creative. It can still appeal to the modern reader: bring together the best minds in economics, from across the ideological spectrum and all spheres of business, including labor. Put them to the task of generating better information. The single overarching goal: "objective and impartial data" on the national economy. Rorty and Stone agreed that, whatever their different respective interpretations, the discussion should proceed not on the basis of speculation but rather on the basis of verifiable facts.

Over the course of the next few years, they successfully brought together a range of luminaries in economics, as well as representatives of business, labor, agriculture, publishing, politics, and finance. In January 1920 they officially founded the National Bureau of Economic Research (NBER) as a nonprofit and nonpartisan organization. In due course, NBER would become one of the most highly regarded economic research institutions in the country. Almost a century later, NBER provides volumes of authoritative economic data. Curiously, as a private organization, it also is the final arbiter on decisions of great political import in the United States. It is the NBER, for instance, which officially determines whether the nation is in a recession or depression.[58]

At the outset, the NBER's nineteen-member Board of Directors immediately proceeded with a large-scale project to determine national income. Under the direction of Wesley C. Mitchell, a Columbia University economics professor, researchers began to collect data. Due to Mitchell's expertise and leadership, however, they did not merely focus on what had been the founders' primary interest, namely distribution of national income. As their first publication noted, the "aim is to ascertain fundamental facts . . . as accurately as may be, and to make its findings widely known . . . to aid all thoughtful men [sic], however divergent their views of public policy, to base their discussions on objective knowledge as distinguished from subjective opinion."[59]

As we trace the development of what would eventually become the GDP, it is worthwhile to recall the tremendous hope that economists such as Mitchell associated with quantitative social science research. To do so, we can listen in on a 1918 lecture Mitchell gave at the Annual Meeting of the American Statistical Association in Richmond, Virginia.[60] The First World War had just ended, and Mitchell reflected on his responsibilities at the War Industries Board. The work showed, in Mitchell's words, the "great confusion" and lack of "good data" that combined to "startling defects of the federal machinery" in its preeminent pursuit of winning the war. The result: more hardship, more cost, and a longer duration of hostilities than necessary, for no one was able "to put before the responsible authorities promptly the data they needed concerning men and commodities, ships and factories."

Having thus reflected on past shortcomings, Mitchell turned his gaze toward the future. What set apart "the present stage of civilization" from "man's savage past," according to Mitchell, was precisely our "attitude toward the use of facts for the guidance of policy." But, he asserted, people had progressed very unevenly. "In science and in industry, we are radicals, radicals relying on a tested method. But in matters of social organization we retain a large part of the conservatism characteristic of the savage mind." Progress in social organization, he suggested, happens usually as a result of crisis and stress. "But when the stress is past we relapse gratefully into our comfortable faith in the thinking that has been done for us by our fathers."

The social sciences, according to Mitchell, promised a better way forward. "Reform by agitation or class struggle is a jerky way of moving forward, uncomfortable and wasteful of energy." He called for "quantitative analysis to point the way" toward a more deliberate future in which social statistics can "render a great service to government" and "to mankind." "Has not the time come," he asked, "to apply our intelligence to taking stock of the resources that the earth still holds and to developing methods of utilization that will protect our future?"

What was the most promising path toward "applying our intelligence," according to Mitchell? The "best hope for the future," he concluded, "lies in the extension to social organization of the methods which we already employ" in industry and science," namely "quantitative analysis" and planning. And "the parts where effort seems most promising" is measurement: "the measurement of social phenomena has many of the progressive features of the physical sciences. It shows forthright progress in knowledge of fact. . . . It is amenable to mathematical formulation. It is capable of forecasting group phenomena. It is objective." Mitchell concluded his address saying that "we may well cherish high hopes for the immediate future of social statistics" geared toward "the task of developing a method by which we may make cumulative progress in social organization."[61]

These were high aspirations, seemingly unencumbered by humility. From today's vantage point, thoroughly in the grip of the "data revolution," one may detect a note of naiveté that should sound very familiar. As a response to frequent chaos and crisis, on the other hand, it is difficult not to sympathize with the larger vision laid out by Mitchell. To prevent unnecessary suffering and needless squandering of national wealth, more and better knowledge of the products of national economic affairs was indeed needed.

As Mitchell had surmised, in the aftermath of World War I, with the urgency of crisis gone, government support for sustained national income efforts yet again largely disappeared. It was not until the next big crisis hit that Mitchell's vision would take more specific shape, and his hopes would be put to a first serious test.

Under the leadership of Mitchell, NBER stayed on topic. Within less than two years, they published their first pioneering work, entitled *Income in the*

United States: Its Amount and Distribution, 1909–1919.[62] Reflecting the diversity of backgrounds and viewpoints on NBER's board, the report explicitly discussed the immense complications in finding agreement on what "national income" is, how to measure it, and what data to use.[63]

In the end, it came down to practicality. It was not an intentional choice of what to value, and what to devalue. No, it was the data available that ended up determining what got measured, and how national income came to be defined. NBER researchers focused exclusively on money exchanged in the marketplace, and tested their approach in a double-entry format familiar to many readers: they figured out "income received" such as wages, salaries, and profits. They separated this from "income produced" such as value of goods manufactured, resources mined, and crops grown. To the extent the two approaches yielded similar figures, the results were thought to be accurate and reliable.

Here is the critical consequence: the NBER report in the end provided a convenient yet narrow answer. It focused exclusively on price as determined by the market in the official economy, tabulated either as production or as income. No clear rationale was given, other than limitations of data and difficulties theorizing other approaches. Practicality won the day. A larger vision of economic activity—one that might include the informal sector, or count depletion as depreciation, or measure human welfare—was left behind.

In its preface, the report did raise many important conceptual questions about what income and product might mean.[64] But they never tried to answer them. Their approach was driven by, and then further facilitated, hard numbers, and with it the illusion of objectivity. The sole focus? The value of commodities as determined by the market.[65]

No doubt, the NBER report was a quantum leap forward in statistical accounting. Today one can read history and economics texts that refer to "growth rates" in the economy, or marvel at "per capita GDP" in different nations over the centuries. One can also apply contemporary knowledge to long past crises—the depression of 1893, say—and study business decline, productivity by sector, negative growth rates, or unemployment. Until the critical contributions of scholars like Willford King, Wesley Mitchell or Irving Fisher in the United States, or Colin Clark, Richard Stone, James Meade and John Maynard Keynes in Great Britain, or Ernst Wagemann in Germany, none of this knowledge was available.[66] For better or worse, they did not possess our instruments. In the evocative language of John Maynard Keynes, the basic statistical apparatus was "deplorably deficient." Anyone seeking economic data of "national importance," Keynes concluded in 1927 with a focus on the British situation, continued "to grope in barbaric darkness."[67]

NBER and similar efforts in other countries began to offer illumination, yet their analytical beam helped elucidate only one narrow sliver of economic life. The sole focus was on value of commodities produced in the formal economy. Everything else remained in darkness. The analysis fell well short of Mitchell's original vision of applying "our intelligence to taking stock of the resources that the earth still holds and to developing methods of utilization that will protect our future."

We turn then to a brief exploration as to how private attempts to account for national income and product finally turned into an official government effort. It required the greatest economic calamity of modern times—the Great Depression—for Congress finally to demand more and better economic measures.

Chapter 3

THE CRUCIBLE OF CRISIS

The Great Depression and the Need for Economic Indicators

The entire economic framework in which our business
processes are set is wholly man made, and there is
nothing sacred about it.

—*Walter Rautenstrauch*

What we measure matters. Agreeing on what to measure requires articulating values, defining targets, and making choices. Once in place, measures establish the ground rules by which we operate.[1]

Outside of the imperative of individual businesses to make a profit, national economies at first possessed no reliable indicators for their performance. Measures that did exist were, at best, haphazard, imprecise, and far from routine. Better measures could be generated only once there was awareness for their need. In order to gain traction, moreover, they required significant incentives and an apparatus capable of undertaking the effort.

A brief reflection on how this works lays the groundwork for why and how national economic measures forcefully emerged during the Great Depression.

Without government, all modern economies would immediately collapse. Its very simplicity explains why this fact is routinely forgotten. Governments provide a series of services to modern economies, but two are decisive: (1) they decide the rules of the game, and (2) they enforce the rules. This is true whether the government is communist or capitalist, democratic or totalitarian.

Outside a government-operated framework, nothing we associate with modern economies would survive.[2] From establishing the basic infrastructure of modern economies—roads, bridges, sewage and water lines—to providing money, public education, establishment and enforcement of laws and regulations, to funding of a social safety net, food inspections, or law enforcement, government, as the political embodiment of the nation-state and a representative of the citizenry, is essential to the operations of modern economies.

The way property is defined and protected provides an illuminating example: whether land is considered public or can be appropriated as private possession or, subsequently, is expropriated again as eminent domain for a different public or private use, all follows an elaborate set of rules established and executed by government. These rules often get confusing: we are allowed, even encouraged, to pick and enjoy the candy on offer at the restaurant register, but when we replicate that behavior in a store, we likely get arrested for shoplifting. As any property lawyer can testify, what is and what is not "private property" is a complicated, completely man-made product that requires a huge governmental apparatus to define, codify, communicate, and enforce.

Recent economic headlines have raised another twisted logic of property relations: the unemployed veteran who goes to jail for sixteen years after stealing $120 from his local 7-Eleven, while the Goldman Sachs CEO retires in lavish wealth after stealing from thousands of clients, enabled by taxpayers who provided him with billions of bailout funds.

Thinking about property on a very basic level, it is worth remembering that the very foundation of property—our planet—not only provides us with everything we need to live, but also was here long before we were, and will be long after we're gone. Yet somehow we don't just borrow its use from our children and grandchildren. Most societies parcel their small part of earth into plots and awkwardly call it "ownership," for use and exploitation as the owner sees fit. One could suspect that more advanced future societies may look upon this arrangement the same way we look at an equally exploitative relationship: the ownership of people, also known as slavery.

One way to capture our unthinking attitude toward private property was highlighted by comedian Dick Gregory. While commenting on textbooks that refer to Columbus "discovering" America (despite the fact that it was already inhabited by as many as thirty million natives), he quipped, "How would you feel if I got into your car, told you that I had 'discovered' it, then kicked you to the curb and drove off?"

Whether private property in the form of people, land, or capital, how modern societies define and enforce notions of property is the result of long, and often acrimonious, struggles. At stake is our relationship with each other and with nature. The resulting rules have been laboriously constructed, codified, and implemented by governments. Only government can legally declare an action either "theft" or "discovery." Indeed, without its enforcement, the safeguards protecting property would be largely meaningless.

What is true for property is equally true for another key component of modern economies—the market. Modern markets and market-based economies are entirely a product of human invention, codified in law and enforced by government regulations. This is true from Beijing to Washington. As economic historians understand, "Previously to our time no economy has ever existed that, even in principle, was controlled by markets. . . . Though the institution of the market was fairly common since the later Stone Age, its role was no more than incidental to economic life."[3]

The modern market is perhaps the single most important political creation for the way economies around the world function today. Unfortunately, what people mean when they employ the term *market* is usually far from clear. This has led to a wide array of confusion. Protesting "government interference with the free market," for instance, is a bit like objecting to "bird interference with egg hatching." From the very beginning, the modern reality of markets has required a tremendous array of human activity—fighting wars, crafting law and public policies, instructing citizens about the latest set of rules, establishing and training enforcement agencies (tax collectors, the police, public jails). *All* of these are government activities. There is nothing "natural" about free market societies. "Free markets could never have come into being merely by allowing things to take their course. . . . *laissez-faire* itself was enforced by the state." In short: no government, no market.[4]

Governments create economic rules. And, short of large-scale self-governing bodies, governments are the only institutions that can and must enforce them, for otherwise the very rules would be meaningless. Among people in leadership positions, this fact is generally well understood. Corporations, for instance, continuously rely on government agencies to facilitate and protect their operations.[5]

Harvard Law Professor and later Senator Elizabeth Warren, after she had been charged with establishing the Consumer Financial Protection Bureau, brought the issue to a point: "There is nobody in this country who got rich on his own. Nobody." In case the deeper point was missed, she added,

> You built a factory out there? Good for you. But I want to be clear: you moved your goods to market on the roads the rest of us paid for; you hired workers the rest of us paid to educate; you were safe in your factory because of police forces and fire forces that the rest of us paid for. You didn't have to worry that marauding bands would come and seize everything at your factory, and hire someone to protect against this, because of the work the rest of us did.[6]

The government creating and enforcing the rules, however, merely established the foundation for modern economies. It did not address the persistently troubling question of what to do when the game itself fails, despite more or less proper enforcement of existing rules. Names commonly used for such failures are "recession" or "depression."

Sometimes the downturn goes well beyond a temporary calamity and threatens the very existence of the system itself, as during the Great Depression, or during the recent Great Recession that started in late 2007. The modern reader may recall the familiar terminology of "too-big-to-fail" and the "impending disaster" that was barely averted by the passage of the $787 billion stimulus package.[7] One could fill libraries with historical records of people in positions of political and economic authority evoking imminent doom for each economic crisis in American history: the "threat of collapse," and, worse, the "threat of revolt" if things could not be turned around.[8]

Our story picks up in the early 1930s, when America had reached such a moment. Exceptional even among the long parade of severe economic crises in American history, the Great Depression challenged the viability of the United States as a democratic nation if government could not swiftly develop new tools to stabilize the economy. The "American way" was in peril—the more so the longer and the deeper the economic slump—for "to the inflamed spirit of a people crushed by hunger and adversity, nothing is impossible, not even revolution."[9]

The Great Depression posed a new set of problems. What started several months before the stock market crash of October of 1929 and lasted almost until the Japanese attack on Pearl Harbor in December 1941, brought the United States and the rest of the industrialized world to the brink of collapse. If the economic floor had not yet caved in, it was certainly buckling. Creating and enforcing rules no longer sufficed. Manipulating public opinion or controlling popular unrest, while certainly a mainstay of politics throughout prior generations, did not address the threats the system itself suddenly faced.

The sheer scale of the failure made it unprecedented. Bankruptcies reached a record high: of the roughly twenty-six thousand banks that existed in early 1929 in the United States, for instance, almost ten thousand had failed by 1932.[10] Investment in the American economy came to a virtual halt, dropping over 95 percent from $16.2 billion in 1929 to a meager $800 million in 1932.[11]

By the end of 1932, output fell to little more than half of its 1929 levels, and international trade plummeted by almost 70 percent. Most ominously, the unemployment rate climbed from 3.2 percent in 1929 to an estimated 25 percent in 1933, with millions more working part-time and almost everyone losing real wages.[12] The number of workers employed in manufacturing was cut in nearly half, with those hanging on to their jobs facing pay cuts and shorter hours. As historian David Kennedy pointed out, half of America's workforce remained "unutilized throughout the Depression decade—a loss of some 104 million person-years of labor, the most perishable and irreplaceable of all commodities."[13]

But the full tragedy of unemployment ran much deeper than what we can, in retrospect, put into neat numbers. People who lost their jobs stayed out of work. "Many lost their skills or the opportunity to develop them or to use them in occupations for which they were best fitted," writes one economic historian. "Many people almost irretrievably lost their faith in themselves. The psychic wounds of the Great Depression were non-measureable but enormous."[14]

Small farm operators were as desperate as workers: not able to make ends meet or pay back their debts, tens of thousands went bankrupt. It created "the bitter irony of starving industrial workers unable to buy food that farmers found unprofitable to sell."[15]

With the benefit of hindsight, we have a fairly good grasp of what happened. Yet citing statistics is also highly deceptive. As the economic stability of the 1920s gave way to chaos, confusion, and suffering, neither the captains of industry nor political leaders had access to basic economic figures, much less to the vast array of data historians can rely on today.

Strange as it may seem today, business leaders knew a great deal about their own shifting bottom lines, but next to nothing about what was happening in the economy at large. Elected officials received reports—increasingly urgent in tone—about unemployment, homelessness, and despair in their districts, but had no concrete data about how widespread this situation was. Policymakers groped in the dark when thinking about what the government could or should do to intervene and help. Whether it came to the number of persons unemployed or the number of families receiving aid, the types of relief available, or the conditions of communities providing any kind of support, "no one person did have detailed and accurate answers."[16]

In the face of increasing human misery, Congress appeared inactive and apathetic. Only a handful of elected leaders appeared sensitive to the needs of working Americans.

Perhaps the most outspoken was a senator from Wisconsin, Robert La Follette, Jr., who became a forceful defender of labor. Son of one of America's best-known progressive politicians, La Follette was neither shackled to party dogma nor beholden to public sentiment. Following his Midwestern sense of right and wrong, La Follette routinely criticized, throughout his career in the Senate, members of both parties, and charted an independent course. As a "progressive Republican," he began to decry what he perceived to be the total inaction of the Hoover government in helping unemployed Americans.

In Congress, as early as 8 February 1930, La Follette stood almost alone in advocating relief for those who suffered unemployment "for no fault of their own." Even progressive colleagues like Nebraska Senator George Norris counseled "to keep the manhood and womanhood of America upon a high standard by not compelling the men and women of our country to become subjects of charity for food and clothing."[17] To La Follette, such reasoning was astonishing. What else was the purpose of government if not to provide relief and support to its own citizens in moments of distress? And was there not ample evidence that government had in the recent past come to the aid of starving Europeans, or victims of the Mississippi flood? What, he asked in Congress, was the difference between a natural catastrophe and an economic calamity when it came to helping people who were drowning?[18]

More than anyone else in Congress, La Follette tried to break through the paralyzed politics surrounding the crisis in order to help people. He put his fingers on a politically sensitive component of the problem: "Can it be that the Republican Party, which has lived on talk about prosperity since 1922, finds itself in a more convenient position *not to have facts* about unemployment," so that it can continue to issue positive statements to the public "based upon absolutely unreliable data?"[19]

Data gave politicians the power of choice: to act or not to act. And here it becomes clear why measuring economic activity was never an objective pursuit, but always a deeply political choice. In this case, inaction did not require data, as La Follette understood. Action certainly did. In order for the federal government to provide relief, offer works programs, or stimulate certain aspects of the economy, it needed reliable, comprehensive, and up-to-date information—not only about unemployment but also about wage levels, investments, productivity, and earnings.

But no such information existed. No federal agency in the early 1930s was tasked with keeping macroeconomic data. Indeed, not paying attention to things like unemployment followed, according to John Kenneth Galbraith, a certain logic: "one did not spend money collecting information on what, in high economic principle, could not exist."[20]

As we have seen in chapter 2, the first organization to put together a set of data on national income—its size, year-to-year variation, and distribution—was a private institution: the National Bureau of Economic Research (NBER).[21] The first time the federal government prepared a national income estimate was in 1926, covering the years 1918–23. Yet the following year, the Federal Trade Commission's funds were cut, and it stopped the estimates. No other federal agency picked up the work. In short, by the time the economic train was racing toward the abyss in 1929, no comprehensive set of data on the national economy existed, either from private or federal sources.[22]

To our present-day sensibilities, this is shocking. For the government to step in and try to slow the economic train's race toward disaster required basic information. What policymakers faced was not just a runaway train without useful gauges, but the pressing need for government to operate as the well-informed engineer, keeping a sharp eye on the track ahead. If the engineer could only peer into the darkness as though blindfolded, this was obviously not a reassuring situation—not for business, not for workers, not for American society.

Who would shine a light? The feds needed basic data on economic conditions: information on employment, on income, on demand, on production. Without such information they were largely impotent to stimulate demand, stabilize finances, to direct investment, or provide aid to the unemployed.

No one in power in the 1930s realized the full degree to which the way we keep score ends up determining the rules of the game. Much less did anyone guess that the gauge that would emerge from the Great Depression would end up fundamentally shaping the course of future global economic decision-making.

As the depression intensified, none of this was understood. The majority of policymakers and economists still believed in a naive version of the laissez-faire market—an economy essentially self-regulating and thus best left alone. Effective tools for those who wanted to avert disaster, or just wanted to help those in dire straits, did not exist.

By today's standards, the government of 1931 was tiny. Very few people thought that government "had either the right or the responsibility to intervene in any meaningful fashion in economic affairs."[23] Aside from printing and regulating the flow of national currency, imposing taxes and a select number of tariffs, the government's toolbox for pulling its national economy out of the ditch was essentially empty.[24]

A few politicians began to demand new tools.[25] First they asked for more money, in the form of aid to the unemployed or to distressed communities, even if it required the government to go into debt. This was new, since most still perceived debt permissible only during times of war. What we recognize today as "deficit spending" did not yet seem culturally acceptable as a possible means to stimulate economic demand. As the descent into economic failure sped up, however, those policymakers unwilling to stand by idly realized something had to be done—and it required more and better data.

Following La Follette's push to generate more information and better accounts proves instructive in several ways. First, it confirms in vivid detail just how little the Washington establishment knew—about economics in general, and, more importantly, about the specific condition of the American economy during the early years of the Great Depression. Second, it helps us trace both the reasons and direction behind the creation of better datasets. Third, it illuminates the intricate relationship between data, theory, and action. More specifically, exploring La Follette's efforts reveals the connection between reliable national income accounts, the rapidly rising currency of the theories of a soon-to-be famous British economist by the name of John Maynard Keynes, and several key programs loosely summarized as New Deal policies.[26]

Finally, by tracing La Follette's actions, we see how GDP came to be constructed. We observe the uncertainties and disagreements among its first and second-generation creators. And we can trace the progression by which a technical instrument initially conceived for very narrow purposes morphed into the world's predominant goal. The fact that this accounting device conquered the world and in the process began to blind entire cultures to possible, and perhaps necessary, alternatives makes the story significant to everyone.

+++

Between the onset of the depression in late 1929 and the election of Franklin D. Roosevelt in November of 1932, Senator La Follette used every opportunity to focus on the plight of the swelling numbers of unemployed. With increasing flourish and anger he and Robert Wagner of New York spoke of the "long and sad procession of weary men in search of work"—people who, from ocean to ocean, in millions of homes, experience "the same human tragedy" of "poverty, idleness and charity."[27]

Several congressional colleagues, however, doubted the severity of the economic downturn—and unemployment in particular—and demanded "proof." Many believed in a set of ideas, broadly associated with laissez-faire capitalism, that considered economic slumps an inevitable (some even opined it a "healthy") part of a functioning market economy. As one historian summarized this view, they thought "a depression was the necessary and unavoidable after-effect of a prosperous era with its accompaniment of personal extravagance, reckless business practices, and financial irresponsibility. It was the time for a beneficial readjustment . . . and for washing away the encumbering debris accumulated by unreasonable expectation."[28] This stance prompted lawmakers to see the proper role of government as doing nothing: stand aside and let the forces of the free market bring things "back into equilibrium."

The reasons for this widespread sentiment varied. The result was the same. Democratic Senator Thomas P. Gore in 1931 stated that government can no more prevent economic crisis than it can outlaw sickness: "You might just as well try to prevent the human race from having a disease as to prevent economic grief of this sort."[29] Herbert Hoover's secretary of the treasury, banker Andrew Mellon, took this sentiment one step further with the following advice to his president: "Liquidate labor, liquidate stocks, liquidate the farmers, liquidate real estate. It will purge the rottenness out of the system." Downturns, he counseled the president, not only were normal, but actually a beneficial and occasionally necessary thing. "High costs of living . . . will come down. People will work harder, live moral lives. Values will be adjusted, and enterprising people will pick up the wrecks from less competent people."[30]

In October 1932, as temperatures dropped into the 20s in New Jersey, millionaire Republican Senator Dwight Morrow aired this piece of wisdom: "There is something about too much prosperity that ruins the fiber of the people." Edmund Wilson, the prominent social commentator, sardonically responded, "It is a reassuring thought, in the cold weather, that the emaciated men in the breadlines, the men and women beggars in the streets, and the children dependent on them, are all having their fiber hardened."[31]

Such sentiments did not provide an environment sympathetic to those suddenly kicked to the curb. To make matters worse, in early 1930, both the White House and the Labor Department issued reports that "unemployment had turned the corner." We now know such statements came three months before the bottom on employment began to fall out. At the time, politicians like Senator David I. Walsh of Massachusetts pointed out that there is a "strong, bitter antagonism to the administration" denying "the facts and diverting attention" to its "complete absence of sympathy with the plight of the unemployed."[32] This may not have been fair to President Hoover, but it accurately reflected the result of his administration's policies.[33]

Less than a year into the slump, few understood its causes. No one accurately predicted the depth the American economy would sink to by 1933. It was unprecedented. As politicians debated what to do, data essential to making sense of what was happening were missing from all considerations; a basic understanding of modern capitalist economies was absent from most. Indeed, given the scarcity of reliable macro-indicators, combined with the lack of regulations and the near total absence of people in positions of authority with a good grasp of basic economic dynamics, it is surprising that the rapidly expanding national economy performed as well as it did for as long as it did.

On the other hand, drastic decline and imminent collapse brought forward a time-honored truth: the views people expressed largely mirrored their own experiences. With few exceptions, elected or appointed officials with secure incomes perceived the day-to-day reality of what was called an "economic crisis" very differently from the swelling ranks of millions of workers who suddenly lost their family income. No available governmental aid yet existed. Things like unemployment benefits, Social Security, or Medicare were all unknown. Outside of aid from communities, churches, families, or voluntary organizations, people without work had no safety net. From the perspective of a mahogany-paneled office suite, some business and government leaders made limited observations about "the less competent" or about the "temporary nature" of the crisis.

At the same time, however, the number of ordinary citizens and rich industrialists who wanted to help the swelling ranks of people in dire straits also rose rapidly. When confronted on a personal level with the hardship of fellow citizens, many Americans tended to rise to the occasion. Daily donations of clothes, preparations of warm meals, a dollar or two for help around the house or the farm skyrocketed. Still, it was like putting Band-Aids on a gunshot wound. Churches, neighborhoods, and municipalities soon found themselves overwhelmed by the sheer number of people in need.

It was the magnitude of the crisis, more than anything, that prompted La Follette to demand help from the federal government. The crisis was national. Clearly, no other institution than the federal government had the power, resources, and legal authority for a national, coordinated response.

But what exactly was the nature of the crisis? How many people were directly affected? On dozens of occasions, La Follette called on the White House, the Commerce Department, and the Senate to create an agency or commission to obtain reliable nation-wide figures on the "labor situation."[34] As he memorably pointed out, "One can get a statement almost down to the minute as to the hog, sheep, or cow population of the United States," but "you can *not* get any accurate information concerning the great, pressing human problem of unemployment."[35] After almost a year of unsuccessful attempts, La Follette went on record stating that "the time has come for the Senate and the Congress to ascertain what are the facts concerning the situation and to act accordingly."[36]

Trying to quell mounting pressure, President Hoover established the President's Emergency Committee for Employment (PECE) in the fall of 1930.[37] Its stated goal was to mobilize and coordinate charitable giving, enlisting hundreds of business and community leaders.[38] Not generally opposed to government regulation or intervention, Hoover was nevertheless adamantly opposed to outright aid to the unemployed. Direct relief, he stated again in 1931, must be avoided at all cost because "the net results of governmental doles are to lower wages toward the bare subsistence level and to endow the slacker."[39] While the Hoover administration encouraged public works programs and urged citizens to extend a helping hand toward the unemployed, it steadfastly resisted any kind of federal support. The work of PECE turned out to be little more than window-dressing.

A year later, serious study of unemployment, as well as any substantive help for the growing army of the jobless, remained in very short supply. When called before a Senate subcommittee in January 1932, Walter S. Gifford, the chair of the successor organization to PECE (POUR), and president of AT&T, bluntly stated that he saw no reason to learn about the levels of unemployment or the needs of the unemployed, for such data would be of no "particular value." He continued to put his trust in volunteerism, self-reliance, and the healing powers of a market economy—a set of beliefs that came easier to a corporate president on loan to the federal government than to the unemployed. "My sober and considered judgment," Gifford opined, "is that at this stage . . . Federal aid would be a disservice to the unemployed."[40] When Gifford repeatedly expressed "great optimism" about the economy and the job market, Senator Edward Costigan of Colorado inquired about evidence or reports on which this optimism was based. Gifford replied, "I have none, Senator."[41]

La Follette, in the meantime, had begun to generate his own datasets. He encouraged relief agencies and labor unions to provide him with information, and his office sent out questionnaires to mayors of all U.S. cities with populations over five thousand. By the end of 1930, this allowed him, on the basis of returns from 303 cities in 41 states with a total population of six million, to conclude that "15.8 percent are unemployed"—a figure substantially higher than Hoover administration estimates.[42]

As reports, letters, and telegrams continued to reach La Follette's office, documenting growing tales of anguish among those desperately searching for work, he carried boxes of documents to the floor of the Senate and, for several hours in December, read them into the *Congressional Record*.[43] With the kind of clarity that comes from sustained reflection, he then asked his colleagues why "there would be no question" that they would "promptly and generously" dispense aid if people were victims of an earthquake, but they refuse to provide essential support when people are victims of an "economic earthquake, caused by bankruptcy in leadership of American industry, finance and Government?"[44]

Congress refused to take action. On 10 February 1931, the senator took the floor again to protest adjournment of Congress in the midst of rising misery without any attempt to provide federal relief. This, he argued, equaled a "breach of faith with the American people."[45]

La Follette pushed forward on several fronts. Immediate relief for the unemployed remained his highest priority, something he thought could best be pursued by providing financial assistance, and by creating employment opportunities through public-works programs. But he continued to run into

seemingly insurmountable obstacles on both fronts. He required the proverbial "proof" requested by his immobilized peers. He needed up-to-date economic data that could inform national policymaking. In February 1931 he
introduced a bill (S. 6215) to authorize hearings to create a national economic
council, which would consist of experts to advise the president on economic
policy. La Follette understood that such a council would need access to reliable
national economic data: number of unemployed, productivity, or national
income—all then unavailable.[46]

It was not an easy sell. His fellow Senators eventually agreed to Senate Resolution 460, authorizing La Follette's committee to hold hearings. But they did
so only after they had cut in half his modest budget request of five thousand
dollars.[47] The debates make clear that the majority had no intention of moving
forward with actual implementation of a national economic council.

Part of the issue was a fundamental conflict in views about the role and
responsibility of government in economic matters. What La Follette had in
mind, and what many of his opponents despised him for, was an increase in
government planning and control. As he told the *New York Times*, "This piece
of legislation is a challenge to the fixed belief that hard times and good times
alternate in cycles. I do not believe hard times are necessary provided it is
possible to look ahead and plan to meet the emergencies that may arise."[48]

Clearly, as the Depression revealed yet again, the interplay of supply and
demand did not guarantee that the economy would serve all people. With a
wary eye on developments in Russia, Germany, and Italy, La Follette sought
a democratic alternative to totalitarian responses to depression and misery.
For him, only a measure of economic democracy could guarantee individual
freedoms and individual economic opportunity for all. The government, as a
democratic representative of the people, needed to step in. The alternatives
were worse. As publisher Robert P. Scripps described the challenge, if Americans could not find a way to shorten work hours and to share both work and
wealth more fairly, "the alternative is the goose step, one way or another, and
Lenin or Mussolini makes mighty little difference."[49]

Scripps voiced his fears at a Progressive Conference La Follette and four
of his Senate colleagues put together in Washington, D.C. [50] Their goal was

to bring together politicians from across the country to outline a legislative agenda to create a "public machinery of planning and control" intended to break the cycle of boom and bust. Without it, La Follette was convinced, "the unequal distribution of wealth now produced will halt the progress of mankind and, in the end, will retard or prevent recovery." [51]

La Follette's subcommittee on creating a national economic council held seventeen day-long hearings from 22 October until 19 December. A high-powered selection of forty-five experts testified—industrialists, bankers, statisticians, economists, labor leaders, industrial commissioners. The outcome was astonishing: the economic elite of the United States was essentially clueless. And, by and large, they knew it.

Frances Perkins, at the time industrial commissioner of the state of New York,[52] put it best when she stated, in response to a question about unemployment figures for her state, "Senator, we have no exact knowledge." In case the larger point was missed, she clarified: "Nor have they [any knowledge] in any industrial State that I know of." Anyone trying to stabilize the economy, she added, was working under a severe "handicap," for information across the board was not "collected sufficiently so that anyone can understand what the economic advice in general ought to be." It was a sobering verdict.[53] If nothing else, it was evidence of the "barbaric darkness" Keynes had described a few years earlier.

The collective testimony clarified how ill-informed all major economic players were. Individual businesses had undergone "revolutionary changes" in planning their own operations, but there was no comparable development visible on a larger, much less a national, scale. Economic data, while available in growing volume, were insufficient, scattered, and not up to date. According to the chief of the economic and research division of the Bureau of Foreign and Domestic Trade, J. Frederic Dewhurst, on vital questions such as employment or wage rates, "no direct measure" existed. The story was no better for production, investment, inventories, commodity orders, or even consumer purchases. Government was "floundering in the dark."[54]

At the close of the hearings, La Follette inserted into the record a document, entitled "The Basic Factual Survey," that specified the information he thought was needed. A "comprehensive survey of economic conditions" must go well "beyond what is now available," including "a summary of past experience and trends" of (1) production, (2) productive power and surplus capacity, and (3) consumption and standards of living, as well as a study of (4) cyclical movements of income, consumers' expenditures, consumers' credit, and savings, and, lastly, (5) potential demand.[55]

Political elites were unmoved. The *Washington Post* opined that the Progressive Conference "rehearsed with renewed vigor" all the "quack remedies for the country's distress."[56] But, other than do nothing, they offered no alternatives. The economy, in the meantime, continued its freefall, unemployment climbed rapidly, and assistance funds effectively ran out. Instead of concerted public action, the result was more politics-as-usual. "And so," concluded a leading historian of the Great Depression, "through the winter of 1931–32, the third winter of the depression, relief resources, public and private, dwindled toward the vanishing point."[57]

Among the privileged, it seemed, the self-serving fairytale that each was his own fate's master was immune to reality. Hundreds of thousands more joined the ranks of the destitute each week, their only sin being that they played by the rules.[58] In a nation of roughly 125 million people, several million workers and their dependent families were simply unaccounted for. The establishment players, shielded from hardship by privilege, trust funds, and taxpayer-funded incomes, did not begin to pay attention until the crisis began to knock on their own doors by threatening to bring down the entire system.

In January of 1932, La Follette introduced another relief bill with two Senate colleagues. He issued this admonition: "Proceed, if you will; make the record that you will extend relief to organized wealth in this situation . . . and that you will turn your back upon millions of upstanding Americans who are suffering want, privation, and misery. But I say that if you fail to meet this issue now, you will meet it later. You cannot duck it; you cannot dodge it."[59]

Shortly before voting on the bill that would have provided a modest $375 million in federal funds for the jobless, Senator Costigan took the floor. The soft-spoken Colorado Democrat, described by colleagues as "shy" and "scholarly," offered a warning that, in hindsight, could just as easily have been articulated during the Depression of the mid-1870s or the Great Recession of the early twenty-first century:

> If, following the legislative record already made at this session, this body refuses to admit the justice of the pending measure . . . a new slogan of sinister significance and far-reaching consequence will be heard in America. That slogan, I fear, may be, "Billions for big business, but no mercy for mankind; billions for doles from the people's taxes for bankers, railroad executives, and financial institutions through government in business and financial corporations, but not one Federal cent for humanity."[60]

On 16 February 1932, the Senate defeated the La Follette / Costigan federal relief bill by a vote of 48 to 35.[61]

Sobered but not yet defeated by Congress's inaction, La Follette's Senate Committee on Manufactures held two more subcommittee hearings. Both addressed the "cooperation by the federal government with the several states" in relieving "the hardship and suffering caused by unemployment."[62]

In a Senate speech on 22 June 1932 that lasted several hours, La Follette offered a historical tour of the Great Depression. He described causes, explained consequences, and provided a detailed outline of what he considered "gross inaction" on the part of President Hoover. He called for a public works programs to create jobs for millions of unemployed. In a dramatic rhetorical flourish, he implored them, saying, "We are facing a grave national emergency, graver than in all the history of the Republic, and I do not except the World War." Reflecting again on the more than ten million men and women out of work, he called for "drastic measures . . . necessary to prevent national paralysis and economic chaos." And in case his sense of urgency was lost on anyone in the Senate, he concluded: "I feel it is my responsibility to . . . warn my colleagues that those who vote against this bill must assume full responsibility for the disaster that will follow."[63]

For millions of Americans, disaster did follow. None of La Follette's legislative initiatives geared at providing support to the unemployed were approved—at least not until after the inauguration of President Franklin D. Roosevelt on 4 March 1933. For the moment, the "quack theories" of established wisdom prevailed.

Yet even before their efforts began to inform the later New Deal legislation, La Follette and his supporters did make their mark. Two weeks prior to his speech, on 8 June 1932, the Senate approved Resolution 220, introduced by La Follette with little fanfare or notice, which officially requested the Department of Commerce to generate a report on national income for the years 1929, 1930, and 1931.[64]

Explaining his request in the Senate, La Follette stated, "In the consideration of legislation in the future, I believe that the data to be compiled . . . will be of very great importance in helping Congress to determine policies relating to fiscal affairs of the Government, as well as to other legislation which is economic in character."[65] For policymakers, his point was both basic and profound: without good sets of data, there was no way to distinguish between quack and sound policies.

At this point, two groups discovered their common interest in better data: congressional supporters of La Follette, and officials at the Commerce Department. Isador Lubin, one of La Follette's economic advisors, managed to recruit the Director of the Commerce Department's Bureau of Foreign and Domestic Commerce (BFDC), Frederick M. Feiker, to endorse the study of the economy, and, more specifically, to ascertain income and purchasing power on a national level. The goal was to obtain up-to-date and reliable data necessary to inform and guide future national economic policymaking.[66]

With approval of Resolution 220, the groundwork for launching GDP was laid.

Chapter 4

BORN FROM DISASTER

The Making of a Key Measure

Much is to be gained by looking not only at the finished
product but also at the original architectural plans.
—*Mark Perlman*

Sometimes it's not what we measure, but what we fail to measure, that gets us in trouble. In the world of national policymaking, action requires measures.

National income and product accounts emerged from deep crisis. Tens of thousands of families had lost their homes. Some found refuge with family and friends, other sought sanctuary in shelters or temporarily lived in their cars. Among the elderly, more and more had to make tough decisions between food or medicine. They could not afford both. Some could afford neither. Perhaps the hardest hit were children, growing numbers of whom saw their parents in despair, their schools beyond reach, their childhood ransacked, and their future imperiled.

It happened in 1932, at the height of the Great Depression. It happened again in 2009, in the midst of the Great Panic. But how deep, and how widespread, was each crisis? What measurement could Americans rely on to find out?

In 2009 the answer seemed obvious. After sharp downturns of Gross Domestic Product in at least two quarters of most of the world's industrialized economies, sighs of relief could be heard around the globe when an "End to Global Recession" was finally announced. The specter of another Great Depression had haunted billions. By the end of 2009, it was finally over. How did we know? GDP had grown again.

Strangely, though, many other indicators—unemployment, poverty, home ownership—refused to get better. Two years later, world leaders thus gathered in a crisis meeting at Camp David. Summed up by the *New York Times* headline, they "urged growth, not austerity." The final statement left no doubt: "our imperative is to promote growth."[1] They did not mention that what they had in mind was nothing other than GDP growth—ironically the very kind of growth that had failed to raise living standards or revitalize the economy. Apparently it seemed too obvious to require mentioning.

But the answer was not always obvious at all. For thousands of years, there had been little or no growth. When large-scale economic growth made an appearance—first in England, then in other European nations and the United States—no one had a clear, let alone standardized or uniform, understanding of either the components or volume of wealth generated. Consequently, as outlined in chapter 3, as late as 1932, no measure existed to determine whether the United States was in a "panic," a temporary economic slump, or what was later called the "Great Depression." No one knew exactly what was going on.

THE CHALLENGE

To find out proved a gigantic task. What La Follette's Senate Resolution 220 requested, "estimates of total national income" for the years 1929–1931," required the proverbial invention of the wheel. Data were ruefully incomplete or too outdated to be of any use. Generally accepted definitions did not exist. Resolution 220 asked for "portions of the national income originating from agriculture, manufacturing, mining, transportation, and other gainful industries and occupations," and to break down this income by type: "wages, rents, royalties, dividends, profits, and other types of payments."[2] On the surface, simple enough. Yet it required far-reaching conceptual decisions: who or what would be included, and on the basis of what?

Few people were better equipped to tackle this challenge than the man eventually selected: Simon Kuznets. Yet many administrative wheels had to be greased before the task could be tackled. Bureaucrats in the Commerce Department, facing smaller budgets for their regular operations, balked at taking on new duties, much less new people and new expenses. Still, in January of 1933, with tireless support of a small staff from the Commerce Department and the National Bureau of Economic Research, Kuznets finally set out on the huge task of finding useful information on the state of the American economy.

As astonishing as it is now to see the gross economic ignorance of policymakers during the early 1930s, it is worth recalling that government, prior to 1933, was tiny by today's standards, in the United States even more than in Europe. As one scholar put it, "It played almost no role in trying to stabilize the national economy, provide support to poor and elderly people, support agriculture or affect policies of state and local governments." In 1929 total government spending was a mere 1.6 percent of total economic output (as compared to over 20 percent today). Income taxes as a minor source of revenue existed only in fourteen states in 1930. Sales taxes were not invented until that same year (in Mississippi).[3]

Except for war, in short, few governments had ever perceived a pressing need for nation-wide economic datasets. Plus, generating reliable figures was labor intensive and expensive. Before 1934, no U.S. businesses or citizens were required to share with government much of the data necessary for the creation of useful national income and product accounts.

Yet since 1890 the American economy had grown by leaps and bounds to become the world's largest producer and market. Between the end of World War I and the onset of the Great Depression in 1929, industrial production as a whole had nearly doubled—both manufacturing and agriculture were bursting at the seams.[4] In ever-greater numbers, Americans purchased cars, phones, washing machines, vacuum cleaners, and other new consumer items. Formerly a debtor nation, the United States had become the world's largest lender during World War I. President Woodrow Wilson was nearly right when he stated in 1919, looking ahead to peacetime commerce, that "the financial leadership will be ours. The industrial primacy will be ours. The commercial advantage will be ours."[5] It was, no doubt, the dawning of the American century.

But there were also signs of trouble. While the decade of the 1920s generated unprecedented growth, with little inflation and virtually no unemployment, it also yielded another, rarely noted development. By 1929 half of the population was classified as urban. As an earlier president, Thomas Jefferson, had warned, a predominantly urban population did not just raise political problems: freedom, he had argued, required people's ability to make an independent living. Urbanization raised lasting economic challenges. The livelihoods of a majority of Americans by 1930 directly relied on the health of the American economy, and, specifically, its ability to provide jobs and income. If businesses did not offer jobs, people had no employment. Without employment, they had no income. Without income, they quickly became destitute, for few any longer had access to the subsistence of Jefferson's yeoman farmers.

The economy had become much more complex and interdependent—and its health much more crucial to people's lives. More than ever before, the national economy relied on growing production, businesses relied on consumer demand, and citizens relied on paid employment in order to survive.

Finally, the Depression raised a critical question: as much as the economy seemed to depend on it, was further economic growth really possible? Or had the economy perhaps reached a state of maturity, where health could no longer be achieved through growth?

Two months before he was elected president, Franklin D. Roosevelt gave full expression to his own doubts about the future. In a campaign address, he contrasted the vigor of America with a world "old and tired." He then proceeded to portray an American economy that had reached its limits, and might in fact be in danger of being "overbuilt." The "last frontier has long since been reached," he continued, free land is "practically no more," and we are now "providing a drab living for our own people." All this, he concluded, "calls for a re-appraisal of values."

Roosevelt then explained what this might mean for the future of the American economy:

> A mere builder of more industrial plants, a creator of more railroad systems, an organizer of more corporations, is as likely to be a danger as a help. . . . Our task now is not discovery or exploitation of natural resources, or necessarily

producing more goods. It is the soberer, less dramatic business of administering resources and plants already in hand, . . . of adapting existing economic organizations to the service of the people.[6]

In hindsight we can say that his remarks were prescient. In terms of predicting the immediate future, however, they could hardly have been further off the mark. Not long before the economy entered its longest stretch of sustained growth, Roosevelt was describing the end of growth, a stationary economy as anticipated by early economists such as Adam Smith and John Stuart Mills, advocated by later thinkers like John Maynard Keynes, and required by the imperatives of sustainability today.

At the time Roosevelt made his statements, however, no one had access to an informed analysis as to what had happened to the economy, how all the moving pieces fit together, or what some possible future courses might look like. Neither politicians nor economists nor accountants knew. In times of national crisis, of course, this information suddenly became an urgent necessity. Roosevelt would have been the first to acknowledge the need for better data and a better understanding of the workings of the national economy. What might a path leading out of "drab conditions" look like?

Given the state of the world economy in the early 1930s, it is therefore not surprising that a national indicator like GDP was an idea whose time had come. Still, what Kuznets' group accomplished between January of 1933 and January of 1934 was extraordinary. The sheer volume and detail of their thick final report to the Senate, simply entitled "National Income 1929–32," was path-breaking.[7] And, though no one knew it then, it represented a giant step toward a very particular articulation of economic objectives. It is no exaggeration to say that today, the entire world economy follows the basic script first drafted in this 1934 report.

In broad strokes, the story goes like this: In June of 1932, the Senate passed a resolution stipulating that the Department of Commerce report on national income in the United States from 1929 to 1931. Under the leadership of Simon Kuznets, a team of researchers produced the first complete national income statistics, which was delivered to the Senate in January of 1934. Their work provided one of the blueprints for later GNP (and GDP) accounts.[8]

The problem is that such a narrative leaves out both meaning and consequence of what had occurred. For starters, almost as soon as they were published, national income accounts began to provide the much-needed data that literally made possible America's innovative economic policies, only later identified with John Maynard Keynes, and popularized as the New Deal.

Then, at the beginning of World War II, this set of numbers drove the unprecedented productivity of American manufacture, decisive both for the stunning speed of American military mobilization and for the eventual victory of overwhelming U.S. military force.

Following the 1944 international agreements at Bretton Woods and the creation of the World Bank and the International Monetary Fund, GDP accounts became an economic version of "magnetic North." They guided economic development policies away from another great depression—in the United States as well as in other major capitalist economies. Indeed, in the United States, with the 1946 Employment Act, national income and product accounts became codified in law as the central goal-post for economic progress. In post–World War II capitalist economies, chief among them the U.S. economy, the overarching purpose of the economic policies, and in short order of politics itself, came to be defined by GDP. For policymakers, the central goal became fostering growth and, by extension, to prevent at all costs a shrinking economy (all defined by GDP). Everything else was secondary.

In historical terms, it was a great transition.

By 1954 all noncommunist economies in the world had signed onto GDP accounts as set forth by the UN in its 1953 publication of the *Standards of National Accounting*. SNA, it is crucial to note, was essentially a replica of America's GDP system. Shortly after the Soviet Union collapsed in 1991, finally, every major national economy was on board—economic success around the globe was henceforth measured by the same set of standards, in fact, by the same number: GDP.

Why so little of this development is part of a public conversation or, indeed, even recognized, much less understood in its wide-ranging implications, remains somewhat mysterious. Given common aversions to the jargon often found in official economics, there are several conceivable reasons. Certainly, that the break-through initially appeared to entail little more than technical accounting procedures did not help. Much of the effort involved tedious work counting and tabulating, and centered on debates about obscure economic concepts. Initially, it also did not produce tangible results for people's day-to-day lives. That, however, would soon and dramatically change.

We return in chapter 9 to the question of what happened to people's lives once countries signed up to follow the magic wand of GDP growth. But first we need to explore how the measure was developed, then refined (chapter 5), before it became the world's single yardstick for success (chapter 6).

THE PLAYERS

Described as quiet with a dry, unassuming sense of humor, Simon Kuznets came across to his colleagues as a meticulous scholar.[9] Though today credited as the "father of modern national accounting," the young scholar was initially thrust more by accident than logic into the role of generating the first-ever set of national economic data that was both detailed and up to date.[10]

Born in 1901 to a Jewish merchant family, Kuznets spent his formative years in his birth city of Kharkov, Ukraine. Early on he developed two characteristics that shaped his life: a real knack for numbers, and a deep concern for the welfare of others. While the latter may have reflected the embattled nature of his ancestry as much as his quiet intelligence, it found resonance in the heady days of the Bolshevik revolution. Whatever one's political views, the community he lived in was suffused by a strong popular longing to escape the hardships of war and build a better peacetime society.

Many of Kuznets' family and compatriots belonged to a Jewish organization called the Bund, beleaguered and persecuted in Tsarist Russia. Yet the Bund also opposed the Bolsheviks. Members advocated reform over revolution, and believed in an inevitable course toward socialism. But in October 1917, the nation plunged into revolution. Civil war came to Kuznets' home. The University of Kharkov, in Kuznets' second year, was forced to close. Young Simon, his education unfinished, joined the Division of Statistics at the Central Soviet of Trade Unions, where he published his first piece, "Money Wages of Factory Workers in Kharkov in 1920."

In 1922, with the country in turmoil and the university closed, Simon and his older brother followed their father to the United States. What exactly compelled and enabled the two brothers to exit revolutionary Russia, learn English in record time, and be admitted to Columbia the same year they arrived remains in a historical fog. Stubbornly private, neither brother left any public record on his reasons for leaving his home country, other than to ascribe it to "the usual economic problems."[11]

We do know that once at Columbia, Simon picked up where he had left off at the University of Kharkov. Though sometimes socially awkward, he was mature beyond his age. His professors found him hard-working, disciplined, and exceptionally intelligent. One faculty member in particular was taken by Kuznets. Wesley Mitchell offered Kuznets a research assistant position in the newly formed National Bureau of Economic Research (NBER). After Kuznets finished his master's degree, Mitchell suggested he continue with doctoral studies. Kuznets eagerly consented.[12] In 1926 he successfully defended his dissertation at Columbia on "Secular Movements in Production and Prices," and in 1927, at the age of 26, accepted a research position at NBER. He would remain associated with the organization until 1961.

The admiration between the two men appeared mutual. Mitchell stood for something Kuznets respected a great deal: a strong focus on empirical evidence. Theories had little value if they were not grounded in solid data. Indeed, it was "observation" and "analysis of mass phenomena," according to Mitchell, which should shape theory, not theory that determined what evidence one sought to find.[13] During years of close collaboration, Kuznets and Mitchell seemed a natural fit: both saw the economy, and particularly economic growth, as a vital foundation for social well-being. Both had grave concerns about the implications of unequal distribution of the fruits of national product. And both considered solid quantitative empirical data fundamental to all economic questions—for the articulation of theories as well as for the advancement of particular policies.

It was no surprise when Mitchell, director of research, asked Kuznets to take over NBER's studies of national income in 1930—an area of research

Mitchell considered central to NBER's mission. Kuznets, however, did not readily accept. Initially he was concerned that Mitchell's request was to divert his attention away from the primary focus of his scholarship: economic growth.[14] Indeed, it was for his empirical studies linking economic growth to social development that Kuznets won the Nobel Prize in economics in 1971.

Mitchell himself had been, in 1919, a cofounder of NBER. The bureau was, as examined in chapter 2, deliberately built around two ideas: an independent collection of reliable economic data, and the inclusion of people from different perspectives. Asking Kuznets to take over the most important section of NBER research was not just an honor. Given the year-old Depression, it was also auspicious.

NBER had acquired a name for impartiality and empirical excellence.[15] But so far, the Congress had not drawn on its information. This changed when one of La Follette's aides, Paul Webbink, strongly recommended Kuznets to his boss after reading an early draft of Kuznets's first publication on the subject, his 1933 "National Income."[16]

Still, the study needed to come from the Commerce Department, since the Senate requested an official government report. Frederic Dewhurst, head of the Economic Research Division of the Department of Commerce, led this early effort. He was widely perceived as an uncompromising expert in his field—a man who, in the words of a top advisor to the departments Frederick Feiker, "combined efficiency, frankness, and broad-gauged outlook" and thus was seen as perhaps the only one to "turn out a detailed survey of national income in which fullest confidence can be placed."[17]

Dewhurst, back in the private sector in 1930, and not interested in returning to the Department of Commerce unless given a "thoroughly worthwhile task,"[18] assigned two researchers to start compiling data on income paid by government and on construction and distribution. He arranged with Mitchell to have Kuznets—based at NBER—provide assistance. Kuznets' job would be "in planning and study, and defining the concepts and methods to be employed." In truth, the Commerce Department had neither people nor money to sustain the effort. This was so despite the fact that internal memos noted that "new purchasing-power and standards-of-living surveys are more needed than studies on any other economic subject." [19] Still, as Director Feiker wrote in a letter to Edwin Gay (director of research at NBER), "Certainly at the moment we have no funds or staff to carry on such a critical analysis."[20]

How few people understood, even in the midst of the Great Depression, why access to national income data was vital becomes evident when we consider that the head of the Economic Research Division himself, Frederic Dewhurst, turned down the offer to head the project. Instead, he resigned. His boss, meanwhile, concluded that without funding, "it is obvious that we cannot undertake any original research to carry through the [Senate's] request."[21]

In America, at least, critical research for the creation of what would later become GDP thus almost did not come to be. Lack of economic expertise among policymakers, bureaucratic in-fighting, and a shortage of resources incapacitated the Commerce Department's ability to go forward with the project.

In the small world of national economic accounting, this essentially left only one person ready to undertake the formidable challenge: Simon Kuznets.[22] He had spent close to a year surveying the existing literature. He had been head of NBER's national income efforts since the end of 1931, and, in this role, identified essential components to the improvement of national accounts. He knew, for instance, they needed clearer definitions and original data. As the person in charge of this work, he had a head start that no one at Commerce possessed: familiarity with the core issues, access to essential data, and support staff at NBER.

Logic aside, however, none of this meant that work could necessarily go forward. Feiker insisted that the Commerce Department had no money, particularly for what he called "significant duplication" of work already done by NBER. When the Senate ordered the Commerce Department to undertake the study, and Dewhurst turned down the offer, Feiker sought support from NBER, and Kuznets in particular. NBER's research director, Edwin Gay, offered "all possible assistance," but insisted Kuznets be paid. Gay sent a detailed offer to Feiker, asking Commerce to cover Kuznets's salary and the costs of one research assistant for the duration of the project. Both Feiker and the acting chief of the Economic Research Division at Commerce, E. A. Tupper, balked. Tupper, in a handwritten note to Feiker, even noted that the request for a modest salary for Kuznets suggested "the National Bureau is trying to 'milk' us."

In one last effort, Feiker tried to convince Dewhurst to stay on "so that you can take charge of the income study."[23] To no avail. Dewhurst left for what he considered "more worthwhile" work.

The leadership at Commerce, of course, knew they were on their way out. In November 1932, the height of the Great Depression, Roosevelt defeated Hoover in a landslide.[24] By March 1933 a new team had arrived, one more sympathetic to economic research and government planning.

In this context, Feiker finally consented to a close collaboration with NBER, and payment of an annual salary for a senior researcher. Kuznets took charge of the effort in the second half of January of 1933, following what he coined, in typical understated fashion, "some administrative difficulties."[25] By June he also managed to get Commerce to assign his former student, Robert R. Nathan, to be a senior aid. (Nathan later took over from Kuznets and became head of the office). By March, meanwhile, as Roosevelt's new administration settled in, Kuznets's NBER colleague, Willard L. Thorp, had been appointed to take over the reins at the Commerce Department's Bureau of Foreign and Domestic Commerce (BFDC).[26] Finally, with lines of communication open, the important work could proceed.

When Kuznets first settled into his small new third-floor office at the Commerce Department, he found that "very little had been done." With the economy in dire straits and political decision-makers desperate for tools to improve the situation, Kuznets possessed powerful motivation but found he had to begin "practically from scratch."[27]

THE METHOD

Today, GDP is represented by a single dollar amount. It is the result of a deceptively simple formula. Economists around the world easily recognize it: $GDP=C+I+G\ (X-M)$.[28] In common English, this stands for: private Consumption plus gross Investment plus Government spending plus (Exports minus Imports). In reality, however, little about this formula is straightforward. On the contrary, it is a result of a history of belabored theoretical disputes and political interests. In the end, as a measure it follows no coherent logic. Indeed, its components are subjective. In many cases, they are arbitrary. How can this be?[29]

As the early architect, Kuznets understood the problem more clearly than almost all of his successors. And he spent much time and effort describing its various facets.

For Kuznets, from the beginning, the central question that should determine all subsequent efforts was this: what was the purpose of measuring national income? Kuznets remained adamant: ultimately, the only valid intent behind productive activities in an economy was to satisfy the needs of its members.

This is worth unpacking. Kuznets's primary interest was in measuring the welfare of a nation. As he stated dozens of times, the "needs of ultimate consumers provide the touchstone by which the results of economic activity are to be judged."[30] But there existed many other real and potential purposes for measuring national income, ranging from taxation to finding revenue for war. As Kuznets and later scholars recognized, economists have variously wanted to use national accounts to measure "(1) the distribution of income and of the costs of government; (2) the extent of unused capacity in various sectors of the economy; (3) the sources of economic growth; (4) pecuniary well-being; . . . (5) the fluctuations of the business cycle so as to design economic stabilization policies." And there were many other conceivable purposes.[31]

But the purpose largely defines the instrument. We measure what we deem most important. We thus gain detailed information only about that which we measure. It's the old dilemma: you can't get answers to questions you do not ask. A focus on possible tax revenue will not say much about satisfaction of consumers. Sources of growth tell you nothing about the quality of growth. A concentration on total amount of money spent in the market will not say much about the standard of living of its members—especially not of those who have little or no money to spend.

Secondly, one can tabulate only data that is available. Areas of productive activity for which no data exist do not show up. Nor do activities for which data are difficult to generate. For example, how does an economist in 1932 measure the economic value of work done by a housewife? Or a barter between a washerwoman and a carpenter who do each other favors in trade? Indeed, especially large economic categories excluded were housework or the informal economy. During the height of the Great Depression, the year Kuznets set out to estimate national income, those two realms of productive activity alone may have yielded more goods and services than the entire official economy. They were excluded simply because reliable figures could not be found.

Even in the "official" market, the one where money is legally exchanged for goods and services, complete datasets on things like "investment," "profit," or "personal income" were notoriously difficult to come by. As Kuznets's personal assistant, Robert Nathan, later commented, "It is hard to believe how limited was the availability of meaningful statistics and basic information in many sectors of the economy."[32]

Third, Kuznets and his team had to settle on a commonly recognized definition of the components that should be counted. As it turned out, a virtually impossible task. After a ten-year struggle with this issue, Kuznets noted in 1941, "For those not intimately acquainted with this type of work it is difficult to realize the degree to which estimates of national income have been and must be affected by implicit or explicit value judgments."[33] Anything resembling "objective" datasets did not exist. The trouble was, and is, that almost everyone thought they did. And this belief had profound political consequences.

Deciding "what to count" was no arcane theoretical matter. Different theoretical choices yielded radically different practical results. Often, as Kuznets noted, if the investigator was not aware of his own subjective assumptions, the results could be worse than meaningless: they could be dangerously misleading. Goods and services might be counted twice, or failed to be counted at all; unproductive activity may be counted as productive, or satisfaction of the social body ignored altogether; depletion or degradation of natural or social capital might go entirely unnoticed; an economy with a larger total income may automatically be assumed to be "better off" without taking into consideration forms of social organization or levels of social cohesion. Distribution of income may be ignored by a focus on overall growth. The potential pitfalls seemed endless, the dangers of misleading data pointing in the wrong direction were real (see figure 4–1).

Writing in the detached voice of the scholar, Kuznets stated in his first official report on national income that "the valuable capacity of the human mind to simplify a complex situation in a compact characterization becomes

Figure 4–1. Simon Kuznets, teaching the intricacies of national accounting. From the Collections of the University of Pennsylvania Archives.

dangerous when not controlled in terms of definitely stated criteria."[34] As if
foreseeing future developments, it was Kuznets's earliest warning against attaching meaning to figures they were never intended to yield. Data on economic
output, especially when limited by availability and continuously shaped by subjective decisions about what to include, was not a reliable measure of success.

Underlying all the problems of conceptualizing national economic accounts were deeper questions, central to the very field of economics. How to
define crucial categories such as income, wealth, and the meaning of "productive" activity?

Here again, answers were not easy to come by. Little agreement among
experts seemed to exist, and there were no standardized definitions.[35] Moreover, attempts by each economist or statistician to generate an operational
definition turned out to be little more than subjective reflections of personal

interests. Willford I. King, who shared Kuznets's interest in questions of economic fairness, noted early on that "each economist is likely to have his pet meaning," and thus "fails to recognize that this is not the same definition used by a fellow-economist." The danger, as King saw it, was that one economist accuses the other of "unsound reasoning because his deductions will not fit in with the definition in the mind of the critic."[36]

When referring to "national income," economists were not speaking the same language. But their definitions did inevitably reflect interests—interests on issues, as Kuznets was keenly aware, that are at "the center of conflict of opposing social groups."[37]

The problems were as profound as they were basic. In the very first comprehensive attempt by the NBER to gauge national income, the 1921 report "Income in the United States," Kuznets's mentor, Wesley Mitchell, highlighted the lack of consensus. The first in a litany of questions was, "Is national income money, or commodities and services, or satisfactions?"[38] A basic question, yet the answer would yield radically different results. And serve very different constituents. And address very different visions of life.[39]

Thus as early as the beginning of the 1920s, economists were arguing about topics that form the center of our political debates today, whether one visits Karachi or Moscow, Tokyo or Johannesburg, New York or Buenos Aires. On one end of the spectrum was the extreme idea that money is the only measure of value. The other end posed the staggering challenge for investigators to find indicators that would allow them to measure things like "satisfaction," or even "happiness." The very direction of economic activity depended on what answers would be provided.

Another question posed by the 1921 report was whether "the national income [is] the sum of the incomes of individuals or may an individual have personal income which is not income to the nation?" In other words, are the needs and desires of the individual the same as those of the society at large? If not, which individual incomes should be included, and which excluded, from an account of national income?

At the end of a long list of questions, the 1921 report asked, "Are there negative incomes to be deducted from the sum of positive incomes?"[40] What about income from selling drugs or bad financial advice or from convincing people to buy things they don't need and can't afford?

Defining purpose or meaning of national income accounts was inherently subjective. In order to obtain any meaningful results, however, it was necessary. To say that Kuznets faced difficult challenges is thus an understatement: lack of sufficient data, conflicting purposes, unclear definitions, all superimposed by an economy in dire need of informed intervention. Just thirty-one years of age, understaffed, and resented by his Commerce administrators, Kuznets nonetheless had to proceed.

In his first major contribution to national accounting, Kuznets defined the scope of national income broadly, as "the end product of a country's economic activity, . . . serving to appraise the prevailing economic organization in terms of its returns."[41] As later scholars have pointed out, most of Kuznets's expressed purposes for such accounts "deal with social welfare and social justice"—data on per capita welfare, distribution of income among social classes, and the proportion of income used for consumption, investment, and savings.[42] Productivity and growth were secondary, important only to the extent to which they informed general welfare.

Still, following in the footsteps of Mitchell, Kuznets believed that national income first had to be accurately conceptualized and described—particularly at a time when "economics was, for the most part, still a speculative discipline [that] proceeded from uncertain premises, by logical deduction, to imperfectly verified conclusions." Such limitations, in turn, made economics virtually "helpless in matters concerned with the aggregative behavior of economies, their growth and fluctuations." In order to be able to address those larger aspects of economic life, economics had to "change from being a branch of applied logic into an empirical science." It is here that Kuznets made his greatest contribution, and here that he laid the foundation for a particular kind of "growth-accounting."[43]

There are many reasons why Kuznets initially settled for a basic market output account at the expense of a more comprehensive set of accounts. Limited by available data, narrowness of widely accepted criteria, and pressing economic needs, it is critical to note that Kuznets's theoretical understanding far outpaced his capacity to express this understanding. As he pointed out repeatedly over the next forty years, much of what he wanted to capture with national accounts was, at first, either conceptually disputed or empirically not yet doable.

His report to the Senate, he stated, provided "an amalgam of . . . estimates rather than . . . a precise measurement," including estimates that were "at best only well-considered guesses." Moreover, Kuznets and his team were under a clear mandate to provide a national income account for the purpose of providing data for policymakers fighting the Depression. The goal was not to develop a national welfare measure, or to craft an indicator of (e)quality or opportunity. The challenge was to find a single measure for the "total economic and business activity" of the nation—the magical whole to which "all of the parts are supposed to add up."[44]

Having thus spelled out the enormous limitations of his initial effort, Kuznets warned against misuse. It was as if he could foresee what was to come: "the welfare of a nation can, therefore, scarcely be inferred from a measurement of national income as defined above."[45]

THE FINDINGS

What did Kuznets and his team find? In the initial report, one has to wade through ten pages to find out. Indicative of how worried Kuznets was about misuse of his data, the first nine pages of Kuznets's report offer no conclusions, but rather focus exclusively on concepts in order to avoid "abuse of findings."

Then, finally, the reader learns about "the striking effect of the present depression." Total national income paid out to individuals declined by 40 percent between 1929 and 1932. Quoting statistics from previous depressions, the report pointed out that the second largest decline had happened between 1920 and 1921, at 14.4 percent. This was, in short, a depression three times as bad as the worst ever experienced before. If nothing else, it was a sobering confirmation of La Follette's most dire premonitions. In terms of output and income, the economy was in a steep nose-dive.

In a bizarre footnote to history, it is worth noting that Kuznets's report almost did not get published.[46] Budget restraints and a general failure to appreciate the significance of its findings required an official request for printing in January by Senator La Follette.[47]

When finally published, the full report explained national income classified by source (manufacturing, agriculture, construction, etc.) and types of payment (wages, salaries, interest and dividend payments, etc.). Moving from concept to findings to methods, half of the report consisted of tables and charts, with dozens of appendices detailing their construction.[48] Twelve major industries were covered in separate chapters.[49]

In a conclusion long since forgotten and buried, Kuznets appealed to the reader to recognize that "the estimates of total national income . . . are of little value in themselves to anyone trying to interpret their significance."[50] Take the distribution of income, for instance. The report's chart on national income by type of payment revealed that, just between 1929 and 1932, inequality had dramatically increased. Income paid out for labor had declined 40 percent, while income from property had declined at a much lower rate of 31 percent. This was significant since both developments mutually aggravated a key problem: lack of demand for the production of goods and the provision of services. It also suggested that income earners—the very people needed most to boost demand in a depressed economy—were more severely hit by the depression than property holders.

When Kuznets further broke down income in basic industries between wages (mostly blue-collar) and salaries (mostly professionals), he discovered that wages had fallen by nineteen percentage points more than salaries.[51] "The cumulative burden of the depression," in short, was much more crushing on lower-income segments of the population. The total numbers of national income revealed no such significant subtleties.

Though admitting possible inaccuracies due to lack of data, Kuznets's report also attempted a first measure of the extent of national unemployment. Excluding labor performed by farm families, his conservative estimates of the number of unemployed went from 2.2 million in 1929 to 5.3 million in 1930. In 1931 they rose to 9.0 million. By 1932 they reached a staggering 13.0

UNITED STATES DEPARTMENT OF COMMERCE

Confidential Data for Use Only in Preparing Estimates of the National
Income by Direction of United States Senate Resolution 220.

(Name)_____Company.   (Address)_____

(Note: Include only salaries and wages which can be allocated to production of oil and gas).
Do not include salaries and wages for refining or distribution of products.

	1929	1930	1931	1932
Total production - oil (bbls.)	....	....	....	....
" " - gas (cu. ft.)	....	....	....	....
" " - natural gasoline (bbls.)	....	....	....	....
Total value oil and gas production ($)	....	....	....	....

1/   (Note: Where drilling done on "contract" please
Drilling   (estimate as near as possible proportion of contract
                      (expenditures which were paid out in salaries and wages)

Number well drilled (both dry and producing)	....	....	....	....
Amount of wages paid	....	....	....	....
Number wage earners (average for year)	....	....	....	....
Amount salaries paid	....	....	....	....
Number salaried people	....	....	....	....

Operating 2/

Amount wages paid	....	....	....	....
Number wage earners (average for year)	....	....	....	....
Amount salaries paid	....	....	....	....
Number salaried people	....	....	....	....

Administrative - Office - Accounting - Land
Geology, etc. 3/

Amount wages paid	....	....	....	....
Number of wage earners (average for year)	....	....	....	....
Amount salaries paid	....	....	....	....
Number salaried people	....	....	....	....
Rentals and Rents - paid	....	....	....	....
Royalties - paid	....	....	....	....

1/ Drilling - This includes general field development and should include such general items as transportation, stock-keeping, tool repairs, and reconditioning, etc.

2/ Operating - Includes those in compressor plants, lifting, general repairs, general labor, etc.

3/ Administrative - Includes those applied to drilling or to operating or allocated thereto.

Filled out by -

Name_____

Title_____

Company_____

Figure 4–2. Sample questionnaire sent out by Kuznets's team to businesses around the country. National Archives and Records Administration, Willard Thorp, Box 160, NC 27 Entry 3.

million. Including population increase, and thus number of persons seeking employment, his estimate for 1932 exceeded 14 million unemployed: a close to sevenfold increase in three years, or about one in four adult Americans. Never before had the nation stood at such a precipice. Again, the findings exceeded La Follette's worst fears.[52]

In the midst of a raging national debate about how best to get out of the depression, these were all findings with potentially far-reaching policy implications. There could no longer be any doubt that the American economy in 1933 was in freefall. Three years into the depression, claims by neoclassical economists that the market would naturally regain equilibrium and again start offering sufficient employment proved fantastical. And the key word here was *proved*. Kuznets had proved it.

The findings provided quantitative rationale for a seismic policy shift on the part of the federal government. The fact that lower-class wage workers were hurting more than comparatively better-off salary earners, and that "payments to property holders formed a relatively increasing cost to the economic system as a whole," finally offered policymakers such as La Follette the numeric justifications for novel initiatives like government-sponsored work relief programs.[53]

The hard data also allowed newly elected President Roosevelt to take aim at "big business." His promise to offer a "new deal" to the American people, one in which government would provide more opportunities, more oversight, and more security, now came sheathed in hard economic facts. Though Roosevelt had been far from clear on his economic policies during the election, he now appeared convinced that any economic revival "cannot endure for long unless we bring about a wiser, more equitable distribution of the national income."[54]

THE BIG CONUNDRUM: TRANSLATING FINDINGS INTO ACTION

This is why Kuznets's final report seized national headlines when released on January 23, 1934. The attention-grabbing title "Our Income Fell 40% in Four Years" in the *New York Times* introduced the report as "the most complete and detailed ever compiled."[55] All major newspapers ran similar stories. Soon thereafter, the new Secretary of Commerce, Daniel Roper, used Kuznets's numbers in a major policy speech supporting the urgent need for New Deal programs.[56] Even among private agencies, businesses, and the public, interest in the report appeared exceptional: within eight months of its printing, almost 4,500 copies were sold at $ .20 a copy. No other government report on the economy had ever sold as many.[57]

With Kuznets's report, "national income accounting" officially entered the language of political debate. It provided a new instrument. Not yet clear were the many ways it could be used, or even whether public attention would last.[58]

Kuznets was much less interested in politics than in the conceptual integrity of national accounts. He quickly abandoned his brief government stint and returned to his two positions at the University of Pennsylvania and NBER. There, he continued to make important contributions to national income studies. His chief assistant, Robert Nathan, left with Kuznets. Though Nathan would soon return to the Commerce Department in a leadership position, he believed at the time that his services could yield more good at the Pennsylvania State Emergency Relief Board.[59] Secretary Roper, in the meantime, had made frequent use of the national income study. But he did not yet appear to understand the vital significance of continuously updated reports. As a result, the Bureau of Foreign and Domestic Commerce, under whose auspices the report was compiled, failed to maintain funding for national income research.

Without plans to turn this one-time study into an annual series, the data compiled would have little to no relevance—certainly not for the purposes of policymaking.[60] For a time, studies on national income accounts were thus in limbo.[61] This could have been a result of personalities, preferences, budgets, and bureaucratic incompetence. Mostly it was not. The main underlying cause for limbo was the fact that the understanding of economists and policymakers themselves had not caught up with realities on the ground. No coherent set of ideas had yet taken hold as to how to deal with the enormous challenges of a global economy that had jumped off its rails.

The stakes could not have been higher. Every plan for the economy had the potential to fundamentally rearrange social relations in the United States. Power, wealth, and future opportunities were at stake. How big would government have to get to allow recovery? What new rules should banks and corporations have to follow? Should the federal government provide citizens a basic safety net? And, after nearly one hundred years of bloody battles between labor and capital, should government finally grant workers the right to bargain collectively? These and many more questions overlay historical battlefields littered with tens of thousands of bodies. They would shape the future course of American society.

What, above all, would get the economy moving again? As the collapse of American businesses and the ignominious defeat of Herbert Hoover demonstrated, doing nothing was no longer a tenable option. As politicians and business leaders belatedly grasped by 1933, hoping for the "invisible hand" to do its magic threatened total disintegration—even revolution.

What the Roosevelt administration attempted with the New Deal was a "barrage of ideas and programs unlike anything known to American history."[62] It started the very day FDR was inaugurated in March 1933. Historians are essentially right when they characterized, in hindsight, much of the New Deal programs as a hodgepodge of measures that were mostly reactive in design. To be sure, the programs did not follow a grand economic theory. They also did not have a clearly defined goal other than to lift the economy out of the depression. Mostly, they responded to a series of escalating crises—bank failures, financial collapse, unemployment, declining wages, lack of investment.

Most New Deal initiatives turned out to be a curious mixture of need and political compromise. They stabilized banks, improved the nation's infrastructure by building and repairing roads, bridges, electric grids, sewage systems, court houses, and airports. They also outlawed child labor, authorized unemployment relief, supported farmers, started social security, and guaranteed workers the right to unionize.

Yet, in retrospect, we can discern a core characteristic of all those programs. New Deal initiatives were Keynesian before Keynes.[63] They stabilized the economy by, in effect, helping to boost demand.[64] They did so by greatly expanding the role of government, paid for with a method that would later be called "deficit-spending."

Most programs were possible only in the wake of the detailed knowledge in Kuznets's national income accounts. They allowed policymakers to discern with some precision what sectors of the economy were bleeding the most. Above all, national income accounts demonstrated the utter inadequacy of the purchasing power of consumers: stunted as it was, it would never suffice to bring the economy back to life. By putting side by side total production of goods and services (gross national product) and total income derived from this production (gross national income), it became "a thought that no one could henceforth escape," in the words of John Kenneth Galbraith, "that the latter needed to be sufficient to buy the former."[65] The underlying problem that had caused the Great Depression: people were not earning enough to buy the products of their own economy. The government had to prime the pump.[66]

Without the kind of data provided by Kuznets, both New Deal policymaking and Keynesian theory were ideas devoid of either compass or clearly specified tools. Neither would have been very effective without empirical evidence to guide them. The New Deal, despite its odd mixture of programs, proceeded much more deliberately than anything Keynes called for.

Infamously, Keynes suggested people be hired to "dig holes in the ground"— or anything, really, that would earn them an income they could, in turn, spend in the market.[67] Whatever one's ideological preferences, the New Deal, on the contrary, at least attempted to promote useful projects intended to benefit society. Kuznets, for one, appreciated this spotlight on social welfare, as his entire national accounting work was focused on "the welfare of the final consumer."

Later uses of national income accounts, focused exclusively on boosting economic output, became increasingly divorced from the goal of human welfare. It is a key distinction. To Kuznets's growing dismay, as the next chapter will explore in detail, rather than following a "more enlightened social philosophy," national accounting deteriorated into an instrument merely in service of "an acquisitive society."[68]

As is often the case when something new and different comes around, public conversations about national income generated far more critical commentary early on than after "instruction and use have made them part of the culture."[69] As a 1936 *New York Times* editorial remarked, "Estimates of national income, once discussed only among a handful of economists and statisticians, are now cited glibly in conversations over cracker boxes and brass rails, and many campaign arguments are based upon them."[70]

Though national income accounts were eventually institutionalized, the combined effect of New Deal programs never managed to lift the American economy out of the depression. In 1939, ten years after the stock market crash, economic output and employment were still well below 1929 levels. In desperation, Kuznets's successor and now chief of the National Income Section, Robert Nathan, continued to reach out to the Secretary of Commerce, Harry Hopkins, to persuade him of the critical significance of accurate national income statistics. People in positions of authority, Nathan argued, needed to use the data correctly to understand the national economic problem. In early 1939 he finally convinced Hopkins to send out the latest figures to key policymakers and department heads, with a letter attached from Nathan explaining what they meant, and how critically important they were.[71]

Once again, however, it was historical circumstances that provided the final boost for national income accounting to become a vital tool of policymakers. Only when faced with the dire needs of war did detailed accounts of production, income, and expenditure become widely recognized as essential. National accountants were able to turn them into one of the most significant weapons for victory. A whole society preparing for war offered another critical insight: New Deal efforts, rather than misguided or flawed, had simply not been big enough to overcome the challenges posed by the Great Depression.[72]

How national accounting was further refined by wartime necessity and then led the country into the longest peacetime period of sustained growth is a story to which we turn in the next chapter.

Chapter 5

FORGED IN WAR

The cost of a thing is the amount of what I will
call "life" which is required to be exchanged for it,
immediately or in the long run.

—*Henry David Thoreau*

In an astonishing example of how quickly GDP had become the key goal-post in the minds of select political leaders, President Franklin D. Roosevelt delivered the following message to Congress and the American people on 14 April 1938: "All the energies of Government and business must be directed to increasing the national income."

After the short boom of early 1936 to mid-1937, the renewed drop in the economy raised fears of a permanently weakened economy and high levels of ongoing underemployment. People were not buying enough. The country, Roosevelt explained, found itself in a situation in which "purchasing power of the consuming public had not kept pace with production." Once again, businesses had gone bankrupt, people had lost their jobs, and national output had declined. To the president's growing conviction, however, this slide back into decline and misery was both unnecessary and preventable. What the country needed, according to the president, was collective action by "government and business" to grow the purchasing power of the American people. With increased demand, this logic suggested, would come jobs, investment, income, and profit.

Above all, for the economy to grow, disposable income for people needed to grow. When private businesses were unable to provide necessary jobs and income, government had a responsibility to step in.

As Roosevelt understood national income accounts, moreover, government investment would more than pay for itself: "As citizen income rises, let us not forget that government expenditures will go down and government tax receipts will go up." The better off the American people, he believed, the more they generate demand and thus boost businesses and provide employment; the more they can pay in taxes and fees, and the less they require necessary services from government.[1]

Roosevelt recommended some $3 billion in additional expenditures, boosting a wide range of New Deal programs, ranging from the Works Progress Administration to the Civilian Conservation Corps. He also included budgets for highways, flood control, and the U.S. Housing Authority. With remarkable clarity, he then provided this summary:

> The higher the national income goes, the faster shall we be able to reduce the total of Federal and state and local debts. Viewed from every angle, today's purchasing power—the citizens' income of today—is not sufficient to drive the economic system at higher speed. Responsibility of government requires us at this time to supplement the normal processes and in so supplementing them to make sure that the addition is adequate. We must start again on a long steady upward incline in national income.[2]

And thus began in earnest a logic of policymaking premised on GDP. It became an essential tool to justify government intervention in a contracting economy. Who would argue with the numbers? In short order, national income accounts were cited more often than any other economic statistics. The data that informed GDP accounts, quite simply, represented the necessary lifeblood for economic policymaking. But that was not all. Since the numbers behind GDP also provided the metrics for what experts considered growth or decline, GDP also morphed into the standard for success and failure.

Since Simon Kuznets's first report in January of 1934, the task of national income reporting had become "professional." Data needed to be collected and reported continually for both businesses and policymakers. By the end of 1934, after experts pleaded with the feds to institutionalize national economic statistics, the Secretary of Commerce officially placed national income accounting under the auspices of his department, albeit with little money and staff to operate.[3] Kuznets's former student, Robert R. Nathan, chaired the effort. Finally, by late 1937, the Department of Commerce began to publish national income reports on a regular monthly basis.[4]

Without Kuznets at the helm, however, the direction of national income accounting changed significantly. Under Nathan's leadership, the original emphasis on the welfare of consumers and society at large was, by 1937, reduced to the much narrower focus on stimulating income and output of the economy. This was particularly true after the economic slump of 1937–38, with Keynesian thinking in Washington gaining influence. Government wanted to boost demand and stabilize employment. Now, since monthly estimates were available, national income accounts became far more useful for that purpose. They provided continuously updated figures on business activity. More importantly, they gave accurate monthly estimates of Americans' purchasing power. But however useful for the purposes of policymaking, this emphasis on total income, or consumer purchasing power, represented a considerable deviation from Kuznets's initial blueprint. As he would later explain, it was also a direction he could not support for post-crisis conditions.[5]

Both businesses and policymakers became eager consumers of the monthly estimates—one in search of potential markets, the other exploring what fiscal stimuli and aid programs were needed for economic recovery.[6] To advance efforts in satisfying the needs of both groups, the Department of Commerce began to publish reports on retail sales, inventories, orders, and shipments in early 1941. If a consumer item like a newly fashionable top-bottom refrigerator made by General Electric was picking up in sales again, yet GE still had a glut of models in storage, sales and shipments would go up, but employment would likely not. Thus, with the economy still lagging, the goal "was to improve the quality of the consumer expenditure data."[7] With better data, the thinking went, opportunities for sales and production and jobs could be matched up more efficiently, in the process increasing overall output and income.

The increasingly widespread use of national income accounts soon worried at least some of its founders. Opening his magisterial 926-page work on national income, published in 1941, Kuznets warned of the "bandying about" of the estimates "to proper and improper ends" by "statesman and economists, politicians and journalists, reformers and cranks, defenders of group interests and advocates of special policies." As he had since 1934, Kuznets appreciated the need for the best possible data during times of "pronounced disturbance in the country's economic life," yet also worried about how "the desire to have a single measure and to read unequivocal meaning into it" could lead to abuse and grave misunderstandings.[8]

What he did not foresee was that events taking place thousands of miles away would once again dramatically shift the debate. In September 1939, Germany invaded Poland. The U.S. military was small and weak, in no position to enter the conflict, or even to help its allies.[9] After a decade of depression, moreover, many Americans were simply demoralized. The much-referenced "can-do" attitude of the world's economic superpower seemed to have lost its vigor. Industrial output in 1939 had not even reached 1929 levels yet.

By the time of the British evacuation of Dunkirk in May 1940, and the German conquest of France, mounting waves of European conflict began to crash onto American shores. Isolation was no longer an option for U.S. policymakers. For a time, both East Coast and West Coast "watchers" patrolled the shoreline on the lookout for German or Japanese warships. Washington was filled with rumors of imminent German and Japanese aggression. After Pearl Harbor, such fears only intensified. In the words of Donald Nelson, chair of the powerful War Production Board and one of the most informed public servants at the time, "We were on the side that was obviously losing—and losing fast—and we were losing along with it."[10]

Most in the civilian and military leadership of the United States felt that a Europe under Nazi rule was intolerable, as was a Japanese domination of Asia. But they wondered, Was the nation, and its economy, ready to respond? How could the United States, in the words of President Roosevelt, be turned successfully into an "arsenal of democracy?"

No one in the military, the private business sector, or the diplomatic corps had ever seen anything like what happened between 1940 and 1944. At first, when the full implications of a global war were not yet clear to Americans, responses were slow and contradictory. By the end of 1940, mobilization began to pick up. But never before in history did a society experience what transpired in the United States after Pearl Harbor: war production took off like a rocket.

What turned out to be an unprecedented mobilization of an entire nation for war, however, posed a radically new set of challenges to economists and national income accountants.[11] The central problems of the Great Depression, lack of demand and overproduction, were suddenly replaced with overwhelming demand and underproduction. Unemployment disappeared almost instantaneously—largely due to the rapidly swelling numbers of citizens in the U.S. Armed Forces. Mass military induction in fact posed temporary labor shortages in several key industries.[12] Now Americans faced a new challenge: How to mobilize effectively? How to finance the war effort? How to prevent inflation?

Was the economy ready to crank out what would be needed to win the war? To put labor, equipment, and material to efficient use required great sophistication. One needed an elaborate system of accounts to keep track of essential investments, productivity, sales, and income.

As the war mobilization effort made clear, the government needed solid data for efficient resource allocation by each sector of the economy. The "invisible hand" did not prevent inefficiency or deep structural crises. The Great Depression had shown that, without serious and wide-ranging interventions by government, the entire national enterprise could end up facing imminent collapse. War preparation provided final and incontrovertible proof of the need for deliberate and informed organization of the economy. Was the nation ready to meet the requirements of the Victory Program?[13]

The challenge was daunting—"a national effort of gigantic magnitude," in the words of President Roosevelt. Military historian Jim Lacey captured the task that lay ahead:

> In his budget message to Congress in January 1940, four months after Germany had invaded Poland, Roosevelt asked for a modest defense supplemental appropriation for fiscal year 1940 and a likely increase in defense spending for fiscal year 1941. In 1940 defense expenditures had reached more than $1 billion, approximately 14 percent of the budget. In his January 1941 budget message, Roosevelt asked for $25 billion in defense expenditures, 62 percent of the budget, reflecting a "world at war." In his January 1942 budget message, President Roosevelt asked for $53 billion for defense, 90 percent of the budget, reflecting "a nation at war in a world at war."[14]

This activity had no precedents, either in size or in terms of required speed. The entire economy would need to be retooled. Millions of citizens needed to be hired, and millions of those already employed would need retraining. The government would have to ration essential resources, and implement wage and price controls. The economy had not yet fully emerged from its worst-ever crisis. Now it needed to perform at its very peak. Millions of lives hung in the balance.

But who could say what war mobilization goals were realistic, and how to accomplish them? In the end, what national accountants were able to accomplish would constitute the most remarkable achievement in its entire history. Some experts even considered it "one of the great technical triumphs in the history of the economics discipline."[15] The government had to devise a system, in close coordination with military command, to establish clear priorities. Then it had to allow for the highest possible output given American resources, capital, labor, production facilities, and strategic needs. What was feasible?

The logistical challenge was staggering. A goal of, say, sixty thousand new tanks might lead to the successful production of that number of bodies and turrets, but because of insufficient production facilities elsewhere these components might be matched with only forty thousand tank engines. Plus, coming up with engine parts necessary to turn those extra twenty thousand bodies and turrets into operational tanks might lead to a crippling shortage of steal for the production of machine guns. Further aggravating the situation, manufacturers, foreseeing such bottlenecks, would be encouraged to hoard materials and parts not immediately needed. Plus a "general scramble" for needed materiel, combined with warring priorities between the civilian and military sectors, would result in mounting inefficiencies.[16]

This was the problem: to set production goals that were too low might unnecessarily prolong war and suffering, and perhaps even lead to defeat. To set production goals that were too high would inflate costs and lead to unnecessary inefficiencies and shortages: "the goods and facilities that were easiest to produce, or those that were locally pushed most energetically, would be the ones finished, rather than those that were most urgently needed."[17] If the government invested in the wrong technologies or innovations when fighting industrial powerhouses like Germany and Japan, it could mean death and defeat for both civilians and soldiers.

World War II provided the existential test for national income accounts. In ordinary life, supply and demand was supposed to determine the price and quantity of goods. In war, mobilization and the necessity to focus on war-related production meant that the government had to plan the price and quantity of goods. America was, in the words of Nelson, the powerful chairman of the War Production Board (WPB), "the free world's last reservoir."[18] By the end of 1941, the United States had to provide essential supplies not only for its own military but also to its key allies, Great Britain and the Soviet Union.[19]

The challenge could thus not have been any more desperate. And it was complicated by a military command that saw little reason to let some "bean counters" in suits tell them about priorities. Detailed accounts of skirmishes between economists at the WPB, especially Kuznets and Nathan, and military commanders, especially Generals Brehon Somervell and George Marshall, illuminated an astounding level of vitriol when established military authority was confronted with the cold logic of national economic accounts.[20]

The clashes began soon after Nathan recruited Kuznets to return to national income computations, this time directly for the war effort. Quickly getting to work, Kuznets wrote a memorandum suggesting that American industry had the capacity to double the army's orders, all without creating inflationary pressure. The military leadership seemed taken aback that American industry showed such capacity.

Then, when realities on the ground yet again shifted in a perilous direction—German invasion of Russia, defeat of British forces in North Africa, and Japanese conquest of islands in the South Pacific—the military, emboldened by Kuznets's estimate, demanded a much "larger force than had ever before been seriously contemplated." The Army Service Forces (ASF), responsible for all army procurements, under the leadership of Assistant Chief of Staff General Somervell, put forth orders triple their original size.[21] Kuznets replied, in his usual understated but stern fashion, "Double does not mean triple."

Weeks of arguments ensued. The Chief of the War Production Board, Donald Nelson, asked Kuznets to put together a detailed feasibility study, using the latest national income data, to compare military goals with actual U.S. production capacity. The report, finished in March 1942, concluded that the military's "three times current rate" goals had to be cut by at least 25 percent. Kuznets had found problems across the board—resource and machine tool shortages, delays in factory construction, and targets that cut too deeply into essential civilian requirements. Implicitly criticizing the military for failing to provide clear targets, Kuznets's report expressed the immediate need for the development of "well-formulated and properly screened and tested objectives." Kuznets understood the domestic economy well enough to know that the military's request for more would actually result in less.[22]

The military leaders' response to Kuznets's report was swift and harsh. Somervell replied, "To me this is an inchoate mass of words. . . . I am not impressed with either the character or basis of the judgments expressed in the reports and recommend they be carefully hidden from the eyes of thoughtful men." Kuznets, who had the support of his immediate superior, Nathan, and the head of the WPB, Nelson, did not back down. Instead, he picked up the gauntlet and replied with a personal note to the general, disputing in detail each of Somervell's objections. Referring to Somervell's biting final commentary, he ended the letter by saying, "Furthermore, your closing argument is a non-sequitur."[23]

Asked by Nelson to clarify and further support his claims in a third memo, Kuznets spent three labor-intensive months gathering and tabulating data. In an era before Excel, it's worth remembering that all calculations were done on ledger paper, with pencil and by hand. Kuznets's papers are chock-full of his feverish calculations and recalculations, well thumbed, and occasionally coffee stained.

Though time and availability of data were not on his side, Kuznets succeeded in pulling together enough to make his point. His concluding memorandum explained in detail how the data revealed where recent capital accumulation had taken place, and thus where greater output could be achieved the quickest. He also demonstrated that the military was frequently relying on outdated production facilities.

As a result of the third Kuznets memorandum, the "imperious" army's Chief of Staff, General George Catlett Marshall, personally came to a meeting of the WPB, requiring every member to attend, and told all present that "the Army didn't need 'a couple of university intellectuals' telling them how to do its business."[24] Soon thereafter, Kuznets and Nathan resigned. Nelson later lamented the "inexcusable lust for power" and "outright ignorance of how industrial production is accomplished" among some of the top brass of the army.[25]

Fortunate for American war efforts, however, civilians in authority understood the need for careful economic planning to prevent "a confused and incalculable production tangle." Without it, immeasurable harm would have come to the strategic position of America and its allies.[26] Upon Nelson's urging, Secretary of War Henry L. Stimson, forced the military to adopt Kuznets's plan.

In hindsight, the contributions of the WPB, and particularly Nathan, Kuznets, and the head of the Office of Progress Reports, Stacey May, can hardly be exaggerated. National planning based on their meticulously generated data translated in greater productivity and much higher output. Military procurement rose from a level of 1.6 percent of GDP in 1940 to an astonishing 48 percent in 1944, or 89 percent of total federal spending—all without civilian shortages of essential goods.

In both speed and volume, America's war production effort was historically unprecedented. From 1941 to 1945, the U.S. economy produced a total of about 300,000 planes, 124,000 ships of all types, 41 billion rounds of ammunition, 100,000 tanks and armored cars, 2,400,000 military trucks, and 434,000 tons of steel.[27]

Significantly, neither Germany nor Japan came close to matching this prowess. In less than three years, the United States had moved from being a minor military power to outproducing the rest of the world.[28]

+++

It was an astonishing transformation of GDP from depression-era policy tool to central weapon against Germany and Japan. Kuznets and his students turned the statistics of the gross national income and product accounts into information essential for planning and wartime production.[29]

In the words of John Kenneth Galbraith, "Simon Kuznets and his talented people had been the equivalent of several infantry divisions in their contribution to the American war effort."[30] Emphasizing the contributions of national accountants, one prominent observer went as far as calling World War II "an economists' war."[31]

Chapter 6

GLOBAL DOMINATION

The Age of GDP

People and nations were to be put into service of the bottom line.

Born as a measure of crisis, refined as a vital tool for military victory, GDP after the war began to be used for purposes that far outstripped its original design. Well before the last bombs were dropped, the measure turned into aspirational goal. The objective of economic activity became growth of GDP. In the process, the logic behind national accounting transformed the world. One result: "We are the first people alive to witness the condition of the entire world being for sale."[1]

FOR RICHER OR POORER

In the United States, national accounting accomplished more than help achieve wartime victory. It revealed a path to pull the nation out of crisis, to provide jobs and an increasing variety of consumer items to its citizens. One member of Simon Kuznets's team in particular had figured out, early on, how to rapidly expand military production at the same time as improving prosperity at home.[2] In an article written three months after Pearl Harbor, Milton Gilbert laid out a comprehensive national income and Gross National Product approach that would allow for both "a record output of many types of civilian goods," and the resources "to provide the overwhelming superiority necessary to insure complete victory."[3]

The approach garnered wild success. Even in the midst of greatest peril to its nation's security, the National Resources Planning Board confidently proclaimed in a 1943 report to the president: "Our expanding economy is likely to surpass the wildest estimates of a few years back and is capable of bringing to all of our people freedom, security and adventure in richer measure than ever before in history."[4]

GDP accountants now played central roles in figuring out taxes, administering prices, keeping score of national economic performance, organizing war production, and, of course, allocating resources and labor necessary for a thriving consumer market. They seemed to possess the keys to prosperity. Long before the war was over, the logic of GDP growth grew into the central target of postwar planning.[5]

After the war, the United States shifted its focus from achieving victory over fascism to safeguarding and expanding its new status as dominant superpower and largest economy in the world. Now Gilbert's recipe took on global significance. "By the end of the war national income accounting had . . . emerged as an essential tool in the formation of economic policy."[6]

America and the world had just barely escaped a global economic collapse, followed by world conflagration that had called into question the very idea of a future, much less a prosperous one. The United States survived both. Indeed, it emerged with renewed optimism and unparalleled strength. Among its elites and policymakers, the newly dominant focus on growth is thus perhaps understandable.[7] America had not just won the war. It had outperformed the rest of the world. It had done so while providing a rising standard of living to its citizens. As such, it represented a shining model of success amid global irrationality and violence. Critically, it was success built on expansion and growth.[8] Meanwhile, all of America's major competitors—economic or political—had been ravaged by war. In this environment, with what appeared to be the magic bullet in hand, no one in power asked economists or their profession for theoretical coherence or democratic accountability.[9]

But when the very different requirements of organizing a peacetime economy reemerged, as Kuznets had argued, certain quick-fix solutions such as counting government output as "final product," including the military, or ignoring a clear definition of function and purpose of economic activity, would cripple the goal of establishing an accurate welfare measure. And so it did.[10]

The pragmatism of meeting the mounting needs of the day prevailed. Long before Japan surrendered in August 1945, the challenges of putting together a stable postwar order seemed staggering, the uncertainties great, and the risks enormous.

Domestic debates in America centered on issues all too familiar from the recent depression: Where will all the returning service men and women find jobs? What will happen to the industries primarily engaged in war production, and to the people who worked there? Policymakers and economists argued over what regulations needed to be in place to prevent market capitalism from driving off the cliff again. Critically, they wondered whether or not sufficient demand could be maintained, particularly for a growing economy.

Two insights, one from the Great Depression, and the other from mobilization for war, came together. The depression revealed the significance of both high levels of investment and employment with adequate incomes in order to generate sufficient demand; in times of severe economic crisis, only government could assure this. War mobilization, on the other hand, had taught planners that having detailed economic data was not just necessary to win the war, it was also far superior to a total reliance on market indicators.

The memories of mass unemployment, long breadlines, fear of social upheaval, coupled with the shock of attack and the experience of war, were vivid and stark. Experiential reality—not theory—focused the American debate in the aftermath of World War II on employment and the role of government.

In the rest of the world, people raised difficult questions about the causes of the deadliest and most destructive international conflagration in history. The incomprehensible toll: over sixty million people had been killed. Persecution had been made scientifically efficient, resulting in the genocide of millions. Dreams about empires and hopes about the nature of progress had gone up in flames. Greed profited mightily. The scale of violence, of sheer human cruelty, reached proportions impossible to grasp.

One conclusion seemed inescapable: if life were to go on after this decade of horror, responses had to be found to some profound questions: What was the role of capitalism—had not the major adversaries, from Germany to Japan to Britain and the United States, been capitalist? How to avoid misguided patriotism or unchecked militarism from pushing people down a path of delusion and destruction? Did some versions of national character—subservience to authority or cultural chauvinism—inevitably lead to conflict and war? How to deal with the rise of technologies that now seemed capable, as the horrifying pictures of Hiroshima and Nagasaki demonstrated, of ending the human project on earth altogether? People from Berlin to Buenos Aires and from Tokyo to Warsaw felt compelled to build a postwar world on a more rational foundation.

Economic growth seemed a straightforward answer in the minds of those responsible for national accounting during and after the war—for men like Milton Gilbert and George Jaszi in the United States, or James Meade and Richard Stone in Great Britain. The rationale was simple: to avoid the calamities of depression, war, and revolution, people needed jobs and incomes, industry needed investment and demand, markets needed to function.

While accountants and economists may not have reflected on the many social and political effects of putting cultures on a regimen of incessant indiscriminate growth, they certainly understood it as effective medicine against a persistent problem: economic downturns and resulting political crises. Such crises routinely produced widespread suffering. They made entire cultures and societies more susceptible to all kinds of crackpot ideas.

Producing more wealth through the expansion of production and trade was less of a political mission as it was an attempt to find more solid footing. The emerging group of leading national income accountants and economists were primarily interested in the "internal workings of the national production." As Gilbert put it matter-of-factly, "I can only repeat that we are not trying to measure welfare, but the value of production from a business point of view."[11]

Among policymakers and accountants alike, larger issues about the future direction of humanity represented questions both abstract and remote. The central challenges in the mid-1940s were practical ones: How to supply the basics for the peoples of Europe and Japan? How to provide employment for the millions of Americans coming back from war? How to generate sufficient demand and investment in economies, all mired in debt, and some in shambles? How to operate thriving economies without the large demands of military production?

How to make sure that national economies remain open to international coop-eration and trade? All questions for which no useful historical models existed.

Expanding value of production and financial wealth along the guidelines established by national income accounts turned out to be a convenient and powerful answer.[12] GDP growth contained promise for everyone: growth in profits for employers, and growth in wages for workers. Growth in tax reve-nue for governments, and growth of available jobs for citizens. Conservatives embraced growth because it generated profits and opportunities for business. Liberals endorsed growth of government as a regulator of business and a pro-vider of basic welfare to all. Progressives advocated growth as an essential means to end poverty and empower the working class.

As a later critic of the "affluent society," John Kenneth Galbraith, noted well before the war was over, "One good reason for expecting prosperity after the war is the fact that we can lay down its specifications. For this we can thank a little-observed but spectacular improvement in the statistical measures of the current output of the U.S. plant."[13] This prosperity was exclusively defined by volume of output as classified by GDP standards. Only a few years later, Galbraith, however, reconsidered: he was one of the first to recognize the in-adequacy of such standards.

For decades to come, the promise of economies moving along a bright path toward more jobs, more revenue, more wealth, and more stuff for everyone ef-fectively allowed political leaders to sidestep deeper questions—about causes of depression and war; about inequality or the role of capital; and, perhaps most importantly, about purpose and direction of work and the content of progress.

Growth of GDP effectively filled the explanatory void.[14]

A STUNTED PRIESTHOOD

Kuznets had repeatedly discussed this dilemma. Well-being of people and vol-ume of output, he argued, were not the same. They were only problematically correlated. As defined by Kuznets, welfare required measures that provided a sounder direction for economic activities; economic output described the limited reality of the monetized marketplace.

Initially, Kuznets himself had argued against the measuring of "subjective feelings . . . whose relation to the objectively perceptible economic goods is not . . . determined with sufficient precision," and thus had to be abandoned in favor of "cruder approximations."[15] Though his views greatly evolved over the years, he early on shared the opinion with a few other economists that growth in GDP did not equal an increase in welfare. "The measurement of economic welfare and the measurement of productivity are in fact quite different things," concluded the British economist Richard J. Hicks as early as 1940.[16]

As one of the first national income and product accountants, Kuznets understood much better than most of his successors the absurdity of ascribing objectivity to the values defined by the market. Or to the numbers aggregated in national accounts. He had been forced to make innumerable subjective decisions about what to include in his "objective" national accounts. He knew he made decisions according to circumstance, political necessity, the availability of coherent models, and the limited data at his disposal. He was, to say the least, fully aware of the subjective nature of all such calculations.

It was a reality few understood, or wanted to accept, then or now. The traditional answer of economists to basic inquiries about well-being is simple: their purpose is not to address complicated "subjective" questions. Economics as a field claims only to describe and analyze economic phenomena based on "objective" criteria. Yet an essential part of this assertion is the claim that the marketplace itself determines what provides utility—what does, and what does not, have value—and thus can be used to gauge welfare.[17]

In real life, of course, this makes little sense. It's like saying the thermometer determines temperature in my living room. If that were true, I could, when cold, simply hold a match under the thermometer and immediately feel warmer. In modern economies, this flawed logic was henceforth repeated over and over again: when nagging problems persist, say poverty or lack of opportunities, even deficient educational quality or environmental decay, economists provide the same answer: turn up market activity as measured by GDP.

The grave dangers of this underlying reasoning became all too evident when the model failed to predict, much less prevent, the S&L crisis of the 1980s, the tech-bust of the 1990s, the economic collapse of 2007–9, or the rising fever of the planet. And yet, the reason for this blind spot is simple: all economic models are based on assumptions. And, the more elaborate the models, the greater the tendency for consequences of flawed assumptions to avalanche.

Some absurdities of mainstream economic assumptions are legend by now: "the rational, calculating, self-interested individual with unlimited wants for whom society is the nation-state" fails to capture the true wellsprings of human motivations and actions. Nor does he reach the nirvana of neoclassical economics called "equilibrium." The point here, however, is more basic: conclusions drawn from a model can never be more correct than the assumptions upon which the model is built. In reality, they are routinely less so.[18]

The model or measure itself is not reality—not growth, not development, not progress. It merely is a narrow and subjective attempt to capture some facet of reality. The moment we allow such a gauge to "represent" reality— like the market determining values, or, in our specific case, GDP representing growth and welfare and development—we get trapped in its logic. What is lost in the bargain is reality itself.

Having traced this development in national accounting, economist Ellen O'Brien concluded that the end result was "a hodge-podge of business, theoretical, and governmental concepts that satisfy no one because they do not mean anything in particular."[19] Nonetheless, this tyranny of bad thinking ended up defining the direction of economic activity.

STOPGAP CONSENSUS

It happened in rapid succession. National accounts moved from crisis response to central purpose of peacetime economies worldwide. In all phases, Kuznets played a critical role. By the mid-1950s, when capitalist economies around the world were captured by the logic of GDP, he had lost more battles than he had won. His gravest defeat centered on how and why the instrument of national accounting should be used in the first place.[20]

Sustained growth provided the easiest and most promising path to avoid the periodic specter of cataclysmic boom and bust cycles. Thus, among policymakers, practical needs of the day closed in on space for deliberations about GDP's purpose or direction.

Pulling together ill-suited bedfellows, otherwise self-declared enemies announced their faith in growth. "Growth" rose to the top of political aspirations, whether the country was socialist or capitalist, secular or theocratic.

Even Soviet leader Nikita Khrushchev agreed with the basic logic when he declared that the Soviet Union "will bury" the West—by which he meant "bury" with larger output of production. As the 1950s drew to a close, Khrushchev seemed confident that the USSR would eventually outperform the capitalist West—by measures following the same logic as those underlying GDP.[21]

In both East and West, the Cold War effectively replaced Depression and war as political rationale for marching orders toward ever more growth. As the dominant of the two remaining superpowers, the United States focused its statecraft on establishing or maintaining military and economic supremacy, which included minimizing the military and economic exploits of the Soviet Union. The rationale created what President Dwight D. Eisenhower would later call the "military-industrial complex." It also led to a radically expanded role of government, very much along Keynesian ideas, in the creation of the welfare state, a larger public role in education and science, a military force of unprecedented peacetime dimensions, and government-controlled monetary policies.[22]

These policies had a domestic and an international component. At home, GDP growth became an essential building block of modern policymaking. In the case of the United States, major examples include the GI-Bill, which offered unprecedented government support for college tuition and housing and business startups; the expansion of government initiatives like social security and unemployment and minimum wage benefits that guaranteed a steady flow of demand for consumer goods; the establishment of a permanent national security / war preparation state, providing millions of jobs through direct transfers of public funds; and the establishment of programs to aid international trade and global growth. Before long, politicians on both sides of the aisle in the United States could no longer imagine fashioning or assessing policy without use of GDP data.

Though there were clear winners and losers of such initiatives, what ultimately determined whether policies were considered successful was their contribution to GDP growth.[23] So pervasive was the goal of growth that Republican President Eisenhower explicitly labeled such government programs as crucial to "maintain personal income and consumption expenditures."[24]

There is no doubt that policies providing opportunity or security to citizens were not just an outcome of cynical calculations to benefit economic output. The point here is more pragmatic: had programs like the GI Bill or minimum wage benefits not also significantly contributed to the goal of GDP growth, they likely would never have seen the light of day.

From 1945 through today, policy initiatives that have little or no impact on GDP growth tend to get little attention and little to no support (like funding for humanities and arts, or early childhood development); plans that may undermine GDP growth are sure never to make it out of committee (strict pollution standards or humanitarian restrictions on weapons exports or environmental cost accounting as part of national accounts); proposals that fly in the face of common sense or science, on the other hand, can succeed for no other reason than that they are seen to boost GDP (fracking or oil extraction from tar sand or deregulating banks).[25] In America, "prosperity, the pursuit of economic growth, and national greatness" began to be defined as one and the same.[26]

It was not just an ideological commitment. The idea of ongoing GDP growth found expression in one of the most consequential pieces of legislation in the history of twentieth-century economics. Introduced by Sen. James E. Murray of Montana, and signed into law in 1946 by President Harry Truman, the Employment Act of 1946 was a classic product of political compromise. Rejecting the mandate of the original Full Employment Act of 1945, which would have required the federal government to provide employment to any interested citizen, the compromise legislation nevertheless forged a different kind of politics in America. It permanently altered the role and size of government, and has rightly been called "the Magna Carta of postwar economic planning."[27] In ways that have been identified but rarely questioned since, it turned economists into key decision-makers. And it officially elevated economic growth as defined by GDP to the central goal of government policy.

"The assumption by the Federal government of responsibility for maximum employment, production, and purchasing power—as embodied in the Employment Act of 1946—gave a new policy significance to national income statistics."[28] Specifically, the Act directed the federal government to use

> all practicable means . . . to coordinate and utilize all its plans, functions, and resources for the purpose of creating and maintaining . . . conditions under which there will be afforded useful employment opportunities . . . and to promote maximum employment, production, and purchasing power.[29]

The Act established two organizations that continue to play a central role in economic policymaking: the Joint Committee of the Congress (JEC), and the Council of Economic Advisors (CEA). The chairman of the CEA routinely interprets the latest GDP figures for the president; and the CEA provides economic advice to the president based on the metrics of the national income and product accounts generated by the Bureau of Economic Analysis (BEA). Every postwar president since Harry Truman has come to consider economic growth the central focus and essential precondition for successful politics.[30]

GDP became a nimble tool serving a wide range of masters—politicians of right, center, and left; generals as well as labor leaders; average citizens, businessmen and women, and, not surprisingly, corporate leaders. Growth of GDP promised to create employment and necessary demand; it allowed the United States to provide vital aid to Europe and Japan and to maintain a large military during times of rising tensions with Soviet communism and growing threats to global resources and foreign markets; it eventually helped the United States win the Cold War and a series of proxy "hot" wars against communism; it helped ease domestic unrest and prevented possible "class wars" by raising the standards of living (as defined by per capita GDP). As Franklin Roosevelt had discovered in 1941, the promise of opportunity through growth could even defuse racial tensions.[31]

It was a powerful weapon indeed. "More rapid economic growth," summarized the economic historian H. W. Arndt, "came to be regarded as a prophylactic or remedy for all the major current ailments of western economies."[32] The national income figures provided by GNP/GDP, meanwhile, were then and continued to be "taken as the chief criterion for national welfare or progress."[33] Underlying all of it, in the words of retail analyst Victor Lebow, was the fact that "in a very real sense the most powerful of all American industries is the manufacture of demand"—demand as the key driver for ever-expanding growth.[34]

In its essence, the story replicated in other cultures. In postwar Germany and Japan, growth-induced "economic miracles" served a range of vital functions: rebuilding war-ravaged economies, stifling anticapitalist dissent, creating new national identities, and, not least of all, moving past the ghosts of fascism and defeat. Throughout the capitalist West, powerbrokers came to see government-supported, anti-austerity and strong pro-growth policies not only as the best antidote to a repeat of depression and misery, but also as a defense against communism.[35] For the Soviet Union, meanwhile, growth became a quasi-religion, a way to show its "superiority" over the West. More pragmatically, growth became the glue holding together its newly acquired empire of disparate, mostly poor, and frequently defiant nations.[36]

In less than a decade after the agonies of world war and the resulting questions about how to build a safer and more just world, GDP growth effectively surpassed aspirations like democracy or human rights as the central political goal. People everywhere began to see it as the precondition for progress, as the ultimate answer to unemployment, poverty, general welfare; as a measuring rod for success; and, finally, as a promise—near or distant—of a better future.

A circular logic took hold: economists began to interpret an increase in the volume of production and consumption (measured by GDP) as successful economics and improved welfare. Robert Nathan articulated it succinctly in 1944: "mass consumption is essential to the success of a system of mass production." Indeed, he called "ever increasing mass consumption" a "prime requisite for prosperity."[37] As explored earlier, it was akin to saying "in order to be healthy, you need to consume calories," before concluding, "the more calories you eat, the healthier you'll be."

GOING GLOBAL

Under the leadership of the United States, the same logic played out in the international arena. The highlights of the postwar world are familiar to many: the American Employment Act of 1946 and the Marshall Plan, the founding of the United Nations, the Bretton Woods financial regime, and the creation of the World Bank. Each contributed to the rise of the international predominance of GDP.

Yet for any of these political milestones to function properly, something else had to be fashioned first: a uniform set of standards by which to account for economic performance. One could only arrive at operational conclusions as long as the gauges were calibrated the same across agencies and countries. In an environment of expanding global markets, working without universal gauges was like being asked to fill a gas tank measured in gallons with a pump calibrated in liters by an attendant who understood neither.

Among Allied accountants in World War II, all understood the vital importance of good economic measures. Mutual aid and collaboration worked only to the extent to which Allied economies spoke the same accounting language. As a forerunner to the UN, the United Nations Relief and Rehabilitation Administration (UNRRA), founded in 1943, immediately ran into a basic problem. Each of the forty-four member-countries committed themselves to paying no less than 1 percent of their national income in dues, yet the majority of countries did not possess a national income accounting system. How could they then figure out what to pay? The Director General of UNRRA asked U.S. Secretary of Commerce Harry Hopkins how to set up national income reports for all member countries. The U.S. supplied both advice and people in aiding this process.[38]

Once the war was over, the need for a uniform system became even more pressing. Should Italy or Britain receive more support to rebuild factories? Should railroad lines be prioritized in France or in Germany? In other words, the Allies needed a way to evaluate respective needs among war-torn nations. They also needed to organize reconstruction in the most efficient way possible, and have a standard measure for their progress. Effective statecraft was premised on knowledge about where employment was available, and where it was most needed. The basic requirement for all those objectives: a uniform set of national income accounts.

International standardization of national accounts had been initiated by the League of Nations in 1939. War put a temporary stop to it. A tripartite commission picked up the cudgel in September 1944. Meeting in Washington, D.C., their purpose, in the words of one of the participants, was "to exchange views on the more difficult problems of national income estimation and, if possible, to bring about uniformity in terminology and in the treatment of controversial items." They agreed "partly through persuasion, partly through compromise."[39] Due to his pioneering work on national accounts, Richard Stone of the United Kingdom played a leadership role. He crafted the key document for discussion at the follow-up meeting in Princeton, New Jersey, in December 1945.[40] Records of the committee in charge of discussing Stone's draft were never made available, and accounts of the meeting in general are sketchy at best.

We know the results, however. In 1947 the committee of statisticians on national income of the newly formed United Nations published a dense, nearly one-hundred-page-long document.[41] With minor alterations and compromises, the document replicated the British/American system of national income and product accounts. Despite the fact that Kuznets considered it "a dubious addition to the theoretical equipment by aid of which we define national income and reckon its distribution," it became the basic design for the metric adopted by the United Nations in 1953. As a result, it has controlled the parameters of macroeconomic thinking ever since.[42]

Though barely noticed at the time, and rarely discussed to this day, it was a momentous event. The world passed a major threshold: the basic structure and focus of national accounting has remained essentially the same since 1953, despite undergoing a wide range of technical alterations. Public deliberations about the metric's underlying purpose never took place.

To a layperson, the GDP seemed as sensible as the blueprints for a building or the procedural guidelines for open-heart surgery: deciding what the GDP encompassed was the work of experts, largely inaccessible, and seemingly objective. Except for a handful of professionals, chief among them Kuznets, no one questioned the measure. The debate over "what should be measured" ended before the public knew it had even started.[43]

Despite Kuznets's central role in developing national accounts, this turn of events explains why he should not be called "the father of GDP." In fact, he was squarely opposed to the postwar incarnation of national accounting.

Nevertheless, the metric approved in 1947 became the foundation for the 1953 United Nations System of National Accounts (UNSNA)—the first international standard for economic accounting. It provided a global blueprint. Even more important, it effectively forced member nations to adopt similar standards.

UN membership was predicated upon accepting this measurement: dues were assessed based on a respective country's GDP. In quick succession, measurement for economic development, including financial assistance and international loans, was determined by GDP, with profound impacts on seven decades of development policies.[44]

NEW RULES

One key example of where the national income standards of the UN found almost immediate and pervasive application was Europe. Perhaps no one better captured transatlantic postwar thinking about the need for economic growth as defined by GDP than Lord Oliver Franks, British ambassador to the United States from 1948 to 1952:

> No government can maintain a high level of employment unless it can secure the corresponding level of economic activity. Unless government intervenes to achieve this, fluctuations will occur. But such intervention will be blind and haphazard in its timing, unless the government is equipped with adequate information. The next consequence, therefore, is that the government needs to compile and to possess national income statistics so that its judgment of when, by what means, by how much to intervene may be well informed.[45]

Europe was a continent in ruin—people were starving, basic production and transportation facilities were destroyed, and the political future of respective

European governments was predicated upon their ability to provide stability, work, and incomes in the midst of widespread chaos.

Within such conditions of need and despair, the American government provided essential economic support. Beginning in April 1948 the Marshall Plan offered European governments a desperately needed infusion of money and goods. Some credited it with "saving Europe" from collapse and communist takeover and for creating the foundation for modern European collaboration through networks like the European Union.[46] As such, it could also be credited for helping to maintain peace.

By making disbursement, administration, and evaluation of aid contingent upon basic shared economic and accounting rules, the U.S. helped reestablish capitalist markets throughout its territories of occupation at the end of the war—southern, western, and central Europe. It also firmly instituted national accounting procedures based on U.S./ UN guidelines. Indeed, the Organization for European Economic Cooperation (OEEC),[47] explicitly requested submissions of national income and product accounts from all its member nations as subsequently set forth in the 1953 UNSNA. The reason: it was deemed necessary "for evaluating the progress of individual countries, and as a basis for allocating . . . aid."[48] Above all, however, the Marshall Plan "sought to spread both the message and the reality of growth to war-ravaged Western Europe."[49]

The United States now possessed an economy that accounted for an astonishing half of the world's total production. It had the only currency that provided both the stability and volume necessary for postwar international trade. In contrast, its former allies and enemies alike faced economies partly ruined, deeply in debt, and starved for the cash necessary for reconstruction and trade. Fully anticipating the consequences of such a disastrous imbalance, the United States had earlier brought together representatives of all Allied nations in July 1944, almost a year before hostilities ceased in Europe. A total of 730 delegates from forty-four nations met in a small town in New Hampshire called Bretton Woods.

Their primary purpose was to prevent another economic collapse like the Great Depression.[50] Following the basic logic of Keynes, the conference established an international currency system in which all member currencies were pegged to the dollar within certain, generally small, exchange rate "bands." The idea was to stabilize exchange rates, and thus the prices for imports and exports. Delegates hoped this would promote both international trade and national economic growth. Allied leaders saw it as a necessary safeguard against a repeat of the Great Depression, when tariffs and currency manipulations had been seen as contributing to the collapse of world trade.[51] Americans in particular asked for, and got, secure parameters for what they called "open markets and free trade."[52]

Under the dominant influence of the United States, the Bretton Woods conference participants laid out the creation of the World Bank and the International Monetary Fund, further spreading GDP metrics beyond the borders of the United States, Great Britain, and Marshall Plan recipients.[53] Following the lead of national accountants in London and Washington, the Bretton Woods attendees adopted a resolution that established the immediate forerunner of GDP as the official guide to policymaking on international monetary exchanges. It also established the metrics to determine which global development projects merited funding.[54]

Global financial support for the GDP regime was to come from a new International Bank for Reconstruction and Development (IBRD, later simply known as World Bank). The purpose of the bank was to facilitate international investment in order to raise "productivity, the standard of living, and conditions of labor" in member nations—the former two measured by the standards of GDP, and thus evaluated by GDP.[55]

One institution in particular emerged from the Bretton Woods discussions as tasked with promoting the values of GDP and the underlying concepts of Keynesianism. Grounded in the perceived need to lower tariffs and trade barriers, the World Trade Organization (WTO) was initially conceived as the General Agreement on Tariffs and Trade, or GATT. Founded in 1948, the primary purpose of GATT was to prevent another steep global economic decline, seen by followers of Keynes as a result of lack of aggregate demand, in part caused by tariff-protected forms of economic isolationism.

After a total of eight rounds of international conferences intended to free up international trade, GATT was eventually reconfigured in 1992 as the WTO, a more powerful and far more corporate-controlled entity than its predecessor.

As a result, countries now "face the ominous dilemma of losing sovereignty for the sake of remaining internationally competitive, because if they choose to resist global integrations, they find themselves in economic backwaters."[56] Invested with disciplinary powers, the WTO can effectively limit governments from enforcing independent national standards, ranging from public health to food safety and protections of workers or the environment.[57]

The end of World War II brought another big dilemma to the surface: steady currency exchanges and standardization of accounts were not sufficient to revitalize economies ravaged by depression and war. Old economic powerhouses like Great Britain, Germany, and Japan were not able to produce or consume enough for economic stability. They desperately needed a vital injection of cash and products in order to rebuild their own economies.[58]

The Marshall Plan made available both. As such, Marshall aid provided the critical trigger for what would be the longest period of sustained economic growth in the history of capitalism.[59] This growth followed the guiding principles of, and was measured by, the metrics of GDP, invisible to all but the accountants and economists who crunched the numbers.[60]

In the midst of postwar instability, in short, talk about GDP as a possibly crippled guidepost for the health of nations was not audible. In any case, it would likely have been seen as hopelessly academic.

David Engerman summarized the result of both domestic and international policies to boost the regime of GDP: it "became the measure of national success, the ranking system for wealth, and a proxy for wellbeing. It ranked developed as well as developing countries, set the dividing line between them, and defined the goals for national economic policies the world over." In his estimation, "not bad for a statistical series that in no sense measures every aspect of economic activity, let alone individual or collective wellbeing."[61]

GDP JUNKIES

Over the course of the next few decades, GDP growth became a global article of faith—independent of whether countries were pushed, forced, or cajoled into accepting its use, or whether they were eager participants in buying into its logic. Japan and China turned out to be fervent converts, making them what Vishakha Desai, the president and chief executive of the Asia Society in New York, has called "GDP junkies." Japan's integration into U.S.- and British-dominated accounting standards happened almost immediately after World War II, implemented through the Allied Supreme Command.[62] China did not adopt national income accounting until after the Cultural Revolution left China poor and in shambles. Major revisions, many in line with the UNSNA, were adopted by the Central Committee of the Chinese Communist Party in 1978. In 1992, China officially adopted GDP as the key measure for its domestic economic performance. Thereafter, according to China experts, gross domestic product was much more than merely a barometer for gauging policies of local officials. Finding ways to increase GDP became the key for advancement in the ruling Communist Party.[63]

Even faster than in the United States, the Chinese growth model ran into serious problems: suffocating smog, toxic drinking water, clogged highways, and skyrocketing cancer rates. Describing Handan, a newly industrialized city in central China, Ian Johnson writes "on bad days you cannot see the other side of a four-lane road. Earlier this year, a factory leaked a toxic chemical into the Zhuozhang River, which feeds the city's reservoir. The river turned brown, dead fish were found floating in the surface, and the city's water was cut off overnight." The effects on people were immediate, and severe. A former civil servant of the Chinese government starkly concluded that "GDP doesn't mean anything if you don't have your life."[64]

To much publicity, in 2004 Chinese reformers thus attempted to implement a Green GDP, factoring into their calculations the environmental consequences of growth. Yet the initial findings, published in 2006, were so devastating—despite the fact that they were considered to have vastly underestimated actual problems—the initiative was quickly abandoned. According to the first estimates, as much as 20 percent of China's GDP was directly based on depletion of resources and degradation of the environment. In several provinces, pollution-adjusted growth rates were negative.

With findings like this, the Central Committee decided to return to an exclusive focus on GDP. If nothing else, it fostered their grip on power. "Delivering growth placates the public, provides spoils for well-connected officials and forestalls demands for political change," concluded two students of the Chinese situation. "A major slowdown could incite social unrest, alienate business interests and threaten the party's rule." Of course, the authors weren't just talking about China. This problem was worldwide.[65]

These days, we read and hear a lot about the threat of China "overtaking" the United States, of becoming "a larger economy" (and thus the "largest in the world"), of having a much more favorable balance of trade and expanding at a much faster clip. The only gauge by which we know this? The GDP.

Ever since the Stalin era, the Soviet Union had joined the club of growth by tying its fortunes to the idea of outproducing and outperforming the "imperialist West."[66] Other countries in the Soviet sphere of domination were forced to join in this overly optimistic endeavor. For roughly four decades, the Soviet orbit experienced a virtual growth mania.

In the context of the Cold War, of course, Soviet growth and development greatly worried the United States. Experts and State Department economists emphasized calculations of Soviet GDP: it was the central measure used to gauge Soviet strength, a potential Soviet threat, and the foundation for Soviet military might. For forty-plus years, the debate raged: which kind of economy fostered more robust growth?

Once Soviet archives opened to historical research in the years after 1991, we learned that American GDP figures of the Soviet national economy had been far more accurate than estimates provided by the Soviet Union's own economic planners, who found it near impossible to come up with reliable data for their centralized planned economy. What did Soviet planners do? They spied on American economists calculating Soviet GDP, and then incorporated what they learned from their American colleagues into their own planning.[67]

When the Soviet empire eventually failed in its endeavor to outproduce the West, and the deeply corrupt walls of actually existing communism were forced open by popular movements from Poland to East Germany, the one transition the successor nations of the former Soviet empire performed without any seeming difficulty was this: adopt the Western accounting system of GDP.[68]

It had happened from Japan to India, and from China to Brazil and the former Soviet Union. By 1992, there was not a single important economy left in the world that did not measure its performance through GDP. Not one major nation had escaped its logic. Globalization became defined by the ingredients necessary for GDP growth: trade liberalization, privatization, expansion of markets, cheap labor, and, always, worldwide commodification and exploitation of resources. A version of globalization that "created a plethora of choice but also a convergence of aspirations and values, which now center around people's desire to own, acquire and—as Adam Smith put it—'truck and barter.' "[69]

In poor and under-resourced nations, people experienced the impacts with devastating effect. Some key elements are important to highlight.[70]

The underlying logic was quite simple. Poor countries contribute very little to GDP—either within their own national boundaries or in international trade. Indeed, poverty itself is defined as a function of GDP: little or no monetary income as defined by national accounts translates as "poor." These are the countries where large numbers are said to subsist on "less than $2 a day." Such statistics are based on GDP. And a low national GDP is prima facie evidence, according to mainstream economists, of economic failure.

If poor countries want to thrive on the world economic stage, they need to open their markets to foreign investment and create a business-friendly infrastructure. Promoting such measures usually requires loans from institutions like the World Bank. As with all loans, however, the lending institution provides a loan only when the recipient can repay with interest, in other words, prosper and grow. When growth, again defined by GDP, is in danger, there are other institutions, like the IMF, that will in turn enforce "structural adjustment" policies to safeguard loans and, more broadly, ensure an economy's continued participation in the GDP regime.[71]

Here is where it commonly gets ugly. Traditional ways of making a living, such as subsistence / small-scale farming or bartering, do not register on the GDP meter. Organized workers or citizens who perceive the logic of markets as a rotten deal also challenge GDP, for the imperatives of GDP tend to undermine things like living wages and environmental protections. In general, when democratic voices in public affairs demand anything other than GDP-based growth, they then appear as "anti-growth." They are not. They are, however, anti-GDP. They are also commonly on the losing side, pushed aside by the triumvirate of the GDP regime–world financial institutions, corporations, and local political elites. "Whether in Africa, Asia, Latin America or post-communist Europe, policies of wholesale privatisation and structural adjustment have led to declining economic activity and social dislocation on a massive scale."[72]

The results of the information provided by GDP are increasingly misleading. In some cases, they go beyond misleading into treachery. World Bank loans by now have a history of directly undermining social and natural capital in recipient countries. Poorer countries are confronted with the reality that short-term gain through natural resource exploitation and depletion is often followed by long-term resource degradation and poverty. A much-cited World Resource Institute study, for instance, documented that the impressive GDP growth rates of Indonesia in the 1970s and 1980s were essentially bought with clear-cutting forests and the exhaustion of topsoil with intensive cash-crop farming.[73] Similar stories of development into dependence and eventual poverty can be told among poorer countries around the world.[74]

A national economy could "exhaust its mineral resources, cut down its forests, erode its soil, pollute its aquifers, and hunt its wildlife to extinction," all while their key performance indicator goes up.[75]

It defies logic. CEOs ordinarily get fired for depleting their own company's capital. Investors and pensioners generally understand that, in order to have a future, you need to live off of interest, not principal. But this basic logic does not apply to national and international accounting.

The response of mainstream development economists has been consistent: if you want social services or environmental protection, you need economic growth to pay for it. A recent study conducted by the World Bank Commission on Growth and Development goes as far as arguing that nothing other than solid GDP growth can possibly solve problems such as world poverty. Remarkably, they suggest that we should double economic output each decade. This is circular logic at its most destructive: they ignore the ways in which GDP growth itself causes social dislocation and environmental degradation.[76] As Nobel Prize–winning economist Joseph Stiglitz summarized, "Market fundamentalists never really appreciated the institutions required to make an economy function well, let alone the broader social fabric that civilizations require to prosper and flourish."[77]

It's the central problem: the very definitions of "flourish," both social and economic, came to be measured by criteria dependent on GDP. Standards of living, within nations and among nations; prosperity; private homeownership and the rise of suburbia; deficits and debts; the welfare state; trade balance; consumer confidence; inflation and international finance; outsourcing and the global economy; mass consumerism; taxes and public transfer payments; wealth and income distribution; exploitation of natural resources—all of this gets defined and understood around the world mainly through categories that collectively make up the system of national accounts and are eventually expressed in the one little big number.[78]

Of course the reader would be right in objecting that none of these things, in the final analysis, depend on GDP. It is certainly true that they might exist, in one form or another, without GDP. This objection, however, would miss a central point. How we think about every one of these aspects of the economy, what significance they hold in political and economic decision-making as well as in the formation of cultural values, and how they have each evolved in size and shape and direction over time—all of it followed the parameters and values inscribed in GDP.

When we use the term "middle class," for instance, we commonly mean some vaguely defined state defined by income level. Income, in turn, is defined by GDP categories. We decidedly do not define middle class, say, by people's level of intellectual development or the state of their health or their degree of happiness or their sense of security. We do not even count things like their social capital or the work performed inside their homes. If we did, there might still be a "middle class," but it would be a very different kind of middle class. The same is true for all other categories, from prosperity to inflation to profit and inequality—all might exist with or without GDP; but currently all are defined by accounting standards and classifications enshrined in national accounting systems that make up GDP.

Not only do we get what we measure. The measure, in this case, also defines our ways of seeing and understanding the world around us.

To appreciate the magnitude of effects, it might be useful to look once again at a powerful analogy otherwise in danger of overuse. As Americans—and, due to American cultural influence, this includes more and more people around the world—we see so-called "black" people. We do so independent of our own skin color or whether we hold conscious or unconscious racial biases. We see race independent on whether we think it's a useful concept or whether we realize that it was a human invention of fairly recent origin. More importantly, in the United States it fundamentally shapes our reality—social identities, places of residence or worship, jobs or educational opportunities, life prospects. Of course people of some brownish or some pinkish hue would continue to exist if we could somehow un-invent race. But here is the point: if people were no longer black or white, just about everything about their lives would change, sometimes dramatically. It is the power of a way of seeing.

In modern economies, as Kuznets understood, the way of seeing that had won the day in the latter half of the twentieth century was growth as promise for a better tomorrow—growth as defined by GDP. In ways largely invisible (not unlike the deep dynamics of race), GDP's core values have by now directed some seven decades worth of peacetime growth. It is the world's controlling ideology, framing both individual and collective ways of seeing and thinking. The institutions and structures that reflected this ideology were just one step behind.

Ruling the world did not bestow coherence to the number, however (any more than there is much coherence behind the concept of race). What GDP has captured, rather, reveals the historical roots of its origins, marked by political compromises and the rationalizations for many ill-designed policies.

SHACKLED IN FOOL'S GOLD

> There is always an easy solution to every human problem—neat, plausible, and wrong.
> —*H. L. Mencken*

Faced with the enormous challenges of providing economic prosperity, employment, and international cooperation after hostilities had ended, talk of the self-healing powers of the free market had all but disappeared after World

War II. Government, it seemed clear, needed to play a much bigger economic role.[79]

The Great Depression had demonstrated that developed capitalist economies were more vulnerable to severe downturns than anyone had anticipated. In the face of enduring crisis, classical and neoclassical faith in the self-healing powers of capitalist markets was hard to maintain. Daily realities on the ground seemed to mock conventional economic wisdom. Keynes, in turn, provided the proverbial nail in the coffin of traditional economics: full employment and eventual recovery, Keynes showed, was in no way automatic. Both the Depression and the war seemed to affirm his theory that government spending—not the market alone—was essential to return to full employment and eventual recovery.[80]

In contrast, the core idea behind neoclassical economics had always been that a "free market" of supply and demand determines prices, outputs, and income distribution—that a "free market" is the most efficient way to produce and disseminate resources.[81] And yet, as a profession, economists had finally proved their mettle in the midst of a command or "planned" economy. "It is one of the great ironies," writes economic historian Michael Bernstein, "that a discipline renowned for its systematic portrayals of the benefits of unfettered, competitive markets would first demonstrate its unique operability in the completely regulated and controlled economy of total war."[82]

The political ramifications seemed obvious to major capitalist nations. Above all, the war, as Kenneth Galbraith noted, had "dealt the classical disapproval of government intervention a heavy blow."[83]

There continues to be much debate about the origins of the basic ideas that made Keynes famous.[84] However, one thing seems beyond dispute: without the people who provided the detailed statistics on output and income, broken down by sectors of the economy and made comparable through conceptual standardization, Keynes' insights would have been another interesting set of ideas without much practical impact—sketches of a house without construction plans.[85] Indeed, since the construction plans were largely drawn up by people like Simon Kuznets in the United States and Colin Clark in Great Britain well before Keynes had even published his master plan, the impact on policymaking might have been similar with or without him.[86]

No matter: once the idea of government planning came armed with incontrovertible national accounts numbers, and proved its mettle during World War II, the effect of Keynesian ideas on economic thinking was indeed what people at the time called "revolutionary." It also created what today is known as big government.

Simply to describe postwar government as larger, or more involved in regulating the economy, however, would largely miss the point. The more significant transformation was that the central function of government became shackled to the imperatives of GDP growth.[87]

Another revolutionary consequence was this: what people meant by "the economy," or whether they even thought about it much, had differed from country to country. Until World War II, a wide range of economies, official and unofficial, existed around the world. Much of what people did to grow food or construct things or take care of family or build community still happened outside official markets. But by 1992, the time Leninist totalitarianism had finally collapsed, only one single definition of national economies had survived, no matter what or where. What is an economy? That which contributes to GDP. We had officially entered the age of GDP.

With the invention of formalized national accounts, the economy could be pictured, for the first time, as a "self-contained 'circular flow' of production, income and expenditure." This means that if something is not tallied by GDP accounts it is, by definition, not part of what is officially seen as the economy. One result in particular should give us pause: the economy suddenly becomes a "separate system, distinct . . . from 'the social', 'the cultural', or 'the political.'"[88]

Societies can exist with different cultures and values, computers with different operating systems. Not so for concepts of the economy. Without GDP, there would be no modern economy.

Defined by GDP as an entity in its own right, the economy can thus presumably be studied independent of social or environmental considerations.

Or effects. It becomes a system strangely divorced from the very foundation upon which it is based—the physical reality of the planet. People enter into it as no more than producers and consumers.

Summarizing years of research on the topic, a team of economists and sustainability experts encapsulated the resulting problem in two sentences:

> By measuring only marketed economic activity . . . GDP ignores changes in the natural, social, and human components of community capital on which the community relies for continued existence and wellbeing. As a result, GDP not only fails to measure key aspects of quality of life; in many ways, it encourages activities that are counter to long-term community wellbeing.[89]

All the while, the reigning hero of the day, around the world, is the one who best promotes GDP growth—as citizen or employee, public servant or entrepreneur. Though likely not fully aware of what exactly is counted as GDP growth, George W. Bush summarized the view in the more common, nebulous language of politics: "We must always act to ensure continued economic growth and prosperity for our citizens and for citizens throughout the world."[90]

Having traced the emergence of national accounting and the rise of GDP to global predominance, it is time to dissect what exactly GDP entails. What, after some seven decades of development and refinement, do presidents and prime ministers and chancellors around the world promote when they collectively tout the benefits of economic growth and prosperity?

Chapter 7

TODAY'S ABC OF GDP

*Whether you can observe a thing or not depends on
the theory which you use. It is theory which decides
what can be observed.*

—*Albert Einstein*

Modern economies require economists to measure an enormous range of widely disparate things—inflation, unemployment, the consumer price index, investment, interest rates, and much more.

As we have explored, the undisputed king among all such measures is GDP. All other measures are a function of GDP—all directly or indirectly derive from it.[1] What is the state of the economy? Are we in a period of growth, or do we find ourselves in the grips of a recession or, worse, a protracted period of stagnation? Are consumers confident? Is the climate good for investments? What are the effects of a particular policy proposal? Can we afford to protect the environment, pay for healthcare, or support the elderly? Are we, in the end, able to do what we think is right?

Listen to the daily news, read the business section of your newspaper, talk to economists or politicians, and you'll quickly discover that all such answers depend on GDP. Scholars think about income or national debt as a percentage of GDP, correlate life expectancy or levels of education to per capita GDP, sometimes even try to gauge life satisfaction as somehow proportional to GDP. Indeed, the only general gauge used, and accepted, to evaluate whether things are going up or down is GDP. This is why GDP has been called "one of the greatest inventions of modern times" and the "best recognized measure of economic performance in the world."[2]

As a measure of the market value of all final goods and services, GDP represents the aggregate figure of the National Income and Product Accounts

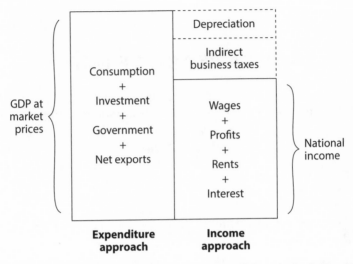

Figure 7–1. In a classic double-entry account, GDP might look like this.

(NIPA). In a classic national double-entry bookkeeping system, GDP attempts to measure the total value of all products as well as the total value of all incomes earned. As in all double-entry accounts, the two should end up being the same (see figure 7–1).[3]

It is a mesmerizing figure, one that can presumably capture in a single number everything from supersized burgers and 9mm semi-automatics to health insurance, education, jails, and therapy sessions, none of them "commensurable, yet there they are, caught up in the same" number.[4]

Let's see how it does that. The amount and variety of things we track in modern economies is dizzying. The U.S. economy, for instance, annually produces some 80 million tons of steel, builds roughly 10 million cars for an annual driving total of about 3 trillion miles, using 139 billion gallons of fuel.[5]

Some 600,000 new homes are constructed. Almost 400 billion cigarettes, some 50 million mobile phones, and over 21 billion diapers (92 percent of which end up in landfills) are sold every year. The average American is exposed to 3,000 ads a day, spends more than 6 hours in front of a screen (TV, computer, smartphone), and consumes 60 gallons of soft drinks a year.[6] And that's just a glimpse of the "goods" in goods and services.

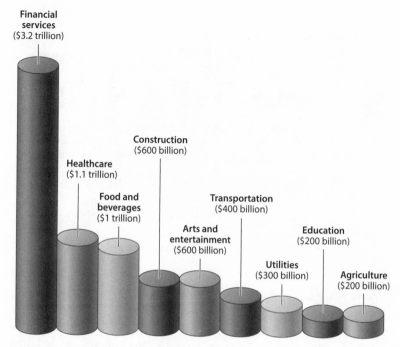

Financial services ($3.2 trillion)

Construction ($600 billion)

Healthcare ($1.1 trillion)

Food and beverages ($1 trillion)

Transportation ($400 billion)

Arts and entertainment ($600 billion)

Education ($200 billion)

Utilities ($300 billion)

Agriculture ($200 billion)

Figure 7–2. U.S. GDP by industry.

What about services? Americans visit a doctor on average 4.1 times a year. About 2 million Americans contract divorce lawyers, while educators teach roughly 80 million students from kindergarten to graduate school. Over 1.4 million men and women are on active duty in the U.S. military, accounting for a small part of the estimated one trillion in annual defense related spending— almost as much as the rest of the world combined.[7] In 2012 one midwife in Kansas helped deliver 234 babies. Indeed, the majority of citizens in highly developed economies now work in the service sector of the economy rather than produce goods. In the United States, only about 12 percent of economic output comes from manufacturing (see figure 7–2).

Money, income, and labor also count. The average American works 1,778 hours a year, about 350 hours more than an average citizen of the European Union. The majority pay interest on credit card debt, while the total overall

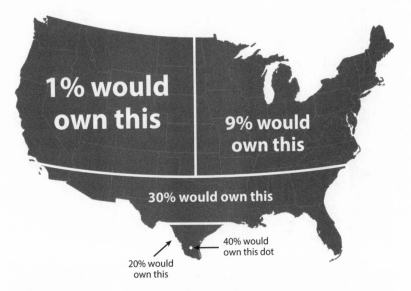

Figure 7–3. If U.S. land were divided like U.S. wealth.

debt burden now stands at close to $200,000 for each man, woman, and child in America. Average wages declined in the 2008–12 period, yet corporate profits reached some $1.7 trillion annually, an amount roughly equivalent to the annual national expenditures on healthcare.[8] Though the trend toward increasing inequality is universal, the largest capitalist economy stands out: in America today, the top 1 percent own almost half of total wealth, while the "bottom" 80 percent, or more than three-quarters of the population, have to make do with a meager one-tenth of the total. The wealthiest family in America (the Walton's of Wal-Mart fame) now controls almost as much net worth as half of all American families combined—a clear case of redistribution from the bottom to the top, as morally reprehensible as it is legal, socially corrosive, and economically celebrated.[9] The bottom line: increasingly, the beneficiaries of growth in GDP almost exclusively belong to the top 1 percent[10] (see figure 7–3).

In order for us to have any understanding of the size and functioning of the national economy, all of the above, and so much more, needs to be counted, tabulated, and compared.[11] It raises difficult questions: What to include, what to omit? What is part of the economy? Should money be our only gauge? Or should we maintain, as the clever ad campaign by Master Card reminds us, that some things are priceless? What happens to things that don't have a price—such as stable families, meaningful jobs, fresh air, or good education? Should they get counted at all?

This much is certain: for anyone to exert any kind of control over local, national, or international economies—to plan, to regulate, to anticipate, to stimulate—the question of what to measure, and how to measure it, is key.

Who makes those decisions? Given the vastly unequal distribution of resources and wealth in modern societies, one might be tempted to think the answer is some version of "the rich and powerful." Not so. Throughout the industrialized world, national accounting is performed by accounting offices of otherwise secondary status. In the United States, it is the Bureau of Economic Analysis (BEA), an agency of the U.S. Department of Commerce, charged by Congress to "promote a better understanding of the U.S. economy by providing the most timely, relevant, and accurate economic data in an objective and cost-effective manner."[12]

We learn about their findings like clockwork. At the end of each economic quarter, accountants of the BEA enter the "Lockup" at the Commerce Department in Washington, D.C. Tabulating the latest national income and output figures, they remain sealed off from the outside world. Even restroom breaks have to be taken in the presence of a companion.[13]

Why such elaborate secrecy? Because the product of their labors—GDP—represents the single most important economic measure.

Once completed, their findings are placed in a sealed envelope and carried over by guarded messenger to the White House. Once there, the Chairman of the President's Council of Economic Advisors examines the computations before giving it personally to the President. Beyond the walls of the White House and the Lockup, no one else knows the contents of that envelope.

The next morning, a similar procedure will lead to the publication of the results. At exactly 7:30 a.m., reporters are led into an electronically sealed conference room. The doors are locked, and no one is allowed in or out. Those present will get advance copies of what will go out to the world exactly one hour later: the initial estimates of last quarter's GDP. For an hour, representatives of the BEA are available for questions and answers. Reporters draft their stories.

At precisely 8:30 a.m., officials flick the switch, reporters connect to their networks, and the figures are officially released to the public. That day, news organizations will run stories on the latest GDP figures. Politicians will comment, Wall Street and global markets from London to Tokyo will respond. The ritual is repeated twice more, in precise monthly intervals, before the end of the next quarter—as the "initial" estimate is followed by the "preliminary" estimate and then the "final" estimate. In each case, revisions routinely send ripples through world markets.[14]

Around the world, nations large and small produce a virtually identical version of their own national GDP. Its release is a monthly ritual of great consequence. Like Groundhog Day, experts track GDP figures to see whether the economy will see its own shadow and go back underground, or whether economic spring will occur. Either way, the world of economics and politics accordingly shifts in its tracks.[15] If something threatens GDP growth—say, a mandate for workplace safety or for toxin-free neighborhoods—it is almost universally dismissed or ignored, however much the populace may hope for it.

The rationale behind what gets counted, and what does not, remains invisible. Outside of national statistical agencies such as BMI-SB in Germany or BEA in the United States, only handfuls of people could explain how the system works, and what, exactly, it does—fewer still have any idea why or how it came about.[16]

On the surface, GDP can be understood as the aggregate national result of what is called a System of National Accounts (SNAs)—the number that summarizes in one metric an enormous amount of data on work, production, investment, income, and consumption. It is a measure of a wide range of economic activity, "some of which is joyful, some beneficial, some regrettably necessary, some remedial, some trivial, some harmful, and some stupid."[17]

One number for an amazing hodgepodge of things—a seemingly great invention.[18] In the words of Paul Samuelson, an eminent economist read by tens of thousands of college students every year, "Without measures of economic aggregates like GDP, policymakers would be adrift in a sea of unorganized

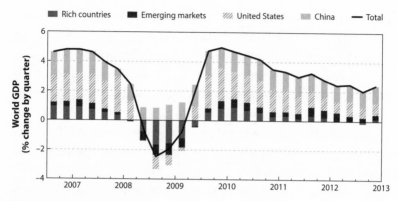

Figure 7–4. World GDP.

data." Or as a long-term scholar of national accounts put it, they are an "indispensable tool for macroeconomic analysis, projections, and policy formulation." Without them, warns Stanford professor and former chair of the Council of Economic Advisors, Michael J. Boskin, "we would be in the economic dark ages."[19]

We traced in previous chapters, how GDP has morphed into the golden arrow of economic activity. It is our one scorecard for national performance. The ultimate target. Up is good. Down is bad.[20]

This is why economists around the world religiously track GDP growth rates. No other data comes close in significance. Everyone understands the imperatives behind the GDP logic: failure to grow spells misery and defeat.

Per capita GDP for the United States today stands at roughly $48,000. In the past, only Luxembourg and Liechtenstein, two tiny countries, outperformed the so-called standard of living of the United States (Luxembourg's has been almost three times larger). This changed after the last recession. The 2011 estimates by the International Monetary Fund now rank U.S. per capita GDP at fifteenth in the world. There has since been a steep decline in public references to U.S. per capita GDP.[21]

People in poor countries like Uganda or Nepal are said to live on "less than $2 a day." It's not clear how anyone could survive on so little. Until we remember that only money exchanged is counted. A Nigerian subsistence farmer or a Greek fisherman, for instance, contributes little or nothing to his country's GDP, though he might be quite content. But GDP-per-capita comparisons don't reflect subtleties such as safety or happiness, or activities like bartering or sharing within an extended family. Actual people and their opinions on quality of life are not considered by GDP accountants—it's not clear, for instance, whether the deckhand on a fishing trawler, making $20 a day for ten hours of labor on someone else's boat is better off than the sixth-generation independent fisherman in Kardamyli making $0 a day.

In its narrow focus, the measure yields remarkable historical advances. How much richer and better off are we today? "Over the past millennium, world population rose 23-fold, per-capita income 14-fold, and GDP more then 300-fold."[22] It sure looks impressive.

National accounting tables published by BEA are organized around broad categories—overall GDP, personal consumption, private domestic investment, net export of goods and services, and government consumption expenditures and gross investment—depicting the relative significance and performance of different sectors of the economy. This allows reporters to trace things like the relative growth of the service sector over manufacturing, or to demonstrate the explosive growth of the financial industry. In each case, what gets measured is value and significance of activity based on its respective contribution to GDP.

Commentators utilize such statistics to show the vital importance of consumer spending: every effort should be made, it is argued, to boost consumption, for it represents over 70 percent of overall demand. Sometimes the consequences are quite revealing: Refusing to run a fully paid ad calling for a "Buy Nothing Day" (which stated that Americans consume five times as much as Mexicans and thirty times as much as Indians, and perhaps could give it a rest for a day), a CBS executive wrote that running such an ad would be "in opposition to the current economic policy in the United States." Apparently, when in conflict, core national values such as freedom of expression lose out to the controlling value of growth.[23]

How important the consumer spending of citizens is to the overall economy, and how much modern American society is willing to push people into

Table 7–1. Consumer Spending and Debt as Proportion of Economy

Year	Total household debt	GDP	Disposable personal income (DPI)	Household debt as a percentage of GDP	Household debt as a percentage of DPI
1975	734	1,638	1,187	45%	62%
1980	1,396	2,788	2,003	50%	70%
1985	2,278	4,218	3,073	54%	74%
1990	3,581	5,801	4,254	62%	84%
1995	4,841	7,415	5,457	65%	89%
2000	6,987	9,952	7,327	70%	95%
2005	11,743	12,638	9,277	93%	127%
2009	13,602	14,119	11,035	96%	123%

Source: Hale Stewart, "Consumer Spending and the Economy," *New York Times*, 19 September 2010

debt to keep the frenzy of growth alive becomes clear in the following chart: between 1975 and 2009, household debt as a percentage of disposable income doubled from 62 to 123 percent (see table 7–1). The engines of GDP need consumers to spend, and go on spending past their income.

This is why President Bush, right after 9/11, urged Americans "to shop" rather than, say, build community, pray, embrace a neighbor, or study history.[24] The last thing he wanted to give Osama bin Laden was the satisfaction of crashing the nation's GDP.

The work of GDP accountants quickly gets quite technical and elaborate.[25] What's important to recognize is that the logic of GDP is employed throughout all levels of the economy. When we read about growth, investment or employment prospects, standards of living, inequality, debt, interest rates, inflation, economic health: in each case we get GDP, a component of GDP, or a function of GDP.[26]

By providing an aggregate number—all goods and services produced—that is said to give "systemic empirical form to the structure, patterns, and performance of an economy," GDP represents the gold standard. As such, it is used as the basis for "judging the level and progress of the wealth of nations, and for identifying the causes of success and failure."[27]

IT'S AN EMPEROR, BUT DOES IT HAVE CLOTHES?

As we have already seen, GDP measures output and income—the total volume of economic activity. But, as a second rule of thumb, it does not measure all volume. With some interesting exceptions, it measures only volume that comes with a price and that is bought and sold in the market. Goods and services without price disappear. Bads are not counted at all. Strangely, the "production of anti-bads" (things like pollution clean-ups or security systems guarding against burglary) is counted as goods.[28]

Here is how this plays out in real life. Taking an imaginary person as a guide—we call her Ms. Golden Arrow—let's assume she gets up in the morning, takes a shower, and has a cup of coffee. If she takes the shower at home, only the water and energy for the hot water heater get measured. What is not measured: the quality of the water, the beauty of her bathroom, or the safety of her home. If she takes the shower at her local health club, only the membership fee is measured. Same for the coffee. At home, what is officially measured is water, coffee beans, electricity; at her local Starbucks, it's the price she pays for the *grande café latte*. If she enjoys a piece of bread with her coffee, it's included if bought in the store, but not if baked at home. If the entire breakfast is served by, say, her stay-at-home husband, GDP remains unaffected. If she prefers the services of a waiter in her local café, GDP goes up by his wages and, unless she is stingy, his tips.

As one male economist once pointed out, if you marry your nanny, you deflate GDP. No market transaction takes place. Perhaps Mark Twain captured this logic even better when he wrote about two women who "earned a precarious living by taking in each other's washing." Only when money changes hands is work counted.[29]

This gets interesting if one has children. If Ms. Arrow stays home with them, perhaps even schools them at home, none of her work is factored into

GDP, and officially nothing grows.[30] If she does any of the things increasing numbers of American parents do—send them to private schools, enroll them in after-school activities, drive them from music lesson to math tutoring to basketball practice, hire babysitters for the much-needed evening out with her spouse—her GDP contribution grows by leaps and bounds. She can become a veritable growth fixture in case the children happen to get stressed from all this activity, eating too much or being diagnosed for depression or a growing alphabet soup of mental disorders—ADD, or OCD, or ADHD. Real or over-diagnosed or pathologized, it is increasingly difficult to know, particularly in light of the fact that every prescription, every treatment adds to the bottom line. All add to GDP.[31]

If Ms. Arrow manages to stay happily married throughout all this, her spousal bliss adds nothing to official accounts of national economic success. If she runs into marital problems, requiring doctors, pills, and therapists, or per-haps even law enforcement, her GDP meter starts ticking in earnest. It hits full stride if she ends up in divorce: lawyers, courts, domestic help, separate living quarters, eating out, membership fees for dating services. A sobering feature of modern consumer culture is a dating website for already married people: with close to twenty-two million dues-paying members, raking in millions in ad dollars, the owner, Ashley Madison, cashes in on loneliness and despair—all a boost to GDP.

According to recent surveys, more and more people in highly industri-alized nations live by themselves—pushing up GDP. Without company of a fellow human being, we need extra living space as well as additional TVs and microwaves, cars and kitchen cabinets—one or more for each individual.

The longer Ms. Arrow works, the better for GDP—her income goes up, as do her contributions to the production of goods and services. On the other hand, time off, taking naps at home, playing a pick-up game of football in the park, marveling at the birds in her front yard, helping her neighbor work through a problem at her job, or taking care of her small garden—none of it gets mea-sured, counted, or recognized as a contribution. GDP remains stagnant.

As it does when she happens to live in a safe and stable neighborhood. But introduce things like severe inequality, social strife, or economic distress, and the resulting need of extra security measures—added police, home security systems, locks, handguns, jails—will advance GDP growth. So does her decision to move to a distant suburb: more roads, more gasoline, more construction, more accidents, more residential services. According to a recent study, one of the fastest-growing labor demographics are so-called "super commuters," people who travel more than ninety miles one way to work. By normal standards, this would seem a deplorable state of affairs for all affected. But, notably, it advances economic health, for it requires an array of services and resources.[32]

The car she needs just in order to get to work? The accident more likely to happen the more she drives? The pill to calm her down or keep her awake? All register as benefit, steadily growing GDP.

Perhaps she had to go into debt in order to build or maintain her lifestyle —a definite plus for GDP. As we measure the goods and services sold, total consumption increases with debt. The new home for which she holds a mortgage? The car purchased on a payment plan? The loan taken out for her child's college tuition? The shopping spree she puts on her credit card? All a net plus on the GDP meter.

Indeed, the financial services industry, whose primary purpose is to provide credit and foster growth, by now accounts for roughly 50 percent of non-farm business profits (up from 10 percent in 1947), and makes up roughly 8 percent of GDP in the United States—almost as much as the entire population spends on food, transportation, and utilities combined, all without creating a single tangible thing that directly improves anyone's lives. But a big boost all to prosperity.[33]

During an average day, Ms. Arrow encounters thousands of ads—on her smartphone, on her computer, on her commute, in the paper, on TV. A multibillion dollar industry that has little function other than to make people unhappy about their current life, advertisements essentially tell people how deficient they are—that is, until and unless they go buy a particular product. Perhaps it should be called "misery production." A roughly $170 billion industry in the United States alone (more than enough money to feed every hungry child on earth), it all counts toward our presumed welfare. As do the layers upon layers of packaging that stand between the consumer and her newly purchased objects of desire. Yes, maintaining the huge landfill, chock-full with packaging materials that will take thousands of years to decompose, also adds to success. And so it goes.

But even the counting does not always follow the same logic. In some cases, GDP accountants do what economists call "impute" a price where none exists. For the house Ms. Arrow owns with her husband, for instance, accountants impute a rent—the amount Ms. Arrow would presumably have to pay if she rented her home. For every homeowner there is thus a monthly "rent" entry in our national accounts, even though no money has exchanged hands. This may seem curious, for national accountants do not impute a price for all the things the Arrows do inside that home—raising their children, cleaning house, growing vegetables. Strangely, accountants also don't impute a price on the ecosystem, even though it provides essentials like fresh air and water, plant pollination or flood control.[34] Those things, national accountants say, are too difficult to impute.[35] If Ms. Arrow is confused about what does and does not contribute to success, she is not alone.

It gets stranger still. Income, according to GDP accounting rules, is not the same as income. Depending on who makes it, it is counted very differently. In the case of businesses, income is the amount left over after all costs are deducted. For businesses, costs include things like labor, material, maintenance, and research. For individual citizens, the same logic does not apply. While Ms. Arrow may be able to deduct certain expenses for tax purposes, most of what's in her paycheck is counted as her actual income—irrespective of whether she needs a nanny to take care of her children when she goes to work, or whether she has to move to a particular neighborhood, get a special certificate, commute by car, or wear certain clothes in order to do her job. Of course she likely realizes that such things constitute little more than what the father of U.S. national accounting, Simon Kuznets, called "the evils necessary in order to be able to make a living."[36] Yet none of them is deducted from her income the way it is in the case of a business: as necessary expenses in your pursuit of providing goods and services.[37]

What about resources, how do they count? Drinking water from the tap, at less than a penny per gallon, adds practically nothing. Bottled water, at a price routinely above what you would pay for the same amount of gasoline, adds a lot. Oil in the ground? Nothing. The seemingly endless flow of gas Ms. Arrow pours into her car's tank? A great boost. The oak tree that she planted in her parents' backyard when she was a teenager, the one that has now grown to a respectable height and reduces noise, provides shade, generates oxygen, re-vitalizes soil, sequesters pollutants, all in addition to offering a home for her younger sibling's treehouse, makes no contributions to GDP. But in case she catches the entrepreneurial spirit, chops down the tree and sells it as lumber or firewood, she will be recognized as a contributor to GDP growth. With money in wallet, though, her gaze out the window may have to settle for a barren stump (of course it might also slightly reduce the "curb-appeal" of her real estate).

At bottom, predominant GDP accounting practices, and thus the measures that guide economic decision-making, are blind to life. The exclusive focus is on volume of output. Success has become a sole function of our contribution to the golden arrow—as producer, consumer, business owner, or politician.

In the words of former Maryland Governor Martin O'Malley, "GDP tells us what we are producing. But it totally neglects what we are using up."[38]

To summarize, the central measure of success in today's modern econo-mies can be described as follows:

1. Quality-blind: As a pure measure of quantity, GDP is entirely oblivious to ques-tions of good or bad: toys, weapons, pornography, organic food, car wrecks—it matters not. Volume (of commercial transactions) is what matters; quality does not.
2. People-blind: As a simple measure of monetized output, everything about people and their lives outside of the cash nexus is ignored, and thus culturally devalued. What counts and what doesn't seems grotesque: lumber but not trees; energy but not vital resources; therapy but not health; Facebook but not community; the nanny, but not the mother.
3. Justice-blind: As a measure of pure volume, GDP says nothing about justice or equality. A community with extreme poverty amidst excessive wealth, ridden with crime and social strife, can have the same GDP as one we recognize as pro-viding fair opportunities in a stable environment. In America today, one person, Bill Gates, owns as much wealth as the bottom 10 percent (or roughly twenty-five million) of Americans combined.[39] GDP has nothing to say about that. The entry for social or human capital is missing.
4. Ecosystem-blind: The planet and all its vital resources and ecosystem functions are not counted in GDP at all—it's like measuring personal well-being without

including health of the body. Damage and depletion are not subtracted from the total, treating the earth like a "business in liquidation."[40] Such neglect robs the poor and future generations of the essentials for a good life. It also "violates both basic accounting principles and common sense."[41] It doesn't add up.

5. Complexity-blind: GDP reduces human and social complexity to a market transaction, and thus is incapable of necessary long-term and large-scale thinking. Short-term financial benefit is rewarded at the expense of investments in crucial developments and benefits such as environmental health, education, infrastructure, or basic equality.

6. Accountability-blind: GDP is accounting without accountability—a small group of experts and their product, GDP—yield immense power over the operation of our economy, yet neither one is responsible to society nor democratically accountable. In the grips of a spell, the underlying logic remains both hidden and immensely powerful.[42]

7. Purpose-blind: In the end, as a simple measure of volume, GDP is entirely blind to the most important question of all: what should be the objective and direction of our economy? GDP counts guns, but not security; medical equipment, but not health; computers, but not education. One cannot measure what one does not ask about. As a result, what gets measured is essentially the speed and volume by which we turn "resources into garbage."[43] Some argue this includes human beings, increasingly driven into "an engulfing sense of purposelessness."[44]

What we get, in the end, may be seen as a gauge that measures the goods life, rather than the good life.[45] Quality of life is not a category. Indeed, as the recent work of Thomas Piketty suggests, GDP growth no longer even reflects the "goods life" for the majority of the population. Instead, its primary purpose stands, in the words of economist Steven Stoll, "naked as a process of wealth creation for the upper 1 percent of the population."[46] The emperor has no clothes.

WHY IT MATTERS

In the end, we may ask, who cares? So what if some economists pay a lot of attention to GDP? What does that have to do with me or my community or my business?

Given entrenched realities of GDP accounting, such questions are akin to a sailboat captain asking, "Who cares that meteorologists keep tabs on weather patterns? Why should I pay attention to speed or direction of the wind?

In many cases the impact is powerful and direct. In other cases GDP accounting harbors results that are one or two steps removed. Either way, as one corporate CEO emphatically stressed, the bottom line is that "business fundamentally depends on GDP."[47]

Why is that? We can think of GDP as the operating system of the economy, "the central statistical construct" of modern economies.[48] As the key indicator for national economic success, it defines both the language and grammar of economics.[49] Except in this case the measure dictates both: definition and desired outcome. What defines a successful job, or business, or nation? What do we need to do in order to be more successful? GDP defines the parameters in which such questions are answered.

Policymakers, economists, bankers, financial experts, and corporations around the globe collectively rely on GDP as a reliable performance measure.[50]

Not a day goes by without news reports such as "Economy in Dire Straits—Third Quarter of Negative GPD," or "Lackluster GDP Projections Seen as Cause for Low Consumer Confidence," or "Country's Credit Rating Downgraded: Ratio of Debt to GDP Seen as Too High," or "Mired In Poverty: Per Capita GDP at Less Than $2 a Day," or, on a presumably more positive note, "Promising Future—Solid GDP Growth-Rates Forecast."

To be clear: quality, size, or style of the sailboat are not at issue here, any more than the values or aspirations of the captain. Individual businesses or citizens don't see themselves working for GDP. But size and direction of wind still determines much of the direction of the boat's journey, or how fast/slow it will get there. It also maps its likelihood to sink. It's hard to stay afloat during times of declining GDP.

Performance is a function of GDP—how much have we contributed? It is the measure of our value—on a personal level as much as on the level of businesses, political parties, states and nations, or international communities. Here is how austerity policies in the United States have been defended by the faithful: "U.S. Economy Shows Greater GDP Growth Rates than European Union." The message: beware of politicians safeguarding social welfare nets—they drag down solid GDP growth. The same logic plays out across virtually every important political issue: wages, equality, job security, taxes, support for families, stewardship of the commons, investments in sustainable technologies, care of the environment. "GDP defines the economic storyline more than any other single thing."[51]

What determines rate or size of taxes, interest rates established by Central Banks, or the amounts of funds spent on welfare or unemployment benefits? Predominantly, the answer is health and size of the national economy as defined by GDP. As the former chairman of the Federal Reserve, Alan Greenspan, put it in the language of detached objectivity: GDP estimates "have a profound influence on markets."[52] Whatever the choices may be—coal-fired power plants or windmills, SUVs or electric cars, intergenerational living quarters or high-end apartment buildings—all depend on whether they are economically viable within markets that are defined by the rules of GDP.

No doubt, we have choices as citizens, particularly in advanced industrialized nations. In some cases a dizzying number of choices. Even choices that reflect values and aspirations—be it vegetarianism, concern for the environment, or gun rights. And yet, to the success or failure of the GDP regime, only one thing matters: that we produce and consume that which is officially counted in our national ledgers.

Given its pervasive reach, GDP imparts its logic throughout modern life:

1. As a gauge for economic success, GDP is omnipresent, both despite and because of the fact that people rarely understand how it functions, or why they follow it.
2. By defining economic success, GDP becomes our operating system: it is both measure and goal.
3. GDP is an extremely reduced proxy for reality.
4. GDP did not invent the fixation on growth, but it does by now entirely define the specific kind of growth we pursue.
5. Since all profit depends on growth, the central goal of (legal) economic activity in modern market economies is a product of GDP rules and guidelines.
6. The very meaning of the term *the economy* is defined by GDP.

Exerting a kind of tyranny by default, GDP operates as an invisible dictator.[53]

In the end, what counts is only that which gets counted.[54] As Einstein understood, what theory does not include will remain unobserved.

Chapter 8

MORE IS NOT ENOUGH

To a man with a hammer, everything looks like a nail.
—Mark Twain

W hat we measure matters—even if it's unclear to us what we're actually measuring. Today, one gauge—GDP—governs economic and political decision-making as much as it dominates public imagination.

A dramatization can clarify GDP's controlling political significance. If a president or prime minister or chancellor of any of the large economies of the world were to present a straightforward "State of the Nation" address that followed the logic of how economic success is currently measured, it would go something like this:

> My fellow citizens, our shared goal is a strong nation and a prosperous people. To achieve this goal, we need economic growth, for growth provides jobs, funds education, finances a better infrastructure, improves budgets, and attracts investment. In short, growth of GDP is the central lifeline to a better future for all of us. And so it is with considerable pride that I can announce today that the state of our nation is strong and prosperous, for our economy has been growing.
>
> Last year, more people around the world were part of the paid workforce. The number of people who were able to stay home with children and family declined. The retirement age is going up, as are the hours worked.
>
> Consumer spending is growing: a multibillion-dollar advertising industry successfully created a multitude of previously unknown desires for new products. Indeed, I am pleased to announce that over 98 percent of what modern consumers purchase today will be used up or thrown away within the first six months, thereby speeding up the cycle of growing demand. Research into planned obsolescence has made great strides: modern products, ranging from cell phones to computers and refrigerators, now last barely a minute beyond what consumers minimally expect—the accelerated turn-over rates that resulted have led to a significant increase in consumption and thus greatly contributed to our economic health. The more quickly things are discarded and replaced with new ones, the better.

We have also experienced great gains in the healthcare sector. In the highly industrialized world, more than 70 percent of mounting healthcare costs are due to preventable diseases such as diabetes, smoking, or obesity: a multiple gain because it reflects significant growth in several sectors, including the fast food industry, advertising, healthcare, pharmaceuticals. Largely due to stress associated with long hours of work, longer commutes, declining job security, and costly health benefits, citizens in developed economies consume drugs at higher levels than ever before, all again leading to robust growth rates across a range of industries.[1]

And, as a possible addition for the American President: [Now, as I am sure you are aware, we are still pursuing various military efforts around the globe: my administration is spending nearly $1 trillion annually in military and defense related expenditures. We spend as much on what one of my predecessors called the "military-industrial complex" as the next twenty-six largest military powers in the world combined. And while the losses in human lives are regrettable and painful, we should remember the multiple gains: not just the manufacture of bombs and planes, but also the reconstruction of damage and the restoration of life and limb—all provide jobs and incomes for our fellow Americans.]

And then there is banking, an industry that has recently experienced some problems. But today I can proudly proclaim that incessant innovation has made the banking sector once again contribute to growth—successful campaigns to distribute credit cards to millions who can't afford them, and who, through the credit card purchases they can't pay for will contribute to growth for decades to come: people will have to work harder and longer hours in order to pay mounting debts and high interest, in the process requiring huge amounts of services. Banks also provide the service of paying a few percentage points interest on savings while charging up to 30 percent when loaning out that same money; and they have invented elaborate systems for charging customers fees and fines in the billions each month—all mechanisms that have contributed to growth in GDP. As banks no longer do much traditional banking, financial speculation in everything from stocks and real estate to derivatives and junk bonds offers virtually endless potential for expansion.

But what fills me with particular confidence about our stable economic growth potential is that we, as a society, still continue to expand our consumption of natural resources and energy. Global warming, and climate change in general, may well be the area with the greatest potential for economic growth. Trading in carbon-emissions permits is already gearing up as a multibillion-dollar financial industry. But that is just the beginning: as we can see from many cases of robust GDP growth in the wake of disasters, an increase in both man-made and natural calamities promise several solid growth opportunities, from cleanup and reconstruction to manufacturing and healthcare.

The future, in short, looks bright, for it is full of economic growth opportunities. As more and more aspects of our lives become part of the monetized

> market—from water and leisure to friendship and community—and as all of us
> work harder, and pay more, to maintain a basic level of comfort, security, and
> opportunity, the future prospects of economic growth are almost endless. And
> since it is common knowledge that economic growth improves our standard of
> living, I say to you tonight that the state of our economy is, indeed, strong and
> prosperous.

Whether growth is achieved through more stuff or more services, more education or more propaganda, more roads or more accidents, more therapy or more guns, more sickness or more pharmaceuticals—it matters not to GDP. Success simply depends on volume of output and activity, no matter the costs to people, communities, or the planet.

In reality, of course, the goals covered in this imaginary political address are not referred to in terms of more stuff, more waste, more work, more depletion. Under whatever banner, political leaders instead spin the language of feel-good obfuscation: apparently everyone is working for prosperity and opportunity, a "brighter future" for a "strong nation" one can believe in.

Less clear is whether those promoting endless GDP growth are fully aware of what they are promoting. Ronald Reagan's former budget director seems onto something in observing "the culprits are bipartisan [or all-partisan], though you'd never guess that from the blather that passes for political discourse these days."[2]

Among leaders and citizens alike, the focus on GDP is so thoroughly ingrained by now that its pervasiveness remains virtually invisible. "By a constant, steady, uniform, insensible operation, like that of the air we breathe in," it is just the way things are done. Of course growth is good.[3]

It is difficult to escape the problem. Well educated, widely traveled, and in the midst of a project on GDP, I was listening to the radio in the car a few years back on the way to pick up my son from an afterschool activity. It was April 2010. America had just been stunned by what most economists had considered no longer possible: a long and deep recession and the near total collapse of the financial system. Unemployment was over 10 percent. The voice on the radio, meanwhile, announced that according to the latest figures released by the Bureau of Economic Analysis, the GDP for the fourth quarter of 2009 had grown a robust 6.1 percent.

Finally! This was fantastic news. I felt immediate relief.

... relief. I did not question the figure even though unemployment had not come down one iota, middle-class wages were stuck in the muck, millions were losing their homes, and the globe kept on warming. It did not even dawn on me to ask, "What exactly had grown?" The number was up; the economy was growing. It felt good.

Later that evening I felt too ashamed of my Pavlovian response to mention it in conversation with my wife. No doubt, deeply ingrained thinking is difficult to shake.[4]

It is unlikely that the citizens of China or Russia or the United States, if asked what they cared about most, would answer "GDP growth." Indeed, there is little indication that people anywhere in the world would deliberately settle for a standard of economic success that entirely skips much of what makes life meaningful to them.

Curiously, the language invented by economists and later adopted by cultures around the globe ignores all such subtleties. In a system supposed to track the performance of capital, most forms of "capital" are missing. Human capital, intellectual capital, social capital, or environmental capital—none of these is counted.[5] Only monetized capital is counted. This type of thinking is akin to a farmer caring only about money in his pocket, without any consideration for the climate, quality of soil or seed, the condition of his equipment, his skill level or experience, let alone his job satisfaction or the purpose of his efforts.

Modern leaders are in effect saying to beleaguered citizens of increasingly depleted communities, "*Qu'ils mangent du PIB*" (Let them eat GDP).[6] Many citizens do. Entire cultures seem "hooked" on GDP growth precisely because it serves as a substitute for greater (e)quality.[7] GDP growth is equated with the (however distant) promise of a better life in the future—more jobs, higher incomes, better choices for tomorrow. Many of the challenges of today—poverty, inequality, waste—remain inadequately addressed (or not at all). Hoping for a better tomorrow based on more growth, the standard mode becomes quiet, even in the face of cultural insanity.

An astounding amount of energy and ink has been spent on establishing a linkage between GDP and human well-being. And, it is true, more often than not, people in countries with higher GDP tend to have more opportunities and report higher levels of happiness than people in countries with lower GDP.[8] But the claim that higher GDP is cause for well-being represents bad reasoning and a serious case of shortsightedness.

That high GDP and opportunities are routinely correlated should not surprise. Both depend on a wide range of things, from a stable body politic to a thriving civil society to good education. GDP rates do not cause such qualities any more than they are a result of them.[9]

And, returning to our farming analogy once more: at first it would seem to make sense that the farmer who was, for whatever good or bad reasons, able to outcompete his neighbors, will be happier than the farmer next door who lost his land in the process. He may even benefit, again short term, from dumping increasing amounts of fossil-based fertilizers into the ground in order to increase yield. To celebrate such fleeting benefits by ignoring human costs to his neighbors, the social costs to the community, or the ecological costs of the land, however, simply does not add up. It doesn't even make sense for the farmer's own children and grandchildren.[10] It's devouring the seed needed for another planting season.

A key concept in economics is "opportunity costs," or the value of the next best alternative to a decision one takes. When you take a trip around the world instead of buying a car, your opportunity cost is not having the new car. Though economists apparently often don't understand or use this concept correctly, it is illuminating when applied to GDP.[11]

Figuring out opportunity costs relies on access to two pieces of essential information: (1) what are my choices? and (2) what is the value of my choices? Without knowledge of either availability or value of choices, one cannot begin to establish a clear sense of opportunity costs. A mainstay of neoclassical economics is to assume that you and I, as economic actors, act rationally (by which they mean in our own best self-interest), and that we are well informed about our choices. But in the case of the single most consequential economic indicator, both are patently untrue: none of us can really say we know about choices (i.e., what would an alternative to the age of GDP entail?); none of us, therefore, has the choice to act rationally.

Whatever economists' assumptions one is willing to follow, not knowing about some of our most fundamental choices represents a crippling dilemma. It robs us of the opportunity to act in an enlightened and rational fashion. In the case of GDP, the opportunity costs by now far outpace its value. Not unlike the smoker who foregoes food in favor of tobacco, pursuing GDP growth accrues more costs than benefits.

Over time, a thickening fog of muddled assumptions seems to have settled over the question of growth. Most fundamentally, we are still not asking, "What exactly are we growing? And why?"

+++

The valuable capacity of the human mind to simplify
a complex situation in a compact characterization
becomes dangerous when not controlled in terms of
definitely stated criteria.
—*Simon Kuznets*

Measures cannot be asked to serve a purpose they do not recognize, nor one for which they were not developed. This does not mean a measure cannot have a profound impact on what lies securely outside its purview.[12]

In late 2011 three well-established economists published an astonishing finding. All three had been troubled by an obvious problem: what people and businesses do frequently has negative effects on others outside of the market transaction, such as pollution, depletion, illness, or accidents. Operating my car, I may cause respiratory ailments in a kid living next to the road, or even injure a cyclist on my way to work. None of these costs or risks is part of my original transaction with GM or Mazda or BMW. The cyclist cannot get compensation for her injuries from the company that produced my car. There are virtually endless potentially negative results from the production and consumption of goods and services (inebriation follows from consuming vodka, pollution from burning gasoline, accidents from driving cars and trucks, health risks from watching too much TV, and so forth).

Many such consequences, however, are incidental—not every driver causes accidents. What is more troubling is when a particular economic activity consistently leads to clear and direct harm to people. Thus the question of the three economists: how big of a problem is this?

In order to obtain solid data and draw reliable conclusions, the researchers focused exclusively on one particular effect: air pollution. For clarity's sake, they ignored many other spillover-effects that cause things like poor soil quality, illness, or community disintegration.

The findings surpassed their worst fears. In some cases, such as coal-fired power plants, the total cost of air pollution damages alone actually exceeded the total amount of value produced.[13]

This is worth repeating in everyday language: the total value of electricity generated by coal-fired power plants is worth less than what it would cost to clean up all the resulting damages of air pollution. It's like the farmer producing a crop of tomatoes but destroying his land in the process. If we were to take into account actual costs, in other words, we would find that coal-fired power plants are a net drain on both economy and society. Given that coal is still the largest source of energy in most industrialized nations, this finding was critically important. If we used better and more comprehensive accounting standards, the economic ripple effects would be enormous.[14]

In fairness, coal-operated power plants may represent a particularly drastic case of economic activity gone awry. Yet the authors concluded the problem is systemic. Based on national accounting data they found that the costs of pollution damage make up a significant proportion of value produced across multiple industries. Entire segments of our national economy, vital to our survival like agriculture and utilities, are currently operated in ways that generate external air-pollution damages valued at roughly one quarter of the entire value they add.

If, as part of the daily operations of the economy, people make bad or harmful decisions based on lack of choices or a shortage of information, economists call it "market failures"—the market was unable to provide an optimal result. In some cases, markets fail more than they function.

Let's say a company releases multiple toxins as part of its operations. The resulting costs for sickness, disability, and death are ordinarily borne by the general public, not by the company, or even its consumers. Economists have a word for that, too: they call such costs "externalities," because such costs lie securely outside of doing business. The child getting sick breathing foul air is the parents' responsibility: no point knocking on the doors of coal companies, or any of the other polluters, from Dow Chemical or Philip Morris to Exxon Mobile or GM.[15]

It's helpful to bear in mind that examples of both market failures and negative externalities can be found everywhere. It is a structural component of an economy in which profit maximization is the overarching goal: one of the most effective ways to minimize costs is to externalize them. Have other people pay the costs; have public health, the environment, or recreation bear the brunt of the burden.

As explored in chapter 3, a common feature of modern societies is that the public pays for the benefits of the privileged few. A shrinking few are benefiting from the efforts of a growing many.

Within the GDP regime we can say, without exaggeration, that businesses, and large-scale corporations in particular, are externality-producing machines.[16] The list is long and getting longer. And the problem is neither exceptional nor marginal. The more a business can get others to pick up the tab for costs—for education, natural resources, social security, healthcare, infrastructure, law enforcement, pollution control, and toxic waste clean-ups—the more profitable the enterprise (and the poorer the community). It goes to the heart of what is commonly considered "economic success" today.

In the case of many modern corporations it is questionable whether they would still be profitable if required to pick up their share of costs rather than dump them on the public.

In fairness, within the regime of GDP, corporations are not the only villains. Citizens also play a role in passing on costs to unwitting or defenseless "others." With the partial exception of goods that carry some heavy consumption taxes in select countries, the following still holds true: when we fill up our cars at the gas station, we don't pay the medical costs of a child's asthma caused by toxic fossil fuels that our cars spew; we do not bear our proportion of costs for roads, bridges, or paved-over arable land. When we buy a cheap T-shirt at the department store, we don't pay for either pollution or the possible emotional and social harm of child labor in the country that produced the shirt—members of the larger community do, whether they drive or not, wear T-shirts or not. When we log trees for timber, no one pays for the loss of recreational areas, loss of good soil or air quality, or the shade, beauty, noise reduction, and water purification provided by trees.[17]

In each case, someone else pays—those who get sick, communities that need to clean up, or future generations that will have to cope with an environment that is both more polluted and more depleted.[18] As the people who benefit from production are almost always not the same as those who may potentially get harmed, it is a phenomenon sometimes described as "privatization of gains and socialization of losses."

How to price that which does not have a price—health, meaningful jobs, safety, an intact environment? It is a tricky and imprecise science. Environmental economists continue to attempt to obtain reliable data on the total amount of "external" costs such as air pollution—an effort greatly complicated by problematic issues such as how to value a human or animal life, how to address pollution that travels across national borders, how to estimate the worth of our shared ecosystem—both intrinsically, as the fountain of life, and essentially as a fountain of necessary resources—or how to "price" damage done to future generations, to people who are not yet born.[19]

The problem becomes more pronounced once we realize that rising negative costs do not just emanate from externalities—dumping costs of production onto others. Increasingly, they are "internal," or so-called "defensive expenditures"—the very existence of the product leads to negative costs. More and more, what we consider "modern" lifestyles in themselves necessitate "internalities," or costs we have to bear just to rectify the expenses of the market system encroaching on our lives. This includes security systems to keep us safe in torn communities, meds for stress, higher mortgages for better neighborhoods and schools, rapidly rising tuitions for college educations of increasingly questionable quality, filters for dirty water, inhalers for polluted lungs. Sure, all these costs increase GDP, but what we're buying is not an improvement, "but the restoration or protection of the quality of life we already had."[20] In each case, a so-called higher standard of living directly leads to additional costs.[21] Why count such things as a plus?

Again, let's see how this plays out in the specific case of the coal-fired power plant. We can see the extent to which our current accounting practices determine how we live, and we can then extrapolate this exercise to broader patterns of consumption.

Let's say the only public source of electricity in your community comes from a coal-fired power plant. Energy production and consumption as measured by GDP are solely based on coal. Also, we now know that the amount of money we spend on a kilowatt-hour of electricity does not reflect actual costs—it omits the cost of environmental and human damage. This fact alone has far-reaching consequences.

If publicly enforced accounting standards were to include all the negative side effects of burning coal, basic laws of the market would thoroughly change the playing field. For one, it would force the power company to invest in power sources that pollute less, thus allowing the consumer to purchase cleaner power.

The community would need to pay less for pollution cleanup and medical treatments. If the costs of toxic pollution were included in the cost of coal-generated energy, several cleaner alternative energy sources would undoubtedly become economically viable. Both consumers and local politicians would make efforts to find more choices.

And the effects keep accumulating. According to GDP, the final product that counts is energy produced. Consumers pay for each kilowatt hour, and the transaction is concluded. But what if your home is in the vicinity of the toxic fumes from the power plant? Not only will your health deteriorate and medical bills likely rise, the value of your home and your neighbors' homes will decline, and with it the appeal of your community. Fewer people will want to move to, invest in, or work there. Every citizen, every politician, every entrepreneur is affected.

But one does not have to live close to the power plant to be affected. Pollution of coal-fired power plants can travel over long distances. You may live in a community that provides the coal for the power plant. People you know may do the high-risk jobs of mining coal. The streams and fields where you took your children to fish and hike have been stripped, or the mountaintop you used to see when looking out your living room window has been leveled.[22]

Then again, you may not be close to either the mining or the burning of the coal. Yet your own retirement account, or your kids' college accounts, may be invested in coal-fired power plants. These are profitable only because the external costs of environmental damage are not counted, and because the mining of coal is registered by GDP as current income rather than as liquidation of assets.[23] You may actually be opposed to coal-generated electricity, yet in reality finance it with your hard-earned income. This is true even if you simply deposit your earnings in the bank, which may also be invested in coal-operated power plants. Of course, the politician who ends up doing the bidding for coal power may, in the privacy of his own conscience, not think burning coal is the best source of energy. Yet he likely is realistic enough not to offend a powerful business lobby, much less advocate alternative energy sources when they are not yet economically viable by the standards of GDP.

Many of the decisions we make as consumers—what size house to buy, what gadgets to put in our homes or pockets, where to reside, what to drive—are impacted by the costs of energy. After all, how many people could afford to keep their thermostat at 69 in 96 degree weather, or keep driving their 16 mpg SUV, if energy sources such as coal or oil reflected their true costs? If the price of unsustainable energy resources went up as a result of different accounting practices, the basic logic of market economies would inevitably start demanding clean power, energy efficient construction, or better public transportation. Who knows, people might even demand that their political representatives reject money from big oil.

But under current accounting rules, even the best-intentioned consumers among us quickly run out of options. Prices not only reflect a rigged game, they don't add up. Things safe and abundant, like solar energy, cost very much; things prohibitively expensive to our communities cost little, like coal. Did you ever notice that the more junk in our food, the cheaper it is? The tasty and pure version of a natural apple or loaf of bread costs the most. Yet you and I need to purchase food, electricity, and means of transportation in the real world of limited choices and limited budgets, no matter how bad or dangerous the product we're purchasing. A privileged few may be able to escape some of the worst offenses, such as steroid-laden milk or coal-generated electricity. But most of us simply can't do without what the market offers as affordable necessities.

The money we hand over each month to, say, the coal-operated power plant in turn pays for ads championing the benefits of coal, for research that downplays the dangers of coal, and for lobbying efforts that push legislation and finance politicians friendly to coal operators. Just consider the fact that, as absurd as common sense and hard science would make it seem, there are politicians who still claim "clean coal" is real.[24]

The reputation and power of the United States is, in part, defined by the fact that Americans make up less than 5 percent of the world's population, but use 30 percent of the world's resources, and generate over 30 percent of the world's pollution—in no small measure due to coal-fired power plants. Of course this bonanza of waste, pollution, and conspicuous consumption is possible only within accounting rules that allow for massive externalization of costs, thereby keeping energy and labor costs artificially low while having the public, people in other countries, and future generations pick up the tab.

American use of energy significantly contributes to daunting changes in the world's climate, yet the biggest and richest economy has taken almost no deliberate action to curb emissions. Few people around the world view this as a fair deal. Be that as it may, Americans and non-Americans alike will experience the consequences of living on a heating planet with shrinking resources.

Sadly, what one values as a human being may not be counted at all in any of these considerations. The only reason the coal-fired power plant is "economically viable" is because we count as a "plus" the mining and burning of coal, but we don't count as a "minus" the depletion of resources or the subsequent pollution of air, water, and soil, or even the illnesses and deaths of people affected. According to reigning accounting standards, clean air, nontoxic soil, safe drinking water, landscapes that are not strip-mined, or simply a pollution-free environment inhabited by a healthy population, all count for nothing.[25]

Such shortcomings not only add up to a "market failure" or a case of imperfect information. They also may well be seen as amounting to a structural failure—a failure so big and consequential that we might be better off without the measures altogether.[26]

It is a failure that is of concern to everyone. It matters little whether we think of ourselves as liberal or conservative, religious or secular. It is of little consequence whether we highlight or ignore consequences like pollution or the decline of strong family units. The effects are all around us, whether or not we think about them. Yet the GDP regime continues to send the wrong signals. Under existing rules, the costs of paying attention to harmful effects of production are higher than the costs of ignoring people and the environment. The GDP logic allowed the coal industry to argue, in 2014, that "the social benefit of carbon-based fuels [is] 50 times greater than its supposed social cost." True indeed, since their accounting methods fail to include everything that really matters: people, communities, and the environment.[27]

The example of the power plant also highlights a conflict of economic interests between the owner of the power plant and citizens working in or around it. As such, it reveals a conflict between microeconomics and macroeconomics.

Let's say the plant, though a gross polluter, is the only employer in town. If citizens were to demand regulations limiting the levels of pollution, the plant operators would likely threaten to cease operations altogether, move to quarters more hospitable to their singular goal of profit maximization, and thus bring to an end the economic foundation of the town. In that case economic interests of individuals (owner and workers) are not the same as those of society at large. By closing or moving their business, and telling workers and communities to accept or forget, "profit maximization on the part of a firm may result in diminishing the gross domestic product. This result is quite independent of the harm done to people."[28] What is good for corporate profits, according to GDP guidelines, is not necessarily good for the communities in which they reside. Sometimes they are in direct conflict: in this case, the choice would be (1) have a job and live in a toxic environment, or (2) be unemployed but have access to fresh air and clean water.

As we have seen, in today's global economy, things without price have little or no economic value. They also tend to have vastly diminished social value. In the realm of economics, something not measured is routinely ignored, and, as a result, it frequently atrophies. As Martin Collier, director of a research foundation created to find better ways to measure national progress, has summarized the scenario, "You are what you measure, you get what you measure, and you fix what you measure." If we don't measure it, in short, it is unlikely to get noticed, or to shape what we do and who we are. Collier's conclusion: if we want what matters to us, "we need to measure what we value."²⁹

Readers can relate to the basic idea: not until the invention of standardized tests did teachers across different schools and communities focus their teaching on test results. Not until the federal government forced car dealers to put "average miles per gallon" stickers on their cars did consumers really start paying attention to gas mileage. Not until Facebook introduced a "friends" feature did the number of one's acquaintances become a publicly competitive benchmark.

Modern economies have turned the world upside down: rather than measure what we value, they value what they measure. We have become prisoners of our own creation.

We do have political means—public policy, regulations, laws—to help us count those values not captured by the monetized market. There are many examples of industrialized countries that put in place public policies geared toward protecting the environment, punishing unsafe behavior, and promoting clean practices. Citizens of all rich industrialized nations are familiar with political interventions like regulations on pollutants, taxes on fuels, subsidies for sustainable energy, or artificially created markets intended to cut carbon emissions. There is little doubt: such political measures can be significant. Some countries, such as Denmark or Germany, now manage to achieve a standard of living equivalent to that of the United States with little more than half of the per capita energy consumption, and a significantly reduced carbon footprint.³⁰

Here another fundamental problem becomes visible. For one, if economic prosperity continues to rely on growth, what we may call "environmental public policies," however significant in their own right, are unlikely to add up to a viable solution. Reducing emissions of ten coal-powered plants by 30 percent does little when we simultaneously add six more coal-powered plants to the grid in order to satisfy mounting demand. Despite all environmental regulations, 2013 saw the largest increases in CO_2 emissions in decades.[31]

Above all, political interventions such as penalties, subsidies, or taxes do not change the basic rules of the game. They function like speed bumps on the multiple lane highways of modern economies. They are not transformative, but merely ameliorative. Above all, they don't change the direction or purpose of the highway. The logic of travel remains the same.

Jonathan Rowe and Judith Silverstein, eloquent critics of GDP, summarized the bizarre result: the unquestioned assumption among reporters, politicians, and economists alike is that we should celebrate all increases in spending. "Expenditures for credit-card interest, obesity medications, gambling, disaster cleanups, even price gouging and fraud are included in the tally of what the media report as economic advance."[32] In the official language of public politics, of course, we speak about it very differently. We say things like "national income and product figures are recognized as the fundamental measurement of the quality of economic conditions."[33]

Our lives, it seems, are held hostage by the GDP regime.[34]

Yet slowly but surely, a growing number of critics have begun to unearth the hidden pillars underneath the illusion of equating growth and success. Let's briefly explore some of their major findings.

THE LITTLE BIG NUMBER: OUR REPORT CARD FOR SUCCESS

If we have the wrong metrics, we will strive for the wrong things.

—Report by the Commission on the Measurement of Economic Performance and Social Progress

One thing long recognized by critics from every vantage point is this: a metric like GDP that exclusively measures volume of output is an unreliable indicator for the quality of what we put out.[35] Quantity tells us little about quality.

Some have understood this from the very beginning. Economist Simon Kuznets was certainly both clear and explicit about GDP's severe limitations. Unlike many of his successors, he understood that what was counted captured only a small sliver of life: things bought and sold in the marketplace.[36]

By now, most economists would agree that GDP is an inadequate welfare measure.[37] Some claim that it was never intended for that purpose.[38] While for the most part historically correct, it's a claim that is both misleading and intellectually dishonest. It's a bit like saying "the institution of marriage was never intended to be anything other than a contractual agreement codifying essential property relations." The key characteristic of GDP is precisely its use as a welfare measure—just like marriage is overwhelmingly perceived, justifiably or not, as an expression of love and devotion.

By and large, the economics profession admits as much. In his best-selling textbook *Principles of Economics*, for instance, Professor N. Gregory Mankiw at Harvard writes that "GDP is the most closely watched statistic because it is thought to be the best single measure of a society's economic wellbeing." In a detailed discussion on the GDP paradox, Dutch economist Jeroen C.J.M. van den Bergh documents the many and pervasive utilizations of GDP as welfare measure, among them the common use of the phrase "standard of living"— something that is entirely defined by GDP.[39]

Still, critics of a system that reduces the good life to the "goods life" existed from the beginning of national accounting. At first they were small in number. Today there is barely an international organization concerned with questions of political or economic governance that has not commissioned reports on the problems with GDP as an appropriate welfare measure. Entire national governments, like those of France and Germany, have recently jumped on board with broad-scale initiatives to generate alternative measures. The European Union even installed a standing commission in 2007 entitled "Beyond GDP."

One of the earliest and best-known critics of GDP was Robert F. Kennedy. During his 1968 presidential campaign, he implored Americans to come together in order to rid America of the "disgrace of violence and poverty." During a speech in Kansas on 18 March of that year, he raised the conversation to a higher plateau. Beyond material poverty, he proclaimed, "there is another greater task," which is "to confront the poverty of satisfaction—purpose and dignity—that afflicts us all." The key problem, according to Kennedy, was that we seem "to have surrendered personal excellence and community values in the mere accumulation of material things"—as measured by GNP (the forerunner of GDP).[40] He went on to explain that

> Gross National Product—if we judge the United States of America by that— counts air pollution and cigarette advertising, and ambulances to clear our highways of carnage. It counts special locks for our doors and the jails for the people who break them. It counts the destruction of the redwood and the loss of our natural wonder in chaotic sprawl. It counts napalm and counts nuclear warheads and armored cars for the police to fight the riots in our cities. It counts Whitman's rifle and Speck's knife, and the television programs which glorify violence in order to sell toys to our children.
>
> Yet the gross national product does not allow for the health of our children, the quality of their education or the joy of their play. It does not include the beauty of our poetry or the strength of our marriages, the intelligence of our public debate or the integrity of our public officials. It measures neither our wit nor our courage, neither our wisdom nor our learning, neither our compassion nor our devotion to our country. It measures everything in short, except that which makes life worthwhile.

Public debates about GDP, however, largely died with Kennedy. In the United States, it took over thirty years after Kennedy's assassination for Congress to hold hearings on the utility of the GDP in 2001, and then again in 2008. Both hearings received miniscule news coverage, and went essentially unnoticed by the public. The 2008 hearing of the Subcommittee on Interstate Commerce, Trade, and Tourism acknowledged major problems, but provided no policy follow-up. Within political circles in Washington, the issue essentially died once again.[41]

Within the economic powerhouses of the world, it turns out, there is strong resistance to challenging the basic logic of GDP. Predictably, those who tabulate GDP defend its global preeminence as an economic indicator. Changing the measure, the argument goes, would "sharply diminish its usefulness." Replacing it would be "a grievous mistake." It would rob policymakers of a much-needed comparative indicator, the measure that Secretary of Commerce William Daley highlighted as his department's most notable achievement with the "the greatest impact on America."[42] Summarizing a common sentiment

Figure 8–1. "Steady As She Goes." www.polyp.org.uk

among macroeconomists, senior Hoover Institution economist Michael J. Boskin argues that "economists and statisticians should be wary of confusing limitations in the GDP accounts . . . with invitations to contaminate them with fuzzy feel-good (or bad) numbers purporting to measure 'happiness' or 'satisfaction.'"[43] Let's stick to handy models and numbers, he seems to suggest, and not pollute them with too much unwelcome reality.

Whatever newly found status economists hold as movers and shakers in the world of politics today, they are by no means the only ones to resist change. Opposition is far more entrenched. As discussed earlier, what's at stake is the viability of all those businesses that have become profitable through externalization of costs—and with it all the incomes, dividends, bonuses, and careers that depend on a model that counts all output, good and bad, as a plus. There are no reliable data on how many businesses would cease to be viable with true cost accounting (or, for that matter, how many new businesses would suddenly realize cost-effectiveness). No doubt, the number is large, and ways of doing business would change throughout the economy. Moreover, and again diffi-cult to estimate, an entire apparatus built upon the GDP accounting regime—world trade organizations, financial institutions, nation-states—would face the need for fundamental change or the possibility of collapse. There is no shortage of vested interests opposed to serious changes.

Nevertheless, and despite the threat of marginalization, a growing number of economists and political analysts have continued to explore the flaws of GDP over the years. GDP, they find, is not just an inadequate welfare measure, but also a deeply flawed economic indicator. Not surprisingly, given the ele-vated status of GDP as the world's measure of economic success, experts on all levels of policymaking and academia have felt obligated to respond. With varying degrees of seriousness, a wide range of investigations has ensued over the past fifty years. Here is a brief summary of the most significant findings.

EMERGING DISSENT

Two eminent economists captured the key problems. Stanford economist Moses Abramovitz, after decades of work on national accounts, concluded that while national income accounts are a valuable tool, "we must be highly skeptical of the view that long-term changes in the rate of growth of welfare can be gauged even roughly from changes in the rate of growth of output."[44] Former senior World Bank economist Herman Daly went further: he con-cluded that growth-centered economies were on an inevitable collision course with nature, thus undermining the very foundations for human existence.[45]

Part of their concern followed an inescapable logic: if we assumed a very conservative economic growth rate of 2 percent annually, large economies like those of the United States or China would double their output every thirty-six years (or every twenty-four years at a 3 percent growth rate).[46] Imagine if you will: in just one long lifetime, eight times as many "goods and services," with the inevitable increase in energy and resource consumption, in pollution, in waste. In two hundred years this would go up to sixty-four times the amount of what we produce and sell right now. If one does the math looking forward, after one thousand years the output of the economy would have to be a staggering one billion times of what it is today.[47] Believing in and promoting such a course of action, of course, is so utterly absurd that the prominent British economist Richard Layard jibed, "Anyone who believes in indefinite growth on a physically finite planet is either mad, or an economist."[48]

But it was not just our ability to survive on this planet that concerned scholars. Picking up on Abromovitz's skepticism, economist Richard Easterlin noted that most in his field still hold the faith that economic growth will increase well-being, despite mounting literature on well-being that "undermines the view that a focus on economic growth is in the best interest of society." Richer people, he found, were generally happier than poorer people. But people in poorer countries were not necessarily less happy than people in richer countries. Above all, after people reach some basic level of comfort, more money or more stuff rarely translates into more happiness.

A central component of the problem is that monetary income does not equal what modern readers might call "quality of life." In fact, it does not even necessarily move in the same direction. This is true within a nation, and more so when comparing different societies. People with lower incomes may be experiencing much higher quality of life than people with more. People with the same income, but in different contexts, may have radically different experiences with quality of life—think living in a rural community in the South, where a comfortable house costs far less than something of the same standard near a city like Los Angeles or New York. Above all, what was sorely needed, according to Easterlin, was an "empirically tested causal model that includes the life satisfaction derived from multiple sources—not just material goods, but also family life, health, work utility, and the like."[49]

Professor E. J. Mishan at the London School of Economics demonstrated how narrow measures such as GDP really are. Imagining two societies, very different from each other yet both market-based democracies, he demonstrated what could be lost. One might be a society of beauty, strong communal and family bonds, and healthy mid-size cities, yet no advertising or TV, few cars or highways, and little crime or drug abuse. The other is a society of vast urban wastelands, ubiquitous consumption of modern technology, personal aggrandizement, clogged highways, and much loneliness, drug abuse, and distrust. We don't have to debate how realistic or desirable either scenario is to appreciate Mishan's basic point: by conventional economic measures, there is no way to tell the difference between the two. Both may have the identical GDP. If economic activity is supposed to have anything to do with our standard of living and our well-being, in short, we need to come up with a very different measuring rod.[50]

A few years later, Marilyn Waring, a feminist, human rights and environmental activist from New Zealand, fired another lightning bolt into the dark labyrinth of national accounting. Catapulted through her community activism into parliament at the age of twenty-three, she later served as chair of the Budget Committee (equivalent to the U.S. Senate Finance Committee). Confronted with her country's full-scale adoption of the United Nations System of National Accounts (the basis for GDP), she underwent what she later called a "rude awakening": everything she cared about as a human being—a pollution-free environment, clean beaches, safe drinking water, healthy communities—was not accounted for in national accounts. GDP was blind to all of it. Moreover, by ignoring not just nature and beauty, but also all the work done outside of the official economy, Waring argued, GDP was essentially a male-centered measure that largely ignored the work of women—as mothers, wives, caretakers.[51] For people—as citizens, mothers, or workers—to have an impact on the direction of national economies, Waring realized, they need to make visible in national accounts that which is important to them.

In the 1980s the prominent economist Amartya Sen, having long thought about the connections between welfare and economics, began to distinguish between "commodities," things bought and sold and captured by GDP, and "capabilities," which are entirely ignored. Sen's primary concern was about people's "freedom to achieve"—to have opportunities and abilities to generate valuable outcomes. The challenge: to devise metrics that could capture capabilities; to transcend the narrow metrics of output and replace it with metrics that capture development, well-being, and quality of life.[52]

Finally, in 1995, three California researchers, Clifford Cobb, Ted Halstead, and Jonathan Rowe, working with all these findings, developed an alternative indicator—the *Genuine Progress Indicator* (GPI). The idea was not to ditch GDP or the idea of a single indicator altogether, but to come up with a much smarter way of calculating. The GPI measures progress and development by incorporating a wide range of social, economic, and ecological variables. Most importantly, it distinguishes between goods and bads. The measure adds items that improve life (like volunteer work or healthy forests), and subtracts items that represent harm (like pollution, crime, or resource depletion).[53] The initial response seemed promising. Four hundred leading economists and business leaders supported the GPI project and declared the following in a joint statement:

> Since the GDP measures only the quantity of market activity without accounting for the social and ecological costs involved, it is both inadequate and mislead-ing as a measure of true prosperity. Policy-makers, economists, the media, and international agencies should cease using the GDP as a measure of progress and publicly acknowledge its shortcomings.[54]

Their conclusion: "new indicators of progress are urgently needed to guide our society." On a trial basis, GPI has since been adopted by Alberta (Canada), Finland, and the state of Maryland.

Around the same time, the German-born California economist Manfred Max-Neef launched the "threshold hypothesis," which states that "for every society there seems to be a period in which economic growth [as measured by GDP] brings about an improvement in the quality of life, but only up to a point—the threshold point—beyond which, if there is more economic growth, quality of life may begin to deteriorate." Using a variety of quality-of-life indicators (including the forerunner to the GPI), Max-Neef argued that in virtually all industrialized nations, quality of life leveled out, or even began to deteriorate sometime between the mid-1950s and the 1970s.[55]

And one other major contribution deserves mention here. Two scholars from British Columbia, William Rees and Mathis Wackernagel, asked how many people at what level of consumption could the planet carry without irre-versible damage and depletion? They called each person's use of resources the *ecological footprint*. Unlike GDP, the ecological footprint allowed each nation, each person, to figure out their impact on the carrying capacity of the planet.

And it allowed for sobering figures: if everyone on earth had the same lifestyle as the average American, for instance, we would need about four planets to support it. Here, then, was science-based, verifiable evidence: the way people currently live in rich countries around the world is not only unsustainable, it also presents a form of theft, from people in poorer countries and from future generations.[56]

Since then, the Organization for Economic Co-operation and Development (OECD), the World Bank, the World Resources Institute, the European Union, as well as think tanks, non-profits, and educational institutions around the world have generated reports critical of the nature and uses of GDP.[57] Major mainstream publications in the United States and Europe such as the *New York Times, Der Spiegel, Le Monde,* or *The Economist* now feature articles and discussions on the shortcomings of GDP.[58]

According to the most highly publicized recent effort to rethink GDP, the French Commission on the Measurement of Economic Performance and So-cial Progress, the predominant idea is to generate a "dashboard of indicators."[59] The result is that most nations now possess several possible dashboards, some with a great number of gauges. There is a wealth of information.

Not all gauges are created equal, however. Some gauges provide informa-tion, like life expectancy or carbon footprint, but have little or no consequence beyond the world of position papers and research projects. Others occasion-ally inform regulatory legislation, like average fuel consumption leading to higher mandated fuel-efficiency standards. Neither type of gauge, however, has moved, much less changed, the central target of economic activity.[60]

There are many indications of how difficult it is to move the "official" con-versation away from maximizing GDP. In 2010 the latest U.S. effort to generate alternatives was snuck into the Patient Protection and Affordable Care Act (better known as Obamacare). Avoiding attention, much less public debate, legislators supportive of the effort instead embedded a small section—section 5605—into the Act. Buried on page 562 of a 906-page bill and with an initial budget of a mere ten million dollars, the section established a congressional commission charged with making "recommendations on how to improve the key national indicators system."

In reality, the section simply made official an effort that had been started in the Government Accountability Office in 2003. A group of researchers established an independent, nonprofit group called State of the USA, supported in part by the National Academy of Sciences. Not relying on one aggregate number, like GDP, the new index encompasses hundreds of indicators, is continuously updated, and allows free public access. Since passage of section 5605, its official mandate has become "to determine how best to establish a key national indicator system (KNIS) for the United States." So far, few have heard of it. Economic policymakers remain unaffected.[61]

Launched in the United Kingdom in 2013, the latest international effort to provide an alternative indicator was developed by a group called The Social Progress Imperative. Based on the work of Sen, Stieglitz, and a range of mostly American researchers, the *Social Progress Index* is intended to measure "the things that really matter to people,"[62] from basic needs to availability of healthcare, a healthy environment, and opportunities for people to improve their lives.

There is, in short, lots of debate, and lots of momentum pushing for change. So far, however, the results are less than encouraging: despite the mounting critique, no government or financial organization or corporation has stopped using GDP as the governing measure for success. Even among its fiercest critics, moreover, few have suggested abandoning GDP altogether.[63] Economic growth still represents the golden arrow of global economic aspirations.

Continued economic growth. By definition exponential in nature, the quietly repressed question, now bursting into the open, is this: how can exponential growth continue to take place on a planet that does not grow? Resulting signs of stress were inevitable. Isolated at first, they began to multiply in number and deepen in intensity. People in different national economies reached their moments of awakening during slightly different moments, and in response to slightly different conditions. But by the time the twentieth century drew to a close, it seemed that only those with a vested interest in denial were able to discount the mounting crisis.

Chapter 9

"THE PEOPLE OF PLENTY
ARE A PEOPLE OF WASTE"*

A nation that destroys its soil destroys itself.
—*President Franklin D. Roosevelt, 1935*

As we peer into society's future, we—you and I,
and our government—must avoid the impulse to
live only for today, plundering, for our own ease and
convenience, the precious resources of tomorrow.
—*President Dwight D. Eisenhower, Farewell Address to the
Nation, 17 January 1961*

Human identity is no longer defined by what one does,
but by what one owns. . . . [P]iling up material goods
cannot fill the emptiness of lives which have
no confidence or purpose.
—*President Jimmy Carter, 1979*

Unless we . . . chart a new course on energy in this
country, we are condemning future generations
to global catastrophe.
—*President Barack Obama, 2006*

By setting a goalpost based on indiscriminate growth, the GDP regime has steadily depleted the resources that subsequent generations will need to prosper.[1]

Underlying all environmental problems is a simple truth: all wealth depends on nature. The services of nature are more valuable than anything humans are able to produce. "Nature's goods and services include producing raw materials, purifying and regulating water, absorbing and decomposing wastes, cycling nutrients, creating and maintaining soils, providing pollination and pest control, and regulating local and global climates."[2] Quite simply, we depend on it. And yet our accounts do not value it at all—GDP counts nature only when it is depleted, destroyed, or polluted.

The first international scholarly investigation exploring the quality of GDP growth appeared in 1972. Published by the Club of Rome, the report was entitled *The Limits to Growth*. It estimated that if human beings continued to consume more than nature was capable of providing, global economic collapse and precipitous population decline could occur as soon as 2030.[3] The implication: today's generations, particularly in highly developed nations, are living at the expense of their children and grandchildren.

Many dire predictions since then have turned out to be inflated, others missed or underestimated. The core of the argument, however, remains solid. The world is running up against real limits and unprecedented threats. There is little disagreement, for instance, that over 60 percent of the world's ecosystem services—including safe food and clean water, fossil energy, climate regulation, and disease prevention—have been used up or seriously degraded since the end of World War II.[4]

Today, every living system on earth is in decline. How did we reach this point? How did we get from victory and seemingly endless promise to the specter of collapse?

In the heady years after World War II, humans seemed well on their way to becoming masters of the globe. We were able to destroy, and then rebuild, entire civilizations; we flew to the moon; we mastered age-old diseases; people with the fortune to be born into industrialized nations managed to put a car in (almost) every garage, and a cell-phone in (virtually) every hand.

There appeared little that could not be accomplished with the tools of progress and growth—with the expanding horizons of science, technology, and capital. Tireless advocates of growth across the political spectrum continued to promise that if we had not yet figured out a problem—say the eradication of poverty or a cure for cancer—with a bit more time and resources, economic growth would create the necessary preconditions for a solution. GDP-growth producers became our national heroes; corporations that registered solid growth rates could do no wrong ("what is good for General Motors is good for

Figure 9–1. "The Same Boat." www.polyp.org.uk

America"); politicians who were perceived as effective growth-promoters were elected; those not were thrown out of office.[5]

But the ostensible victory proved short-lived. Beginning in the late 1960s, disconcerting signs of growth excesses began to emerge. Young people dropped out of the consumer culture, Rachel Carson illuminated the threats of species extinction through pesticides, pollution sickened children and cut short the lives of the elderly, rivers turned into flowing trash repositories.[6]

A simple MORE, it turned out, could no longer deliver on its promise of better. MORE began failing to raise quality of life—not happiness, not job satisfaction, not standards of living, not health, not education. Inequality in income, and even more in wealth, actually rose in all advanced nations while wages began to stagnate and public infrastructure began to deteriorate. Only the richest of the rich still benefited from GDP growth.[7]

Year after year, successive studies revealed new aspects of social dysfunction: wives drowning in unhappiness and lack of meaning in their increasingly well-equipped little homes, unable to find fulfillment in housework and consumption; phenomenal growth in agricultural output bought with toxic pesticides leaching into our soil, water, and bodies; a consumers' middle class constructed with what one scholar called "white affirmative action," successfully creating a surge in demand and wealth, but further exacerbating racial inequality; citizens drowning in an onslaught of sophisticated advertising, manipulated into consuming ever more and, as a consequence, going deeper into debt.[8]

Consumption became the predominant marker of status and identity in the late twentieth century. Those who couldn't participate were left behind. Almost inevitably, what sociologist David Riesman and his colleagues in the 1950s began to call "other-directed" human beings were the result, perpetually trying to fit into an ever more rapidly changing world, losing sight of self in the process.[9]

The energy crisis of the early 1970s intensified a sense of foreboding. It revealed the Achilles heel of all modern economies: the pillars of growth were built upon a single resource—oil. Worse, the most privileged nations (chief among them Japan, the United States, and the countries of Western Europe) increasingly depended on other countries for access to this vital resource. If the major oil-producing countries (OPEC) cut off the economic powerhouses of the world, modern life itself would begin to limp, and then collapse. The consequences of this continuously deepening oil addiction were as inevitable as they were predictable: not only smog and toxins and environmental degradation, but also debt, dependence, and endless foreign entanglements costing thousands of lives, trillions of dollars, and a failure to invest in a sustainable future at home.[10]

President Jimmy Carter addressed the dilemma in a 1979 speech that later became known as the "malaise speech." In the third year of his presidency, and after months of having listened to a cross-section of U.S. decision-makers, Carter laid out what he considered the key challenges. Much maligned at the time, he counseled the nation "that piling up material goods cannot fill the emptiness of lives which have no confidence or purpose." Claiming that America stood at a "turning point in our history," he then warned against

> a path that leads to fragmentation and self-interest. Down that road lies a mistaken idea of freedom, the right to grasp for ourselves some advantage over

others. That path would be one of constant conflict between narrow interests ending in chaos and immobility. It is a certain route to failure.[11]

Among other things, in order to promote the country's independence and security, Carter advocated a drastic decline in oil consumption. Almost four decades later, one is sobered reading his statements: in the United States, a half dozen subsequent presidents have come and gone promising to get us "off our oil addiction." The nation, and the world, still finds itself caught up in oil wars. Americans consume, despite advances in science and technology, more oil today than in 1979. Efficiency has greatly improved, the citizens of highly developed nations consume less per capita, but world consumption continues on a steep incline.

Neither his warnings nor his suggestions, perhaps needless to say, were heeded.[12] Instead, unlike their European counterparts, American citizens did the opposite. After the unwelcome maturity of Carter had been kicked out of the White House, Americans shifted their splurging into higher gear, doubling the size of their houses, replacing cars with SUVs, cranking up the A/C while average temperatures began to climb. The amount of trash produced by each citizen doubled within thirty years, most of it based on nonrenewable resources.[13]

The shopping mall became a central gathering place for this consumption craze. In an illuminating study on one hundred years of consumerism, Gary Cross concluded that "the effect was a near obliteration of the culture of constraint . . . Only growth without limits was consistent with American optimism." As a people, it seemed, Americans had a hard time reaching some basic level of maturity.[14]

Not helping matters, meanwhile, was the fact that the dominant economic success indicator remained unaffected by mounting problems and crises: aside from a few dips, it kept rising. Mass consumption cranked up the meter. GDP, meanwhile, remained indifferent to the planet catching a fever.[15] As did most business and economic leaders. Before he became top economic advisor to President Obama, then chief economist of the World Bank, Lawrence Summers, asserted the following in 1991:

> There are no . . . limits to the carrying capacity of the earth that are likely to bind any time in the foreseeable future. There isn't a risk of an apocalypse due to global warming or anything else. The idea that we should put limits on growth

because of some natural limit is a profound error and one that, were it ever to prove influential, would have staggering social costs.[16]

Whether informed by blind faith in the wonders of growth or simply un-encumbered by facts, his statement represented a stunning assessment. In fairness to Summers, national and international economies did not operate with indicators able to inform about anything other than monetary market transactions. Only the cold numbers of economic output charts mattered. And Summers was good with abstract numbers. He had trained with the students of Gilbert, Nathan, and others to be a macroeconomist.

Almost unbelievably, our national economic scorecard continued to plow ahead measuring success without entry for the nation's overall physical, men-tal, and economic health. Reigning economic logic turned nature into a repos-itory of exploitable resources, and reduced human beings to consumers and producers. It was a process that economist and Nobel laureate Joseph Stiglitz later aptly characterized as "GDP fetishism."[17]

In 1989, the same year that capitalism appeared to triumph at last over communism, conferences in many Western capitals began to address the dire state of the planet. "By seeking to reorient man's exploitation of man toward an exploitation of nature by man," wrote the French sociologist Bruno Latour, "capitalism magnified both . . . : the multitudes that were supposed to be saved from death fall back into poverty . . . ; nature, over which we were supposed to gain absolute mastery, dominates us in equally global fashion, and threatens us all."[18] Things, in short, did not work out as anticipated. Communism was dead. Capitalism, meanwhile, seemed bent on self-destruction.

By the time our ever expanding array of electronic gadgetry set its clocks for Y2K, once-disparate warning signs began to converge into a reality hard to deny: endless growth as the magic formula for global advancement was no longer pos-sible. Heat waves, droughts, and floods exacerbated by global warming provided a stark backdrop. But signs of distress could be found everywhere.[19]

In hindsight, the biggest question will be why we did not realize two obvi-ous things all along:

1. People generally value what they measure—or, if they don't measure it, they tend to ignore it or relegate it to wishful thinking. Measures provide tangible

markers for otherwise elusive goals. Once recognized as an important marker, a measure such as income, grades, or growth becomes the focus of cultural attention, which loses sight of the rationale behind the measure. An exclusive focus on output does not, and cannot, take into account social or environmental health.

2. We inhabit a planet that is "finite": there is only so much clean water, arable land, fossil fuels. The more we use up, cut down, burn, trash, pave over, the less there will be. The economy may grow, but the planet cannot grow with it. Every gallon of oil we burn takes earth millions of years to regenerate. Each ton of greenhouse gas we emit into the air increases global warming. Each parking lot and highway we pave gobbles up acres that can no longer be used to grow food or generate fresh air or sustain wildlife or run clean rivers or provide a playground. Growth has natural limits.

By all available estimates, people have used up more resources since the Great Depression than in all of prior human history combined. Worldwide, exploitation of natural resources has doubled roughly every twenty-five years since.[20] During the same time the world's human population has more than tripled (see figure 9–2).

The multiple effects of expanding human consumption and growth are by now common knowledge: they forever alter our environment. On the one hand they prompt technological advances, they allow industrial-scale agriculture, they create unprecedented material wealth, and they afford a seemingly endless amount of consumer choices. But on the other hand, they trash, pollute, sicken, make toxic, and kill. In the process, climates change and the essential sources of life itself disappear.[21]

Human consumption—however unevenly divided—today far exceeds what ecologists call the "carrying capacity" of our planet. When the Iroquois nations counseled to consider consequences for the seventh generation, they were not just wise, they also realized that all of their actions were likely reversible within a few generations. Modern societies have exacerbated the problem in both directions: we produce and consume far more in the here and now, while our actions, from climate change to nuclear waste to depletion of vital resources, will have consequences for thousands of future generations. Indeed, climate experts are unclear as to whether they will ever be reversible.[22]

The signposts of social distress are equally mounting: exhaustion, illness, stress, but also loneliness, cynicism, anger. One among many, Roger Cohen eloquently captured it as "frenzied individualism, solipsistic screen-gazing, the disembodied pleasures of social networking and the à-la-carte life as defined by 600 TV channels and a gazillion blogs" in which "feelings of anxiety and inadequacy grow in the lonely chamber of self-absorption and projection."[23] Turn on Fox or MSNBC, and you can see one result: frustration that is vented in various blame games—of each other, government, or the decline of values.

The papers of record provide little solace. As Mark O'Connell vividly recounted the experience of reading the newspaper next to his new-born son: "massacres, rapes, recurrent outbursts of savage recreational violence, a world built on a seemingly unshakable foundation of economic cruelty and injustice, the continuing project of environmental destruction." The whole paper, he lamented, was a "dispassionate catalog of brutality, perversity, stupidity and greed, capped off with a couple of pages of TV listings—and there was nothing good there either."[24]

A culture unhinged. Citizens lost in the maelstrom of accelerating consumption, weighed down by the hopeless battle against obsolescence, losing sight of anchors that could provide meaning or stability, hanging on to their smartphones for answers and solace.

The tragic irony is that our collective pursuit of MORE had become responsible for many forms of LESS.[25] People everywhere were beginning to experience the voracious appetite for MORE as something that directly created their own poverty, loneliness, and dependence. Growth of GDP had turned into the Trojan horse of prosperity.

Around the world, hundreds of millions continued to live in poverty, lacking essentials such as food, healthcare, or education. Indeed, as Yale professor Thomas Pogge documented, all the economic growth of the past thirty years, instead of alleviating poverty, had actually increased the number of poor and chronically malnourished.[26]

At best, GDP growth offered a devil's bargain: "wages and riches now; disease and death down the road."[27] Uprooted and unsupported, many were simply left with the latter. To borrow the language of Occupy Wall Street, for the "bottom" 99 percent, GDP growth became an empty promise.

There is growing awareness that the nature of MORE must change. There was a time and need for increased material output, however crudely defined. For the young as for the poor and starving: a diet of increasing calories entailed the promise of health and opportunity. Today's voracious consumers are turning the world into a heap of trash in their addiction for more. The young and poor, meanwhile, are running out of options. And continuing population growth adds to the squeeze. Despite ongoing debate about numbers, there is a limit to how many people the earth can carry sustainably, and we have likely surpassed that limit. Rather than adhering to indiscriminate output, a smart version of MORE would address quality, capabilities, and development.

A British economist was one of the first to document the widening disconnect between growth and well-being. In a detailed study, Richard Douthwaite explored the effects of a doubling of national income in Britain between 1955 and 1988 and came to the sobering conclusion that "almost all the extra resources that growth had created had been used to keep the system functioning in an increasingly inefficient way." More cars, more roads, more energy, more plastic bottles, more medications—all to achieve a result in no way superior to what people had before, yet with great costs to humans and environment, and at great expense to stable and safe communities, free time, and physical health.[28]

Today, the story replicates around the world, from Brazil to South Africa to China. In all these "developing" countries, consumer choices are expanding. The middle class is growing, and so is the girth of people's waistlines, the amount of medications needed to get through the day, the dependence on goods and services provided by the market, the rates of cancer, the piles of waste, and the number of pollution-related illnesses. A boom all to GDP.

This is not an issue of somehow denying today's poor the benefits acquired by today's rich. Our wagons are hitched together. Both are racing toward the cliff on the rails of GDP growth. Unless we get off the track, the options are limited, and the prospects grim. We can temporarily ignore the inevitable results of GDP growth the same way we can ignore the results of gravity when jumping out of a twentieth-story window. For a while things will look pretty good. The result is inevitable in either case. Intelligently calculating capitalists, such as investment banker Jeremy Grantham, see the writing on the wall:

> With incredible good fortune we inherited a remarkable but finite stock of resources and an amazing biodiversity. All free. This was our capital account, yet as we run our assets down we are not accounting for the losses. Free clean water becomes expensive recycled water. Free fish and free trees become expensive fish farms and tree farms. A free mountainous watershed area in China becomes a deforested invitation to a ruinously expensive flood.[29]

It is a story of physical limits as much as a story of failed social and cultural promises, even in the richest of rich nations. Surveys suggest that most citizens of highly industrialized nations have stopped believing that things are getting better.[30] And no wonder: work became longer and harder, yet provided less job security and less confidence that people could take care of themselves and their loved ones in either sickness or old age. The faith that today's children will have a better life than their parents has been on its deathbed for quite some time. Hope that a doctor can be found to revitalize the patient is dimming.[31]

In the largest capitalist economy, the bottom 80 percent of income earners have not seen real wages go up in more than forty years. Over the past thirty years, virtually all the material benefits of U.S. economic growth—and they were significant—have gone to the richest 1 percent of Americans. CEOs who made about thirty times as much as their average employees in 1970 now make about four hundred times as much. This means that the top guns "earn" as much in an hour as minimum wage workers make in an entire year.[32] Globally, the wealth of the richest five hundred people exceeds the wealth of the bottom 50 percent of the world's population. Think of it this way: a small group of rich guys (and, yes, they're mostly guys) who could comfortably fit into an average grocery store, own more than 4.5 billion of us combined (that's roughly fifteen times the population of the United States). If you picture the world as a village of one hundred, just one resident owns two-thirds of the village.

This level of gluttony and inequality has consequences way beyond the pocketbook or bank account. Our jobs come and go ever more quickly—an average of nine times in each of our careers. Stable communities of any kind are as difficult to come by as a sense of purpose beyond MORE. What research consistently highlights as the main components of human happiness—an active, curious, and giving lifestyle in a well-connected community—is in decline on all fronts.[33] For the great majority of the world's population, business as usual is bankrupting us.[34]

Important to note: the concern here is not about the environment or about the planet. Mother earth will do fine with or without us.

The concern is about us. Our collective challenge is to find a way to sustain human life on earth, and, most taxing of all, to do so in a way that can provide basic security and a decent standard of living for everyone (all seven billion of us, expected to be about nine billion by 2050).

In all of this, "it remains a paradox," in the words of two prominent paleoanthropologists, "that so many centuries of science have led us to know what any Kalahari Bushman, any Australian Aborigine, or any of our ancestors who painted bison in the caves of Altamira knew full well: that it is not the earth that belongs to man, but man who belongs to the earth."[35] Growing our way out of a denial of this basic relationship is bound to end in tragic failure.

Treating the earth as a business in liquidation, acting as if we are masters without limits, can only lead to bad results.[36] Reporting on the fact that, over the past fifty years, "humans have changed ecosystems more rapidly and extensively than in any comparable period of time in human history," a five-year Millennium Ecosystem Assessment commissioned by the UN ominously concluded, "The ability of the planet's ecosystem to sustain future generations can no longer be taken for granted."[37]

It's no longer a radical conclusion. Careful and conservative chroniclers of the interaction between human affairs and the environment by now argue that "humans have upended hosts of ecosystems and are exerting a growing and potentially calamitous influence on the climate." A steadily growing number of prominent researchers are ringing the alarm bells. Concluding sixty years of research in climatology, the distinguished former NASA scientist James Lovelock starkly predicted that "before this century is over, billions of us will die."[38]

The World's Carbon Problem

1. Consensus among scientists: a 2.0°C (3.6°F) increase in average global temperatures is the absolute limit that provides any chance of avoiding very serious climate damage.
2. Our emissions of greenhouse gasses have increased global temperature by 0.8°C since 1850.
3. How much CO_2 would it take to incur another 1.2°C increase? Answer: 565 gigatons.
4. How much CO_2 is in the already-proven reserves of oil, coal, and gas? Answer: 2,795 gigatons, or roughly five times our maximum target allowance (and there are much larger, yet undetected, reserves).
5. To have any chance of avoiding catastrophic climate change, we thus need to leave in the ground at least 80 percent of all proven reserves.
6. By today's market values, 2,795 gigatons are worth about $27 trillion.

Source: All figures are from Bill McKibben, "Global Warming's New Terrifying Math" (2012).

Some leading politicians are taking note. "The issue of climate change is one we ignore at our own peril," stated President Obama. "[Unless we chart a very different course,] we are condemning future generations to global catastrophe."[39] After a three-day summit in 2000, government leaders from around the world declared "the current unsustainable patterns of production and consumption must be changed in the interest of our future welfare and that of our descendants."[40]

The most powerful military on earth is also beginning to pay attention to resource scarcity and an ecosystem in distress. The *Observer* published excerpts of a secret 2004 Pentagon report in which American defense experts, addressing the impacts of climate change, concluded, "Disruption and conflict will be endemic features of life," and, once again, life will be "defined by warfare." Very publicly, a 2014 Defense Department report again warned of the "security threats presented by climate change." In the preface to an international 2010 study of the flaws of GDP, French President Nicolas Sarkozy brought it all to a point: "growth is endangering the future of the planet and is destroying more than it is creating."[41]

As the second decade of the twenty-first century picked up speed, reports from around the world, and from across the professional spectrum, got worse. While headline news remained superficially and comfortingly focused on economic travails and political dysfunction, those willing to read past page two found reports on "superbugs" threatening national health, business predictions of severe oil shortages causing major disruptions in the very near future, and scientific findings that the world is warmer than at any time during the past four thousand years, currently increasing at an alarmingly rapid clip.[42]

Of course, one did not have to be a scientist, politician, or military strategist to see the writing on the wall. Looking at the evidence, the Reverend John Stott, a leader of the worldwide evangelical movement, urged his followers to act, for "Christians cannot regard with equanimity the injustices that spoil God's world and demean his creatures." In the words of Duke University Divinity professor Norman Wirzba, the situation is "alarming" for a simple reason: "we are quickly burning, bulldozing and consuming ourselves out of existence." [43]

The environmental historian John Robert McNeill finds in his magisterial work on human impact on the environment that "the human race, without intending anything of the sort, has undertaken a gigantic uncontrolled experiment on the earth. In time," he suggests, "this will appear as the most important aspect of 20th century history, more so than World War II, the communist enterprise, the rise of mass literacy, the spread of democracy, or the growing emancipation of women."[44] History, we may discover, is not merely about human beings. Nature (and its condition) emerges as a topic vital to human affairs.[45]

What humans are doing to their ability to thrive on this planet, it would seem, is not a liberal or conservative issue. Pushing forward in the direction of GDP growth affected all of us. Gated communities built far away from industrial waste and social decay could provide only limited and short-term shelter. Due to warmer ocean temperatures, Hurricane Sandy's left turn, slamming into the Jersey shore and New York City in late October of 2012, merely provided further evidence: privilege and wealth can only protect you so far. Multimillion-dollar mansions were simply washed away by the onslaught. As

Ronald Wright dryly noted, "Wealth can buy no refuge from pollution . . . and wealth is no shield from chaos, as the surprise on each haughty face that rolled from the guillotine made clear."[46]

It is not too much to say that our economic value system resembled the textbook definition of a psychopath: cold, egocentric, superficial, irresponsible, remorseless, and violent. We might note in passing that disregarding, depleting, and destroying the very things we need in order to survive may also serve as a solid working definition of ignorance.

Nature's services are not free. The longer we treat them as if they were free, the steeper the costs, and the more harmful the consequences for the poor, the young, and future generations.[47]

+++

Among experts, the debate is largely settled. The literature reporting on research about our collision course with planet earth is enormous, and steadily growing, despite its glaring absence from most political debates. The emerging scientific consensus seems to be that "our old world, the one that we have inhabited for the last 12,000 years, has ended, even if no newspaper has yet printed its scientific obituary." After careful review of ten years' worth of peer-reviewed scientific journal articles, the science historian Naomi Oreskes found broad consensus: while we can find ongoing debate about "tempo and mode," there is general agreement "on the reality of human-induced climate change."[48]

Each of the first twelve years of the twenty-first century were among the hottest fourteen years ever measured. Scientists say that the point of no return is about 350 parts per million of heat-trapping greenhouse gases—above that, life as we've known it is no longer sustainable; and no change of human behavior, no matter how radical, will be able to turn things around. For thousands of years the level has been around 280 parts. In 2013, for the first time, we surpassed the 400 mark. Just melting the permafrost in Alaska, Canada, and Siberia could get us above 500. Among many other factors, anything above 400 will lead to a significant rise in seawater levels. At just six feet, most coastal

(a) Socioeconomic trends

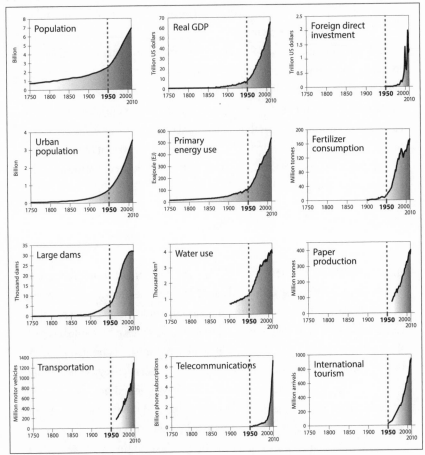

Figure 9–2. Great Accelerations. (a) Socioeconomic trends. (b) Earth system trends. International Geosphere-Biosphere Programme (IGBP) © 2014

metropolitan centers around the world would be swamped.[49] As a recent scientific paper further argued, even a mid-level scenario of predicted temperature increases would create conditions that humans will likely not survive.[50]

Put together by the International Geosphere-Biosphere Programme (IGBP), the above set of graphs (see figure 9–2) reveal the obvious interconnections between human actions and the health of our spaceship earth.

(b) Earth system trends

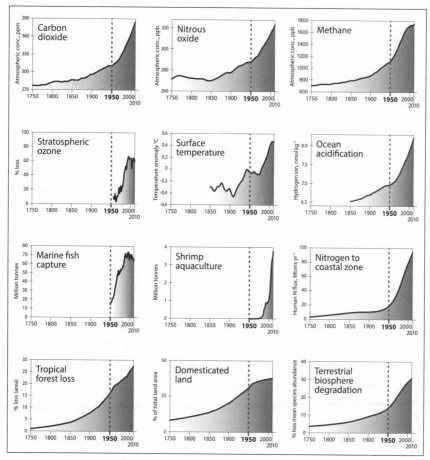

One way to capture the growing disconnect between GDP growth and quality of life is to call it "uneconomic growth." Five areas stand out:

- Jobless growth (GDP grows, but expanded job opportunities do not follow)
- Ruthless growth (GDP grows, but benefits are mostly or exclusively for the rich)
- Voiceless growth (GDP grows, but is not accompanied by empowerment or an extension of democracy)
- Rootless growth (GDP grows and in the process destroys communities and people's cultural identities)
- Futureless growth (perhaps most significant of all, GDP grows at the expense of opportunities for future generations)[51]

For Americans, it has already resulted in what the economist Gar Alperovitz has called a "long and dreary list" of consequences:

> The United States now ranks lowest or close to lowest among advanced "afflu-ent" nations in connection with inequality (21st out of 21), poverty (21st out of 21), life expectancy (21st out of 21), infant mortality (21st out of 21), mental health (18th out of 20), obesity (18th out of 18), public spending on social pro-grams as a percentage of GDP (19th out of 21), maternity leave (21st out of 21), paid annual leave (20th out of 20), the "material wellbeing of children" (19th out of 21), and overall environmental performance (21st out of 21).[52]

Taking into account things like political freedom, job security, and qual-ity of family life, *The Economist* comes to the conclusion that the United States, despite its top position in per capita GDP, ranks only 13th in the world. Countries with little more than half the per capita GDP outscore the United States.[53]

To clarify: whether our GDP-growth orientation has caused the bulk of problems listed here is a question that researchers and political activists will probably ponder for a long time. It is, however, also a fairly useless question, akin to wondering whether calories are to blame for the eventual death of the morbidly obese patient. The answer: definitely yes, and probably no. The over-all health of the patient on a continuously expanding diet was undoubtedly determined by the growing amount of calories consumed. And yet, calories were likely not the immediate cause of death.

If the goal is either quality of life today, or a future for our children, GDP is the wrong metric. When a prominent conservative research fellow wrote in late 2012 that "routine redistribution of wealth from future generations to our-selves is undemocratic, corrupting, and ultimately impoverishing," he was ad-dressing the problem of financial deficits.[54] The threat, however, runs deeper. It is the environmental equivalent of financing our current consumption with the income of future generations.[55]

Under the regime of GDP values, wrote the award-winning investigative reporter John Pilger, "democracy has become a business plan, with a bottom line for every human activity, every dream, every decency, every hope." Pol-itics, under this regime, becomes "devoted to the same economic policies—socialism for the rich, capitalism for the poor—and the same foreign policy of servility to endless war. This is not democracy," Pilger concluded. "It is to politics what McDonalds is to food."[56]

Yet he too merely described the surface of a deeper problem. The issue is not only about what we are doing to ourselves. Sure, we may, at some point, find a way to improve on our politics, to make politicians more accountable to their constituents. But like sailors on an increasingly storm-battered boat, our improved sailing skills will help us only if we can figure out how to prevent the boat from sinking. The plunder of the planet, together with the accelerating destruction of an ecosystem that would allow future generations to thrive, constitute the deeper legacy of GDP values. Life, under this regime, becomes devoted to endless indiscriminate growth. This is not prosperity. It is to quality of life what the waste dump is to nature.

A business plan that counts as a plus the arable land turned into parking lots, the air into smog, the water into toxic sludge, the steel into weapons, and ultimately life into commodities, inevitably lives in conflict with nature and human existence. It is the logic of war. For the winners, it may be profitable in the short run. In the long run it robs all humanity of its future.[57]

Why, then, is a fundamental course correction not on top of most people's agenda? The sheer scope of the problem represents one likely answer. The question becomes, "what can we possibly do?" Unless there is a common cause for the seemingly endless array of problems discussed above, the prospect of meaningful intervention indeed seems dishearteningly slim. Another problem, discussed by the veteran entrepreneur and environmentalist activist Paul Gilding, is that most of us harbor the false impression that catastrophe is still far away. In the face of something so big that it requires us to change just about everything, he argues, "denial is still the dominant response."[58]

A cynic may argue that "warnings of future catastrophe hold no sway in the human mind against the immediate gratification available in profusion from modern consumer society," in the words of community planner William E. Rees. "The explosive fossil-fuelled growth of the human enterprise may be gradually destroying the planet, but today's market economy is unequalled in its capacity to satisfy both the basic needs and the trivial wants of billions of people 'right now!'"[59]

But for that to be true would fail to explain the millions of citizens around the world who are actively engaged in the struggle for a more sustainable world.

The biggest obstacle, perhaps, is uncertainty. Trying to hold on to what is familiar comes easier than trying to comprehend or embrace change. What exactly will happen if we continue on the path of GDP growth? The short answer: we don't know for sure.

Unlike the doctor who can tell the alcoholic with reasonable certainty what will be the result of continued drinking, the precise impact of our collective growth addiction is much more difficult to predict. There exists plenty of disagreement among experts about exactly when, and how, we will hit the proverbial brick wall. What will we run out of first: land to cultivate, food to eat, air to breathe, water to drink, or resources to maintain any semblance of a modern society? How will nations and societies respond when they fall short of essentials for their survival? Are global wars inevitable?

The one thing that science and logic offers as a virtual certainty by now is this: unless we get off the train of escalating GDP growth, a collective wreck is inevitable. Our own species is neither separate from, nor immune to, nature and its condition.[60] No realistic scenarios exist that hold the promise of decoupling growth and its ill-effects—depletion of nonrenewables, pollution, and destruction. Technology offers no panacea—indeed, it will live up to its promise only if uncoupled from expansion and growth and put into service of much smarter models of development.

The human capacity to predict the future, and, more particularly, to figure out what is, and what is not, possible, is very limited. The ability to travel back in time a mere hundred years would quickly reveal that efforts to describe to our ancestors the life of today—its science and technology as well as its customs and laws—would have been met with utter incredulity. Even the sharpest and most educated minds of yesteryear could not have fathomed it. Women were still struggling to get the vote. America was securely in the grips of Jim Crow. Cars were a rarity, mostly confined to a few big cities. The vast majority of people had no access to electricity. Our ancestors wrote letters with pen and paper, the fastest responses not arriving before the week was out.

But admitting to serious limits in imagination and foresight does not mean we should not explore possibilities, or even probabilities. Not knowing for sure whether we will get into a car accident should not prevent us from putting on our seatbelts or keeping our breaks in good working order. It does seem wise to be wary of both extremes on the spectrum of possible answers: those who cheerfully declare their full faith in human inventiveness and modern technologies and science to fix all of our problems; and those who essentially declare the human experiment to be doomed.[61]

But there are a few things, I believe, we do know with a reliable degree of certainty. The following list is neither exhaustive nor prioritized. It is, however, a list of items central to addressing questions about a viable future beyond GDP.

- As long as growth depends on material throughput (and most of GDP growth does), we are, logically and inevitably, running up against the natural limits of a finite planet. Those limits include the levels of CO_2 beyond which fresh water supplies, arable land, and human life itself are threatened.
- For the roughly two billion of the world's poor (a larger number than the world's total population in 1900), major improvements in standards of living remain one of the most pressing tasks of modern politics; and some of those improvements will undoubtedly require physical growth.
- Combined, global economies currently produce significantly more than enough for every man, woman, and child on earth to have access to all the basics: housing, food, healthcare, education, jobs; quantity is not the problem—short-sighted goals, corruption, inefficient development, and inequality are.
- In developed nations in general, and for all people worldwide who have access to the basics, GDP growth has long ceased to translate into increased welfare, much less increased security or health or happiness.
- In accelerating fashion, growth of GDP is making things worse, rather than better (for both the rich and the poor).
- Throughout the world, spanning the political spectrum from right to left, "growth" remains the overarching goal (even if desperately ill defined); by default, growth is thus determined by the values embodied in GDP.
- Whatever the future may hold: being wrong on the side of caution (getting off our growth addiction of resource depletion, waste, and degradation) has few, if any, downsides; being wrong on the side of continued growth (based on faith in future discoveries and extraordinary self-healing powers of the planet) may doom the entire human enterprise.

The price tag of "modern progress" is steep, even if not always readily visible to its main beneficiaries. Having studied the larger global arc of national developments, historian David S. Landes cautiously concluded that "wealth entails not only consumption but also waste, not only production but also destruction. It is this waste and destruction, which has increased enormously with output and income, that threatens the space we live and move in."[62]

Which brings us back to the vital importance of metrics. Within the operating logic of modern economies, what matters is missing in action. "People" in their full humanity are absent from the very measures and structures supposed to serve them. The resulting key challenge is this: without a target guiding us toward a sustainable future, and thus without any effective feedback mechanisms on whether we are on the right path, there is little hope to get off the runaway train of reckless growth and land on ground that nurtures the well-being of people.

Following the logic of the GDP regime, we currently destroy, like Easter Islanders some 150 years ago, the very foundation we stand on. Details and debates aside, even those blind to the readily visible consequences should appreciate the basic truism: modern civilizations can survive only if they live off of the interest, and not the capital, of our planet. Whether growth is conceivable without destruction of our natural capital is a secondary question. Once we started using up, depleting, trashing, and polluting at a faster rate than earth could replenish and clean up, the timer on our collective existence started ticking.

What's most urgently needed, thus, is a better goalpost. Now.

BREAKING THE SPELL

If we could first know where we are and whither we are tending, we could then better judge what to do, and how to do it.

—Abraham Lincoln

Here we are, reams of studies detailing the urgency of our predicament—devastating climate change, the desolation of our planet's oceans and forests, mass extinction of vital species at the hands of human civilization; soil eroded and farmlands turned into deserts while the toxins contained in pesticides and fertilizers bleed into rivers and leave dead zones in our oceans; poisonous chemicals entering our bodies as part of our daily routines, exposing even the most innocent—our babies—to dangerous levels of toxicity. Under the guidelines of the GDP regime and legal constructs providing them privileges as persons, corporations in their actions *increasingly* embody the pathological characteristics of the GDP regime—reckless and exploitative, relentlessly plowing forward in search of expansion and profit without care or remorse for the consequences on either nature or people.[63]

We may already have passed critical thresholds, yet many of our economic experts tell us that to avert problems we should actually speed up. Most of our political leaders, meanwhile, remain safely muted in the prison of the "practical." Within the logic of the GDP regime, politics is as wedded to the imperatives of mindless growth as are businesses.

Perhaps we are looking for solutions in the wrong places. Perhaps we should not worry too much about an entire cadre of politicians and pundits who make a career belittling or denying our collision course with nature and the human spirit, poking fun at assorted "tree huggers," blithely dismissing "fact-based science." Or complain about experts not providing all the answers. Or despair over the inaction of our fellow humans, those "others" out there who presumably don't pay enough attention or simply don't care.

The real problem is that, whatever our level of understanding or concern, we are all passengers on the train. We may be better or worse stewards of our cabins, some enjoying servants and conspicuous consumption while others reduce, reuse, perhaps even repair. We may find ourselves in leadership positions or merely function as producers, consumers, or educators. It is important to acknowledge, however, that even the most powerful, in business as in politics, are effectively hamstrung. Political leaders may at times be able to affect the speed of the train, but rarely the direction. Powerful or not, nobody has yet figured out a way to get off the train, or change its course.

The logic of the GDP regime is, above all, a systemic problem.

Awareness is important, but not enough. Neither is awareness coupled with extraordinary personal efforts—cutting down on waste, buying local, reducing one's footprint. Even getting organized in the rear carriage can never be more than a first step as long as we don't find effective means to change the direction of the train.

Robert Jensen, one of a growing number of authors who struggle with this conundrum, writes that "pointing out that we live in unsustainable systems, that unsustainable systems can't be sustained, and that no person or institution with power in the dominant culture is talking about this—well, that's obviously crazy." When he asked readers to report on their reactions to this condition of seeming collective irrationality, one wrote back, "I feel hopeless. I feel sad. I feel amused at the absurdity of it all. I feel depressed. I feel enraged. I feel guilty and I feel trapped."[64] This is as good of a summary of our collective state as I have seen.

What this book suggests is that we are in the presence of an enormous opportunity. We can get off the train by articulating better goals, and implementing measures that correspond to those goals. This would fundamentally redirect our journey away from indiscriminate growth and toward smart development.[65] "What if we defined success not by the money we spent and the goods we consumed but by the quality of life we create?"[66]

We already possess most of the necessary tools to accomplish this.[67] What is missing above all else is the articulation of a new direction, one with a central focus on sustainability and quality of life. Once a clear direction is mapped, clear metrics can be established that reliably tell us about success and failure.

However useful its data may have been in capturing volume of output, GDP needs to be exposed as a measure that, in the twenty-first century, is both primitive and dangerous. It is nothing other than a "great delusion" that jobs, the good life, or progress itself "depend on GDP growth."[68] GDP as primary guide to economic and social success is bankrupt. The spell of GDP needs to be broken.

The challenge goes well beyond exposing GDP as a dangerously flawed accounting mechanism, however. As the globally dominant measure of success, GDP, perhaps more than anything else, has "the potential," in the words of the accounting historian Jane Gleeson-White, "to make or break life on the earth."[69]

As of today, not a single nation, governing party, or policymaking multinational organization in the industrialized world has replaced the logic of GDP with sustainability as its core organizing principle. It is not just the idea, but the regime that is based on the idea, that needs to come to an end.

But what, then, in the face of seemingly insurmountable obstacles, can be done? As a historian, I cannot help but be hopeful. The record of human struggle contains a wealth of examples of how fast deeply ingrained ways of thinking and doing business can get thrown overboard in the face of crisis.[70]

We are facing a crisis of potentially unprecedented magnitude. Yet once this crisis is understood as deriving from a common cause—entire societies organized around the goal of mindless growth—the lens through which to view life inevitably changes. Our way of thinking can shift.[71]

That moment is here. Macroeconomic theories based on the logic of GDP no longer account for reality—economic, social, or otherwise. It is time for outdated "truths" to be discarded and make way for a new paradigm, a clearer way of seeing, and a set of metrics that can actually point us toward a better future.

Chapter 10

FROM ALCHEMY TO REASON

What If? A Thought Experiment

*A system without feedback eventually fails. . . . Life
creates the conditions that are conducive to life.
Period. Full stop.*

—Martin O'Malley

Measures are an attempt to reflect our aspirations. They are supposed to define, clarify, and embody what we set out to do. To the extent they succeed, they can also tell us how far we've come. Or they can start sending us down a blind path.

Nothing promotes the status quo more than stifled aspirations, fed by a crippled sense of opportunity. It does not matter whether it is fed by cynicism, ignorance, dogma, or a lack of imagination.

The results of denied possibilities are as grand as they are tragic in scale. Day in and day out, the amount of human and natural capital wasted in modern societies is, quite simply, staggering. Every mind that is not educated and trained; every life whose basic needs are not nurtured; every resource that is wasted and every human rotting away in jail; every ecosystem that is destroyed—all represent a theft of future opportunities. On the scale in which GDP-driven nations squander possibilities, they cripple not only our imagination but also our prospects. It is no exaggeration to say that modern societies live in slavery to a false promise—the promise that more output will translate into a better life.

Given the enormous opportunities we possess, it is sobering to acknowledge how truncated our conversations about possible futures tend to be. Discoveries are made, breakthroughs achieved, and innovations introduced at ever greater speed. It seems our aspirations cannot keep pace.

It is thus important to engage, if only for a moment, in a different kind of exploration, one that borrows from a wide range of disciplines, ranging from psychology to politics to sports. How can we explain the growing divide between reality and possibility? What barriers and opportunities do we face in an attempt to move forward?

To begin with, a fundamental task seems to elude the human species: how to articulate smart goals that make good use of what we know and have. Our sense of the possible seems mired in the past. It's as if accelerating change, often experienced as disruptive and unsettling, makes people return to the false comforts of yesterday. Faced with a range of prospects, we tend to hunker down and make peace with the familiar, even if this includes conflict and war, inequality and poverty, alienation and loneliness, and the suffocation of nature under a pile of discarded consumer items.

Routinely, we can't see what seems to be right in front of us. This truth was driven home to me in the late spring of 1989 when I asked East European dissidents, shortly before Soviet control had begun to crack visibly, "How much longer do you think communist one-party control will last?" Without fail, they looked at me as if I had lost my mind. The few who bothered to respond to such a seemingly insane question said something along the lines of "it will certainly not end in my lifetime." Both they and I had spent much, if not all, of our lives under the stifling realities of the Cold War. It was how the world worked. Six months later the Berlin wall came down. The Soviet empire collapsed soon thereafter. Communism was dead. The Cold War was over.

In late October 2008 eminent scholars and political experts were still betting against Americans being ready to elect an African American president. A month later people did, by a wide margin. As Kuznets commented in his own time, "It would have been a wise prophet indeed who, 25 years ago, had foreseen the major changes in the country's conditions."[1]

Blindness to possibility, even in the face of logic and new insights, runs deep in all aspects of life, from the extraordinary to the mundane. One does not have to be a baseball fan, for instance, to appreciate the meaning of a minor revolution that happened despite the concerted resistance of fans and players and scouts deeply wedded to tradition. For over a century, baseball enthusiasts had measured the quality of players by batting averages or stolen bases, until such concepts became deeply ingrained in the psyches of millions of managers and followers alike. Then a baseball aficionado by the name of Bill James came along with more methodical, if less flamboyant, statistical data like On-Base plus Slugging percentages (OPS). The new data showed that the old way of thinking was neither accurate nor a good predictor of a player's or a team's future performance. Particularly managers and scouts fiercely held on to the old ways. Privileged knowledge confers power—until it is revealed as deeply flawed.

Now commonly known as sabermetrics, the new statistics eventually transformed baseball. At first its rationale was resisted, prolonging the time necessary for its logic to settle in well beyond what reason would suggest. Sure, perhaps some of the magic of the old spell was lost. What was gained, moreover, was a mixed bag. It brought more rationality and a "ruthless drive for efficiency" to the game. On the other hand, it democratized the sport. Among other things, it showed why success in baseball had resisted "so many rich men's attempts to buy [the game]."[2] And so it goes: the promises and dangers of expanded possibilities.

There is something in this resistance that goes beyond a general failure to comprehend future possibilities: it is a deep-rooted tendency to deny possibility. Frequently, this denial is cloaked in the garb of realism and sophistication, or what Nobel Prize–winning psychologist Daniel Kahneman calls "the illusion of validity."[3] "You must be naive to believe this could happen," people are told when proposing a fundamental departure from some kind of social pathology, be it male supremacy or corporate personhood or mass incarceration. Or continued GDP growth. The more widely shared denial of possibility is, of course, the more it tends to become self-fulfilling. We can't realize what we can't imagine.

Perhaps there is consolation in denying possibility: it asks less of us and provides an easy rationale for blind acceptance. References to history or imagined characteristics of human nature serve as favorite excuses. "It's never been done," it is said, or "People are too selfish for that." The tyranny of dead and unexamined ideas.

It is thus a matter of practical concern to reject the lazy response of "there is no way" when the conversation turns to exploring changes in our economy's direction. Instead, why not follow a path that underlies all good planning and development: first, figure out where we want to go; then think about how we can get there. Perhaps Paul Hawken said it best: "Don't be put off by people who know what is not possible. Do what needs to be done, and check to see if it was impossible only after you are done."[4] Or as Nelson Mandela reminds us, "It always seems impossible until it's done."

But where to start a conversation about goals, about "what needs to be done?" Unless we want to resemble teachers discussing how best to improve SAT scores among their students, in the process failing to explore what matters—quality of education—it makes sense to start with a simple yet basic question: what do we want from our economy?

This fairly straightforward question, however, quickly reveals itself to be more like a march through rugged terrain after two hundred years of battle. Navigating ruins and craters from countless historical struggles, we encounter landmines and the stench of old corpses. But we can also detect new life breaking through the debris, and excavate discarded old ideas that may prove newly valuable, "a minefield studded with pots of treasure."[5] Each step of the way, we are confronted with choices about which way to turn, whose ideas to learn from, and what strategies to adopt.

Merely asking the question about goals for a modern economy already reveals a basic truth: any deliberate answer is better than what we have today— blind and indiscriminate volume of output.

Let's begin our investigation by figuring out what we know about the terrain as currently configured, then move to central elements of the landscape we need to keep an eye on, before exploring Simon Kuznets' roadmap—incomplete as it may be—of how to move beyond the old battlefields. Finally, after having assembled tools and guides and historical experiences, let's see whether we can glimpse a more promising landscape—an economy that works for what we want.

+++

When a measure becomes a target, it ceases to be a
good measure.
—*Charles Goodhart*

At the outset, we should reiterate a basic assumption of this book: the sole object of our efforts should be to sustain and expand human well-being, not simply to promote income or growth.[6] As we have seen, the two are not the same. Income and growth, as defined today, can enhance, take away from, even undermine well-being. Both should therefore be, at best, of secondary concern.

We collect more data than ever before—on personal behavior, on business transactions, on patterns of consumption. On some level at least, we probably possess more knowledge than at any other point in history. But herein also lies the problem. Data are useful only if put into models. Models, however, inevitably simplify reality. They miss connections. They can never substitute setting priorities and targets. Ask yourself this: do you want Google, based on its sophisticated algorithms analyzing previous patterns of your search and purchasing behavior, to decide what you should buy next? Or what to read and think about next?

This is a dilemma. By defining and limiting our choices, models steer both our thinking and our behavior. Data scientists call it a *behavioral loop*. There is no shortage of tragic examples: the Great Recession of 2007–9 was the first global economic catastrophe triggered by faulty financial models, all based on data captured by refined algorithms.[7]

The historical evolution of GDP provides further evidence: by defining the pathways of economic activity and profitability, it defines our choices. And it steers our thinking and behavior—or, more precisely, *narrows* and *falsifies* our thinking and behavior.

Rather than seeing the model as a subjective attempt to approximate reality, the model becomes our reality. GDP is identified with volume and success of the economy. It is the idea shaping the brain—the creation imprisoning the creator. GDP represents the ultimate behavioral loop.

Even in the short run, the damage can be breathtaking. Prior to the financial collapse of 2008, the acrobats of modeling had magically created trillions of dollars of assets or securities by doing nothing other than entering numbers into digital programs that followed the algorithms of ever more fanciful models.[8] Most of it, of course, was astonishing, immature make-believe, entirely disconnected from physical reality—the perfect bubble. And the acrobatics involved trillions of dollars, representing little more than the imaginations of global financial wizards and all those who fell under their spell. But when the bubble of foolishness burst behind the walls of expert mathematical sophistication, it destroyed many of the more practical minded, namely those who produce and occupy reality. In addition to the human agony, the quants run amok managed to destroy homes, businesses, investments, jobs, retirement accounts, and with it families and lives.[9]

Generally, what gets lost in the maniacal pursuit to produce greater numbers—profits, bottom lines, output, growth—is the question about initial purpose. It gets lost because human deliberation about goals and preferences are replaced with statistical models based on faulty assumptions. And, though this may seem obvious, it is useful to remember that statistical models do not have feelings or intuitions. Models may be developed or refined with additional data, but they cannot process experience or evaluate choices that lie outside their narrow confines. No model can be better than the ideas and choices that have gone into it.

So, descending the ladder of make-believe in an effort to find some ground of reality under our feet, let's ask, What do we know about human well-being?

Most fundamentally, what scientists realize and economists tend to forget is that quality of life is grounded in a physical reality, without which all questions about welfare or development become moot. Geneticists tell us that life on earth requires information, energy, and catalysis. Physicists might say that earth-type life depends on six essential elements (carbon, hydrogen, oxygen, nitrogen, sulfur, and phosphorus) and the presence of liquid water. For our purposes, it is sufficient to say that life and well-being most essentially depend on a viable ecosystem (and not on human abstractions like free markets or government regulations). What is necessary for this viability can be described today with an unprecedented degree of precision.

What environmental scholars call the "ecological footprint," for instance, measures "how much land and water area a human population requires to produce the resources it consumes and to absorb its waste." Beyond that, the ecological footprint can also "track how much productive area—or biocapacity —is available."[10] Despite continuing errors and adjustments, we are close to reaching a point that allows us to say quite precisely what it takes to sustain the physical basics of life. We pretty much know what different lifestyles and economies require in order to be viable. And we know about thresholds—the point at which we begin to live beyond our ecological means.

As we have seen, applying the available data to our situation reveals bad news: according to the most recent reports, worldwide humanity "demands over 50 percent more than what the planet can regenerate."[11] Anyone running a business understands that you cannot live off of your capital. Any citizen understands that it's not real income when you live off of your savings.

The idea of indefinite economic growth of GDP is thus not only, as we have seen, patently irrational. It is also a form of intergenerational tyranny. For our children and grandchildren, it is exploitation without representation.

We've run out of time to lament ecological destruction while driving a Prius to the health food store. As gratifying, even useful, our attempts at recycling or buying fair trade or using low-energy light bulbs may be, they barely scratch the surface of both challenges and opportunities at hand. Perhaps Ronald Wright captured a valid starting point when he wrote that "the reform that is needed is not anti-capitalist, anti-American, or even deep environmentalist; it is simply the transition from short-term to long-term thinking. From reck-lessness and excess to moderation and the precautionary principle."[12]

The first and most obvious goal, therefore, has to be for each country to bring down its demands on nature and resources to a sustainable level. The basic truth is that we can't use up more than we can regenerate.[13] The pathology of compound growth of material through-put has to stop. The primitive Wild West economy of voracious expansion has to be replaced with an intelligent spaceship economy of qualitative development.[14]

Setting aside specifics for the moment, of course, one should assume that the underlying objective of global sustainability is not controversial, as it is essential for human survival.[15]

Sustainability does not preclude growth and development. On the contrary. Few people would say "no" to more stability, more independence, more freedom, more time—all goals not in necessary conflict with the ecosystem or future generations. Many sustainable growth and development opportunities can also be achieved through economic means—more efficient technology, better organization of work, scientific breakthroughs in communication or energy generation.

Most qualitative accomplishments, however, will likely lie outside the realm of classical economics. With increasing efficiency and growing populations, necessary work (what for most people today is "wage labor") not only can, but will have to be, reduced and more equitably distributed. As a species, we produce too much and waste too much. And we do it while largely separated into two groups: those "overworked" and those "unemployed." Both groups are stunted in the expression of their capabilities. Both are stifled in their potential contributions to sustainability, equity, and civil society.

Spending less time doing necessary work, in turn, will offer opportunities for people to expand their lives outside of markets and competition and deal-making. Family, neighborhood, community, the commons—all forms of social and voluntary networks will gain in significance. The "love of money as possession," what Keynes called a "disgusting morbidity, one of those semi-criminal, semi-pathological propensities" characteristic of growth economies, could be left behind. No longer the principal goal of a new economy, those who continue to define their life goals by the pursuit of wealth and money might safely be handed "over with a shudder to the specialists in mental disease."[16]

The promises of sustainability, a way of life that doesn't steal from future generations, can be found precisely in the realization of goals that lie beyond mere accumulation. It's not a particularly controversial point: the person who works less has more time to take care of herself and her family. The person who drives less and walks more is healthier and more relaxed. The person who

Figure 10–1. Taken on 7 December 1972 by the astronauts of the Apollo 17 spacecraft from a distance of about 28,000 miles, this iconic picture became known as the *Blue Marble* and constitutes one of the most widely used images ever.

lives in a safe and stable community is happier and more creative. The person who eats better is not only healthier but also more energetic. The person who can rely on having a job and access to healthcare and quality education is not only better off, but also more productive. The person who lives in a connected community that offers emotional support and opportunities for meaningful engagement not only feels better but also wastes less time and resources on things like housing, commuting, or shopping.[17]

Above all, only the pursuit of quality of life (rather than quantity of consumption) offers the chance to stop the plunder of the planet. It's a realization made visible by the first full-earth shot taken by Apollo 17 in December 1972: in a vast universe, we all occupy the same small planet (see figure 10–1). One people, one planet. Unless we have the goal of being the last to die on a sinking ship, there is no future in the depletion of mother earth or the primitive competition for more.

For the house we want to build, in short, sustainability represents the plot of ground supporting everything else. Without it, no lasting development can take place.

Once we have a lot that can sustain our house, what about the foundation? Are there aspirations that can be enshrined in our economic measures that have a legitimate claim to universality? Goals, in short, that define the aspirations of people worldwide and could thus fashion new economic measures that reflect them? Goals that offer solid ground below whatever edifice different cultures may decide to erect on top?

One good starting point for establishing a common goal is the International Bill of Human Rights, "one of the highest expressions of the human conscience of our time."[18]

Explore them.[19] For one, they go well beyond rights and aspirations spelled out in most national constitutions, including the U.S. Constitution.

Moreover, when the drafters declare in the preamble that "the freedom of speech and belief and freedom from fear and want have been proclaimed as the highest aspiration of the common people," they deliberately echoed a U.S. president who rose to prominence during the same moment in history that generated the GDP regime: the Great Depression. His lesson was straightforward. It was during a 1941 State of the Union Address that Franklin D. Roosevelt famously called for the worldwide protection of four freedoms: "the freedom of speech and expression, the freedom of worship, the freedom from want, and the freedom from fear."

By establishing a wide range of basic human, social, and economic rights and freedoms, including a right to work and organize, or to have access to the best available education and healthcare, the universal declaration provides an excellent foundation. It allows us to define targets around which we can then design economic measures intended to facilitate and support the realization of our goals. The declaration's near universal ratification, furthermore, would suggest that the values it professes enjoy broad support.[20] Its values certainly represent a good embodiment of what Kuznets called a "more enlightened social philosophy."[21]

The reader will note that dominant economic performance measures, chief among them GDP, cover none of the Human Rights declarations. In fact, as

Kuznets noted, they do not address human welfare at all. It is as if our house contains a well-equipped kitchen, large bowls of delicious ingredients placed before some brilliant chefs, and a diverse coterie of gifted guests awaiting their meal in the dining room, yet the best goal we can come up with for the occasion is to reward those who can eat the most food the fastest. Sure, some of the guests will get fed. But it wastes good food and talent, leaves behind the less greedy and the less muscular, corrupts the privileged few, and passes the kitchen on to future generations in a depleted state of shambles. It affords no comfort that our economic experts assure us that "the greatest good of all" is presumably best served by the acquisitive greed of each.

We should also note that, obviously, human development is not to blame for this astonishing discrepancy between our social values and our economic goals: the articles spelled out in human rights declarations are, by any standard, a remarkable achievement. Given the course of human history over the past two thousand years, they also justly deserve to be called "progress." Our economic goals, on the other hand, remind us more of what Thomas Hobbes might have called "poor, nasty, [and] brutish," or what Keynes simply referred to as "semi-pathological."[22]

How then can we best align our social and cultural accomplishments with how we make a living? How can we organize our economy to reflect our social and political accomplishments?

A central suggestion of this book is that our performance indicators need to reflect what we want, for we get what we measure. The central goal of preserving and supporting life and its free expression should not be negotiable. By the same token, no one should be allowed to pursue this goal at the expense of others or future generations.

The new overarching standard could be quite simple: penalize everything that harms present or future generations; reward all that is beneficial to future generations. Within that framework, allow as much opportunity as possible for people to develop their fullest potential, and promote as much freedom as possible for people to express themselves. Let the market operate freely wherever it does not interfere with human rights and a sustainable economy. Let human rights worthy of a civilized culture provide us with the guidelines for a much freer market and a more vibrant democracy.

Of course, the reader might object, as important as broad principles may be in guiding our actions, they say little about what, specifically, to do. True. But, unfortunately, in order to get to some possible specifics, we must first lift a few mental cobwebs that political and economic pundits continue to spin. Otherwise we cannot access a clear pathway to imagining an economy organized around performance goals that measure what we want.

MENTAL COBWEBS

The difficulty lies, not in the new ideas, but in escaping from the old ones, which ramify, for those brought up as most of us have been, into every corner of our minds.

—*John Maynard Keynes*

The first mental cobweb is both basic and profound: it is pointless to blame a structure or a system for failing to do what it was not set up to do. It is basic because few would argue with its logic. It is profound because we tend to forget, and the implications reach far and wide.

Whatever the precise makeup of a sustainable economy, markets or governments, laws or regulations, technological inventions or scientific breakthroughs are not the solution. Nor are they the problem. They are merely tools. All are as good or as bad as we make them—empty vessels whose quality is determined by their makeup and implementation. Or, to be more precise, all are as good or bad as the performance measures and enforcement mechanisms put in place to guide them.[23]

When government primarily defines its responsibility as boosting economic growth and securing the rights of private corporations, as it arguably has for quite some time in advanced economies around the world, it cannot be blamed for failing to rescue people who were drowning in New Orleans in the wake of Katrina, much less for relegating sustainability to an afterthought.[24] When markets function under rules that count accidents as benefits or resource depletion as an asset rather than a liability, they cannot be blamed for people pursuing destructive goals. When the Fourteenth Amendment, which was passed to protect the rights of free blacks by prohibiting state and local governments from depriving persons of life, liberty, or property, is, in turn, commandeered by the Supreme Court in order to expand the rights of private corporations, the law cannot be blamed for its perverse consequences, turning modern-day mega corporations into entities with more rights and privileges than those of citizens.

Good goals, clearly defined, can come to fruition only if coupled with performance measures that track their progress.

If government had a well-defined and enforceable set of responsibilities to provide for the welfare of its citizens in times of crisis, the immediate response to citizens drowning in New Orleans would have been different. The same is true for private corporations: unless they are mandated to assure that their waste leaves water as clean downstream as it was upstream, or that the health of their workers is as good after work as it was before, they cannot be asked to take responsibility for the quality of either water or health. But without measures in place that clearly show both successes and failures, the goals themselves are nearly useless.[25] Without definition and enforcement, the "pursuit of happiness" becomes a rote invocation on the Fourth of July, empty of substance.

Unlike the Declaration of Independence, of course, modern accounting standards don't articulate good goals. On the contrary, as discussed in chapter 8, they are explicitly set up to encourage profit-oriented businesses to pursue harmful goals: externalize as many expenses, and ignore as many harmful consequences as possible. Wherever the accounting rules allow, dump on the public and the commons. The privatization of gains and the socialization of losses is a pervasive problem. It is also a logical result of a system that rewards such practices. Business executives, meanwhile, are as people no different than anyone else—but they do serve a pathological system. Some are aware of it. And, torn between their values as individuals and parents and community members on the one hand, and their actions and responsibilities as corporate managers on the other, they agonize over it.

It's really quite simple: the more a business can do to pass on to society such large costs as security or roads or education or healthcare or law enforcement or pollution cleanups, the higher their profit, according to current rules. Since profit is the central goal of any private business, it is inevitable that businesses have become experts in externalizing costs. It is "profitability without accountability."[26]

The example of coal-operated power plants, explored in chapter 8, is merely a case in point. There are many others. Who knows how much a hamburger at McDonalds would cost, for instance, if the chain had to pay its full share of the roads leading up to its franchises, the healthcare or education of its workers, or the greenhouse gas emissions of the millions of steroid-boosted cattle-camp cows needed for its beef patties. No matter whether prices were to go up 50 or 250 percent, it's doubtful the king of global fast food would remain profitable.[27]

We should emphasize, again, that focus on profit is not the main culprit. The problem is bad measures, and thus bad results for people. The alternative: if you make the mess, clean it up; if you need something in order to become profitable, pay for it. Once you have fulfilled your obligations and responsibilities to the common good, keep all the profit you want. In the process, let those who produce much of the wealth enjoy it. Let the commons and the people who inhabit it take pleasure in the products of their own labor. We could call it privatization of costs and socialization of gains.

The challenge of evaluating our goals, and of figuring out whether we are moving toward or away from them, brings us to measures. As mentioned in the introduction, all measures are a means to an end, something allowing us to compare or evaluate or appraise. Without agreeing on a common metric, people could not come together to build or calculate or price anything. I painfully learned this lesson when trying to apply my hard-earned European knowledge of the metric system to construction work in the United States. Many a miscut 2 x 4 landed on the waste pile.[28]

My foibles in construction, of course, pale in comparison to the larger point. Here is an example of much greater import: people used to measure the size of land by how many people it could sustain—how much access to water, how fertile the soil? It was a central measure for survival. Today we measure land by hectares or acres, often entirely independent of its fertility. Different purposes, different concepts, different measures, and different consequences for what appears to be the same thing.

All measures are a product of choice—choosing to measure one thing over another; serving one purpose or master over another. By definition, they cannot thus be objective—correct, yes; but objective, absolutely not.[29]

Here, then, are two more cobweb-clearing exercises. When it comes to economic activity, we are faced with fundamental choices: first, do we focus on quantitative or qualitative measures, say ounces of food versus taste or dietary contribution to health? Is one more reliable than the other? And which can provide better performance indicators for our economy?

And, second, what to do about the fact that some things are much easier to measure than others, like money earned versus job satisfaction? Do we measure only that which is easily measureable, and ignore that which is hard, even if the hard-to-measure performance indicator may be of great importance?

As a result of choices made in the past, and detailed in this book, current economic measures are all built on the assumption that price is a reliable quantitative measure for value: only those things that have a price, therefore, have value. It is prioritizing, if you will, the exchange value of goods and services over the use value of the same. In real life, of course, this faith rarely makes sense. Few people would have to think long when faced with a choice between either $10 million of cash or, say, oxygen. Which would they value more? Of course the answer is obvious. GDP-driven markets, however, consistently defy common sense.

It's a central problem: how to evaluate things that are priceless? Clearly, there are things, like air, that are essential yet priceless. Not everything that is both crucial to the economy and to life has been financialized—given a price, for it is not bought or sold in the marketplace.

What to do about that? Theoretically, we have three options:

1. Money Standard: We can try to fix the failures of GDP by a smarter, "true cost" pricing system and a different set of goals;

2. Quality Standard: We can ditch GDP and other money standards and replace them with qualitative measures; or

3. Dashboard Standard: We can mix and match GDP with other indicators, turning it into just one among many important measures.

Over the course of the past four decades, all three options have been explored. There are, today, well over a hundred measures that have been developed around the world in response to the failures of GDP.[30]

Following the logic of option 1 (Money Standard) is the idea that we should "impute" prices—a fancy term for attaching an artificial or "shadow" price to things like unexplored resources, or parenting, clean water, and pollution.[31] On the plus side, this would force players in the market to pay more attention to such vital items. It might also allow us to correct current GDP accounts, without entirely giving up on existing national accounts and the convenience of a single metric.

On the minus side, it remains exceedingly difficult to find agreement on how to value things like parenting or resource depletion. Or to decide which activities to promote as beneficial (like volunteer work), and which to subtract as harmful (junk food? gambling?). Above all, imputing prices for previously nonmonetized aspects of human existence would represent a further expansion of the commodity logic to social life and nature. Every part of living could end up being turned into a commodity, properly financialized, and, in many cases, accessible to privatization.

Still, much can be learned from such efforts. Developed by the World Bank, the Genuine Savings Indicator (GSI) is a metric that, like all others that fall into this category, starts with the existing GDP, and then subtracts imputed costs for resource depletion and environmental degradation, but adds all investments in social and human capital (like education, effective government, safety, and so forth). One logical and consistent finding of such accounts is that selling off and depleting natural resources actually takes away from future welfare. This tragic reality particularly affects poor countries. Investing in people and communities, on the other hand, adds to future welfare.

Very similar to GSI are a variety of Green GDP indicators, all of which emphasize costs of resource depletion and ecosystem degradation.

The most highly developed indicator in this category is the *Genuine Progress Indicator* (GPI). Based on an elaborate set of criteria that cover a wide range of life, GPI attempts to determine what activities provide *goods* and what activities inflict *ills*. GPI adjusts GDP values by making "deductions to account for income inequality and costs of crime, environmental degradation, and loss of leisure." On the other hand, it adds to GDP figures by counting "the services from consumer durables and public infrastructure as well as the benefits of volunteering and housework."

As an experimental alternative to GDP, the Genuine Progress Indicator has found a following in many nations. The primary reason, according to its authors, is that "by differentiating between economic activity that *diminishes* both natural and social capital and activity that *enhances* such capital," GPI is designed to "measure sustainable economic welfare rather than economic activity alone."

Its most significant finding to date is that, in all industrialized countries, GPI grew in proportion to GDP until the 1970s, at which point the two began to diverge. GDP kept on going up. GPI, on the other hand, began to stagnate, and in some cases even declined (see figure 10–2).[32] Due to its much more comprehensive coverage of vital indicators, progressive states like Maryland and Vermont have officially adopted GPI, and others are considering similar moves.[33]

Following option 2 (Quality Standard) are a great variety of indicators that use nonmonetized quality indicators. For the sake of clarity, let's briefly review the main two kinds: one is based on "objective" scientific data, and the other primarily informed by a series of subjective records.

A prime example for the first has been mentioned before in this book, and is called the *Ecological Footprint* (EF). In essence, it is a gauge of human demand on the earth's ecosystem. It measures how much biologically productive land is needed to provide the resources and absorb the wastes of individuals, locales, or nations.

In each case, the central question is: are resources used up faster than the supporting ecosystem regenerates? Based on current estimates, the world uses up ecological resources a little less than twice as fast as the earth is able to renew them.

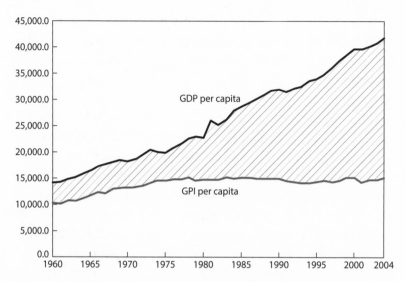

Figure 10–2. The widening gap between growth and progress.

An interesting outlier to ponder: if every global citizen consumed and polluted and trashed like the average American, we would need a total of about five planets to sustain our habits. Given that versions of American consumer culture are still seen as models for development, especially in some rapidly growing countries with much larger populations, this fact alone should give us serious pause.

The second form of nonmonetized indicators attempts to measure broad qualities like human happiness, quality of life, or life satisfaction.[34] All are, it would seem obvious, highly subjective. As explored earlier, of course, the so-called hard numbers of national income accounting are no less subjective.

Directly measuring quality of life just avoids the detour of questionable assumptions. It also makes evident what otherwise remains hidden: quality cannot be reduced to a mathematical number. Figuring out how to define and measure quality is a messy process, one better undertaken in broad daylight and with democratic input.

In general, quality of life indicators attempt to measure the extent to which economic activity meets human needs. They do so through direct survey methods, or through proxies such as life expectancy, gender equality, or rates of violence. Over the past few decades, happiness and life satisfaction studies have been pursued by economists as well as by psychologists, sociologists, and neuroscientists. They have, in the meantime, generated increasingly sophisticated evidence.[35]

One core finding of happiness research: beyond a certain level of income and GDP, happiness no longer increases. Ever more, wealthy nations waste inordinate resources just to maintain basic levels of life satisfaction in the face of environmental degradation, the breakdown of social cohesion, and the loss of cultural purpose among an endless quest for more stuff. The returns (or, in the lingo of economists, marginal utility) are not just diminished. More and more, they disappear. Or turn into additional costs. It is akin to the addict finding himself spending more and more time and effort and agony managing his affliction. Soon, the temporary satisfaction (or utility) gained from consuming the drug of choice declines, then disappears altogether, and eventually turns into a liability.

Option 3, combining different indicators into a Dashboard Standard, has generated a wide following. It can build on what already exists, and has the great advantage of potentially capturing a much wider range of criteria than any single metric. By potentially allowing everyone to measure whatever they consider most important, dashboards can also effectively serve as tranquilizers of discontent—measure what you want, policy will still follow the growth imperatives of GDP.

The best known, and perhaps most consequential of such measures, is the United Nations *Human Development Index* (HDI). A composite of life expectancy, education, and income (based on GDP), it represents the attempt, in the words of its creator, Pakistani economist Mahbub ul Haq, "to shift the focus of development economics from national income accounting to people centered policies."[36] HDI is a central component of the annual Human Development Report of the United Nations.

Another significant attempt to generate a meaningful composite indicator is the *Happy Planet Index* (HPI). Advertised as the "leading global measure of sustainable wellbeing," it is a creation of the London-based New Economics Foundation (nef), an independent "think-and-do tank," which, in its own words, "inspires and demonstrates real economic wellbeing." HPI focuses on global data from three perspectives: life expectancy, experienced well-being, and ecological footprint. Since it does not address many of the areas that enhance, in Amartya Sen's words, "human capabilities"—things like gender equality, human rights, or participation in democratic governance—nef cautions that HPI should never be the only measure of nations. In a statement addressing single-indicator efforts in general, nef warns that "blind pursuit of a single objective, whilst disregarding the means to achieving it, is dangerous."

Primarily due to one of the world's worst ecological footprints, the United States currently scores a 37.3 out of 100 on the HPI scale, and ranks 105th out of 151 countries measured. According to nef, countries worldwide would have to achieve an average of 89 points on their scale in order to reach sustainability.

The dashboard option is pursued in recognition of the fact that human life cannot be reduced to a single figure, and cultural priorities should not be reduced to the lowest common denominator. Implementation is the biggest challenge of such dashboard indicator sets. As they are much more explicitly contentious than numerical indicators with a pretense of objectivity, none has ever acquired much influence in the realm of policymaking.

So-called national "satellite accounts" are a prominent case in point. First developed in France in the 1960s, these accounts are tellingly named this way because whatever they measure—education, health, happiness—they merely circle around the main account, which, of course, is GDP. They are also measured by their respective impact on GDP.

In part due to political advocacy of the women's movement, which promoted the inclusion of unpaid labor, and to pressure from the environmental movement, which fought for inclusion of data that portrayed the state of the ecosystem, the United Nations began to encourage nations to include satellite accounts in their new Standards of National Accounts (SNA), revised in 1993.[37] Still maintained in many countries, satellite accounts have had minimal impact on political or economic decision-making. The United States stopped supporting and funding social and environmental satellite accounts in the early years of the first Clinton presidential term.[38]

The United Nation's Millennium Development Goals, signed in 2000 by 189 nations, represent a recent international example of integrated satellite accounts. Broken down into eight distinct categories, the manifesto includes four dozen indicators that allow national and international statistical experts to track progress of nations and regions in each category. Signatories agreed to promote a "world with less poverty, hunger and disease, greater survival prospects for mothers and their infants, better educated children, equal opportunities for women, and a healthier environment." Nations also pledged to help create "a world in which developed and developing countries worked in partnership for the betterment of all."

Subsequent declarations included the right to development for all, and freeing everyone from want. Also resolved was an international call "for halving by the year 2015 the number of people who live on less than one dollar a day."[39] Especially tragic for poor countries, the goals of promoting gender equality, empowering women, and improving maternal health appeared most resistant to progress.[40]

The largest ongoing effort to address the multiple inadequacies of GDP accounts is the *Beyond GDP* initiative by the European Commission. Though not yet clear what will come of it, the EU commission has stated clearly that GDP is an insufficient measure, and needs to be supplemented by "social, environment, and wellbeing indicators." According to its own mission, however, the plan does not seem to include replacing GDP, as much as to find additional measures that would "allow politicians to better monitor and evaluate progress in our society," as well as to "better communicate in a clear way that a given policy may target or affect many other elements of the society than economic activity."[41] In other words, no major policies have shifted as a result. GDP reigns on.[42]

It becomes readily apparent that all three options—improving GDP through a better pricing system, ditching GDP and replacing it with purely qualitative measures, or finding composites as either additions to, or a replacement of, GDP—face at least three basic problems.

First is *selection of criteria*. Second is the *quality of data*. And, perhaps most importantly, third is *usefulness of data*. In short, how do we create a system in which indicators, once we've decided what we want, actually define what we do? How do we set priorities and find metrics that adequately measure those priorities? And, finally, how do we make sure that the information we're getting is solid, meaningful, and enforceable?

Using the analogy of health once more: Once we've realized that calorie intake is not an adequate indicator, then what? Should we instead measure, say, level of education, amount of exercise, and quality of diet? If so, how do we rank those criteria? Since what we measure defines what is important, how do we best capture our goals? Lastly, how do we account for the inevitable change in priorities and circumstances over time—how do we not get locked into static and increasingly outdated metrics, like we did with GDP?

Even if we agreed on broad categories—say, quality of diet and health— the next question is just as critical: how best to measure them? What are good datasets that reflect what we want to know? How can we assure ongoing improvements in the way we conceptualize and generate data? After all, yesterday's ideas about a healthy diet may not be the same as tomorrow's.

Last but not least, once there is some agreement on what to measure, and how to measure it, the mere existence of the measures is not likely to alter behavior. As in the case of GDP, the new measures need to inform and shape policy—laws, regulations, incentive structures, cost evaluations, taxes. In a world that pushes junk food, cars, and a sedentary life on stuffy couches as a profitable way of life, no awareness of better health can alone move us from a path that has long been rewarded and is thus deeply ingrained, no matter how debilitating.

At this point in history, the basic choice among national performance indicators seems to come down to this: either priceless values are entirely ignored in economic accounting, and thus will continue to be depleted, trashed, and disregarded. Or we attempt to turn even things like nature or happiness into commodities. The latter threatens to turn the world on its head: rather than the economy being a subset of the overall ecosystem—both dependent upon and subservient to it—it becomes its master. Nature and most forms of social life, once turned into a subordinate status to a profit-driven economy, all potentially find themselves being up for sale. Neither path alone promises a sustainable way forward.

Are there alternatives? Yes, but. . . . Alternatives to commodification and financialization of nature and society exist, such as the ecological footprint metrics or indicators for happiness. How to turn such metrics into economic indicators that will actually be used to make and enforce policies nationally and internationally is much less clear. At a minimum, the collective focus would have to move away from the narrow goal of financial gain.

Obviously, it is easier to measure what comes with a price determined by the market. Metrics that attempt to get a handle on the strains we put on our ecosystem, or that attempt to capture life satisfaction, do not come with a price. They are not traded on the stock market. They are not commodities that could be bought and sold. Yet both examples—footprint and happiness—provide essential information for any responsible economy. The first tells us whether we are living beyond our means. The second tells us whether our labors are paying off: does the economy actually improve our welfare? Clearly, without such vital gauges, we may well continue to speed up our journey, yet fail to notice that we are heading toward the cliff.

The point of this exploration is not to determine whether quantitative or qualitative measures are better. It is to demonstrate that both provide valuable information. And both are highly subjective: in all cases we first have to determine *what* exactly to measure (and thereby what to ignore), and then figure out *how* to measure it. Whether we are aware of it or not, to borrow from the old master again, measures are "affected by implicit or explicit value judgments."[43]

So, in chambers of commerce, business schools, civic clubs, city halls, library panels, state houses, classrooms, the halls of Congress, and in international forums, let the necessary conversations begin.

ONE MORE TIME: SIMON KUZNETS

> You can never get enough of what you
> don't need to make you happy.
> —*Eric Hoffer*

Like many profound thinkers of the "good life," from Aristotle to Confucius to Bentham to Marx, Simon Kuznets was more precise, and more specific, about the theoretical conditions necessary, than about the practical steps required to get there. Though he explicitly wanted a society that would follow a "more enlightened philosophy," what exactly he meant by that can only be guessed from his theoretical principles.

As an economic historian, it was encouraging to muse on the old master's wisdom for a thought experiment. A lecture note I found in his personal papers had this to say: "It is not only quantitative data . . . that the economist needs but also qualitative information; for obviously there are important facets in economic life that have not been and perhaps never will be subject to quantitative measurement." Wise and encouraging words, followed by, "For this reason a great cognizance of the possible contributions of historians to the economic study seems to me an indispensable step towards a sounder development of such study."[44]

In combination with his published work, there is profound importance in these statements. They represent an acknowledgment that the pursuit of a "more enlightened philosophy," as much as it will rely on verifiable quantitative data, can never be reduced to it. On the contrary, "important facets" can be captured only through careful study and analysis of historical experiences, and evaluation and constant reevaluation of qualitative standards.

And to what end? Kuznets' writing, both published and unpublished, reveals that he spent more time thinking, and came to much clearer conclusions than most economists today, about the ultimate goal of his efforts—and by extension the goal of an economy. It was to expand human welfare. Anything else had to be subservient. Only to the extent to which data was verifiable did Kuznets deem the information valuable. His interest piqued when he could establish a causal connection between things like volume of output or growth on the one hand, and welfare on the other. Various claims and theories about welfare unsubstantiated by data irritated him.

Both science and economics, at their best, are good at asking *how* something works. They are bad at asking *why* something works a certain way, much less how or why it should work a certain way. Kuznets understood this. When it came to a national economy, he insisted, "distinctions must be kept in mind between quantity and quality of growth, between its costs and return, and between the short and the long run." What ultimately mattered were quality, context, and purpose.

Something as multilayered as a national economy, Kuznets realized, was almost infinitely complex. The best one could do was to figure out approximations of the total by generating data that most closely correlated with the ultimate purpose of economic accounting: human welfare. After years of study, Kuznets tentatively concluded that the best available path, one for which actual data could be obtained, was to study broad flows of identifiable income. Compiling data on consumption, business spending, income, and government transfers, Kuznets believed that one could get a reasonably good sense of the general level of national economic activity. What he called "national income accounts" could, he believed, generate much of the needed data to tackle the evaluation of welfare.

For Kuznets, the purpose of such accounts was by no means only to serve as a reflection of what was happening in the larger economy. By attempting to provide a representation, national accounts are as much a product as they become, in turn, a producer of economic reality. Detailed knowledge of investments and consumption by date, sector, and region was essential to inform economic decisions intended to serve the common good.

How could the greatest proportion of economic potential be recruited into service to humanity? There was no ready-made answer: "individual judgments differ and a social consensus must be sought on what is needed and desirable." Attaining this social consensus, Kuznets knew, would never be easy. Yet it was vital for a democratic society, and should thus be of "continuous concern."

But this raised another, equally complicated question. Throughout his entire work on national income, Kuznets's focus remained on the question as to what exactly provided a "service" to human welfare. Not all goods provide a good. Not all services provide a service. Mere growth of output, however accurately tabulated, would therefore never be sufficient. As he emphatically stated, on the contrary, "Objectives should be explicit: goals for 'more' growth should specify more growth of what and for what."

It was this very question of purpose that made him a member of a very small minority among economists. To him, post–World War II accountants and economists confused means and ends, and never addressed the most important question: "growth for what?" It was also the primary reason why he dropped research into national accounting altogether.

Not surprisingly, as an economist Kuznets thought about "human welfare" in terms of goods and services. To be more precise, he thought about it in terms of both the components and preconditions of goods and services that could be measured. Investment, for instance, was important to him as a necessary precursor to production and consumption that, in turn, could lead to increased human welfare. But what components of investment or production, exactly, would do so? "It is scarcely helpful to urge that the over-all growth rate be raised," he argued, "without specifying the components of the product that should grow"—without asking, in other words, what are we growing, and for what?[45]

Here we need to revisit and elaborate on a key feature of Kuznets's critique of the system of national accounts as defined after the war. In economic terminology, it is the difference between "intermediate" and "final." In common English, it's the difference between "means" and "ends."

If someone wants to sell tables, she or he needs tools and wood to produce them. The table is the final good. Tools and wood are merely intermediate goods, a means to an end. This distinction gets complicated quickly. The saw used in order to produce the table is intermediate. The saw bought by itself is final. What about the lock purchased to secure the workshop from uninvited intruders? Not so clear.

It gets more complicated once we realize that there is, logically, no discernible point at which something moves from intermediate to final. The table, for instance, could also be seen as a means for me to have dinner with my family. The dinner, in turn, could simply be a means for us to remain productive citizens. And so forth ad infinitum.

The broader our definition of the end or final product—happiness, welfare, even life itself—the more goods and services turn into intermediate products: merely a means to some higher end.

This led Kuznets to a further distinction—between products that actually provide what he called a "net service" to the final consumer, and those that do not. Within his voluminous writings, however, there are but a few places where he attempts to spell out this distinction. The clearest explanation can be found in his 1937 *Studies in Income and Wealth*. It deserves full quotation. Here he advocates national estimates that would

> subtract from the present national income totals all expenses on armament, most of the outlays on advertising, a great many of the expenses involved in financial and speculative activities, and what is perhaps most important, the outlays that have been made necessary in order to overcome difficulties that are, properly speaking, costs implicit in our economic civilization. All the gigantic outlays on our urban civilization, subways, expensive housing, etc., which in our usual estimates we include at the value of the net product they yield on the "market," do not really represent net services to the individuals comprising the nation but are, from their viewpoint, an evil necessary in order to be able to make a living (i.e., they are largely business expenses rather than living expenses).[46]

These are profound distinctions—"the evils necessary in order to be able to make a living." Today "the evils necessary" make up an ever greater proportion of the Gross Domestic Product—they all count as a good, yet according to Kuznets, they should never have been counted at all. As we have seen, the measure that conquered the era since World War II indiscriminately included almost all goods and services, necessary evil or not, as "final product."

Eleven years after he penned this clarification, at a point in time when he had won many a battle but lost the war, Kuznets concluded that what ends up being counted is essentially a result of what one judges to be the "end-goal of economic activity." It was a debate, he understood, that "cuts right through the philosophical and methodological roots of economic study."[47] The results were a reflection of subjective value judgments, irrespective whether they were driven by ideology, convenience, or pragmatism.

What, Kuznets inquired, was the ultimate purpose of economic activity? The question boiled down to this: if it doesn't make our lives better, what good is it?

His concept of "net service" was an attempt to clarify the nebulous distinction between intermediate and final goods. As long as something provided a verifiable good to the consumer, it should be counted, even if it might still be seen as a means to some larger end. Consequently, Kuznets argued that we should subtract all those market transactions that merely represent "necessary evils"—things we only have to do in order to be able to participate in the market system in the first place. While he used the example of subways and expensive housing, we could today add many more examples, from cars to professional clothing to computers.

Easy to overlook, the predominant use of such items is to meet necessary requirements to participate in the marketplace. Taken together, it is questionable whether, say, the car bought primarily to commute to work some twenty miles away or drive to the shopping center some ten miles away provides a "net service." Even if we were to assume the car is occasionally used for enjoyable purposes, its main function remains being a simple means to an end. It should also be noted that it is a drain on our income, time, and resources, which otherwise could be used on more obvious net services. It may even endanger our lives—directly through accidents, indirectly through pollution and global warming. What, then, is a car's "net service?"

One thing was clear to Kuznets: the way national accountants in the U.S. and Britain had resolved the issue was of no use. He found little in their rationalizations that proved helpful in determining which observable flows represented net service, and which represented costs. His ultimate verdict of the accounts as they existed (and would continue to exist around the world) was witheringly dismissive: "the system of accounts was constructed to fit the solution." The Keynesian solution, of course, had been to crank up income, and thus purchasing power. The more was counted as net service rather than cost, the higher the income. It was a system, according to Kuznets, that allows one to "write in it anything one wishes."[48]

Obviously, Kuznets did not reject the usefulness of good data on production "from a business point of view." For specific purposes, they might well be essential. During the crisis of mobilization and war he had helped create them. Yet he explicitly disputed that "output" was a useful social measure. It was certainly inadequate to capture public welfare. Despite what many economists believed, GDP was not "a sound measure of the utility of goods and services," but rather an indiscriminate concoction of costs and goods and ills that provided bad incentives and led to unreliable results.[49]

The larger question remained unresolved: who or what might define and measure public welfare? A particularly difficult question, for no amount of economic data, no matter how good, could ever provide a full answer.

Kuznets was a firm believer in economic growth. To him, it was a necessary prerequisite for human welfare: employment, freedom, and, as he later argued (incorrectly, as it turned out), increasing levels of equality. We can speculate what he might have said in light of climate change, species extinction, depletion of resources, and escalating inequality. Given his emphasis on human welfare, it seems doubtful that he would have upheld his focus on growth. But we cannot know.

What we do know is what he said about the process of defining what growth we want, and why. "If economic growth is to be more deliberately geared to what is wanted," he argued, "effort must be exerted to formulate a consensus."[50] The answer he gave in his 1948 piece, his last lengthy analysis of national accounting, was that "the final goal of economic activity is provision of goods to consumers."[51] Certainly, he stated, "the total we are seeking [in national accounts] is that of *product*—of the end-result of activity—not of the volume of *activity* itself."[52]

What Kuznets deemed essential above all, namely that there would be an ongoing public discussion about the proper goals of an economy, and that only a clear articulation of such goals could lead to meaningful accounting categories, disappeared behind the curtain of ever more obscure models and calculations.

To his great dismay, GDP—a measure of the volume of activity—won the day. And it cast the veil of pseudo-objectivity over a range of highly subjective decisions, in the process becoming "one of the most used, and misused, sources of economic information."[53]

CLEARING A PATH

Having tackled some major conceptual cobwebs, and with a clear Kutznetsian roadmap, let's move on to experiment with a possible path forward.[54]

Three of humanity's core challenges today are inequality, growth, and sustainability. Growth of GDP remains the most important overarching goal, but one that we now understand also propels inequality and undermines any hope for sustainability. Creative ideas like a global wealth tax might address inequality, but have no discernible impact on sustainability.[55] Carbon taxes may begin to address some of the worst threats to sustainability, but have little impact on inequality.

Historically, the GDP regime has laid down the tracks for those three challenges to hurdle toward a head-on collision. Indeed, within the logic of the GDP regime, there is no way to prevent the collision. As long as indiscriminate growth of output remains the lifeblood, inequality will worsen, and sustainability will remain little more than a slogan, with potentially tragic consequences for future generations.

GDP is not just a measure of the economy. It defines the economy.[56] And the one place in which the key challenges of growth, inequality, and sustainability coalesce is precisely in the way we define the economy (and then, in turn, measure what was defined). The central challenge is thus to generate a different concept of the economy.

As long as fossil fuel consumption, for instance, is rewarded as profitable because it allows higher output of goods and services, political intervention may succeed in slowing down the train, but never reach sustainability. As long as indiscriminate output is rewarded in an environment in which fundamental human needs (such as safety, security, happiness) remain unaddressed, or even systematically excluded, inequality is an inevitable outcome.

By failing to address any of the three challenges—inequality, growth, and sustainability—the logic of GDP, once the presumed harbinger of prosperity for all, today translates into an international race to the bottom. Primarily valued by their direct contribution to GDP growth, people and nature are increasingly reduced to commodities, in danger of being used up, and, if necessary, discarded. No one seems responsible because the whole process follows what is perceived to be a systemic imperative: growth of GDP.

Our measure of success thus provides the key for a more sustainable and humane future. The history of how GDP came to rule the world suggests a path forward that is, at least theoretically, simple. The challenge is to measure what we want, and use that measure not only to replace GDP but also to redefine the economy.

As daunting as such a challenge may seem in today's political environment, it is helpful to keep in mind that GDP was designed as a descriptive measure, well before it turned into global goal for economic activities. Significantly, however, it was initially not a tool created by those in positions of wealth and power, but rather by accountants eager to meet the needs of depression and war.

With the reality of unsustainable growth, rampant inequality, and climate change, today's world faces challenges of equal proportions.

Local and regional attempts suggest that it might become possible to replace the national and international accounting regime with one that accounts for "true costs" of economic activity, including things like resource depletion, pollution, and social decay (along the lines of GPI). It would require a herculean regulatory task: not just a fundamental revision of the six-hundred-page UN System of National Accounts and all its national versions, but also implementation of an entirely different structure of incentives and regulations, reconstituted political and legal enforcement agencies—national and international—as well as the creation of improved business models. The way "success" is defined and measured would fundamentally have to change. Sustainability, social equity, and democratic accountability would have to be put on equal footing with profit as essential requirements—a goalpost with four equal sides rather than a flat bottom line.

Within globally interconnected economies, changing the rules by which the game is played can only happen on an international level. It is not likely undertaken by world leaders lacking confidence.[57] Yet one could speculate about the outcome of several international leaders of either the caliber or political understanding of a Nelson Mandela, Robert Kennedy, Mohamed Nasheed, Aung San Suu Kyi, or Elizabeth Warren, coming together to tackle this central challenge. At a minimum, such leaders could take critical first steps toward better models and metrics in such a top-down fashion.

One could also imagine a major climate crisis exacerbating an already-existing global economic crisis, threatening the livelihoods of tens or hundreds of millions. How much would it take before people succeed in forming large social movements and electable political parties demanding a radical course correction toward sustainability of life?

Millions of seeds for this to happen have already been planted. People everywhere are making efforts to jump off the train of stupid growth and mindless consumerism, devising more meaningful goals in the process. It's happening in every major city bloc, among small businesses and, yes, even in the corridors of power. What it still lacks is a common language, organization and a unifying voice. Replacing the GDP regime with a democratically articulated smart metric that promotes general welfare could provide a unifying goal.

One could also envision a scenario in which enlightened bureaucrats and academic elites pull together to fashion new performance measures from the inside. This could take the form of incremental changes geared toward something like true cost accounting. Or a complete overhaul of the logic of GDP growth. How, in the current political climate, such efforts could go much beyond the French Commission on the Measurement of Economic Performance and Social Progress is more difficult to imagine.

In the end, good analysis, even a great plan, is not enough. Neither will it suffice to create a potentially endless variety of new and illuminating measures, from literacy to women's empowerment to resource use, if we don't change the very definition of a modern economy. Insights need to be translated into policymaking, nationally and internationally.

+++

You never change things by fighting the existing reality.
To change something, build a new model that makes
the existing model obsolete.
—*Buckminster Fuller*

There is no shortage of talented people who have attempted to tackle the big issues of our collective predicament, trying to figure out underlying causes, suggesting solutions. Some prominent examples are useful to review, particularly in light of what they say about goals and direction of our collective activities.

Given the tendency of capitalism to widen the gap between the owners of capital and everyone else, Thomas Piketty in *Capital* suggests a straightforward if not difficult-to-implement solution to growing inequality: a tax on wealth and excessive income. Wealth, according to Piketty, needs to be taxed at 15 percent, worldwide and every year. Incomes over $500,000 should be taxed at 80 percent. The combined effect would be twofold: it would stop rising inequality, and it would generate vital revenue for a variety of much needed programs, from education to infrastructure build-up to eradication of poverty. Piketty does not question content and direction of economic growth, however. On the contrary, part of his critique of inequality is that it is bad for growth. "Inequality is okay up to a certain point," he clarified in an interview, "as long as it is in the common interest, as long as it promotes growth, innovation and entrepreneurship."[58]

A new economic Marshall Plan would provide millions of jobs and provide the income needed to boost economic activity, according to Hedrick Smith, author of *Who Stole the American Dream*. It should be followed up by a fairer tax system, less military spending, and the safeguarding of things like home ownership, Social Security, and healthcare for everyone. Smith suggests a public-private partnership to rebuild infrastructure like bridges, sewer systems, high-speed Internet access. Combined, such measures would not just create a fairer and more stable economy; they would also allow citizens to reclaim democracy and the American dream.[59]

Nobel laureate Joseph Stiglitz starts with the observation that modern markets don't work—they are not efficient, not stable, not fair. Huge needs, from poverty to environmental destruction, are unmet. And, despite growth in GDP, standards of living are deteriorating for everyone but the richest few. The political system is equally broken, often beholden to "moneyed interests." Stiglitz calls the result a state of "moral deprivation." What is at stake, he argues, is not just prosperity, but the very foundation of democracy: a belief in opportunities for everyone, a system of justice, and a common purpose. By trying to reintroduce a sense of morality into capitalism, Stiglitz believes that government and markets and corporations can be remodeled to serve the public good. Unlike Piketty or Smith, he calls for an "improved-upon" GDP because we've been in "hot pursuit of the wrong goals." Nevertheless, Stiglitz also remains a growth proponent. In his view, it provides "the resources with which to tackle some of society's most intractable problems."[60]

With less faith in top-down solutions, and a clear focus on grassroots efforts already underway, political economist Gar Alperovitz lists a wide range of solutions, from worker-owned enterprises to co-ops, social enterprises, and government-owned businesses that not only can be further developed but might, at some point, succeed in replacing "corporate capitalism." For all intents and purposes, Alperovitz concludes, corporations have rigged economics and effectively own politics. The top 1 percent are the only remaining beneficiaries of how things are done today. Systemic change, he argues, is thus essential. In part, Alperovitz urges us to move away from the "grow or die" imperative that corporations follow, for in areas such as energy, minerals, water, and arable land, growth is no longer possible. He seems less interested in exploring why and how economies follow a very particular kind of growth, or how essential it would be to fashion different indicators for economic activity.[61]

Emphasizing the role of business, Paul Hawken, in his best-selling *The Ecology of Commerce*, advocates for a kind of capitalism where markets are effectively liberated from their destructive tendencies. As currently organized, he argues, what's good for business and the economy is almost always bad for nature, often bad for people, and, by being harmful and wasteful, inherently uneconomical. How to accomplish this liberation? Hawken proposes three key approaches: (1) "entirely eliminate waste from our industrial production"; (2) rapidly transform the economy from one based on fossil fuels to one based on "current sunshine" (such as solar, wind, waves etc.); and (3) create a legal and political system of accountability that "supports and strengthens restorative behavior." For Hawken, this kind of change will not come from traditional, top-down channels. The primary drivers will be reorganized businesses and the self-organized people who run them.[62]

A few thinkers call for a complete redirection of economic activity, away from a focus on markets, growth, and the exploitation of nature. Perhaps the best-known proponent of a radical departure from money-driven economics is David Korten, former Harvard business professor, later government advisor, now political activist and prominent critic of corporate globalization. Today's "global capitalist economy is destructive of both life and the human soul," he argues. Policies to help the poor, regulations to protect some aspects of the environment, or laws to restrict the power of global corporations—none, according to Korten, can successfully address the larger problem: an economy organized "for the benefit of Wall Street bankers and speculators."

Asking what people really want from life, Korten concludes that "major improvements in our health and happiness come not from more money and consumption, but rather from relationships, cultural expression, and spiritual growth." In this, he deliberately stays outside the false dichotomy of capitalism versus socialism—both banked on growth as measured by financial indicators. Putting forth a myriad of proposals, Korten instead proposes a radical shift of focus toward "real-wealth indicators," cultivating "our possibilities rather than our pathologies," by which he essentially means fostering community, sustainability, and equity.[63]

In sum, there is no shortage of valuable ideas. None of them fall into the old and tired categories of liberal versus conservative. By the same token, few address the triple challenges of growth, inequality, and sustainability, or call for a fundamental redefinition of economic activity. How realistic any of the suggestions put forth are today, or perhaps tomorrow, is impossible to know. Yet dismissing the ideas because we do not yet know how to translate them into practical policies seems ill advised, and bad politics at that. Confining ourselves to today's pragmatically truncated range of sanctioned mainstream political debates is unlikely to provide direction, much less answers. If nothing else, they are ruefully inadequate to the task.

The experiment of the next chapter takes a different approach. Rather than add another version of a specific list of things to do, it outlines clearer goals and envisions a different kind of economy—one that squarely addresses the triple challenges of sustainability, equity, and growth. Learning from the history of GDP, borrowing from many creative thinkers, it creates a basic map with several routes. As it requires holding political cynicism at bay, I invite the reader into a space where thinking can take place "as if" more is possible.

When considering how "realistic" certain suggestions are, it might be worth remembering that today only one thing seems demonstrably unrealistic: a continuation on the path of indiscriminate GDP growth.

Chapter 11

LOOKING FORWARD

We live in capitalism. Its power seems inescapable. So
did the divine right of kings. Any human power can be
resisted and changed by human beings.
—*Ursula K. Le Guin*

The ideals of freedom and democracy surely have one thing in common: impermanence. To advocate a free and democratic society means to accept the idea that there are no permanent answers, no final solutions. New experiences and fresh contexts will provide new insights and alternative perspectives. The ability of people to govern themselves is, by necessity, a work in progress. Regimenting answers for others and future generations violates this logic.

This raises important questions not only about the structures people build but also about the ideologies they fashion in order to justify and rationalize those structures, often in their attempts to make them permanent. Build a MacMansion in some disconnected suburb and raise a family in it, and the children will likely associate home with something other than vibrant interconnected communities. Have children experience all their lives that milk comes in plastic gallon jugs placed in refrigerator stalls at the grocery store, and it's unlikely that they will associate this nurturing white liquid with living animals and a complex natural environment. The common problem is this: common experiences are routinely defended as common sense, as something that should continue because it's commonly seen as normal and right. If it's all you've known, why not live a twenty-minute car ride away from everything and get your milk from plastic jugs?

As a people, it seems, we rather like the idea that things make sense, that there are good reasons for why things are the way they are. Even if we disagree with a particular thing, we tend to assume that it makes sense for someone, that there are some clearly defined interests behind it—government, rich people, the working class, white folks, consumers. And, presumably, that this group has a clear idea how best to pursue that interest.

But what a claim it is. The idea that things generally makes sense—and that people with clearly defined interests, cognizant of how best to pursue them, are behind them—does not stack up well to historical evidence. No doubt, there are the crass examples in which people, and particularly people in power, have effectively tried to push their interests by pushing their own kind—rich people only inviting other rich people to the country club; white people only hiring other white people; men excluding women from consideration. There is also no doubt that such conduct has significantly shaped our social environment. Rarely for the better.

What's lost in such group and identity thinking, however, is a recognition of greater significance. More often than not, things don't make sense. More often than not, people have only the faintest grasp on what their interests might be, and usually have little idea how best to pursue them. Indeed, what shapes people's thinking and conduct is routinely not deliberate action, but rather things like habit, tradition, and fear—following what has been put in place before we were born; following custom without knowing where it originated, or why. And such deeply internalized behavior leads people to accept certain aspects of life as a given—thinking, to return to our previous example, that home is experienced in oversized houses in suburbs and milk comes from the grocery store; thinking that rich people probably deserve to be rich, and GDP is a good measure of success. Even, it is important to note, if these secular versions of faith make little sense, much less do a good job of promoting self-interest.

Commuting drove our parents crazy, sunk huge amounts of resources into cars and gasoline, stole time from family activities, polluted our environment; the milk is laden with antibiotics and growth hormones, comes from cows who are kept in ghastly conditions, and the milk jugs take thousands of years to decompose, foul up our waters and coastlines, not to mention waste precious resources that future generations will need for pharmaceuticals and computer parts. Whose best interests does this serve?

We need an open and deliberate conversation about the direction of economic activity. It is a conversation that does not require agreement on the age-old question of whether people like to be consulted on the key decisions of their lives. Seventy years under the GDP regime should settle the issue: we no longer have the option of leaving it up to elites or to bureaucrats and blind metrics.

Today's collective challenge is how to make intelligent and equitable use of what we have. Broadly speaking, the new objective needs to be quality, not quantity; development rather than expansion and growth; conservation rather than extraction and depletion; learning from nature, rather than conquering and crushing it.[1] In short: the articulation of a meaningful goal for economic activity. Quality of life, rather than volume of output. And this challenge requires broad and ongoing democratic input.

As the tensions between reality and possibility pull toward the irreconcilable, more and more people begin to return their focus to values that sustain healthy lives and well-being. Evolutionary biologists discovered it first, now business consultants are catching on: cooperation is generally more productive than competition, sharing is more efficient and more life-enhancing than the endless pursuit of self-interest.[2]

The practical use of history illuminates what can happen when people focus on what makes them thrive. It would be difficult to imagine a sound objection to the conclusion that human beings, when organized around the pressing purpose of surmounting oppressive obstacles, can initiate momentous change.[3]

The outcome is never exactly what initiators had in mind—but sometimes it comes close.

Tomorrow may show developments to be realistic that just yesterday seemed utterly fantastical. What happens next depends in large part on how prepared current societies are. It took American revolutionaries over twenty years to compromise on a set of comprehensive rules to govern their future. But they held fast. Civil rights activists are still struggling with an obstreperous culture of racial privilege, but that hardly takes away from their accomplishments. For global citizens witnessing the inevitable end of GDP growth, it is thus not a fortune cookie quote, but an ethical imperative: one has to reach for the impossible in order to reach the possible.

Our collective collision course with the future is not a problem we can simply blame on others, or relegate to some future resolution. As consumers, producers, parents, or children, we rightly suspect that responsibility also lies within us, now.

I am writing this on a laptop, inside a plane, returning home from a conference in Berlin on sustainability. That, too, is a kind of absurdity. After flying some twelve thousand miles to discuss options for the future with friends and colleagues, I will have to work hard on getting my carbon footprint anywhere near sustainable levels.

The history behind the GDP regime suggests that many of the problems discussed have a common origin: the failure to articulate good goals for economic activities—objectives that go beyond mere "output" and begin to address future prosperity, real development of capabilities, and, above all, sustainability.

It may well be the central contradiction of our time: on the one hand, the broad realization of the limits and dangers of GDP growth; on the other a politics that remains hostage to the imperatives of GDP growth.[4]

Operating inside such cultures, the problem does not lie with people who are somehow deficient or bad, nor is it simply caused by incomplete or misguided ideas. The primary problem originates within the very structure that continuously generates, promotes, and rewards bad behavior and bad ideas. Like an operating system in a computer, the logic of GDP remains largely invisible, but it is in charge of how the system works. There is no stepping outside of the logic within existing economic structures. Change will come only by changing the logic, by building a stronger and more intelligently designed foundation. But therein also lies great promise.

The previous chapter explored the fact that, in and out of government, more and more concerned observers have begun to explore alternative options, a possible "bridge at the edge of the world" connecting an "economy for the common good" with the imperatives of "sustainability" brought to life either through smart "cradle to cradle" design or through a realization that "enough is enough," all helping us create "prosperity without growth." They have much to offer.[5]

Rather than listen to mainstream debates that are stuck in a crippled sense of possibility, why not imagine how liberating it would be to have a conversation about future prospects without tired references to such labels as liberal or conservative, capitalist or socialist, or without asking yet again why so many ideas are presumably "unrealistic" or how there are "no viable alternatives." No doubt, there is comfort in such platitudes, as they can effectively rationalize inaction and lack of deep thought.

Surely it is time to retire the old chestnuts. So-called conservatives promote economic policies that don't "conserve" but relentlessly change the social fabric of our communities. Liberals support big government, regulations, and, in some cases, an overbearing security state. Economists speak of "rational actors" operating in a "free market"—although neither are more than figments of imagination for those of us in search of simple answers. Contrary to mainstream economic doctrine, modern governments, not private markets, by now generate almost half of GDP; the public sector is responsible for many of the key innovations of the past century; and capitalism's most recent "success story" happens in "socialist" China. Economic growth has marched on unabated, yet the problems are growing faster than the solutions. There is no way to capture such realities with yesteryear's abstractions or with thinking confined to narrow disciplines.

Above all, prevailing ideologies and assumptions are grounded in the struggles of past centuries, struggles that primarily centered on wealth creation. The core premise, despite all other disagreements from right to left, was that a rising tide lifts all boats.

Today's world faces a very different set of problems. Despite distressingly persistent levels of poverty, there is actually more than enough material goods to go around. But the rising tide has become an increasingly toxic sludge. A fairer distribution of the fruits of our collective labor, though undoubtedly a good and necessary start, does not address the deeper problems.

During its very first national political campaign in 1983, the German Green Party put forth the slogan "Not right, not left, but forward," a reaction against a style of politics in which parties from right to left had signed up for prosperity based on growth, gambling the future while ignoring mounting evidence of distress.

Raising the possibility of a fundamentally different path forward that does not depend on GDP growth, of course, invites the ridicule of those who deem themselves the guardians of responsibility—economists who raise the specter of opportunity costs and the loss of utility maximization, and, of course, worst of all, the end of their central claim to legitimacy: growth; parents and educators who worry about job opportunities and earning potentials; leftists who insist on their tired claim that growth is the only answer to poverty.

A fundamental course correction away from our central focus on GDP growth is often associated with pain, suffering, and loss. But intelligent design and the imperative of sustainability by no means necessarily translate into less. Giving up on our excessive consumption habits may well provide us with a net gain. No longer prisoners of frazzled lives, endless work, constantly changing fashions, lousy quality, planned obsolescence, and growing debt, we could even begin to engage in the "joyful discovery of our own sovereignty."[6]

Systems engineers, for instance, understand that the quality of a system can be properly evaluated only by how well it serves its objective. Until the goal is clearly defined, there is no point designing measures (unless one wants the measure to fill in for the missing goal).[7]

When it comes to goals, history provides a rich tapestry to learn from. Building from the bottom up, the foundation—both ethically and practically—for any viable future is justice, the broad aspiration to treat people fairly. Only then, as international economists Philip Smith and Manfred Max-Neef put it, can people "live in dignity, without fear and with adequate means for satisfying the universal needs of humankind." In practical reality, this may take many different forms, will never be fully accomplished, and thus will always remain, at least in part, aspiration. And yet, two central preconditions for justice stand out in our context: (1) the more that economic and financial power is concentrated in the hands of the few, the less justice there can be; (2) without a comprehensive concept of sustainability that includes a deep understanding of the interdependence of humans and nature—justice can never be more than a hollow dream.[8]

What then, in a smarter world, might become the core objective of an economy? To provide secure livelihoods? To nourish and protect? To allow for the enjoyment of long and rich lives? To foster social and cultural wealth? The answers are not yet clear, except that they will vary over time, and differ from place to place. Unless this broad public conversation emerges, however, the answers will be determined by large corporations and governments that pursue the global logic of profit and growth. The answers, in short, will serve neither justice nor democracy, nor can they meet the requirements of sustainability.

The record is quite clear: the democratic voices of people are far less chaotic and dangerous than the logic of the GDP regime. People generally agree on many basic criteria routinely trampled by GDP growth. Who, for instance, would deliberately advocate an economy that plunders the planet and robs future generations?

Whatever an eventual compromise grounded in the broad principles of justice and sustainability may entail: the result will at least be intentional, rather than the result of a narrow and corrupted market. Perfect? No. But guided by human goals rather than accounting logic. Thus pointing in the right direction. And, of course, always improvable.

Our personal lives offer insights. People tend to feel well when they live the attributes of healthy relationships and cooperation: kindness, generosity, respect, honesty, care. When it comes to our economy, on the other hand, people are told to feed on longings for gain and competition: greed, selfishness, envy, and concern only for exchange value and the short term. As the logic of the economy seeps into more and more aspects of our lives, both individuals and communities increasingly suffer from being pulled into two mutually exclusive directions—pursuing self-interest at the expense of the broader good, the personal at the expense of the social, the private at the expense of the communal, the now at the expense of tomorrow. In the aggregate: our lives at the expense of our children (and other species).

But the train of indiscriminate GDP growth keeps chugging along, only occasionally slowed by the rare effective mandate or regulation.

Knowledge is not the problem. Millions are working on potential solutions. They allow us to outline with a remarkable degree of "potential realism" what a society might look like that does not follow GDP growth targets. A society that, instead, follows the criteria set forth by Kuznets—built around a focus on the welfare of people, grounded in new insights about sustainability, justice, neuroscience, and human happiness.

In the end, what matters is whether "an economy supports or destroys healthy communities," not whether it can be described as capitalist or socialist, left or right, growing or shrinking.[9]

The goal is a much broader and creative concept of sustainability, one that shows how our well-being depends not only on a healthy ecosystem, but also on justice, vibrant communities, stable cultures, political openness, and safety. As the key to human survival, sustainability is "a concept which needs to be nourished from every discipline, every culture and every tradition."[10] Including a redesigned economy.

What then might it look like to make use of available knowledge, rather than hunker down in self-prescribed dogma or denial?[11]

A DARING VISION

The Ethics of Basic Security and Fairness
The past reveals to the present what the present is
capable of seeing
—*R. H. Tawney*

The great promise of industrialization and capitalism was that it would conquer scarcity, that it would provide people around the world with various cultural versions of a chicken in every pot. Growth in wealth would translate into general prosperity.

In that respect, capitalism has succeeded, and failed, spectacularly. No system in history comes close to the amount of wealth and freedom created. No other system can match its capacity for destruction.

From a basic quality of life perspective, capitalism's biggest failure lies in its structural inability to provide material and social security to its subjects. One out of two children continues to live in poverty worldwide—one out of four in the richest country on earth. Job and income insecurity are endemic.

But what if we took capitalism's major advances, and left behind its crippling shortcomings; expanded its freedom and creativity by putting it on a foundation of security, not fear? [12]

Due in large part to capitalist growth, providing basic dignity for each woman, man, and child is eminently possible.[13] But dignity requires a certain level of security and well-being, including sufficient nourishment, shelter, education, healthcare, political freedom, and a right to work.

Not having to worry about the essentials of one's existence, of course, also provides the necessary foundation for community, democracy, art, culture, or simply one's ability to learn, develop, and grow. Dependent people cannot be free, much less members of a flourishing civil society. Dignity is a necessary precondition for freedom. Providing basic security and fairness for everyone, however, would not only offer dignity, but it would also unleash unprecedented levels of creativity, innovation, and civic participation.[14]

For a time, GDP growth made inequality tolerable—a growing pie, it was assumed, would provide bigger pieces for everyone. Having by now reached the limits of growth, inequality is becoming intolerable.[15]

The verdict is in: less inequality is a win-win proposition—more security, more justice, and better motivation all around. Bringing down historically high levels of inequality can thus improve living conditions without "economic growth."[16]

The way out of this our collective predicament is a question of intelligent political design. Take an idea such as the basic income guarantee. Seen from the perspective of today's predominant values of competition, self-interest, and endless self-promotion, it is an idea that, indeed, seems far out. Yet the idea is steadily gaining ground among people from the political right to left. It is one of those rare ideas that could represent a game changer, for it could fundamentally alter what many have come to accept as the laws of politics and economics. It is also an idea that has the benefit of being practical. In brief, here is what it might entail: Each citizen could have a right to a "basic dignity income" (in American society, say $15,000 for each adult, and $4,000 for each child in the household).[17]

A basic income would also address the shortcomings of a narrow focus on inequality. Even if income and wealth were distributed far more equally, it would not, in itself, address the indiscriminate nature of economic growth, the stultifying narrowness of dominant performance measures, or the relentless reduction of human beings to producers and consumers. Above all, it would not address basic security. However critical in its own right, reducing inequality does not provide us with better goals for economic activity. It does not adequately address questions of happiness or sustainability, of development that has a future.[18]

A basic income guarantee would, however, fundamentally alter the logic of the GDP regime, and thus human aspirations. This would likely yield multiple benefits. It could provide the security necessary for people to become empowered citizens, free to speak their mind, to explore, and to participate in a democratic commons. It could fundamentally alter the dependent relationships between government, business, and citizens.[19]

Many government agencies and programs (such as welfare and unemployment benefits), for instance, would no longer be needed. Businesses could no longer bank on despair among the needy to get away with poverty wages, lack of benefits, or dangerous working conditions. But the rewards would be far greater. Research increasingly shows that poverty amidst plenty, as much as insecurity and injustice, wreak havoc on the health of our communities. They breed alienation and violence; they require us to focus on ourselves rather than the common good; they stifle creativity; and, by forcing us to worry about the here and now, they leave little room for considerations about a sustainable future.[20]

The data is solid and makes sense: the more equitable, prosperous and free a society, the more creativity and social mobility can be detected. As an added bonus, equality and stability also reduce violence and end population growth. It is almost too obvious to require emphasis: sustainability is impossible within a culture focused on the bottom line, one that breeds poverty amidst plenty, rampant inequality, and existential insecurity.

The challenge is to allow motivation to come from the place where it is most likely to generate productive results: ourselves; our own intrinsic desire to contribute something positive, to enhance the common good. To be sure, fear and competition can also serve as effective motivators. But since such motivation is external, the results tend to be narrow, exclusive, and unreliable.

Imagine the difference between trying to be good in something because it feels really good to be good, or just trying to be better than someone else, in large part because your existence depends on it. Inevitably, the latter motivation thrives on the defeat, exclusion, and low performance of others. Psychologist Tim Kasser has called this "the high price of materialism." Today's dominant performance measures consistently squash intrinsic motivation, the kind that leads to more creativity and more productivity.[21]

Once a basic income guarantee exists for everyone, and the central goal of the economy is built around smart metrics based on sustainability and human dignity (rather than volume and profit), the dynamics of supply and demand will likely play out differently than in the past: essential work (childcare, farming, IT, and so forth) would likely be valued more highly, unessential work (entertainment, financial speculation, lobbying) would become less lucrative, done by people willing to settle for lower wages and increased hours. It might even be the beginning of a market we could recognize as "free."

It is entirely up to human communities to determine what goals and performance measures are in place. How the market works depends on the regulations and incentives we establish. As we have explored, people tend to follow what they measure. If contribution to sustainability were our performance measure (rather than, as today, contribution to indiscriminate output), then a functioning market would automatically begin to prioritize contributions that add most to our new performance measure. The new glamour would be teachers and sustainable farmers and battery power researchers and systems engineers; insurance collectors or ad agents peddling fast food would likely receive the social pity of today's garbage collectors.

As a democratically organized people, we could for instance prevent any organization, political or economic, from growing beyond effective transparency and public controls. No more "Too big to fail." All entities, especially corporations, could once again be chartered, and allowed to operate, only with clearly articulated goals of how to serve the community.[22] Once they begin to violate their provisions, their charters could be revoked by democratically elected regulators. All organizations might undergo periodic performance evaluations, and be closed down by democratically legitimized oversight committees when they stop serving their mission of contributing to sustain-ability, equity, and happiness. This is not a new idea: it largely describes the reality of the first chartered corporations in America.[23]

History also shows that democratic oversight in itself is no guarantee against corruption or patronage. But in the context of existential security and reduced inequality, transparent and democratically legitimized deliberations constitute a decisive leap forward compared to decisions made on golf courses or in luxuriously appointed boardrooms where only one thing matters: how to im-prove the bottom line as defined by GDP—growing output rather than quality.

Current political reality guarantees the unconditional existence of corpo-rations. What if instead one would guarantee the safe and sound existence of all fellow citizens? Rather than making survival of people conditional on their contributions to GDP growth, why not make survival of corporations and gov-ernmental agencies conditional on their contributions to sustainability and equity, or simply the common good?

It is, above all, a question of political will.

"Equal Opportunities" that Deserve the Name

The paradox of our time in history is that we have
taller buildings but shorter tempers, wider freeways,
but narrower viewpoints. We spend more, but have
less, we buy more, but enjoy less. We have bigger
houses and smaller families; more conveniences,
but less time. We have more degrees but less sense,
more knowledge, but less judgment, more experts,
yet more problems, more medicine, but less wellness.
We've learned to rush, but not to wait; we build more
computers to hold more information to produce more
copies than ever, but have less communication; we've
become long on quantity, but short on quality.

—Bob Moorehead

Freed from work as a burdensome necessity, citizens could begin to pursue a wide range of activities, releasing creativity unstifled by the threat of poverty.[24] Salaries and product prices could be set by a market of supply and demand within the confines of measures and regulations promoting sustainable development. The labor market, liberated from the distortions of poverty and dependency, could begin to resemble a free market.

Imagine we considered everything over twenty hours of work full-time. Wage labor, after all, is not a particularly satisfying goal of life, nor is its current volume sustainable. A drastically reduced workweek could address a range of challenges, all of which are related: overproduction and overconsumption, depletion of resources and high carbon emissions, stress and low well-being, worn-out communities and rising inequality.[25] As already the case in several modern economies, top incomes could be limited to twenty or forty times the lowest wage within an establishment, compared to the three hundred to five hundred times that represents current practice. Within those parameters—basic income guarantee, minimum hours, and a gliding scale of top wages—wages and working hours are freely negotiated.

The rationale for setting an upper income in the same company would be simple, and would follow the imperatives of logic and ethics developed by conservative economist Willford King (see chapter 2): some people are perhaps ten times more competent or make fifteen times as much of an effort. But is there anything that justifies, as it was in 2014, someone making one thousand times as much as a full-time worker in the same business? If society allows and promotes such disparities, it should at least acknowledge that it has abandoned any claims to equal opportunity, freedom, or ethics.[26]

A central element of human existence is the need to be a contributing part of a larger social whole. Why not give everyone the right to a job, whether full- or part-time, serving the diverse needs of everyone from teenagers earning some money on the side to heads of households and retirees who are not quite ready to stop working altogether. It should be a shame to waste the energy and creativity of the young, or the wisdom and experiences of the old. Unemployment would essentially disappear, and with it most social services and all unemployment benefits.

It would also create a far more stable and viable economic system. By finally decoupling income and employment from economic growth, it would end the fundamental contradiction of modern capitalist economies that created an endless series of boom and bust cycles, accompanied by a massive destruction of capital and the infliction of both needless and pervasive human suffering.

The reason behind such a result is straightforward: we would no longer produce more than we decide is good for us; and we would stop producing more than the planet can sustain. In the past, the health of the economy depended on what consumers were able to purchase based on their incomes (aggregate demand), while profitability depended on paying workers/employees as little as possible and dumping as many external costs onto the public as possible. The result was inevitable: both people and the ecosystem suffered; the next major crisis was always just around the corner. Community, or the commons, was reduced to the marketplace; citizens mattered primarily as consumers; and the public good shriveled to a concoction of private gains.

If we were to take the notion of historical progress seriously, the rights to employment and a basic income should be the foundation for any civilized society. They end welfare, handouts, and special privileges. They also drastically reduce the size of government. Once we give ourselves permission to exit the narrow parameters of debate sanctioned by the institutional icons of the GDP regime—corporations, mainstream parties, the dominant news outlets—people form Occupy Wall Street to the Tea Party may discover a surprising range of commonalities. It is only in the interest of those in power to highlight differences.

At work as in all other aspects of social life: through an intelligently designed national accounting system, innovations toward improved sustainability could be rewarded in the same way as the other sides of a viable goalpost (social equity, democratic accountability, and economic viability).

Take healthcare, for instance. The needs of citizens could be provided by a national one-payer system, one that does not pit our health against the profits of some behemoth insurance company. The key difference, however, would be another principle of sustainability: doctors and healthcare facilities could be reimbursed based on their successes in keeping patients healthy, not based on the number of procedures they perform or the amount of medications they prescribe. It is a question of intelligent design: the measure defines the outcome.

John F. Kennedy was onto a deeper truth with his famous appeal: what makes a social community thrive is not just what people get out of it, but, critically, what they contribute to it. "Ask not what your country can do for you; ask what you can do for your country." It would likely make sense to revisit ideas about requiring every able-bodied citizen to contribute two full-time community enhancement years between the ages of, say, eighteen and thirty. Care is a direct function of belonging and understanding. Such community service could provide a range of essential experiences in different areas of welfare improvement, from elderly care and infrastructure maintenance to sustainability research and green energy projects.

Stressed out and overworked as most of us are, it may be difficult to imagine, but no less real: time and energy that would be freed up if we provided basic social security and a much-reduced workweek for everyone would undoubtedly translate into an explosion of community projects and volunteer efforts, from technology startups to community gardens, education centers, and programs for children and the elderly. For a wide variety of such services, costs would likely plunge.

Finally we would be able to put substance behind our claim that we are committed to providing equal opportunities to all of society's children. Aside from receiving a basic income, each child could have a constitutional right to have access to safe communities, a healthy diet, and a quality education from the ages of two to twenty-two. No longer would we have to accept the disgrace of segregated communities—one made up of trust fund babies with access to the best educational opportunities money can buy, the other comprising low-income children facing violence, decay, and the exclusion from opportunity.

Being serious about opportunity requires being serious about safe communities, equal access, and the independence that can come only from having a proverbial plot of ground to stand on.

Money and Credit for the Common Good

If economic success of a nation is only judged by
income . . . the important goal of wellbeing is missed.

—*Amartya Sen*

In today's economies, there are two dominant metrics: on the macro level, GDP; on the micro level, profit.[27] Both can only be articulated in monetary terms, both have only one goal: growth. As we have seen, most things that really matter to people are left out of how modern economies are organized (things like safety, cooperation, community). Moreover, essential preconditions for a future, such as a viable ecosystem, are consistently violated.

This is not to say that money does not possess some useful qualities. But when money "makes the world go around," as the old lyrics suggest, it has turned into a pathological fetish.[28] The financial bottom line—GDP or margin of profit—can never tell us more about the health of an economy or business than calories consumed can tell us about the health of a community or person.[29]

Modern economies need money to function. Modern societies need money for exchange and development. But money should never be more than a means, and its operations should be democratically regulated to assure they serve their purposes.

Today, well over 90 percent of money and credit is created and controlled not by governments, central banks, or any other body with any democratic legitimacy. Money and credit is created and controlled by private institutions, mostly banks. One result is that financial assets around the world far outpace global output of goods and services as defined by GDP—in 2012, there were some estimated $650 trillion in financial assets in a world with a global GDP of roughly $80 trillion. Another result is that most power is controlled by private business interests, which in turn are run by an ever smaller number of people.

As described in this book, some two-thirds of financial assets, and some 50 percent of global wealth, are controlled by the top 1 percent, while half of the world's population owns just 1 percent of the wealth. This is a rude wakeup call to anyone interested in freedom or democracy or equal opportunity or sustainability, none of which can exist in the presence of such disparities. It is also, quite simply, mindless for people who want a future. In 2040 the epitaph on the age of GDP could read as follows:

> In relentless pursuit of profit, the holders of financial assets had decided to put more and more money into bets rather than investments, "chasing yields but catching bubbles," turning much of the economy into casino capitalism. In the meantime, concentrated financial capital in the form of banks and insurance companies had become not only "too big to fail," but also "too big to jail"— slaves to concentrated wealth, communities and nations effectively abandoned accountability of any kind.[30]

These were the symptoms of an economic system run amok—undemocratic and unsustainable. Blinded by bad measures, people continued to play the game even though it created untenable results.

Historically, money has served multiple functions. Its role as a medium for exchange and a provider of credit needs to be enhanced. Its ability to be stockpiled so some can own a potentially infinite amount of labor and capital, and thus be used for the purposes of speculation and control, needs to be severely restricted in order to enhance the stability of markets and the common good.[31]

Money and credit can be organized to serve civic goals of sustainability and public welfare, not just the bottom line of profit-seeking private banks. Individuals and businesses, for instance, could receive loans from the federal government or private entities for interest rates equivalent to the administrative costs of the loans (including enforcement).[32] Right now, the federal government continuously affords effectively free public money to profit-seeking private banks. In contrast, a democratic government could provide low-cost loans directly to its people, cutting out the waste and fraud in the middle. Such loans could be used for purposes such as small-business startups, research and development projects, purchases of homes, or capital enhancement needs of small businesses or environmentally friendly farms. Delinquent loans could be paid off through work for the government and/or community enhancement projects.

Money creation in general could become a public, not a private-only, enterprise. Its role and utility thus could be regulated by standards and measures that follow the goals that a democratic body politic has set for itself. As in all other areas of life, a means (in this case money) could be measured and evaluated according to its performance in achieving a goal (as in a free, sustainable, and equitable society). As such, money should be treated the way we treat biological cells: they are vital for our well-being, but when they turn cancerous we try to get rid of them.

Living within Means

If civilization is to survive, it must live on the interest,
not the capital, of nature.

—*Ronald Wright*

Growth of output does not translate into either prosperity or progress. Through higher efficiency, smarter organization and, above all, clearly articulated goals that go beyond mere growth of quantity, it is possible to do much better with less. [33]

Growth of output, with no concern for the quality of that output, is a problem systemic to the way in which our economy is organized today. It is not a problem that somehow emanates from human nature. The choice between GDP growth and prosperity on the one hand, and depression and misery on the other, is false. It is also of our own making. With goals no longer exclusively fixated on volume, we can wean ourselves from collective GDP addiction.[34]

In this kind of future, a new set of measures could reward communities that physically bring together people's living arrangements: residence, work, leisure, and consumption (essentially how the world was organized before we started to build communities around the needs of cars rather than people). Those communities and citizens who exceed their share of the ecological footprint could be asked to pay increasing fees in proportion to their use of resources, while communities and citizens who manage to fall well below their share could reap the benefits. This would dis-incentivize sub/urban sprawl, and incentivize intelligently designed, tight-knit communities that integrate all aspects of life, and provide services based on the latest technological knowledge about sustainable living.

If the dumping of environmental and social costs on the general public was no longer rewarded, a new network of environmentally friendly public mass transportation systems could begin to crisscross the country. With sustainability as our core metric securely in place, people would be able to get from one population center to the other faster and more comfortably than by plane today, and do so on near-zero emissions. The results would be dramatic: far fewer deaths from accidents, less illness caused by pollution, much less stress for commuters, and rising access to fertile land for purposes of physical and social nourishment.[35]

Measures that reward sustainable technologies also lead to a range of zero-emission commuter vehicles for personal use. To cover costs of roads and bridges, construction, maintenance, loss of arable land and environmental degradation, private users of highways and interstate travel could be charged based on miles and ecological footprint of their vehicles.

If we could begin to measure not blind quantity and growth, but rather quality and development, the buildings we inhabit would be constructed or retrofitted to energy self-sufficiency standards. In general, energy generation would become cheaper, decentralized, and largely controlled by local communities. Education, science, and development would receive a cultural and economic boost not seen since the Manhattan Project or the early days of space exploration—except this time the boost spreads throughout society and comes from economy-wide market performance standards, rather than from singular and limited government initiatives.

If we developed new market criteria that no longer allow the costs of waste and depletion to be dumped on the public, the manufacture of sustainable products and sustainable energy could boom because it would become profitable. Scientists, professionals, and skilled workers might well find themselves in a race to develop products that support better stewardship of the ecosystem as well as provide greater welfare to the public. Intelligent performance measures would make sure that job opportunities, income, and profits depend on it. As a result, job satisfaction and personal integrity would also flourish.[36]

Local Where Possible, Global Where Necessary
We don't inherit the world from our ancestors; we borrow it from our children.
—*David Brower*

Such a vision would not be pro- or anti-globalization.[37] We have always lived in a globalized world, even when we did not yet know or understand it. Similarly, we are all part of local economies, and our well-being depends on them.

Shoes can serve as a good example for the problems and complexities that a globalized economy poses today. Currently, we produce some twenty billion pairs of shoes annually for a total population of about seven billion (many of whom still cannot afford shoes). Most of these shoes are produced in low-wage countries such as China, India, and Bangladesh. The vast majority of shoes are not worn or consumed by people who live close to the point of production—in fact, many of the shoe-production workers don't make enough money to be able to buy their own product.

If we were to trace the journey of an average shoe from production to consumption—materials that go into the shoe, workers traveling to the shoe factory, packaging for the shoe, shipping from production to warehouses to place of sale—we arrive at a distance that would allow us to travel around the entire globe twice, for each pair of shoes. Originally, shoes were locally produced with natural materials that were biodegradable at the end of the shoe's lifetime. No longer. Modern shoes are full of toxins—chromium, lead, plastics—which eventually degrade as pollution into the atmosphere and soil.[38]

We are used to buying shoes that last no more than a year or two. All the energy and resources that went into the shoes' production and sale end up, in short order, at the dump. Of course, in our economy, that's the whole point—both planned and perceived obsolescence promote growth of GDP: the faster a product becomes waste, the better. And since most of us would rather pay $90 for a pair of shoes that lasts a year than pay $300 for a pair that lasts ten, local shoe manufacturers in places from Athens or Berlin to Sydney or Washington have all but disappeared. Local communities are the poorer for it.

This is what we call progress: workers who have been displaced from the land that used to sustain them, often in large-scale efforts to generate the raw materials necessary to manufacture things like shoes, are working long hours under deplorable working conditions. They produce cheap shoes for the ever-changing tastes of a mass market thousands of miles away consisting of people most of whom have long lost decent production jobs to lower-wage competitors in developing nations. To make this all work, we use up huge amounts of nonrenewable energy and raw materials and annually create mountains of discarded shoe piles.

It is a problem that requires both local and global solutions.

Efficiency and division of labor can be very good, provided we use the right measures. But the Walmart model of modern economies only works based on bad accounting: people who have lost skilled jobs in economically diverse communities "benefit" from cheap prices based on the labor of people who have lost their skilled jobs and are now employed as cheap, "unskilled" labor. And, as discussed earlier, the whole operation is made possible only by nature's and society's "free" services. Based on standards that account for the ecosystem and prioritize quality of life, for both current and future generations, the Walmart model is wasteful, inefficient, and unsustainable.

The solution: accounting standards with a focus on long-term sustainability. First and foremost, standards created and maintained to assure the ecological foundation behind "development that meets the needs of the present without compromising the ability of future generation to meet their own needs."[39] Secondly, standards that maintain or help improve the basic pillars of civic life, as determined by an ongoing democratic dialogue.

Creating such standards is no more difficult than determining what counts as income or investment. Both efforts are complex and fluid by nature. It will entail creative thinking and revisions (as it did, and still does, defining income and investment). Standards with a focus on sustainability do, however, require a very different understanding of what an "economy" is—one dependent upon a healthy ecosystem as well as a free social organization. An economy that can fulfill the long-term needs of both local and global communities.

There are many models. Started in England by Permaculture teacher Rob Hopkins, for instance, and now with over 350 projects in thirty different countries, so-called *Transition Initiatives* are transforming towns and neighborhoods into well-organized, tight-knit communities striving for self-sustainability.[40] Not an easy task, and perhaps impossible to succeed fully without a larger political and economic network of support and incentives. But they show what can be done even on a small scale and, most importantly, what would be necessary to be in place on a larger scale for people to live sustainably, without dependence on fossil fuels, big centralized structures, massive consumption, and the destruction of the commons.

Above All: Measuring What We Want

Sustainability is not a "niche." The old way of measuring
value is becoming irrelevant.

—Al Gore

Figuring out a desirable direction for economic activity may turn out to be easier than finding adequate indicators for the quality and direction of performance. Some measures, however, define far more than others. From individual firms all the way to the level of international policymaking, new economic performance indicators need to do more than inform. They need to define the parameters of decision-making—regulate, incentivize, reward, and, if necessary, penalize. And they need to be consistently refined to reflect democratic goals—social, political, environmental, cultural.

We currently have a wealth of indicators—life expectancy, income and wealth distribution, pollution, crime, literacy, carbon output, hours worked, rate of unemployment, old age security, and thousands more. But they rarely inform, and never determine, speed or direction of what drives modern capitalist economies.

This, more than anything, has to change. Across the entire spectrum of life, both costs and benefits of economic activities have to be, as best as possible, recorded and made transparent. It is only then that we can intelligently define the regulatory structure in which economic decisions are made.

Take gasoline, for instance. It's difficult to figure out its true costs. Much ink has been spilled on it. There are hidden costs that can be tallied, such as air pollution or traffic congestion. Many others are far more difficult to specify with accuracy. What is the value of clean air or the availability of fossil fuels to future generations? What part of the American $1 trillion military and intelligence budget is spent on securing oil as a vital resource to the American economy? What price tag should we put on each of the thousands of birds, sea turtles, and marine mammals killed by the 170 million gallons spilled by BP's Deepwater Horizon explosion in the Gulf of Mexico?

Conservative estimates suggest that each gallon should be taxed by an additional $1.65, which includes only known and measurable costs. Including hidden costs may raise a gallon to as much as sixteen dollars.[41]

This could generate many short-term problems, including a possibly crushing burden on poor people. Smart regulatory design can likely avoid most problems.

Here are the larger points:

- Consumers, in order to make intelligent decisions, need ready access to information on a full cost accounting of a gallon of gas (as, indeed, on all other products and services they purchase).
- Basic market fairness requires that producers can no longer dump social and environmental costs onto the public.

- Internalizing hidden costs creates the necessary market incentives for products and services that do not dump, destroy, and deplete.
- A full accounting of costs would likely result in the prohibition of certain aspects of exploration, refining, and use of oil—oil rigs without functioning emergency protocols, or extracting of oil from tar sand, requiring vast amount of water and energy in a process that lays waste to millions of acres of fertile land.

The basic logic applies to all goods and services. Only transparent accounting of true costs provides producers and consumers with the information necessary to make intelligent decisions in the marketplace. Only a regulatory structure that no longer allows businesses to externalize costs can incentivize and reward sustainable market transactions. All require measures that reflect what we want, and metrics that shape economic decision-making accordingly. To say it again: we need to begin measuring, and then enforcing, what we want.

A MOMENT OF POSSIBILITY

When the forms of an old culture are dying, the new culture is created by a few people who are not afraid to be insecure.

—*Rudolph Bahro*

Set aside for a moment what you or I might like, or dislike, about the scenarios outlined above. The larger point is this: assuming we put in place different performance indicators and different political regulations—if we began to measure and encourage what we want—the scenarios above would surely be realistic. The means and the know-how are there. The changes necessary would be less drastic than what we have experienced in many areas of daily life just over the past hundred years, and in some cases in just a matter of decades.

No doubt, many objections can be raised—details overlooked, priorities misplaced, claims unsubstantiated, expert testimonies neglected, entire areas of life ignored. I readily grant all. If nothing else, I am not interested in playing the role of the grand master planner, nor am I expert in all the many fields that will have to come together for better alternatives to work.

What interests me is expanding the boundaries of what we think possible, to overcome the stunted narrowness of most contemporary political debates. After all, it seems obvious by now that "those who can't imagine change reveal the deficits of their imaginations, not the difficulty of change."[42]

As I have suggested throughout, it is both essential and helpful to start the conversation with the sound historical realization that things like the market, corporations, and the GDP are all products of our own creation—some more deliberate than others. However much this history has faded into the background, the fact remains: we made it; it's ours to change, and ours to shape. If the goal is to broaden human capabilities, to sustain life in richer and freer varieties, then the renowned political theorist Roberto Unger is right: "nothing is more important than structural change. Our ideals and our interests remain always nailed to the cross of the institutions and practices that represent them in fact."[43]

The inevitable question then becomes, How to bring about such change? No one can know for sure. History, however, may offer some illuminating lessons when thinking about how to move forward.

A central argument of this book is that an economic measure, the Gross Domestic Product, though itself a product of crisis and war, subsequently defined the direction and goals of economic activity during times of peace. By doing so, it increasingly began to define many of our values and steer many of our actions. By now it shapes how we think about progress itself.

The values that inform how GDP is assembled are not the result of a public dialogue. Nor have they ever been part of a political campaign or a congressional debate. Decisions on how to construct GDP were not the outcome of broad deliberations, or of political negotiations and compromise. Unlike debates about civil rights or women's equality or the right of workers to bargain collectively, people did not die on the frontlines in a brutal struggle that took over a century to come to fruition. No major legislation was ever passed on behalf of GDP. As the expression of a system of national accounts, GDP has no democratic legitimacy.

Unknown to, and unelected by, the public, a dedicated team of accountants and economists constructed a measure initially intended to represent economic reality. Yet from the beginning, as soon as they decided what to count and how to count it, the measure itself began to define the reality it was supposed to reflect. By defining it, it also told us how best to make a living in it. It thus began to establish our goals, and shape our values—a classic behavioral loop.

Having decided during times of crisis, war, and starvation that more calories were the key to future health, the simple amount of calories became the guiding principle of collective action. Soon enough, amount of calories began to shape our culture, which in due course descended into caloric mania, signs of fraud and misallocated resources and rampant health risks notwithstanding. Our own creation "comes back to us as if it were an alien fate and acquires the mendacious semblance of naturalness, necessity, and authority."[44]

This brief reiteration of key findings suggests that we are in the presence of a great opportunity: by changing our performance measures, we can alter what people might be able to do. A teacher instructing his students that they will be tested on how well they intelligently question rules will get very different results than the teacher rewarding obedience. The doctor who is told that she will be paid for the health of her patients will treat them differently than a doctor evaluated and paid for number of patients seen, procedures completed, medications prescribed.

For this to work, neither teacher nor doctor has to be convinced of the superiority of the new performance measures. At first, something will operate with which economists are familiar: self-interest. But it will not stop there, any more than the idea to put a fence around a piece of land and call it "private property" stopped there. In short order, it will inevitably lead to regulations and then laws and associations and then political parties and entire constitutions that sanctify sustainability (as they once did with private property), until it becomes generally recognized as a basic human right. If it can be done with private property (it took some three hundred years), there is no reason why it cannot be done with sustainability. It does, however, have to start with well-defined performance measures. Proponents of private property, after all, were quite clear about what they wanted.

Such discussion leads to the question of who, then, should design such measures, as well as maintain and continuously refine them? If what we measure significantly shapes what we do, those who articulate the measures by definition possess great power—for good or ill. This is true independent of whether they were aware of this power or not, or whether or not they were granted a democratic mandate to begin with.

Here we run into a dilemma. On the one hand, if new performance indicators for a national economy are hashed out by a small number of people behind closed doors, it is easier to get them implemented. Yet this small, unaccountable group poses greater dangers of error and abuse. On the other hand, the more the discussions about new performance measures for a national economy are part of a sustained public dialogue, the more difficult it will be to reach consensus. And the greater the danger of racing off the cliff in our continued pursuit of GDP growth.

It might be best to think about the process of generating new performance measures as something like a Second Constitutional Convention. Clearly articulated rights and privileges and obligations mean little without enforcement mechanisms. Enforcement mechanisms, in turn, serve the purpose of ensuring that rights, privileges, and obligations are actually followed. But if the enforcers are not continuously checked and evaluated by clear performance indicators, the results can easily be worse than noncompliance. At best, if we have nothing that tells us how well or how badly we're doing in the pursuit of our stated goals, there is little left to enforce. At worst, lack of clear standards can lead to abuse and tyranny—French peasants experienced that as clearly as American sharecroppers, Soviet workers, or Congolese miners.

Performance indicators are thus as important as the Articles of the Constitution—one cannot work well without the other. The founders of the new American republic came together to build a "more perfect union." They were explicit in identifying the qualities they considered essential preconditions for this union, among them justice, tranquility, security, general welfare, and the blessings of liberty. Worthy goals indeed. Yet the central economic measure, the little big number that rules our lives more than any of the well-rehearsed goals of the constitution, does not cover a single one of these political goals.

The naked fact is this: our national economy provides neither substantive goals nor meaningful performance measures. We don't have an economic constitution that clearly describes what we want as a people. Our ruling number measures output, not quality or development.

Around the world, countries continue to discuss and pass new or significantly altered national constitutions. They do so when a critical number of citizens no longer think that the old constitution is a viable document. The process is never easy. The outcome is not always good. But the arc of history tends toward improvement whenever people begin to ask questions and become involved.

GDP no longer is a viable indicator. It does more harm than good. It should therefore be abandoned.

Broadly based on the guidelines provided by the International Bill of Human Rights and the existential as well as ethical imperative of sustainability, we need a national dialogue about goals of an economic constitution based on the four essential sides of our goalpost: sustainability, equity, democratic accountability, and economic viability. Simultaneous to this dialogue, taking place nationally and internationally, we can have "experts"—legal scholars, economists, ecologists, climatologists, medical professionals, philosophers— begin the process of figuring out how best to measure the performance of the goals embedded in our new economic constitution, and thus establish structures and regulations that support and incentivize the pursuit of these goals.

Above all, we need to keep trying. As Harvard economist David Landes noted in his acclaimed work on *The Wealth and Poverty of Nations,* we should not expect miracles or perfection or, for that matter, the apocalypse. But "we must cultivate a skeptical faith, avoid dogma, listen and watch well, try to clarify and define ends, the better to choose means."[45] We can move forward once we finally break the GDP spell and begin to construct measures that actually represent our vital goals. As we have seen, we can build on much work already done.

When America's Founders came together in Philadelphia in May 1787, the task was to create a constitution that would bring forth a viable nation. Our task is to create an economic constitution that will bring forth a viable future.

Let's get to it. If we don't want to share the fate of the Easter Islanders, this is our chance to get it right. Is there a task more important?

Appendix A

THE MEASURE AS GUIDE

Every measure is an answer to a question—a decision to focus on some things at the expense of others. Indicators define what is important, and what is not: they establish goals. Using income as a measure of personal success, for instance, privileges money over other possible options such as health or happiness. As such, all measures are both limited and subjective attempts to represent reality.[1]

It's a common problem: what tells me that I am going where I want to go? As a business owner, how can I tell that my decisions will lead to future success, and perhaps even prosperity? In our attempts to find answers, we often try to quantify our success: we latch on to numeric measures for almost every purpose. Once stockbrokers are paid commissions for the number of trades rather than their performance, the outcome is volume, even if that means bad service. Oil company workers monetarily rewarded for barrels of oil extracted are not likely to take all necessary precautions to protect the natural environment. All this happens, moreover, largely independent of who people are, what values they hold, or what individually motivates them.

Whatever gauge is applied, most measures fail to account for everything that matters. Our business bottom line may tell us about cash flow and profit, but not about productivity, job satisfaction, or employee retention. Our children's grades and SAT scores may tell us about their ability to retain information or follow directions, but are poor indicators for their character and development as citizens, or their ability to solve the problems of adult life in the twenty-first century.

Sometimes prominent measures of success have only a very tangential connection to what really matters. More income does not denote quality of life. Longevity of marriages does not necessarily imply happiness. More output does not translate into more development or quality. Businesses, of course, depend on measures to keep track of a wide range of things—quality, performance, costs, market shares, and many more. Not so clear, in many cases, is whether such measures actually represent the goals and values of those who use them in order to gauge their performance.

Use or misuse of measures can have consequences large and small. CEOs required by corporate performance measures to pursue goals at work that violate what they believe as private citizens end up with a bruised personal integrity. Stockbrokers being paid commissions on each and every trade necessarily taints the quality of services provided to groups of clients.[2] British Petroleum's grossly negligent conduct in pursuit of a measure called profit resulted in death and the destruction of entire habitats and communities.[3] Research physicists using "light-nanoseconds" to measure the distance a photon can travel in one billionth of a second, on the other hand, is likely to be of limited consequence to most of us.

Independent of consequences, measures are more than an intended reflection of reality. They also shape the very reality they are supposed to represent. Whether it is the bottom line for CEOs, or standardized tests for teachers, or paychecks for workers, measures define what we do (and perhaps who we become), even though they may have little to do with what we initially wanted. The CEO may have wanted to be an innovative industry leader, the teacher an empowering mentor, the worker a skilled master of her trade: all nevertheless end up working for the targets established by our measures (profit, test scores, income respectively).

One could say measures speak back to us. By giving us the limited reality we inquired about, measures highlight and exaggerate some aspects while downplaying and ignoring others. Our actions, in turn, tend to pursue the measure's lead. Once we follow standard measures of educational achievement and buy into the notion, say, that our children's future is best served by attending a private elite university, many of our, and their, futures will follow a very particular path.

To summarize: measures are attempts to represent reality. Once established, they in turn begin to define reality. They determine lens and categories through which we see reality, and then shape it. But they tell us only what we asked for, however limited that may have been. Measure the bottom line, and the bottom line is what you get. No more, no less.[4]

What does GDP measure? Volume of output. No more, no less.[5]

Note that immediate consequences of GDP on things like interest rates or investment climate or consumer confidence are virtually impossible to nail down in precise numbers. Yet the effects are ubiquitous. And they take place independent of whether citizens, consumers, economists, accountants, and politicians are aware of it. It is a kind of tyranny by default.

The standards by which GDP are calculated serve as a good example. By some estimates, "if the economy were to grow one percentage point more than expected in each year over the next 10, the deficit would shrink by more than $3 trillion"—all without cutting a single social program or raising a single dollar of taxes.[6] The opposite, of course, is equally true: one percentage less than expected, and financial quagmire becomes a virtual certainty. The slightest alterations up or down in the way GDP is computed, in short, could yield either figure, all independent of what is happening in the actual physical economy. It's as if your daughter, by getting an A, suddenly becomes smarter. It's also the primary reason why both the United States and China quickly abandoned attempts to count resource depletion and environmental degradation in their national accounts: it obliterated their positive growth rates, with potentially devastating results for economic activity.[7]

Politicians cannot allow that to happen. In modern economies throughout the world today, GDP growth is considered to be the paramount condition for success.

Adjusting its calculations forward and backward, the Bureau of Economic Analysis, one day in July 2013, made the U.S. GDP suddenly grow by about three percentage points. How did they do that? By including things like research and development expenditures, art, music, film and book royalties, and the promise of future pension payments. Sure, there may well be good accounting arguments for and against such adjustments—but it was decidedly not an objective representation of economic health.

Three analysts who studied the problem of GDP adjustment for decades summed up the dilemma with rare clarity:

> By the curious standard of the GDP, the nation's economic hero is a terminal cancer patient who is going through a costly divorce. The happiest event is an earthquake or a hurricane. The most desirable habitat is a multibillion-dollar Superfund site. All these add to the GDP, because they cause money to change hands. It is as if a business kept a balance sheet by merely adding up all "transactions," without distinguishing between income and expenses, or between assets and liabilities.[8]

Neither politics nor markets seem particularly concerned about such accounting shenanigans. Both respond to BEA's announcements as if they were divine truth uttered by the oracle herself. Profit, employment, prosperity depend on GDP's numbers. "The country's real problem is the economic growth deficit," proclaimed the conservative *Wall Street Journal* on the day of this writing. It decides major political debates, as it affects the course of our actions and the content of our beliefs. "The promise of America depends on sustained economic growth," politicians routinely declare.[9] Frequently, it is peddled as the miracle that can cure all social ills. "The Road to Better Jobs through Economic Growth," headlined the liberal *Huffington Post*. "Wealth undoubtedly leads to health," postulated the World Health Organization in an official report. A *World Bank* Report, chaired by two Nobel laureates, simply declared: "growth is a necessary, if not sufficient, condition for broader development, enlarging the scope for individuals to be productive and creative."[10]

Following an extensive review of the impacts of GDP accounting over time, Elizabeth Dickenson proclaimed in a review, aptly entitled "One Stat to Rule them All," that GDP "is the ultimate measure of a country's overall welfare, a window into an economy's soul, the statistic to end all statistics"—in short, she wrote, it is "the defining statistic of the last century."[11]

All this has one decisive consequence: independent of what GDP actually measures, or whether you and I would consider it a good representation of what matters to us, in today's economies the failure of GDP to grow necessarily spells trouble, for it represents the very operating logic of the entire system. It's a connection that is well understood within the corridors of power and sanctioned thought. Anything less than robust GDP growth is perceived as a central threat to the vitality of the economy, endangering the health of society. Merely the discussion of possible downturns translates into headlines such as "Dismal Data and Gloomy Forecasts."[12]

To be sure, there is debate about the best path to promote GDP growth. Careers and reputations wax and wane based on whether to support more or less austerity, more or less economic stimulus. Should government become more involved? Are investments in green technologies a good idea? How much of a problem is inequality? Parties and political ideologies are in large part defined by such debates.

The idea that GDP growth itself is possibly at the heart of the problem continues to be beyond the pale of mainstream political debate. Among experts, doubts about GDP as a valid welfare measure are by now widely accepted. Questioning its underlying logic, however, still incurs the ridicule of the high priests of economic doctrine. With good reason. It represents a core challenge to the existing economic apparatus and its various proponents, from business to politics to academia.

What GDP represents, in short, is more than the power of an idea. It is the power of a system built on ideas that are no longer visible. Neither original purpose nor initial direction of the ideas is part of a public conversation. By setting the rules by which economies function, GDP defines global economic realities. We are collectively sailing west because the weatherman tells us the wind is blowing west.[13]

A critique of GDP consequently has to address far more than the fact that it represents a flawed or dangerous measure. It has to explore and reveal the measure's function as the organizing logic of modern societies. How did a measure come to rule the world?

NOTES

INTRODUCTION

1. Philip G. Smith and Manfred Max-Neef, *Economics Unmasked* (2011), 69.
2. Even though national income and product accounts were not technically called GDP at first (first using GNP, most industrialized countries switched to GDP in the 1980s—the United States in 1991; for the difference between the two, see box in this introduction), for sake of consistency I have used the acronym GDP throughout the book.
3. GDP is the undisputed king of economic measures. Health of the economy is primarily defined by GDP. Most other and more specific economic measures either derive from, or are a direct component of, GDP. The government's debt is defined and evaluated as a ratio of GDP. How we define and count income or profit is regulated by GDP. So is welfare. Even how we think about our standard of living is almost exclusively a function of GDP. Nobel laureate Paul Samuelson summarized the significance of GDP accounts in the fifteenth edition of his widely read textbook coauthored with William Nordhaus, *Economics,* ([1948] 1995) as follows: GDP gives us "an overall picture of the state of the economy." Without it, "policymakers would be adrift in a sea of unorganized data. The GDP and related data are like beacons that help policymakers steer the economy toward the key economic objectives." He concluded that GDP is "truly among the great inventions of the twentieth century."
4. As this book explores, faith in economic growth that follows the logic of GDP is as widespread as it is deeply ingrained in cultures around the globe. While it may no longer be universally trusted as a welfare indicator, it still performs like an invisible dictator when it comes to policymaking. Questioning its basic logic comes close to economic treason, a betrayal of future prospects for prosperity.
5. Moses Abramovitz, *Thinking about Growth* (1989), 343.
6. As economist Herman Daly has repeatedly pointed out, money is a strange symbol for wealth, for unlike the material foundations of wealth, it does not follow the laws of physics; for a brief overview, see Maywa Montenegro, "Herman Daly Applies a Biophysical Lens to the Economy and Finds that Bigger Isn't Necessarily Better" (2009).
7. The literature on this point is too vast to cite here. A few examples suffice: for Soviet-style mis-measures, see Lawrence Goodwyn, *Breaking the Barrier* (1991). For the financial shenanigans that led to the downturn of 2007–9, see Matt Taibbi, *Griftopia: A Story of Bankers, Politicians, and the Most Audacious Power Grab in American History* (2011). Even simple conversion errors from one measure to the next, such as from imperial to metric, have resulted in financial loss and death.

8. "Value" carries multiple meanings: it defines an amount of goods and services as well as the general concept of material worth; usefulness or utility or importance; a numerical quantity; and, of course, cultural standards and principles. Remarkably, what to count, and how to count it, helps define all the different aspects of the meaning.

9. An argument made by Paul A. Samuelson and William D. Nordhaus in celebration of GDP; see further discussion on this in chap. 1 of *Economics*, 16th ed. (1998), 390.

10. This is true not only for economic performance but also for cross-cultural objectives such as "meaningful work" or "freedom of expression." Using faulty measures, or, worse, measures designed for entirely different purposes, on the other hand, one runs the risk of ending up like the captain who, trusting his outdated map rather than his eyes and intuition, ran his ship into a boulder and sank.

11. Calories are as vital to our physical condition as output is to a nation's economy; neither provide good or reliable indicators of overall health.

12. Vandana Shiva, "How Economic Growth has Become Anti-Life" (2013a).

13. In his best-selling *The Ecology of Commerce* (2010), Paul Hawken proposes a number of sustainable growth models (68).

14. Some would say it is the logic of a cancerous tumor: growth, no matter the consequences (which include destroying the very organism on which it depends). This analogy also makes clear that growth per se is not necessarily the problem—what we grow is.

15. William Greider, *One World, Ready or Not* (1997), 11.

16. This critique includes some of the most noted economists, such as Kenneth Arrow, Herman Daly, John Kenneth Galbraith, Ezra Mishan, William Nordhaus and James Tobin, Paul Samuelson, Joseph Stigliz, and, first of all, Simon Kuznets. For a good recent overview, see Joseph Stiglitz, Amartya Sen, and Jean-Paul Fitoussi "Report by the Commission on the Measurement of Economic Performance and Social Progress" (2009), 85–142; 143–232. Chapters 2 and 8 provide an introduction to many sources; for a full list, see bibliography.

17. Andro Linklater, *Measuring America: How the United States Was Shaped by the Greatest Land Sale in History* (2003), 4.

18. Lewis Dartnell, "Civilization's Starter Kit," (2014); the consequences of separating thinking from doing in the endless quest for "more" is brilliantly explored in Matthew B. Crawford, "Shop Class as Soulcraft" (2006), 7–24; see also his more developed book version, *Shop Class as Soulcraft: An Inquiry into the Value of Work* (2009).

19. Neil Postman, *Conscientious Objections* (1992), 25.

20. Following a logic very similar to what we currently experience in America with fossil fuel extraction (fracking, sand oil)—heightened resolve to get to the last drop with little or no foresight for long-term consequences.

21. See Ronald Wright, *A Short History of Progress* (2004), 57–64. As his books makes clear, the Easter Islanders were by no means the only civilization that marched off the cliff in their pursuit of bad goals; most major civilizations have

done so. For further specific evidence, see Rachael Beddoe et al., "Overcoming Systemic Roadblocks to Sustainability" (2009), 2483–89. As Jared Diamond suggests in his book *Collapse: How Societies Choose to Fail or Succeed* (2005), environmental factors have frequently been cause for collapse, and modern societies are on track to replicate such disasters.

22. While I have used predominantly American examples, it would be easy to find a wide range of examples from around the world; some widely known would include Hitler's rise to power, the Bolshevik Revolution, or Gandhi's march to the sea.

23. Simon Kuznets, "National Income, 1929–1932" (1934), 7.

24. The report was a logical extension of his own research, in part informed by early giants in the field of national income accounting such as Willford King, Colin Clark, and Wesley C. Mitchell.

25. See, for instance, another important figure in national accounting, the British economist Richard Stone, who said in his 1984 Nobel acceptance lecture, referring to newly generated national accounts in countries such as Great Britain and Holland: ". . . the idea was in the air and made its appearance in several guises at the same time;" Richard Stone, "Nobel Memorial Lecture 1984. The Accounts of Society" (1986), 20.

26. The claim that rational accounting was essential for the development of capitalism is not new, but had previously been made only in reference to individual businesses; see Bruce G. Carruthers and Wendy Nelson Espeland, "Accounting for Rationality: Double-Entry Bookkeeping and the Rhetoric of Economic Rationality" (1991), 31–69.

27. Strictly speaking, national income is not identical with GDP: the latter measures all goods and services, while the former subtracts from GDP depreciation of capital (things like buildings and machines), which is the same as Net Domestic Product (NDP). Also, as explained in the box in this introduction (on the difference between GNP and GDP), national income adds or subtracts income made abroad: a country's national income grows or declines in part depending on how much income is received from capital/assets owned abroad, and how much capital/assets is owned by foreigners at home. For the purposes of this critical reflection, however, the two are used interchangeably.

28. Whether the Great Recession of 2007–09 and its aftermath will change this narrative remains to be seen; as explained in chapter 1, per capita GDP in the United States has almost tripled since the end of World War II.

29. The UN passed its version of GNP accounting standards in 1953 as the United Nations System of National Accounts (UNSNA), a system that governs global investment and trade to this day. For further detail, see chapter 5.

30. By 1993, the entire international community had switched from GNP to GDP (for an explanation of the difference, see box in this introduction).

31. J. Steven Landefeld, "GDP: One of the Great Inventions of the 20th Century" (2000). In a comprehensive survey of international economic measures, economists Katherine Scrivens and Barbara Iasiello conclude, quite simply, that "GDP has

been the most influential indicator of the last century" and "the foremost indicator of national progress;" see their "Indicators Of 'Societal Progress': Lessons From International Experiences" (2010), 18.

32. Select scholars of course have long recognized this, yet it has not penetrated the consciousness of those engaged in positions of economic or political decision-making. For examples, citations, and a fuller discussion, see chapters 8 and 9.

33. Austrian economist Oskar Morgenstern, "Does GNP Measure Growth and Welfare" (1974), 23. For a very good summary exploration of the shortcomings and dangers of the GDP regime, see Lorenzo Fioramonti's recently published book *Gross Domestic Problem* (2013).

34. A classic economics' textbook definition of GDP is "The market value of an economy's domestically produced goods and services over a specified period of time"; see Robert J. Barro, *Macroeconomics* (2008).

35. As one sympathetic economist and historian of national accounts put it, "National income estimators sometimes have to engage in rather elaborate gymnastics in order to keep their definitions reasonably realistic"; see John P. Lewis and Robert C. Turner. *Business Conditions Analysis* (1967), 26; or as Richard Stone, a leader in the international institutionalization of national accounts put it when he addressed the question of definitions for consumption or production, "The answer is that the matter is still being debated but that in the meantime most people are agreed that the definitions adopted in the United Nations system of national accounts are serviceable and flexible enough to cover a wide range of situations;" see Stone, ibid. (1986), 22.

36. In a compelling and thought-provoking short book, Diane Coyle recently published a "Brief but Affectionate History" of GDP that covers some of the critical reflections developed in this book, but arrives at a very different conclusion: "GDP, for all its flaws, is still a bright light shining through the mist." While Coyle discusses in eloquent prose many of GDP's shortcomings as an accurate measure of success or well-being, she maintains, contrary to the arguments developed herein, that GDP is "an important measure for the freedom and human capability created by the capitalist market economy." A key difference between her work and this is that she maintains that GDP, as a reasonably accurate measure of economic growth, is closely correlated to human satisfaction. See Diane Coyle, *GDP: A Brief but Affectionate History* (2014), 140, 5.

37. Perhaps the most famous economist of the twentieth century, John Maynard Keynes, thought it would be "splendid" if "economists could manage to get themselves thought of as humble, competent people, on a level with dentists," rather than the wizards and sages they like to think of themselves as today—providing useful services, yes; but not determining the health of the entire body. "Economic Possibilities for Our Grandchildren" (1930), reprinted in Keynes, *Essays in Persuasion* (1963), 373.

38. See Robert Higgs, "Military Spending / GDP = Nonsense for Budget Policy Making" (2008).

39. During the unexpected collapse of 2007–9, all key economic variables fell at a faster rate than during the beginning of the Great Depression in the early 1930s; see Nicholas Crafts and Peter Fearon, *The Great Depression of the 1930s—Lessons for Today* (2013), 6. The corruption of some of *Wall Street's* most powerful institutions has been well documented by, for instance, Kevin Phillips, *Bad Money* (2008), Dean Baker, *Plunder and Blunder* (2010), and Matt Taibbi, *The Divide: American Injustice in the Age of the Wealth Gap* (2014).

40. According to the most conservative estimates, banks received some $5 trillion in public help. One research institute concluded that the price tag in the United States for shoring up the fabric of GDP growth alone was close to $30 trillion—or about twice the total of American annual output as measured by GDP. As unemployment remained high, millions continued to lose their homes, inequality reached Gilded Age proportions, and real wages actually declined, it became clear that such enormous amounts were not spent for citizens and their needs; see James Felkerson et al., "$29,000,000,000,000: A Detailed Look at the Fed's Bailout by Funding Facility and Recipient" (2011). Whatever the real figures will turn out to be—no one appears to keep a precise count any longer—the amounts are staggering. The sheer magnitude of frantic efforts provided a stark reminder of our collective desperation to hold onto GDP growth. Little else seemed to matter.

41. Alan Greenspan, "Testimony of Dr. Alan Greenspan in front of House Committee on Oversight and Government Reform, 23 Oct. 2008."

42. Timothy Geithner, interviewed by Jon Stewart, *Daily Show* (2014).

43. Karl Polanyi, *The Great Transformation: The Political and Economic Origins of Our Time* ([1944] 2001); Rachel Carson, *Silent Spring* ([1962] 2002); Thomas Piketty, *Capital in the Twenty-First Century* (2014). Perhaps the most insightful thinker on the impossibility to comprehend large phenomena yet keep distinct the study of human and thing, nature and society, artificially organized in categories and disciplines, is Bruno Latour; see particularly his *We Have Never Been Modern* (1993).

44. I am belatedly heartened by Thomas Piketty's explicit call for this kind of research in his widely read recent work. In particular, he encourages social scientists not to leave "economic facts to economists" and encourages broader historical research by asking scholars "to make use of whatever tools are available" in order to reach a fuller understanding rather than simply "abandon the terrain to others"; see Piketty, ibid. (2014), 574–75.

45. It is perhaps a case of tragic irony that Kuznets, resisting to the end to fall in line with economic orthodoxy on national accounting, himself sparked another false truth. Much better known for his work on economic growth, Kuznets received the 1971 Nobel Prize in economics for what became known as the "Kuznets U-curve," or the idea that inequality in national economies decreases in advanced stages of development and growth. As the work of Thomas Piketty demonstrates, Kuznets in this case engaged in the very thing he consistently

criticized in others: drawing conclusions that went well beyond his available data. The false notion of declining inequality through growth and development was nevertheless enthusiastically embraced by much of the economics profession.

CHAPTER I

1. Karl Polanyi, *The Great Transformation: The Political and Economic Origins of Our Time* ([1944] 2001), 35.
2. See 2013 World Hunger and Poverty Statistics, http://www.worldhunger.org/articles/Learn/world%20hunger%20facts%202002.htm.
3. One of many misconceptions of early cultures concerns life expectancy; new research suggests that the typical lifespan for an adult hunter-gatherer was nearly the same as that for modern humans, though child mortality was much higher; see, for instance, Michael Gurven and Hillard Kaplan, "Longevity among Hunter-Gatherers," *Population and Development Review* (2007), 321–65.
4. William J. Baumol et al., *Productivity and American Leadership: The Long View* (1989), 9.
5. Steven Stoll, *The Great Delusion* (2008), 15.
6. For an excellent overview, see Polanyi, ibid; Jared Diamond, *Guns, Germs, and Steel* (1999); and Robert C. Allen, *The British Industrial Revolution in Global Perspective* (2009). It may be worth keeping in mind that, as persistent poverty in countries around the world starkly confirms, growth has always been, and continues to be, very unequally distributed. Today, roughly half of the world's population still lives in poverty, or, perhaps worse, has become the direct victim of development. Either way, the problem of survival is far from resolved. Poverty still exists in the richest nations.
7. Ronald Wright, *A Short History of Progress* (2004), 47.
8. Among many places, this development is described with clarity and economy in Robert Heilbroner, *The Nature and Logic of Capitalism* (1985), chap. 3, pp. 53–77.
9. The separation of producer and product went hand in hand with another significant separation, that between philosophy and science. For a good introduction to the origins and consequences of both developments, see Immanuel Wallerstein, *World Systems Analysis* (2004).
10. See, for instance, E. P. Thompson's attempt to rescue their resistance "from the enormous condescension of posterity," *The Making of the English Working Class* (1966), 12; see especially chap. 16.
11. The same, of course, is true for other forms of social organization, such as churches, inventing the tithe as a reliable form of wealth extraction.
12. Alexander Hamilton, Report on Manufactures (1791).

13. "National income" is here broadly defined the way it was understood in seventeenth-century England, as a "set of data which show the consolidated sales and expenses of business, the receipts and expenditures of government, and the receipts and expenditures of individuals in their interrelation"; see George Jaszi, "The Concept of National Income and National Product," (1946), 147.

14. Paul Studenski, *The Income of Nations* (1958), 13.

15. Tony Aspromourgos, "New Light on the Economics of William Petty (1623–1687)" (2000), 54; Henry Morley, introduction to William Petty, *Essays on Mankind and Political Arithmetic* ([1888] 2006), 13. Most work about Petty focuses on his conceptual contributions to the study of national wealth. Karl Marx called Petty the "founder of political economy," and the later Director of the Bureau of Economic Analysis, George Jaszi, wrote in his 1946 dissertation that Petty "was the originator specifically of the national income concept and that therein lies his outstanding contribution to the quantitative world"; see Jaszi, ibid. (1946), 36.

16. See Sir William Petty, *Political Survey of Ireland* (2nd ed., 1719), 17; see also Ted McCormick, *William Petty and the Ambitions of Political Arithmetic* (2010), 79–117; John Kenyon, Jane Ohlmeyer, and J. S. Morrill, *The Civil Wars: A Military History of England, Scotland, and Ireland, 1638–1660* (1998), 278.

17. According to geographical surveys, Kerry County encompasses 4,746 square km, or almost 1.2 million acres. For background, see Wilson Lloyd Bevan, "Sir William Petty: A Study in English Economic Literature" (1894), 379; John C. Adams, "Sir William Petty: Scientist, economist, inventor, 1623–1687" (1999), 12.

18. McCormick, ibid., 304.

19. Karl Marx and Friedrich Engels, "The Communist Manifesto" [1848], in Robert C. Tucker, ed., *The Marx-Engels Reader* (1978), 475.

20. Charles Tilly, *Coercion, Capital, and European States—AD 990–1992* (1992), 12. In addition to the occupation of Ireland, Petty's work also informed the need for revenue during the second Dutch War (1665–67), in much the same way that, thirty years later, Gregory King's estimates were used to address the fiscal problems during the wars with France.

21. For the argument that Petty greatly advanced the role of empirical evidence in economic thinking, see Benjamin H. Mitra-Kahn, "Redefining the Economy: How the 'Economy' Was Invented in 1620" (2011).

22. The "national income" concept as first developed by Petty, and soon thereafter refined by Gregory King, was of interest not only to national elites, but also to people concerned about the origins or distribution of national wealth. As quantifiable output totals, national income accounts could yield potentially powerful information to military leaders, entrepreneurs, and social reformers alike.

23. Aristotle, as quoted in Jerome M. Segal, "Alternative Conceptions of the Economic Realm" (1991), 287.

24. R. H. Tawney, *Religion and the Rise of Capitalism* ([1926] 1958), 38.

25. For historical data, see Richard Sutch, "Gross Domestic Product: 1790–2002" (2006). A sobering fact for Americans: labor productivity increased by a factor

of about 10 over the past forty years, while labor income remained essentially the same.

26. For a sample of excellent studies on this question, see Richard Nelson, *The Sources of Economic Growth* (1996); and Joel Mokyr, "The Intellectual Origins of Modern Economic Growth" (2005).

27. Polanyi, ibid., 49.

28. A term used by the Cambridge Trust for New Thinking in Economics, founded by Cambridge economist Terry Barker; see http://www.neweconomicthinking .org/ (accessed 20 Feb. 2013).

29. Perhaps the best-known book exploring the irrationality behind the concept of rational market actors is Dan Ariely's *Predictably Irrational—The Hidden Forces that Shape Our Decision* (2010). The book provides a wealth of examples, including "the power of the free cookie," which shows that considerations we have for others when offered free cookies essentially disappear once we pay for the cookie.

30. Money, of course, is the symbol of this incursion of economic values into our lives. Economists are fond of claiming that the way we spend money is somehow a good expression of our values and wishes. Through our purchases we presumably establish the demand that then spurs the most effective supply. As a culture, we have largely accepted this claim, despite the obvious fact that our spending habits are "certainly idiosyncratic, frequently wasteful, occasionally counterproductive," all in addition to being routinely irrational—not to mention that those short on money seem to have no voice in any of this; see George P. Brockway, *The End of Economic Man: An Introduction to Humanist Economics* (2001), 46. To argue, as many economists have, that market behavior is a sign of "revealed preference," in other words, presumably showing that by making the choice to purchase the consumer maximizes utility, is a clear case of circular logic. By this logic, behavior is explained by preference, which in turn is defined by behavior. But such circular theorizing simply avoids the issue: choice is both more and less than an indication of self-interested behavior. In addition, "the rationale of this approach seems to be based on the idea that the only way of understanding a person's real preference is to examine his actual choices, and there is no choice-independent way of understanding someone's attitude towards alternatives." For a fuller development of this point, see for instance Amartya Sen, "Rational Fools: A Critique of the Behavioral Foundations of Economic Theory" (1977), 317–44.

31. See for instance, Thomas R. Malthus, *An Essay on the Principle of Population* ([1798] 2004), chap. 2, p. 19.

32. They produced goods and services that, in today's economic parlance, would be called "intermediate"—merely a means to an end.

33. Adam Smith, *Inquiry into the Nature and Causes of the Wealth of Nations* ([1776] 2009]), 208.

34. Ibid.

35. John Stuart Mill, *Principles of Political Economy* (1848), 116. Today's sustainability economists, of course, argue that Malthus was still essentially right: beyond a certain number, earth's resources cannot sustain populations. For a good summary of recent debates, see Elizabeth Kolbert, "Head Count" (2013).

36. A similar point is made by Gar Alperovitz and Lew Daly in *Unjust Deserts* (2008), 22–29.

37. In an excellent collection of essays entitled *Erasing the Invisible Hand: Essays on an Elusive and Misused Concept in Economics* (2014), Warren Samuels and his collaborators provide a far more comprehensive interpretation of Smith's work, effectively ridiculing simplistic modern uses of the "invisible hand" for ideological purposes of defending equally simplistic notions of the free market.

38. Smith, ibid. ([1776] 2009), 215.

39. Ibid., 196. In today's economic lingo, what the service sector provided, according to Smith, would be considered "intermediate" rather than final services—a means to an end.

40. There is no indication that he would have had anything other than disdain for today's concentration of wealth in the hands of a few, or the abuse of the planet without concern for future generations. Ibid., 255.

41. Ibid., 509.

42. Ibid., 248.

43. Polanyi, ibid., 111.

44. Smith, ibid. ([1776] 2009), 312.

45. After the pioneering work of Petty and King, national income work in the eighteenth century apparently was characterized by a "marked decline in the skill, originality, and understanding," thus presumably providing little impetus for Smith to consult its findings; see Jaszi, ibid. (1946), 114–18.

46. Marshall became a leading scholar with his 1890 publication of *Principles of Economics*, providing a comprehensive theory of national economics, parts of which are now familiar to readers, such as "costs of production" or "supply and demand"; see Marshall's *Principles of Economics* ([1890] 2009).

47. Polanyi, ibid., 73.

48. Human beings, in turn, were increasingly seen as primary, no longer part of the natural world.

49. Marshall added the word "net" in order to highlight the need to avoid double-counting: as he put it, "raw and half-finished commodities [and] the wearing out and depreciation of plant which is involved in production . . . must of course be deducted from the gross produce before the true or net income can be found." Marshall, ibid., 434.

50. As the post–Great Panic of 2007–9 debates reveal, this is cause for an ongoing controversy in politics: much complaint has recently been published about all the "unproductive" activities of bankers and speculators who are "essentially producing nothing." The political debates, however, have had no impact on national accounting, on how we measure our national wealth.

CHAPTER 2

1. Long before this logic began to permeate modern culture, and even before it defined neoclassical economic thinking, Western philosophers, particularly Jeremy Bentham and John Stuart Mill, laid the ideological foundation. Bentham's concept of "utilitarianism"—the idea that policy should be directed toward "the greatest good of all"—subsequently morphed into his student's liberal economic doctrine of "utility maximization," not only as the be-all and end-all of economics, but as the only guarantee of "liberty" itself (see especially John Stuart Mill's *On Liberty*).
2. This is not to say that people did not continue their attempts to inject and reintroduce moral values into the market. For a development of such arguments, see Paul J. Zak, *Moral Markets* (2008).
3. Tim Jackson, "Let' Be Less Productive," (2012).
4. In a book aptly entitled *A Consumers' Republic* (2003), Lizabeth Cohen shows how consumerism eventually became an inherent part of what it means to be an American citizen.
5. Terry Bouton, *Taming Democracy: "The People," the Founders, and the Troubled Ending of the American Revolution* (2007), 9, 258.
6. Werner Sombart, "Medieval and Modern Commercial Enterprise" (1953), 38.
7. Most small-business owners are dependent on the larger economy no less than wage earners.
8. Bain Report, "A World Awash in Money" (2012), 3.
9. The richest 1 percent own about 50 percent of global wealth, and the top 10 percent account for almost 90 percent of global wealth. Half of the world's population owns essentially nothing. If one were to subtract housing from the calculations, the discrepancies are even more pronounced. About three-quarters of the total global wealth is owned by the top 10 percent of America, Europe, and Asia-Pacific. See World Institute for Development Economics Research of the United Nations "Personal Assets from a Global Perspective" (2005).
10. Karl Marx, *The Communist Manifesto* ([1848] 2008), 35.
11. For a good discussion of Weber's thinking, see Bruce G. Carruthers and Wendy Nelson Espeland, "Accounting for Rationality: Double-Entry Bookkeeping and the Rhetoric of Economic Rationality" (1991), 31–69.
12. Karl Polanyi, *The Great Transformation* ([1944] 2001).
13. Sam Gindin and Leo Panitch, *The Making of Global Capitalism* (2012), 3.
14. As quoted in Richard Layard, *Happiness: Lessons from a New Science* (2006), 235.
15. Wil S. Hylton, "Broken Heartland: The Looming Collapse of Agriculture on the Great Plains" (2012), 27.
16. For an excellent discussion of this point, see Peter Linebaugh, *The Magna Carta Manifesto—Liberties and Commons for All* (2008).
17. R. H. Tawney, *Religion and the Rise of Capitalism* ([1926] 1958), 228–29; 235.

18. George P. Brockway, *The End of Economic Man: An Introduction to Humanist Economics* (2001), 45. The broader literature ranges from moral philosophy to cultural anthropology and psychology, and from neuroscience to economics. At this point in time, one can safely assert that the myth of rationality in the pursuit of self-interest has been fully debunked by scholars. For good examples, see Dan Ariely, *Predictably Irrational—The Hidden Forces That Shape Our Decisions* (2010); Justin Fox, *The Myth of the Rational Market: A History of Risk, Reward, and Delusion on Wall Street* (2009); Ha-Joon Chang, *23 Things They Don't Tell You About Capitalism* (2011); A. G. Sanfey, "Social Decision-Making: Insights from Game Theory and Neuroscience," *Science* (2007), 598–602; Colin Camerer et al., "Neuroeconomics: How Neuroscience Can Inform Economics," *Journal of Economic Literature* (2005), 9–64; and Oshin Vartanian, *Neuroscience of Decision Making* (2011).

19. Karl Polanyi, *Primitive, Archaic, and Modern Economies* (1968), 68.

20. Much work on how truncated and primitive economic models of human behavior are has been nicely summarized in Mehmet Karacuka and Asad Zaman, "The Empirical Evidence against Neoclassical Utility Theory" (2012), 366–414.

21. As quoted in Gar Alperovitz, *America Beyond Capitalism* (2011), 34. Alperovitz collects similar sentiments from other American historical icons, including Supreme Court Justice Louis Brandeis, who pointedly asked "Can any man be really free who is constantly in danger of becoming dependent for mere subsistence upon somebody and something else than his own exertion and conduct?" Jefferson was not the only founding father who considered economic independence as vital to political freedom. James Madison wrote in 1792, "The class of citizens who provide at once their own food and their own raiment, may be viewed as the most truly independent and happy. They are more: they are the basis of public liberty, and the strongest bulwark of public safety. It follows, that the greater the proportion of this class to the whole society, the more free, the more independent, and the more happy must be the society itself." James Madison, "Republican Distribution of Citizens" ([1792] 1983), 246. I thank my graduate student, Christina Patterson, for bringing this quote to my attention.

22. Linebaugh, ibid., 6.

23. For the definitive history of this movement, see Lawrence Goodwyn, *The Populist Moment—A Short History of the Agrarian Revolt in America* (1978).

24. Examples include environmental movements (from deeply conservative to radical); civil rights and Black Power movements; the student movements of the 1960s, from Mexico to Japan; independence movements from the Philippines to Iran and South Africa; democracy movements from the Haitian Revolution to the Prague Spring and current-day popular movements in the Middle East; and of course global justice movements around the world.

25. Goodwyn, ibid. (1978), ix.

26. Jerome M. Segal, *Graceful Simplicity: The Philosophy and Politics of the Alternative American Dream* (2003), 120.

27. Daniel Breslau, "Economics Invents the Economy: Mathematics, Statistics, and Models in the Works of Irving Fisher and Wesley Mitchell" (2003), 379.

28. Ibid., 380; see also Benjamin H. Mitra-Kahn, "Redefining the Economy: How the 'Economy' Was Invented in 1620" (2011), and the work of Daniel Hirschman, who is currently finishing his dissertation at the University of Michigan: "Inventing the Economy: Or, How We Learned to Stop Worrying and Love the GDP."

29. In his latest book *Capital in the Twenty-First Century* (2014), French economist, philosopher, and mathematician Thomas Piketty shows little more than derision for this newly predominant branch of economics. He writes, "For far too long economists have sought to define themselves in terms of their supposedly scientific methods. In fact, those methods rely on an immoderate us of mathematical models, which are frequently no more than an excuse for occupying the terrain and masking the vacuity of the content" (574).

30. André Vanoli, *A History of National Accounting* (2005), 4; see also Paul Studenski, *The Income of Nations* (1958), 11–78.

31. According to Studenski (who gives examples from each of these countries), the first attempt in the United States to estimate national income seems to have been made by George Tucker at the University of Virginia in 1843, though the effort was limited by lack of data and a concept of income restricted to material production; Studenski, ibid., 30.

32. Mark Perlman argues that King's effort was a direct response to a 1896 study of national income done by Charles B. Spahr, a labor advocate who was trying to show that the working class was carrying a large and growing share of the cost of federal government; see Mark Perlman, "Political Purpose and the National Accounts" (1987), 135.

33. Willford I. King, *The Wealth and Income of the People of the United States* (1915), 2. King was in part motivated by an earlier study, Charles B. Spahr's 1896 *An Essay on the Present Distribution of Wealth in the United States*, a book that not only found great inequality but also emphasized that a growing share of the cost of federal government was borne by common laborers.

34. Later research revealed that King was right on target—the actual figure was slightly higher at 18 percent; see Anthony B. Atkinson, Thomas Piketty, and Emmanuel Saez, "Top Incomes in the Long Run of History" (2011), 3–71.

35. King noted that the gap in wealth—all the assets people hold, everything from valuables to real estate to stocks—was even more pronounced. Some individual wealth, moreover, was obtained at the expense of the public. As he explained, "Certain individuals may profit enormously by the increase in land values due to the growth of a great city, but the masses of people will probably be forced by this same growth to travel far to their work or to live in crowded quarters amid the smoke and dust of busy thoroughfares." King, ibid., 6.

36. Ibid., 60; emphasis in original. It is safe to assume that King, who would play a significant role in the formulation of national income accounting after World

War I (he became one of NBER's earliest research associates), would have been less than pleased to discover that by 2010, the wealthiest 1 percent possessed roughly 24 percent of total income, 35 percent of total wealth, and 43 percent of financial wealth. All these figures are higher than what King found to be true for 1915, a time partly known for its robber barons, labor agitation, and widespread fear that the social fabric of American society increasingly began to resemble old European aristocracies.

37. Though Piketty acknowledges that "for countries as well as individuals, the wealth hierarchy is not just about money; it is also a matter of honor and moral values." See Piketty, ibid., 509.

38. Though the author himself never makes this point, the most detailed background of historical accounting efforts remains the dense, almost encyclopedic work of Paul Studenski, *The Income of Nations* (1958). A more recent study by the former head of the official French Statistical Agency, André Vanoli, also provides valuable background, but despite extensive discussions on methodology and cultural differences in approach, he equally assumes that national accounting can presumably be based on market prices only. It is the bread and butter of business and national accountants alike. See Vanoli, ibid., particularly box 74 on pp. 438–42.

39. Robert Heilbroner, *The Worldly Philosophers* (1999), 272.

40. For a good introduction to the problem of demand and growth as measures of well-being, see E. J. Mishan, *The Economic Growth Debate* (1977).

41. Francis, "Apostolic Exhortation Evangelii Gaudium of the Holy Father Francis to the Bishops, Clergy, Consecrated Persons and the Lay Faithful on the Proclamation of the Gospel in Today's World" (November 2013).

42. Mark Sagoff, "On the Economic Value of Ecosystem Services," *Environmental Values* 17 (2008), 244.

43. Ibid., 242.

44. Adam Smith, *Inquiry into the Nature and Causes of the Wealth of Nations* ([1776] 2009]), chap. 11; Karl Marx, *A Critique of Political Economy* ([1848] 2008); John Maynard Keynes, *The General Theory of Employment, Interest and Money* ([1936] 1965), chap. 24; Joseph Schumpeter, *Capitalism, Socialism, and Democracy* (1942), chaps. 12–14.

45. Robert Heilbroner, *The Economic Transformation of America* (1998), 283.

46. When contemplating the rationale of the great economists on the end to growth, in fact, one might be tempted to argue that the icons of presumed ideological differences—Smith, Marx, Mills, and Keynes chief among them—essentially shared a common vision of the future. In his *Principles of Political Economy,* for instance, Mills wrote of how "the end of growth leads to a stationary state." And he explicitly argued that "the stationary state of capital and wealth . . . would be a very considerable improvement on our present condition." To him, the reason was obvious: "It is scarcely necessary to remark that a stationary condition of capital and population implies no stationary state of human improvement.

There would be as much scope as ever for all kinds of mental culture, and moral and social progress; as much room for improving the Art of Living, and much more likelihood of it being improved, when minds cease to be engrossed by the art of getting on." John Stuart Mill, *Principles of Political Economy* (1848), book 4, chap. 6, pp. 336, 339.

Writing a little less than a century later, Keynes vividly anticipated the benefits of social organization beyond the growth era. What people would realize when growth is no longer our central goal, Keynes believed, is "that avarice is a vice, that the exaction of usury is a misdemeanour, and the love of money is detestable. . . . We shall once more value ends above means and prefer the good to the useful." Even more emphatically, he later wrote that "the day is not far off when the economic problem will take the back seat where it belongs, and the arena of the heart and the head will be occupied or reoccupied, by our real problems—the problems of life and of human relations, of creation and behavior and religion." While they would no doubt insist on minor corrections or clarifications, it seems safe to assume that both Smith and Marx would have signed off on either Mill's or Keynes' statements. John Maynard Keynes, "Economic Possibilities for Our Grandchildren" (1930), reprinted in Keynes, *Essays in Persuasion* (1963), 358–373.

47. Heilbroner, ibid. (1998), 38.

48. And, of course, there were many other questions that followed, such as: What was national income or product? How productive was each sector of the economy? What was distribution of income by wages, salaries, profits, and rents? Who or what, for that matter, determined what was a final and what an "intermediate" product, or how depreciation might be defined?

49. Individual businesses ordinarily generated information on things like how many people they employed, amount and proportion of wages, or how much of their profit was used for investment in future production. None of this existed on a national level. No one had ever determined, moreover, what could, and what could not, count as profitable economic activity. By and large, if it could be bought and sold, it was a commodity—and thus a potential source for profit. Government did occasionally impose clear restrictions on this anarchy of the market, such as when it prohibited prostitution and the sale of alcohol, or when it regulated gambling.

50. Today, total U.S. government spending as percentage of GDP stands at about 40 percent. Except for times of war, this percentage had never been above 5 percent until the Great Depression; for figures, see http://www.usgovernmentspending.com/.

51. Many explorations into the working of national economies were essentially impossible without solid statistical data. This included studies that most economists would consider basic today: things like consumption-savings ratios, government spending as percent of GDP, capital formation, profit-investment ratios, or the relationship between employment and national income.

52. According to Studenski's monumental study, *The Income of Nations* (1958), the very first official government studies of national income were generated in Australia in 1886, followed by Canada in 1925, and then, in relatively short sequence, by most other industrialized nations between 1925 and 1940. See also the account by Richard Stone, "Nobel Memorial Lecture 1984. The Accounts of Society" (1986), 5–28.

53. The National Bureau of Economic Research (NBER) offers a comprehensive list of monthly data on the national economy. According to their chronology, between 1854 and 1919 the United States experienced sixteen business cycles, in which the average recession lasted twenty-two months, and the average expansion twenty-seven months. Between the end of World War I and the end of World War II, there were six cycles: recessions lasted on average eighteen months and expansions thirty-five months (http://www.nber.org/cycles/recessions.html). During the Great Depression, according to the Bureau of Economic Analysis, it took a full eleven years (1929–40) before the American economy recovered its 1929 levels of output and employment (http://www.bea.gov/national/nipaweb/SelectTable.asp?Selected=N).

54. The same year Willford King had published his national income estimates, though I have found no indication that either man was aware of King's work at the time.

55. Even though the struggle for the eight-hour day had been in full force since the 1880s, American workers still worked twelve- to fourteen-hour days. Despite decades of struggles, workers had not yet gained the right to bargain collectively, nor had government put in place comprehensive wage or workplace safety laws, or provided benefits for the old, the unemployed, or those unable to work. Yet American manufacturing outperformed every other major industrial power by 1915.

56. See, for instance, David Kennedy, *Over Here: the First World War and American Society* (2004); see also David Noble's work *America By Design* (1979) on the role of science and technology in the growth of a corporate kind of capitalism.

57. Malcolm C. Rorty, as quoted in Nahum I. Stone, "The Beginnings of the National Bureau of Economic Research" (1945), 6.

58. NBER associates make up twenty Nobel Prize winners in economics, and thirteen past chairs of the President's Council of Economic Advisers. More than 1,100 professors are research associates at NBER.

59. Together with fellow economist Edwin Gay, Mitchell had been recruited by Rorty and Stone and subsequently had taken the lead during World War I in laying the groundwork for this organization, an effort that promised to fulfill his dreams. More than merely agreeing with Rorty and Stone on the need for verifiable knowledge as the foundation for debate, Mitchell viewed quantitative data as the core of his intellectual universe. Good data, he was convinced, promised a better future guided by knowledge rather than ignorance. Lack of data, in turn, would likely result, as social organization became ever more complex,

in increasingly disastrous failures. Edwin Gay was Dean of the Harvard Business School, and later NBER's first director. The idea was to generate information on the national economy that would be useful for a wide range of purposes. Their efforts expanded to include basic information on size, composition, growth, and fluctuation over time. Wesley Clair Mitchell, Willford Isbell King, and Frederick R. Macaulay, *Income in the United States: Its Amount and Distribution, 1909–1919* (1921), 1: v.

60. Arthur F. Burns, *Wesley Mitchell and the National Bureau*, National Bureau of Economic Research (1949), 5.

61. Wesley C. Mitchell, "Statistics and Government" (1919), 223–35.

62. Mitchell et al. (1921).

63. For a further discussion on this point, see chapter 4.

64. It should be noted, though, that the methods were meticulously revealed throughout. As one economic historian wrote, "Never before, nor since, has such a frank and detailed revelation been made of the actual methods of estimation and compilation"; see Palmer, *The Meaning and Measurement of the National Income and of Other Social Accounting Aggregates* (1966), 27.

65. Indeed, it is curious to read the introduction to NBER's volume *Income in the United States, 1909–1919*. While it acknowledges "most serious difficulties" of coming up with widely recognized definitions, and even allows for things like "services" or "satisfaction" to be legitimate forms of income, it then proceeds, without clarification or acknowledgment, to tabulate only money income of the official economy; see pp. 1–6. The report was published in two volumes—comprising detailed analysis and a wealth of data. At least among economists and a small cadre of policymakers, it also established NBER's reputation for thorough and impartial work. It certainly succeeded in garnering ongoing support from academics and private funders. For a good short history of NBER, see Solomon Fabricant, *Toward a Firmer Basis of Economic Policy: The Founding of the National Bureau of Economic Research* (1984).

66. Mark Perlman and Morgan Marietta, in a 2005 piece on the politics of social accounting, claim that "American statistical efforts" of the 1920s and 30s "pale by comparison with what was undertaken and, to an amazing degree, realized by a group of German statistical entrepreneurs immediately after the First World War and throughout the 1920s," whereas the UK did not "move toward creating its own national accounts system until after the fall of France in the summer of 1940." See Perlman and Marietta, "The Politics of Social Accounting: Public Goals and the Evolution of the National Accounts in Germany, the United Kingdom and the United States" (2005), 213, 216.

67. John Maynard Keynes, "The British Balance of Trade, 1925–27" (1927), 551–65. A significant early proponent of statistical data on the economy, the widely respected economist Irving Fisher concluded that so-called "index numbers"—prices or quantities over time—were not seriously considered until well after World War I. What we take for granted today, the familiar measure of GDP, in-

cluding its array of detailed economic indexes, was thus a surprisingly recent development. Remarkably, it subsequently spread across the industrialized world and moved from rudimentary calculations to intricate world system in less than an average American's lifetime. See Irving Fisher, *The Making of Index Numbers. A Study of their Varieties, Tests and Reliability* (1927), 460.

CHAPTER 3

1. The opening quotation is from Walter Rautenstrauch (Chair of Columbia University's Department of Industrial Engineering), letter to Senator Robert J. Bulkley, Chairman, Committee on Manufactures (1938).
2. Even the ideological icon of small government, Adam Smith, realized that the state is essential for economic development. In the notebooks that predated his famous *Wealth of Nations,* he wrote that "little else is requisite to carry a state to the highest degree of opulence from the lowest barbarism, but peace, easy taxes and a tolerable administration of justice"—all three functions, it should be noted, that only the state/government can guarantee. Adam Smith, *An Inquiry into the Nature and Causes of the Wealth of Nations* ([1776] 2009), xliii.
3. Karl Polanyi, *The Great Transformation: The Political and Economic Origins of Our Time* ([1944] 2001). 45.
4. Ibid., 143. Again, markets existed before governments, but this fails to take into account that they did not define the economy, but rather were as significant or central to social and economic life, prior to government regulations, as the average community farmers' market is today. On the general myth of "free markets," see James Kenneth Galbraith, *The Predator State: How Conservatives Abandoned the Free Market and Why Liberals Should Too* (2008); Ha-Joon Chang, *Bad Samaritans–The Myth of Free Trade and the Secret History of Capitalism* (2008); George P. Brockway, *The End of Economic Man: An Introduction to Humanist Economics* (2001); Dean Baker, *The Conservative Nanny State* (2006); Thomas Palley, *Plenty of Nothing* (1998). In a recent piece, former Secretary of Labor, Robert Reich, succinctly summarized the fallacy of free markets: "markets aren't 'free' of rules; the rules define them." Providing a wealth of pertinent examples, he further explained that "the 'free market' is a bunch of rules about (1) what can be owned and traded (the genome? slaves? nuclear materials? babies? votes?); (2) on what terms (equal access to the internet? the right to organize unions? corporate monopolies? the length of patent protections?); (3) under what conditions (poisonous drugs? unsafe foods? deceptive Ponzi schemes? uninsured derivatives? dangerous workplaces?); (4) what's private and what's public (police? roads? clean air and clean water? healthcare? good schools? parks and playgrounds?); (5) how to pay for what (taxes, user fees, individual pricing?)"; see Robert Reich, "The Myth of Free Markets" (2013b).

5. In a telling incident, early in his term President Obama displayed a moment of clarity rare for Washington politics when he told the top bankers assembled in the White House on 27 March 2009, at the height of the most recent Great Recession, "My administration is the only thing between you and the [common citizens'] pitchforks"; *ABC News*, 3 April 2009, http://abcnews.go.com/blogs/politics/2009/04/obama-to-banker/ (accessed Aug. 2013).

6. Elizabeth Warren, campaigning for U.S. Senate in Andover, Mass., August 2011. For a detailed historical and philosophical exploration of this point, see Gar Alperovitz and Lew Daly, *Unjust Deserts—How the Rich Are Taking Our Common Inheritance* (2008).

7. Officially entitled the "American Recovery and Reinvestment Act," it was signed into law by President Obama on 13 Feb. 2009.

8. A good example (out of literally thousands) would be AFL President William Green, an otherwise conservative labor leader, who warned in 1931 "when despite every effort to get employment, men and women find no opportunity to earn their living, desperation and blind revolt follow." Quoted in Robert S. McElvaine, *The Great Depression: America, 1929–1941* (1993), 91.

9. Robert M. La Follette (U.S. Senator from Wisconsin), *New York Times*, 27 April 1931.

10. Data from table V 20–30 in U.S. Bureau of the Census, *Historical Statistics of the United States: Colonial Times to 1970* (1975), 912.

11. McElvaine, ibid., 73.

12. U.S. Bureau of Economic Analysis, *National Income and Product Accounts*, tables 1.1, 1.2, and 3.2.

13. David M. Kennedy, *Freedom from Fear* (1999), 166–67.

14. John P. Lewis and Robert C. Turner, *Business Conditions Analysis* (1967).

15. Nicholas Crafts and Peter Fearon, *The Great Depression of the 1930s—Lessons for Today* (2013), 10.

16. Albert U. Romasco, *The Poverty of Abundance: Hoover, the Nation, the Depression* (1965), 166.

17. George W. Norris, as quoted in Patrick J. Maney, *"Young Bob" La Follette* (1978), 83.

18. *Congressional Record* 71:3, 1930–31, 697–710, 1173–222, 4431–38.

19. Senator Robert Wagner, in "Conflict in Senate on Unemployment Delays Tariff Bill" (1930), 1. Emphasis added. Given the state of the economy, unemployment numbers remained a politically highly sensitive topic—the numbers could be used as rationale for a wide range of programs, but also as an excuse for doing nothing, and they could break political careers. Three-and-a-half years later, President Franklin D. Roosevelt signed an Executive Order prohibiting the release of any statistics prior to their clearance by the Chairman of the Central Statistical Board. See Frank C. Walker, letter to the Secretary of Commerce (1933).

20. John Kenneth Galbraith, *Economics in Perspective* (1987), 245

21. As explored in chapter 2, this was its 1922 report *Income in the United States, Its Amount and Distribution, 1909–1919*. The report was published in two volumes, both edited by the lead NBER researcher Wesley C. Mitchell. NBER did not for-

malize their work on national income until, following a Jan. 1936 meeting of the Conference on Research in National Income and Wealth, it initiated in 1937 a series entitled "Studies in Income and Wealth."

22. Carol S. Carson, "The History of the United States National Income and Product Accounts" (1975), 154–55.

23. Hugh S. Norton, *The Employment Act and the Council of Economic Advisors, 1946–1976* (1977), 9.

24. Mark Blyth provides an excellent summary of contesting theories among economists and politicians trying to explain the Depression, ranging from a call for "sound finance" to what he calls a policy of "growthmanship;" see Blyth, *Great Transformations: Economic Ideas and Institutional Change in the 20th Century* (2002), 49–95.

25. Chief among them Senators Robert Wagner of N.Y., Edward Costigan of Colo., George Norris of Neb., Burton Wheeler of Mont., John Morris Sheppard of Texas, Representatives LaGuardia and Mead of N.Y., Kelly of Pa., Cutting of N.M.—all sponsored major relief and public works bills

26. Within the context of a global recession, Keynes first fully explicated his ideas about the critical role of government in the creation of demand in his *The General Theory of Employment, Interest and Money* ([1936] 1965). His theories essentially generated the field of macroeconomics, and have greatly shaped economic policymaking ever since.

27. Robert Wagner, as quoted in "Senators Demand Action to Check Unemployed," *New York Times*, 4 March 1930, p. 1.

28. Albert U. Romasco, ibid. (1965), 4; see also Mark Blyth's detailed account of such theories, ibid. (2002), 49–64.

29. Thomas P. Gore, Democrat from Oklahoma, as quoted in Arthur M. Schlesingner, *The Crisis of the Old Order* ([1957] 2002), 226.

30. Herbert Hoover, *The Memoirs of Herbert Hoover* (1952), iii, 30.

31. Edmund Wilson, *The American Jitters: A Year of the Slump* ([1932] 1968), 3.

32. *Congressional Record-Senate*, 72nd Congress, 3 March 1930, 4596–97.

33. Ironically, Hoover had long shown great interest in obtaining better economic statistics (as Treasury Secretary, he was instrumental in getting the "Survey of Current Business" started in 1921), primarily in order to "mitigate booms and crises," but above all in order to lessen the effects of economic downturns on employment; for an excellent historical review, see Michael Bernstein, *A Perilous Progress* (2001), 51–64.

34. "Senators Demand Action to Check Unemployment," *New York Times*, 4 March 1930, p. 1.

35. *Congressional Record-Senate*, 72nd Congress, 3 March 1930, p. 4609, emphasis added.

36. *Congressional Record-Senate*, 74th Congress, 15 Dec. 1930, p. 702.

37. In August 1931, PECE was transformed into the President's Organization for Unemployment Relief (POUR).

38. In an almost tragically ironic twist, just before the voluntary aid campaign was to be launched, many large corporations that were part of the initiative, such as United States Steel, Ford, and General Motors, announced wage cuts of 10 or more percent. See Robert H. Bremner, *American Philanthropy* (1988), 139.

39. Herbert Hoover, as quoted in Carl N. Degler, "The Ordeal of Herbert Hoover" (1963), 570.

40. Walter S. Gifford, as quoted in McElvaine, ibid., 79.

41. Gifford, as quoted in Schlesinger, ibid. ([1957] 2002), 173.

42. "Congress Wrangles, Drought Aid Waits," *New York Times*, 10 Jan. 1931, p. 1.

43. On 15 Dec. 1930, La Follette spent several hours reading into the record telegrams from labor organizations across the country, all demonstrating the severity of unemployment and rising poverty. Robert M. La Follette, Jr., Papers, 1895–1960, Library of Congress,; C556 (speeches and writing during 1930–31).

44. *Congressional Record*-Senate, 71st Congress, 15 Dec. 1930, p. 703.

45. Robert M. La Follette, as quoted in Edward Newell Doan, *The La Follettes and the Wisconsin Idea* (1947), 164.

46. Hearings would be held by the Committee on Manufactures, which he chaired. See *Congressional Record*-Senate, 25 Feb. 1931, p. 5944.

47. *Congressional Record*-Senate, 26 Feb. 1931, p. 6100.

48. Robert M. La Follette, as quoted in Maney, ibid., 92.

49. Robert P. Scripps, as quoted in the *Pittsburg Press*, 12 March 1931, p. 1.

50. They were George Norris of Neb., Edward Costigan of Colo., Bronson Cutting of N. M., and Burton Wheeler of Mont. The conference was held in Washington, 11–13 March, and was attended by progressive national and state politicians, mayors, labor leaders, writers, and activists.

51. Robert M. La Follette, as quoted in Doan, ibid., 165; and quoted in McElvaine, ibid., 230.

52. After his election as President of the United States, Franklin Roosevelt appointed Perkins as Secretary of the Labor Department, a position she held throughout all four terms of FDR's presidency. She was the first woman to be appointed to a cabinet position, and a member of the cabinet who decisively contributed to New Deal policies.

53. The 777-page transcript of ten full days of hearings represents a goldmine of similar statements, at times leaving chairman La Follette in a state of seeming exasperation. Hearings before a Subcommittee of the Committee of Manufactures, U.S. Senate, 72nd Congress, on S. 6215, 23, Oct. 1931, U.S. Government, pp. 133, 129, 141.

54. As Dewhurst characterized it: "Our lack of information has been woeful." John Maurice Clark, Professor of Economics at Columbia University, Hearings before a Subcommittee of the Committee of Manufactures, ibid., 211; J. Frederic Dewhurst, Chief of Economic Research Division, Bureau of Foreign and Domestic Commerce, Department of Commerce, ibid., 572–80; Ralph E. Flanders, Chairman of the American Engineering Council, ibid., 243.

55. Part of the November report of the Progressive Conference, the document expressed appreciation for the immense difficulties in generating such material; it also emphasized the "great value" it would have as essential guides to policymaking. A report by a Subcommittee of the Committee on Unemployment Stabilization of the Progressive Conference, in U.S., Congress, Committee on Manufactures, Establishment of National Economic Council, Hearings before a Subcommittee of the Committee on Manufactures, Senate, on S. 6215 (71st Congress), 72d Congress, 1st sess., 1931, pp. 746–47. National accounting scholars may note that "national income" was not an explicit category in the report, though all major components of later national income accounts are mentioned.

56. *Washington Post*, 20 Aug. 1931, p. 6.

57. Schlesinger, ibid. (2002), 174.

58. Official disregard for the realities of unemployment shone through even when addressed. The *New York Times* reported that "unemployment among all classes of workers in the United States now ranges between 9,000,000 and 11,000,000, according to the most reliable estimates. Official, up-to-date information as to the exact figure is lacking, however." See *New York Times*, 20 June 1932.

59. *Congressional Record*, 72nd Congress, 1st sess., 2 Feb. 1932, p. 3095; La Follette's speech took up the better part of two full days.

60. *Congressional Record*, 72nd Congress, 1st sess., 3 Feb. 1932, 3307; between Costigan and La Follette, they recorded a full 408 pages of testimony into the *Congressional Record*.

61. The bill was sponsored by Senators Robert M. La Follette, Jr., of Wisconsin, Edward F. Costigan of Colorado, and Bronson Cutting of New Mexico, S. 3045, *CR*, Vol. 75, 4042–4, and Reports on Public Bills, etc., Senate Report No. 135, Vol. 1, 72nd Cong., 1st sess., Senate; for debate see *CR*, Vol. 75, 3067–3260, 3306–3327, 1760–1763; 3314, 3516–3525; and 3658–3677, 6203–6206.

62. U.S., Congress, Senate, subcommittee of the Committee on Manufactures, Hearings, on S. 174 and S.262, Unemployment Relief, 72nd Congress, 1st sess., 28–30 Dec. 1931, and 4–9 Jan. 1932; Ibid., on S.4592, Federal Cooperation in Unemployment Relief, 9 May–4 June 1932.

63. Hoover, he claimed, supported a "doctrinaire economic philosophy" of "nonintervention" which utterly failed to "break through into the world of reality." *Congressional Record*, 72nd Congress, 22 June 1932, pp. 13685–86.

64. Carson, ibid. (1975), 155–56; *Congressional Record*, 72nd Congress, 1st sess., 1–11 June, 1932, p. 12285. (U.S. Congress, Senate, Resolution 220 [1932]). The resolution as introduced by Sen. La Follette is printed on page 12285, and there is discussion about the resolution on pages 12285–86 (8 June 1932). The resolution was again brought up on 13 June, at page 12748, and passed the Senate on that date. It was a simple Senate Resolution, not legislation that needed to be passed by both chambers.

65. *Congressional Record*, 72nd Congress, 8 June 1932, p. 12285. Passage of the resolution is recorded on 13 June, p. 12749.

66. As one of Feiker's aids at Commerce put it in a memorandum, such "surveys are more needed than studies on any other economic subjects." Both groups realized that while there was no consensus on government's role in the economy, few disagreed with the need for better economic data. Memorandum dated 24 Feb. 1932, National Archives, Record Group 151, Frederick M. Feiker File. The BFDC was renamed to the "Office of Business Economics" (OBE) in 1947. In 1971, it became the Bureau of Economic Analysis (BEA), which continues to be its current name. All operated within the US Department of Commerce.

CHAPTER 4

1. *New York Times*, 20 May 2012. It should be noted that about half of the world leaders in 2008 had since lost elections and were no longer present at the 2012 meeting, in no small part due to lack of GDP growth in their respective countries.
2. Senate Resolution 220, submitted 8 June 1932, passed on 13 June 1932, 72nd Congress, 1st sess.
3. Ron Snell, "The Great Recession" (2009), 17, 15.
4. According to the U.S. Department of Agriculture, productivity in many areas more than doubled between 1890 and 1930. See "A History of American Agriculture, 1776–1990," available at http://www.usda.gov/history2/text4.html.
5. Woodrow Wilson, as quoted in Robert Heilbroner, *The Economic Transformation of America* (1998), 256.
6. Franklin D. Roosevelt, *The Public Papers and Addresses of Franklin D. Roosevelt* (1938–50), 1:743–52.
7. Only because of significant disagreements later on between the Commerce Department accounts and Kuznets's concepts (see chapter 5), it should be noted that the final report led to considerable acrimony between the senior economist of the Division of Economic Research at the Commerce Department, Robert F. Martin, and Simon Kuznets. In essence, Martin felt disrespected by Kuznets, and considered the work of his team largely unacknowledged. In a letter to the acting Chief of the Economic Research Division, Martin called the report a "grab" and spoke of the "singular ungenerousness" of Kuznets; see letter from Martin to Mr. Tupper, dated 22 Jan. 1934, National Archives, Record Group 151, Thorp File. After Kuznets's departure, Martin took over the reins of national income accounting at Commerce, before leaving in June 1935 to join the National Industrial Conference Board as their lead national accounts expert.
8. As will be discussed later, it also ignores that Kuznets fundamentally disagreed with key components of how GDP was eventually defined.
9. For one of many obituaries that express such characterizations, see Morris Hamburg, in Simon Kuznets, unprocessed papers, Harvard University Archives, Box 1 of 2.

10. Kuznets, of course, was not the only one critical to the creation of national accounts, though it is safe to say that his contributions were central, perhaps even decisive in generating the general accounting model after which GDP was fashioned. Of similar significance in the United Kingdom was Colin Clark, by many believed to have been the first to develop and use the concept of GNP (Gross National Product). Important earlier contributions in the United States were made, in historical order, by George Tucker (1859), Willford I. King (1915), and Wesley C. Mitchell (1921). For a brief review of developments, see Joseph W. Duncan and William C. Shelton, *Revolution in United States Government Statistics* (1978); for a detailed discussion, see Paul Studenski, *The Income of Nations* (1958).

11. As quoted by James H. Street, "The Contribution of Simon S. Kuznets to Institutionalist Development Theory" (1988), 501.

12. His dissertation, published in 1930 as "Secular Movements in Production and Prices," was an effort to discover the causes and costs of business fluctuations, and was awarded the prestigious Hartshaffer and Marx Prize.

13. As quoted in Malcolm Rutherford, *Institutions in Economics* (1996), 41.

14. He had just published his first major piece in English on the topic. Simon Kuznets, *Secular Movements in Production and Prices, Their Nature and Their Bearing upon Cyclical Fluctuations* (1930).

15. As mentioned in chapter 3, to this day, NBER—a private institution—remains the final arbiter to determine whether the U.S. economy is in a recession or not.

16. An entry in the *Encyclopedia of Social Sciences*, vol. 11 (1933b). For Webbink account, see Vibha Kapuria-Foreman and Mark Perlman, "An Economic Historian's Economist: Remembering Simon Kuznets," (1995), 1530. Webbink later drafted Senate Resolution 220 as well as La Follette's accompanying remarks in the Senate.

17. Dewhurst had earlier testified before La Follette's subcommittee on Manufactures about the inadequacy of economy-wide statistics. For almost a decade, he had also been in charge of providing economic reports to the public on what meager information was available. For quote, see Calvert Judkins, memorandum dated Feb. 24, 1932.

18. Ibid.

19. "Memorandum on the History and Progress of the Study of National Income for 1929–32," attached to a letter from Simon Kuznets to Dr. Willard L. Thorp (1933a). See also Carol S. Carson, "The History of the United States National Income and Product Accounts" (1971), 78. For memo, see Judkins, ibid.

20. Letter from Frederick M. Feiker to Dr. Edwin F. Gay, 13 April 1932, National Archives, Record Group 151, Frederick M. Feiker files.

21. Ibid.

22. Lillian Epstein, Kuznets's "assistant" at NBER, had more years of experience and background in national income accounts than Kuznets himself, but in a very male-dominated environment, she was apparently never considered for the task. Yet again she did, however, provide vital assistance to the project.

23. Letter from F. M. Surface to Mr. [E. A.] Tupper, 19 Nov. 1932, National Archives, Record Group 151, Frederick M. Feiker files; letter from Edwin F. Gay to Frederick M. Feiker, 18 November 1932, ibid. (Gay asked for $5,000 annual salary for Kuznets, which, in 2012 dollars, roughly equals $84,000); letter from Frederick M. Feiker to Frederic Dewhurst, 14 Dec. 1932.

24. FDR won over 57 percent of the vote, and carried forty-two of forty-eight states.

25. Kuznets, ibid. (1933a).

26. The BFDC was the predecessor of today's Bureau of Economic Analysis (BEA).

27. Kuznets, ibid. (1933a).

28. It was probably British economist J. R. Hicks who first theorized this formula in "The Valuation of the Social Income," 105–24. Another formula used by accountants that leads to the same result is taking GDP (Y) as the sum of *final consumption expenditures* (FCE), *gross capital formation* (GCF), and *net exports* (X–M), or Y=FCE + GCF + (X–M).

29. Most of the literature credits British economists James Meade and Richard Stone with the basic concepts behind this formula. In an unpublished Ph.D. diss., Benjamin H. Mitra-Kahn convincingly argues that, contrary to such scholarly claims, the person singularly responsible for the basic concept behind the formula is British economist John Maynard Keynes; see Mitra-Kahn, "Redefining the Economy: How the 'Economy' Was Invented in 1620" (2011), 210–25.

30. Simon Kuznets, *National Income and Its Composition* (1941), 57.

31. Mark Perlman, "Political Purpose and the National Accounts" (1980), 134.

32. Robert R. Nathan, "GNP and Military Mobilization" (1994), 3.

33. Kuznets, ibid. (1941), 5.

34. Kuznets, Senate Report, "National Income, 1929–1932" (1934), 5.

35. For an excellent updated summary discussion on this point, see Robert Eisner, *The Misunderstood Economy: What Counts and How to Count It* (1994); for general background on this question, see Alonso and Starr, *The Politics of Numbers* (1987); Paul Studenski, *The Income of Nations* (1958); Duncan and Shelton, *Revolution in United States Government Statistics* (1978); W. W. Rostow, *Theorists of Economic Growth* (1990); and André Vanoli, *A History of National Accounting* (2005).

36. Willford I. King, "Income and Wealth," (1925), 457.

37. Kuznets, ibid. (1941), 6. For economists, income provides a wide range of interest and significance: it is used to establish a tax base, to measure the ability of persons, companies, and nations to receive or pay back loans, to figure out "income parity" or social equality, to judge the feasibility of investments or construction projects, and so on. Practical applications of income concepts in government are nearly endless, yet the character of each application thus depends on the very definition of income that informs it.

38. Wesley C. Mitchell, Willford I. King, Frederick R. Macaulay, and Oswald W. Knauth, *Income in the United States* (1921), 3.

39. As we have seen in chapter 2, , the father of classical economics, Adam Smith, excluded services from his notion of national income—as did Karl Marx, and,

following his lead, most nominally communist countries during the twentieth century.

40. Mitchell et al., ibid. (1921).

41. Simon Kuznets, "National Income" (1933b), 11: 205.

42. Mark Perlman and Morgan Marietta, "The Politics of Social Accounting" (2005), 219.

43. Moses Abramovitz, "Simon Kuznets, 1901–1985" (1986), 242.

44. The "whole" could be arrived at in several ways. Two measures the report featured were *national income produced* and *national income paid out*. The broader of the two, national income produced, soon turned into the primary focus of national accounts. Defined by the report as "all commodities produced and all personal services rendered . . . at their market value, [minus] value . . . of stock of goods expended in producing this total," it is this version that became generally associated with the short-hand "national income." What Kuznets attempted, in short, was not a gauge of the welfare of the nation. Based on what data was available to him, he attempted to provide a limited "index of productivity." He defined income as covering only those activities that happened in the marketplace (thereby "lowering," by Kuznets's ready admission, "the value of national income measurements"). In essence, he followed an earlier economist of national accounts, Arthur C. Pigou, who had argued that national income comprises the goods and services that "can be brought directly or indirectly into relation with the measuring-rod of money"—price would determine value. This was contrary to what Kuznets believed was the ultimate purpose of national income accounts. Thus, based on prices determined by the market, national income did not account for the level of inequality or income distribution. Satisfaction of consumer needs, moreover, remained unaddressed. So did social or personal well-being. Kuznets repeatedly stated that a "student of social affairs" legitimately interested in any aspect of national income other than productivity of the market would "have to qualify and change our estimates, possibly in a marked fashion." John P. Lewis and Robert C. Turner, *Business Conditions Analysis* (1959), 15; Arthur C. Pigou, *The Economics of Welfare* ([1920] 2013), 11, 31.

45. Kuznets, ibid. (1934), 9, 6, 4, 7.

46. The extent to which it was only Kuznets's report has been somewhat controversial. The head of the initial effort at the Commerce Department, then senior assistant to Kuznets at Commerce, and later Director of the Bureau of Foreign and Domestic Commerce, Robert Martin, early on disputed lone, or even primary, authorship by Kuznets. Martin wrote that he is experiencing "the unpleasantness of resisting what is turning out to be a 'grab,'" and complained about the "singular ungenerousness" accorded to him by Kuznets; Robert F. Martin letter to Mr. Tupper, 22 Jan. 1934, National Archives, National Income collection, box 160.

47. See Carson, ibid. (1971), 84.

48. Unprecedented in its extensive revelation of sources used, the report vividly portrays the difficulties Kuznets and his team faced: in addition to census data,

the report cites city and state estimates, "Census of Occupations," tabulations of income tax returns, returns of thousands of questionnaires, and even things like "letter from Mr. Purves of the Department of Agriculture;" going through roughly 100 pages of appendices on data used, one finds that the two words that stand out the most are "estimated" and "assumed," for nowhere was Kuznets working with reliably accurate or definitive datasets; Kuznets, ibid. (1934).

49. The Department of Commerce was authorized by the initial Senate resolution to obtain necessary data from other government and private organizations (which they extensively used in cases such as the Income Tax Unit, the Federal Reserve, or the Department of Agriculture, as well as several trade and industrial associations); where data were not available, they used the powers of the government to request information via questionnaires (to obtain, for instance, income statements from oil- and gas-producing industries, income of professionals, or compensation payments for injuries); see Kuznets, ibid. (1933a).

50. Kuznets, ibid. (1934), 13.

51. The reason these figures add up to more than the 40 percent mentioned in the previous paragraph is that they do not, unlike the totals, include payments for pensions and injury; ibid., 14.

52. The depression, furthermore, had dramatically distinctive effects on different industries. Employment in construction, for instance, declined by almost 60 percent (with a concurrent decline of 73 percent income paid out), in mining by 40 percent (with 61 percent less income paid out), whereas in government it had actually increased by 4 percent. Overall, income paid out declined faster than employment, suggesting depressed wage scales and an increase in part-time work. Among those who still had a job, most nevertheless saw their incomes decline; unemployment figures were based on Census data; family farm labor had also declined significantly, but he did not have access to reliable figures. Figures are for 1929 to 1932; ibid., 14–25.

53. Ibid., 13.

54. Frank D. Roosevelt, as quoted in the *Washington Post*, 9 March 1933, p. 1.

55. *New York Times*, 24 Jan. 1934, p. 4

56. Rosemary D. Marcuss and Richard E. Kane, "U.S. National Income and Product Statistics" (2007), 36.

57. Adjusted for inflation, roughly equivalent to $3.40 in 2012 terms. For background, see Carson, ibid. (1971), 97.

58. The language of the iconic "GNP" did not appear in public, at least in print, until Clark Warburton's publication in December 1934, "Value of the Gross National Product and Its Components, 1919–1929" (1934), 383–88.

59. Arnold J. Katz, "A Tribute for Robert R. Nathan," (2002), 8. When funding and support staff were finally secured, Nathan returned in December 1934 to Commerce as chief of the National Income Section (NIS), which carried on the earlier work of Kuznets and his staff.

60. Ibid., 96–99; Duncan and Shelton, ibid. (1978), 78–79.

61. The National Income Collection at the National Archives contains a wealth of correspondence revealing the uphill struggle to get Congress and the White House to support and fund ongoing work on national economic statistics. See, for instance, the letters from William Thorp, Director of the Bureau of Foreign and Domestic Commerce; National Archives, Box 160, Willard Thorp files.

62. Arthur M. Schlesinger, *The Coming of the New Deal* ([1957] 2003), 20.

63. John Maynard Keynes's famous magnum opus *The General Theory of Employment, Interest, and Money* was not published until February 1936. It should also be noted that there are many claims to the originality of Keynes's ideas. Economist J. Adam Tooze, for instance, makes the case in *Statistics and the German State* (2001) that much of the Keynesian revolution was presaged in Weimar Germany; John K. Galbraith argues that what was attributed to Keynes should, in fairness, have been called the "Stockholm Revolution," as Swedish economists had largely anticipated Keynes; Galbraith, *A Life in Our Times* (1981), 82.

64. The flip-side of boosting demand was restricting supply in order to stabilize prices. In 1933 the newly established Agricultural Adjustment Act started with two highly controversial programs: the first came to be known as the "Great Pig Slaughter of 1933," the other was forever burned into the minds of the destitute as newspaper reports showed corn being plowed under—hungry and homeless, many did not grasp the finer economic points of price stabilization. Both programs were designed to help farmers make a living in an environment of radically reduced demand (corn crops were to be reduced by 20 to 30 percent, and the number of hogs farrowed by 25 percent, or what amounted to about six million pigs slaughtered). Later declared unconstitutional, the program did succeed in stabilizing prices.

65. Galbraith, ibid. (1987), 245.

66. Or what Keynes later explained as the need for boosting "aggregate demand." The point that the "statistical revolution" of national income accounting preceded the "Keynesian Revolution" is most clearly explained in Don Patinkin, "Keynes and Econometrics: On the Interaction between the Macroeconomic Revolutions of the Interwar Period" (1976), 1091–123. As Tooze claims in *Statistics and the German State* (2001), furthermore, macroeconomics not only had many roots predating Keynes, the so-called "Keynesian Revolution" was "in many respects the least revolutionary of a variety of possibilities on offer in the interwar period;" Tooze, ibid., 290.

67. John Maynard Keynes, *The General Theory of Employment, Interest and Money* ([1936] 1965), book 4, chap. 16, section 3, p. 220.

68. Simon Kuznets, discussion section, in M. A. Copeland, "Concepts of National Income" (1937), 1:37.

69. John Kenneth Galbraith, "The National Accounts: Arrival and Impact" (1980), 80.

70. Many economic claims are grounded in the information derived from national income estimates, the article continued. With a familiarity almost eerie for a

reader today, the authors cited as an example the claim that we do not need to "worry about the increase in the national debt" because of an even greater "increase in national income." This was troubling. If people "examined a little more closely the way in which these figures are arrived at," they would "probably be more careful." The authors then argued, correctly, that "national income is not . . . a definitely known total." Rather, it is "an estimate, subject to a wide margin of error and a wide range of possible interpretations." One searches in vain for a comparable level of clarity in today's newspaper reports on national income. *New York Times*, editorial, 6 Sept. 1936.

71. Letter from Robert Nathan to Harry Hopkins, 27 Jan. 1939, and Hopkins letter to Congressional leaders, 31 Jan. 1939, National Archives, National Income Files, Box 692, Willard Thorp files.

72. The role of government during World War II raised two more related questions of profound significance: (1) could some version of a command economy actually work long term, and (2) was it possible that government could have prevented the routine, and routinely devastating, economic downturns of the previous century by concerted efforts to stimulate demand?

CHAPTER 5

1. As many scholars have pointed out, Roosevelt probably never possessed, or perhaps never ascribed to, a comprehensive "economic philosophy." Rather, he responded to circumstances and needs, and, following the renewed sharp downturn of 1937–38, the most sensible explanation seemed to come from Keynes: that essential deficit spending, through the multiplier effect, would increase national income significantly more than original spending. This allowed even those in favor of balanced budgets, like FDR himself, to advocate more government spending. For a particularly good discussion on this point, see Herbert Stein, *The Fiscal Revolution in America* (1977), and particularly chap. 7, "The Fiscal Revolution and the Keynesian Revolution." A similar account is provided by Mark Blyth, who argues that officials in the Treasury Department "began bombarding the White House with memos advocating greater spending," or, as one telegram stated, adopting a socioeconomic policy that would direct government toward "the increase in production of goods and services and the elimination of physical and human waste"; as quoted in Blyth, *Great Transformations: Economic Ideas and Institutional Change in the 20th Century* (2002), 74.

2. All FDR quotes from Franklin D. Roosevelt, Message to Congress, 14 April 1938, available at The American Presidency Project, http://www.presidency.ucsb.edu/ws/print.php?pid=15626 (accessed 4 July 2012). For a good brief review of the economic context as seen by policymakers, see Gerald Colm, "Experiences in the Use of Social Accounting in Public Policy in the United States" (1951), 75–111.

3. Robert R. Nathan, who agreed to head national income work at the Bureau of Foreign and Domestic Commerce (BFDC) after Robert F. Martin's departure, worked with a staff of three for the next two years; see Joseph W. Duncan and William C. Shelton, *Revolution in United States Government Statistics, 1926–1976* (1978), 80.

4. Carol S. Carson suggests that lack of necessary budgets and personnel, coupled with a dearth of reliable data (annual estimates were largely based on annual data such as census totals and corporate income tax returns), constitutes the main reasons as to why it took almost four years for the monthly income series to come to fruition; see Carson, "The History of the United States National Income and Product Accounts (1971), 103. By 1938 the BFDC added a state-by-state series, and by 1939 the Economic Research Division, responsible for national accounts, was abolished to make way for the National Income Section, which became its own division within the Commerce Department. It should also be noted that as accuracy and speed of reporting constituted an obvious trade-off, the decision was made to publicize new data in "preliminary" form as soon as it was processed, and to report revised figures as more information became available.

5. Mark Perlman makes a similar point in "Political Purpose and National Accounts" (1983), 140–41; also see the section "One More Time: Simon Kuznets" in chapter 10, this volume, for further discussion on this important point.

6. See Duncan and Shelton, ibid., 81.

7. Mark Perlman and Morgan Marietta, "The Politics of Social Accounting" (2005), 220.

8. Simon Kuznets, *National Income and Its Composition, 1919–1938* (1941), xxv–xxvi, 3–6.

9. According to military historian Richard Overy, the U.S. military was rated eighteenth in the world in 1939; see Richard Overy, *Why the Allies Won* (1995), 190.

10. Donald M. Nelson, *Arsenal of Democracy: The Story of American War Production* (1946), 3. Nelson, who had been executive vice president of Sears Roebuck, accepted the position of director of priorities of the U.S. Office of Production Management (1941–42), before serving as chairman of the powerful War Production Board (1942–44).

11. Mitra-Kahn argues, correctly I think, that Kuznets gave up his own definition of a national economy in favor of the British GNP metric (which included government expenditures) during this time of necessary war mobilization; see Mitra-Kahn, "Redefining the Economy: How the 'Economy' Was Invented in 1620" (2011), 236–71.

12. The unemployment rate of nearly 20 percent in 1938 dropped to 4.7 percent by 1942 and essentially disappeared to a historical low of less than 2 percent by 1943. See Department of Labor, Bureau of Labor Statistics.

13. The term originated with Lieutenant General Albert Wedemeyer, whose September 1941 report, entitled "The Ultimate Requirements Study" but soon referred to

as the "Victory Program," outlined strategic and economic goals that had to be met in order to achieve victory in war. For a good discussion, see James Lacey, *Keep from All Thoughtful Men: How U.S. Economists Won World War II* (2011).

14. Ibid., 46.

15. Perlman and Marietta, ibid., 221.

16. John E. Brigante, *The Feasibility Dispute* (1950), 35–36. In a memorandum to Nathan, Kuznets explained the significance of feasibility studies: "An attempt to secure unattainable goals is likely to result in an unbalanced performance in the sense that facilities will be built for which there will not be enough raw materials; that semi-finished products will be produced which it will be impossible to finish; and that finished products will be produced for which indispensable complements will be lacking." Quoted in Lacey, ibid., 138.

17. Brigante, ibid., 3.

18. Nelson, ibid. (1946), 377. Nelson provides several pages of examples as to why and how careful planning based on accurate statistical income and product data was essential, and, specifically, why "a production program which goes substantially beyond the limits of feasibility" would be highly detrimental to the war effort.

19. Through a program called "Lend-Lease," the United States exported about $32.5 billion worth of goods, mostly military equipment, between 1941 and 1945, of which $13.8 billion went to Great Britain and $9.5 billion went to the Soviet Union; see Alan Milward, *War, Economy, and Society, 1939–1945* (1979), 71.

20. For a detailed account, see Brigante, ibid.; Nathan was selected by Nelson to head the Planning Committee of the War Production Board. In May 1942 Nathan secured the services of his former mentor, Kuznets.

21. Brigante, ibid., 32.

22. Kuznets's data also revealed essential labor shortages, for workers seemed to desert hard and badly paid jobs like mining for the higher wages of war plants and shipyards. Ibid., 69.

23. As Kuznets's immediate superior at the WPB, Nathan replied to Somervell that "in view of the gravity of the problem discussed in these documents, I hesitate to take your memorandum seriously." For quotes (p. 108) and a full account of battles between economists and military leaders, see Lacey, ibid.; see also Mark Perlman, After dinner speech (2003).

24. According to Nelson, the army also engaged in a vicious media attack on the role of the WPB, and on Nelson in particular, including a public request for his resignation; see Nelson, ibid. (1946), 384–89.

25. Ibid., 390.

26. Ibid., 379.

27. One military historian characterized World War II as the "gross national product war"; see Russell Weigley, *The American Way of War* (1973), 146. See also John Paxton, "Myth vs. Reality: The Question of Mass Production in World War II" (2008), 91–104; Arthur Herman, *Freedom's Forge: How American Business Produced Victory in World War II* (2012); for figures, see Nelson, ibid. (1946).

28. Two experts in the field conclude that "national income and product account not only for Germany but also for all of 'fortress Europe' would have been of great use to Hitler, Speer, and others in the latter part of the war if they had been familiar with the concepts and had had the basic data." Duncan and Shelton, ibid., 91. Furthermore, as Michael Edelstein points out, the U.S. economy accomplished this while only devoting "about 31% of its labor force to war production and the military, while Germany committed 38%, Britain, 45% and Russia, 54%." See Edelstein, "The Size of the U.S. Armed Forces during World War II: Feasibility and War Planning" (2001), 48.

29. The focus on the war's immediate needs meant that even leading practitioners such as Milton Gilbert or George Jaszi effectively rejected any and all larger conceptual questions about the GDP. Technical questions about how to define "final product" were answered by the needs of the moment: more output of war-related production. When he first joined the Bureau as an economist in 1941, Jaszi described his role as resisting the "forging [of] national output into a measure of economic welfare." He clearly noted that his position was, at the time, a minority position that opposed "such mental giants as the late Professor Kuznets and Professor Hicks." He also had to "defy a forceful secretary of Commerce who had 'instructed' BEA to prepare a measure of welfare;" see George Jaszi, "An Economic Accountant's Audit" (1986), 411–17.

30. John Kenneth Galbraith, "The National Accounts: Arrival and Impact" (1980), 80.

31. Paul Samuelson, "Unemployment Ahead" (1944), 298; Paul A. Samuelson and William D. Nordhaus, *Economics* (1985), 102.

CHAPTER 6

1. Wendy Jehanara Tremayne, *The Good Life Lab* (2013), 23.

2. Domestically, the efforts of key players like Robert Nathan, Simon Kuznets, and Stacey May were not possible without the national income data provided by the Commerce Department. After Nathan had left to work for the War Production Board (WPB), another former student of Kuznets, Milton Gilbert, took charge of the National Income Division in 1941. Gilbert, editor of the *Survey of Current Business* from 1939–41, was an avowed Keynesian and, even more than Nathan, interested in a more detailed breakdown of national accounts. He believed that such detail could provide government with the necessary tools to convert a depressed peacetime economy into a successful wartime economy, all without depriving the civilian sector of essential consumer items. Thus, both the Commerce Department and the WPB pulled in the same direction at a key time of crisis and war mobilization. In peacetime, national income accounts had focused primarily on income flows. To be useful to wartime production planning,

Gilbert understood, national accounts needed to provide much more detailed information on product flows. In a "thrilling process" of data-gathering and retooling, the first American version of GNP accounts were thus created by economists at the Bureau of Foreign and Domestic Commerce. George Jaszi, "The Quarterly National Income and Product Account of the United States, 1942–62" (1965), 102.

3. Making full use of available national income statistics, Gilbert demonstrated what could lead to victory: a combination of higher employment, increased output, a reduction of fixed capital formation and consumer expenditures and, above all, a significant shift in production from civilian to military goods, all at pay rates higher than in the civilian sector. See Gilbert, "War Expenditures and National Income" (1942b), 9. It should also be noted that his approach was greatly influenced by the writings of several British economists: aside from Keynes himself, two economists in particular had made significant contributions to making national income accounts operational for war mobilization, James Meade and Richard Stone.

4. As quoted in Bill McKibben, *Deep Economy: The Wealth of Communities and the Durable Future* (2007), 8.

5. National income and product accountants occupied leading positions in the Treasury Department, the Office of Price Administration, the Federal Deposit Insurance Corporation, the National Defense Advisory Council, and the War Production Board; for further details, see Carol S. Carson, "The History of the United States National Income and Product Accounts: The Development of an Analytical Tool" (1975), 189–99.

6. Richard Ruggles, *National Income Accounting and Its Relation to Economic Policy* (1949), 14; and Ruggles, "The United State National Income Accounts, 1947–1977" (1983), 18.

7. Economist Richard Ruggles shows that, until World War II, national accounting in the United States did not yet follow a fully developed "system." That system did not come into place until Richard Stone and James Meade, both economists working on national accounts for the British government, "put into operational terms the concepts laid out in Keynes's *General Theory*." It was also the system that was then "rapidly adopted" by those in charge of national income work in the United States, and later adopted by the League of Nations. See Ruggles, *National Accounting and Economic Policy* (1999), 75.

8. More than anything, the accomplishments of data-driven national accounting work explain the sudden, almost meteoric, post-1945 rise in influence of economists. Their new seats at the tables of power were premised on mathematical models that could assure ongoing growth. "Experts had strikingly proved the effectiveness of a new wisdom by which the nation's productive capacity could be accurately measured, configured, and utilized for military purposes." It was a powerful weapon. Michael Bernstein, *A Perilous Progress* (2001), 93. Economists not only provided the data for wartime production but also played essen-

tial roles in the Office of Price Administration, making sure the civilian sector did not collapse due to the drain of resources to the military, and the Department of Treasury, where they were charged with figuring out ways to finance the war. Almost as important as their role in organizing war production was their function in the Office of Strategic Services (the predecessor of the CIA). "Economists in that agency planned the daily bombing strikes of Nazi territory on the basis of an analysis of which targets, if destroyed, would most damage war-making capacity." Robert W. Fogel, "Simon S. Kuznets" (2000), 12.

9. Initially, according to a leading economist of the time, "The theory of growth [was] an underdeveloped area in economics." Moses Abramovitz, *Thinking about Growth* (1989), 133. Learning from the application of selective stimuli to the depressed economy of the 1930s, and then generating unprecedented output by applying fresh accounting measures to the task of mobilization for victory, firmly established growth as the central underlying logic of modern economic thought; this history is quite well documented in Robert M. Collins, *More—The Politics of Economic Growth in Postwar America* (2000).

10. The profession of economics, argues Bernstein, "no longer the study of 'the nature and causes of the wealth of nations' (as Adam Smith suggested), or 'a critical analysis of capitalist production' (as Karl Marx suggested), . . . had become the formal study of 'the adaptation of scarce means to given ends.'" Bernstein, ibid., 95. As if following the law of unintended consequences, the result was a far cry from what pioneers like Willford King or Wesley Mitchell or Simon Kuznets sought to accomplish.

11. Mark Perlman and Morgan Marietta, "The Politics of Social Accounting" (2005), 222; Milton Gilbert, "National Income: Concepts and Measurements" (1945), 5.

12. Yale economist Richard Ruggles described national accounts, as if devoid of all value judgments, as "a system of classification that permits the making of a descriptive and factual record of what has happened in the economy." See Ruggles, ibid. (1999), 9.

13. John Kenneth Galbraith, "The Job before Us" (1943), 65.

14. According to Carol S. Carson's extensive study, even before the war was over, some two hundred public and private organizations in the United States were engaged in planning for postwar problems. At least forty-five were using national income statistics to devise strategies for industrial, agricultural, and financial growth and stability; see Carson, ibid. (1975), 200. For an official summary, see S. Morris Livingston, *Markets after the War* (1943).

15. Simon Kuznets, "National Income," (1933b), 11: 205–224. For a thorough discussion of the changes in Kuznets views on national income as an indicator of welfare, see Abe Tarasofsky, "GDP and Its Derivatives as Welfare Measure" (1998).

16. J. R. Hicks, "The Valuation of the Social Income" (1940), 122.

17. Among many critics of this claim, the economist Daniel Bromley responded, "To believe that markets determine value is to believe that milk comes from plastic bottles." See Bromley, "Resources and Economic Development" (1985),

781. Michael Bernstein notes that contemporary policy debate, framed within the categories of mainstream economic theory, has assumed a very narrow view: "ends, objectives, goals fall from view; means, techniques, trade-offs become the sole object of discussion," all grounded in "a vast array of unspoken and frequently unconscious beliefs," Bernstein, ibid., 4.

18. For a wide-ranging discussion on the shortcomings of economics, see Stephen A. Marglin, *The Dismal Science* (2008), 36. David Orrell's book *Economyths* (2010) goes further by arguing that neoclassical economics is little more than ideology pretending to be science. Based on similar reasoning, Yves Smith questions the key role of economists in policymaking, since their conclusions are routinely based on doctrine rather than evidence; see *ECONned* (2011). For a short exploration devastating to the core assumptions underlying neoclassical economics, see Alex Rosenberg, "From Rational Choice to Reflexivity" (2014), 21–41.

19. Ellen O'Brien, "Contested Accounts: The Evolution of the Meaning and Measurement of National Accounts" (1998), 11.

20. It should be noted that it is therefore erroneous to call the father of modern national accounts "the father of the GNP." The logic that emerged victoriously, and in the end informed GNP and GDP, was of predominantly British origin before gaining a significant following in the United States. It seemed to serve U.S. interests well. Yet it was a logic fundamentally different from the one advocated by Kuznets. Publications, interviews, and personal correspondence of Kuznets merely offer a sketchy portrait on why he gave up on national accounts, and particularly on accounts with a final product orientation that was clearly focused on human welfare. The clearest account comes from an interview he gave shortly before his death, in which he said that he "had underestimated the logical and causality-related difficulties inherent in the analysis" of his preferred focus; see Christian Leipert, "A Critical Appraisal of Gross National Product" (1987), 362.

21. For a brief history of the main developments, see John W. Kendrick, "The Historical Development of National-Income Accounts" (1970), 284–315; for Khrushchev quote, see "We Will Bury You!" *Time* magazine, 26 Nov. 1956.

22. See Collins, ibid. (2000).

23. For powerful sample accounts of winners and losers, see Ira Katznelson, *When Affirmative Action Was White* (2005), and Lizabeth Cohen, *A Consumers' Republic: The Politics of Mass Consumption in Postwar America* (2003).

24. Dwight D. Eisenhower, as quoted by Lizabeth Cohen, ibid., 118. Cohen's third chapter, entitled "Reconversion: The Emergence of the Consumers' Republic," provides an excellent account of the broader social and cultural impacts of our GDP fixation.

25. For a good summary of examples, see Robert Costanza, Maureen Hart, et al., "Beyond GDP: The Need for New Measures of Progress" (2009); for a more extensive and conceptual discussion, see Tomáš Hák and Svatava Janoušková, "Review Report on Beyond GDP Indicators: Categorisation, Intentions and Impacts" (2012), 20–28.

26. The story of this development is well told in Andrew L. Yarrow's book, *Measuring America: How Economic Growth Came to Define American Greatness in the Late Twentieth Century* (2010), 2, 196. As Yarrow argues, economic growth became America's key identity, and "tended to assume greater importance" than other issues such as civil rights or equality, resulting in "widespread disappointment, anxiety, and unhappiness."

27. Cohen, ibid., 118.

28. Carson, ibid. (1975), 210.

29. Public Law 304, 79th Congress (1946).

30. Jimmy Carter is a possible exception to this general phenomenon. Leon Keyserling, the second Chair of CEA, was perhaps the first to articulate in explicit terms the role of economic growth in American politics. He noted that "we need more than a slight upward trend of business and employment.... Economic stability requires economic growth, and the maximum employment and production objectives of the Employment Act require an expanding economy." Quoted in H. W. Arndt, *The Rise and Fall of Economic Growth* (1984), 35.

31. When the black president of the Brotherhood of Sleeping Car Porters, A. Philip Randolph, had threatened a "March on Washington" if the President did not eliminate racial discrimination in war production, FDR backed down and issued Executive Order 8802 in 1941, banning discrimination in defense industries and establishing the Fair Employment Practice Committee. For more detail, see Cornelius Bynum, *A. Philip Randolph and the Struggle for Civil Rights* (2010).

32. Ibid., 43. Historian Lizabeth Cohen's excellent book *A Consumers' Republic* (ibid.) not only traces why and how economic growth turns into a key goal of postwar policies, but also convincingly explains, in vivid detail, how America turned into a consumers' republic in the process.

33. Edgar Z. Palmer, *The Meaning and Measurement of the National Income* (1966), 2.

34. Victor Lebow, "What Makes the Consumer Buy?"(1958), 28.

35. This point is well developed in Mark Blyth, *Austerity: The History of a Dangerous Idea* (2013).

36. According to economist Angus Maddison, "Japanese postwar growth has exceeded that of any other country, and the Soviet growth rate has been as high as [that of] the highest West European performers." See *Asia: Economic Growth in Japan and the USSR* (2006), xxiii. Postwar growth rates for the Soviet Union, particularly since it did not employ GDP metrics, remain controversial; for an updated summary, see Martin Kragh, "The Soviet Enterprise" (2013), 360–94. Though the Soviets used an accounting device different from GDP (with a larger focus on goods than services, central planning rather than markets determining prices and production, etc.), their Material Product System (MPS) shared in common with GDP a singular focus on output.

37. Robert R. Nathan, *Mobilizing for Abundance* (1944), 98.

38. For the original written request for support, see letter from Herbert H. Lehman to Secretary Harry Hopkins, 29 Dec. 1943; NARA, National Income collection,

Thorp files, Box 2566. Simon Kuznets's personal files at Harvard contain dozens of letters to economists and accountants in countries ranging from Iceland to Jordan, Turkey, Austria and Japan advising them on their respective efforts to set up national income accounts.

39. Edward F. Denison, "Report on Tripartite Discussions of National Income Measurement" (1947), 3. The leading representatives were Milton Gilbert (United States), Richard Stone (Great Britain), and George Luxton (Canada).

40. Meeting of the Subcommittee of National Income of the League of Nations, December 1945; notable additions to the original three—the United States (now represented by George Jaszi), the Great Britain, and Canada—were representatives from Australia, the Netherlands, and Mexico. Stone, as the lead economist in charge of the British national accounts (also sometimes referred to as "the British Kuznets"), was the first to put accounts into an internally coherent system that were closely modeled after the concepts of Keynes's *General Theory*. It was the model that would, in the end, win the day, defeating Kuznets's broader notions of social accounts that would more comprehensively measure welfare. See, for instance, Ruggles, ibid. (1999).

41. The document was entitled *Measurement of National Income and the Construction of Social Accounts;* for further details, see Kendrick, ibid., 309. In September of the same year, national income accountants from around the world met in Washington and formed the International Association for Research in Income and Wealth, modeled after the Conference on Research in Income and Wealth in the United States (established in 1936). Simon Kuznets played a key role in bringing scholars together. The purpose of the association was to provide an international forum for scholarly exchanges and research in the national income field. Its proceedings were subsequently published as the "Income and Wealth" series.

42. Simon Kuznets, "National Income: A New Version" (1948), 154.

43. National income and product accounts came to be seen as a mere tool intended to capture the workings of the economy; a description of *what was*, not a prescription of *what we wanted*. Textbooks tell us that after the Depression and World War II, "the economy was never the same again." See Jonathan Hughes and Louis P. Cain, *American Economic History* (2003), 598. In the specialized language of economics, as explored in chapters 7 and 8, GNP was a basic double-entry account that measured the monetary value of output of final goods and services, as well as the distribution of incomes that such production of outputs generated. Data were allocated by sector, industry, state, and nation. Yet both of the basic terms that underlay the entire system—*final goods and services*, and *income*—constituted a severely truncated version of Kuznets' original definition.

44. For a good summary of key issues, see Joseph Stiglitz, "Development Policies in an Age of Globalization" (2002). For an excellent broader historical context, see William Greider, *One World, Ready or Not* (1997); see also Michel Chossudovsky, *The Globalization of Poverty and the New World Order* (2003); for a

world historical perspective, see Amiya Kumar Bagchi, *Perilous Passage: Mankind and the Global Ascendancy of Capital* (2008).

45. Lord Franks, "The Evolution of Twentieth-Century Capitalism" (1967), 10.

46. The case for "saving Europe" has most recently been made by Greg Berman in *The Most Noble Adventure: The Marshall Plan and the Time When America Helped Save Europe* (2008); for a detailed historical study of the Marshall Plan, see Nicolaus Mills, *Winning the Peace: The Marshall Plan and America's Coming of Age as a Superpower* (2008).

47. The OEEC emanated from the original Committee for Economic Development, or CEEC, and was the predecessor of today's EU.

48. Ruggles, ibid. (1999), 77.

49. Collins, ibid. (2000), 22. For further details, see Michael J. Hogan, *The Marshall Plan: America, Britain, and the Reconstruction of Western Europe, 1947–1952* (1987). Angus Maddison describes the standardization of OEEC accounting procedures under American guidance in *Economic Growth in the West: Comparative Experience in Europe and North America* (1964).

50. As the influential development economist Albert O. Hirschman was the first to point out, Bretton Woods was also motivated by interests to prevent another war, "inspired by the belief that the achievement of plenty and of stability constitute the necessary and sufficient condition for a lasting peace." *National Power and the Structure of Foreign Trade* (1945), 80.

51. For a good introductory overview, see Frederick S. Weaver, *The United States and the Global Economy: From Bretton Woods to the Current Crisis* (2011); for an excellent detailed discussion, see Barry Eichengreen, *Globalizing Capital: A History of the International Monetary System* (2008). For a discussion highly critical of the role of the IMF, the World Bank, and the World Trade Organization in institutionalizing dominance of the United States in the postwar international economic agenda, see Richard Peet, *Unholy Trinity: The IMF, World Bank, and WTO* (2009).

52. For a detailed account of discussions between representatives of an exhausted former world empire, Great Britain, and those of the undisputed new economic world power, the United States, see Benn Steil, *The Battle of Bretton Woods* (2013).

53. Designed as twin pillars to foster global economic growth, the IMF promotes international monetary cooperation, while the World Bank primarily provides loans to poor countries for long-term economic development and growth. Voting power in both institutions is based on capital contributions, not population of member nations. Effectively curtailing the input of competing nations, "the United States required an international agreement and wished to secure it even while hostilities in Europe prevented enemy nations from taking part in negotiations and to minimize the involvement of the allies on whose territory the war was fought." See Barry Eichengreen, "Hegemonic Stability Theories of the International Monetary System" (1989), 267. For a more extensive discussion

of U.S. dominance over the deliberations, see Lloyd Gruber, *Ruling the World: Power Politics and the Rise of Supranational Institutions* (2000).

54. See Maddison, ibid. (1964); Berman, ibid. (2008); Mills, ibid. (2008); and Hogan, ibid. (1987).

55. International Bank for Reconstruction and Development, *Articles of Agreement*, Article I, "Purposes" (1944). For a good overall introduction to the history and purposes of the World Bank, see Katherine Marshall, *The World Bank: From Reconstruction to Development to Equity* (2008).

56. Paul Hawken, *The Ecology of Commerce* (2010), 109.

57. See Lori Wallach and Patrick Woodall, *Whose Trade Organization?* (2004). China became a member of the WTO in 2001, Russia in 2012, which leaves no large economy outside the WTO.

58. German economist Utz-Peter Reich calls U.S. Secretary of State Robert Marshall "the political father of the official German national accounts"; see Utz-Peter Reich, "German National Accounts between Politics and Academics," in Zoltan Kenessey, *The Accounts of Nations* (1994), 161.

59. For supporting evidence, see Berman, ibid. (2008); United Nations, Statistics Office, *Statistical Yearbooks* (1960, 1970, and 1980). See also Mills, ibid. (2008); Clifford Cobb, Mark Glickman, and Craig Cheslog, "The Genuine Progress Indicator 2000 Update" (2001); Noreena Hertz, *The Silent Takeover: Global Capitalism and the Death of Democracy* (2003); World Bank, *World Development Report* (2000).

60. A widely cited student of national income accounts, Richard Ruggles of Yale University, writing about essential international readjustment measures such as the Marshall Plan, argues that they have meaning only "in terms of the relevant economic magnitudes in the different countries . . . adjustment within any country must be defined in terms of full utilization of capacity, workable trade patterns, and . . . allocation of production between investments and consumption . . . information provided by national income accounts is essential for achieving such a balance." Ruggles, ibid. (1949), 8.

61. David Engerman, "American Knowledge and Global Power," (2007), 615.

62. See Kyojiro Someya, 'Accounting 'Revolutions' in Japan" (1989), 75–86.

63. For quotes, see *New York Times*, 18 July 2010; see also Minxin Pei, "The Dark Side of China's Rise" (2006), 32–40; L.H.M. Ling, "Hegemony and the Internationalizing State: A Post-Colonial Analysis of China's Integration into Asian Corporatism" (1996), 1–26; Yan Wang and Yudong Yao, "Sources of China's Economic Growth 1952–1999: Incorporating Human Capital Accumulation" (2003), 32–52; Kam Wing Chan, "Economic Growth Strategy and Urbanization Policies in China, 1949–1982" (2009), 275–305; David Lampton, *The Three Faces of Chinese Power* (2008); Martin King Whyte, "Paradoxes of China's Economic Boom" (2009), 371–92; Chris Bramall, "Sources of Chinese Economic Growth, 1978–1996" (2011); Huang Xiaoming, *The Rise and Fall of the East Asian Growth System, 1951–2000* (2013); Connie Carter and Andrew Harding, eds., *Special Economic Zones in Asian Market Economies* (2010).

64. Wang Xiaohong, as quoted in Ian Johnson, "In the Air" (2013).

65. Joseph Kahn and Jim Yardley, "As China Roars, Pollution Reaches Deadly Extremes" (2007). See also Jianguo Liu and Jared Diamond, "Revolutionizing China's Environmental Protection" (2008), 37–38. Many countries have tried similar routes; see, for instance, Mark De Haan, "On the International Harmonisation of Environmental Accounting" (1999), 151–60.

66. For a good recent exploration of the role of growth, including in the Soviet Union, see Andrew J. Sutter, "Unlimited Growth and Innovation: Paradise or Paradox?" (2010); for a full exploration of growth in the Soviet sphere, see Paul Gregory, Robert C. Stuart, and Steven L. Husted, *Russian and Soviet Economic Performance and Structure* (1998); Jeffrey Sachs, Wing Thye Woo, Stanley Fischer, and Gordon Hughes, "Structural Factors in the Economic Reforms of China, Eastern Europe, and the Former Soviet Union" (1994), 102–45; Gur Ofer, "Soviet Economic Growth: 1928–1985" (1987), 1767–833.

67. For a summary account and a wealth of references, see David Engerman, "American Knowledge and Global Power" (2007), 620–21.

68. Transitions from state-communism to Western-style capitalism were otherwise often painful and fraught with tension. For a full account of one such example, see Dirk Philipsen, *We Were the People* (1993).

69. Hertz, *The Silent Takeover: Global Capitalism and the Death of Democracy* (2003), 39. One important vehicle for the spread of universal accounting standards based on the UN System of National Accounts is the International Financial Reporting Standards (IFRS) as the global accounting benchmark; for a summary of research, see William Judge, Shaomin Li, and Robert Pinsker. "National adoption of international accounting standards: an institutional perspective" (2010), 161–74. According to Indian economist S. G. Tiwari, India's concerted effort to generate national income accounts compatible with the British and American models was greatly assisted by the two creators of the first comprehensive accounts, Simon Kuznets from the United States and Richard Stone from the United Kingdom; see Tiwari, "Development of National Accounts in India," in Zoltan Kenessey, *The Accounts of Nations* (1994), 127.

70. For a good introduction, see Noami Klein, *The Shock Doctrine* (2007); see also Greider, ibid. (1997); Noam Chomsky's *Profit Over People* (1999); Joseph Stiglitz, *Globalization and Its Discontents* (2003); Chossudovsky, ibid. (2003); for detailed accounts of the devastating effects of growth policies on the world's poor, Joyce Millen, Alec Irwin, and John Gershman, eds. *Dying for Growth: Global Inequality and the Health of the Poor* (2000). All provide insightful case studies from around the world, though most ascribe too much intent on the part of political and financial leaders, neglecting the dominant structural logic of the GDP regime.

71. So-called Structural Adjustment Programs (SAPs) have no other function than to facilitate a country's long-term growth as defined by GDP; programs are intended to make local economies more market oriented and open them up to outside investment and trade, which routinely includes measures such as

privatization of national assets, resource exploitation, cuts to welfare programs, and destruction of local small-scale businesses.

72. John Gray, "The End of the World as We Know It" (2007).

73. See Robert Repetto et al., *Wasting Assets* (1989).

74. SAPs, based on GDP criteria and prescribed by the IMF and the World Bank as conditions for loans and repayment, have resulted in widespread cutbacks in health, education, and other vital social services around the world. They have, at times, also directly resulted in critical resource depletion. For a sample of recent studies, see SAPRIN, *Structural Adjustment: The SAPRI Report—the Policy Roots of Economic Crisis, Poverty, and Inequality* (2004); Éric Toussaint and Damien Millet, *Debt, the IMF, and the World Bank* (2010). For a balanced review that analyzes the IMF and the World Bank as something not merely beholden to U.S. interests, but rather to a set of criteria I have here described as "GDP logic," see Ngaire Woods, *The Globalizers: The IMF, the World Bank, and Their Borrowers* (2006). It is easy to see how the GDP logic also leads to what in Africa is called the "resource curse"—many countries, from Nigeria to the Democratic Republic of Congo (formerly Zaire), Liberia, Somalia, Uganda, and Sierra Leone, have been torn apart by civil wars, successive military coups, and poverty, all as a direct result of economic rules that allow national parties and international corporations to make huge profits on resource depletion and human exploitation. It is what Kamari Maxine Clarke has called a "vast and unregulated system of extractive capitalism." See Clarke, "Treat Greed in Africa as a War Crime" (2013).

75. Repetto et al., ibid. (1989), 2.

76. See Commission on Growth and Development, World Bank, 2008. See chapter 8 of this volume for an explanation as to why assuming indefinite growth is both insane and absurd; for a brief exploration of uneconomic growth—yielding more costs than benefits—see Herman Daly, "What Is the Limiting Factor?" (2013).

77. Joseph Stiglitz, "Bleakonomics" (2007).

78. Indeed, the very quantities that economists use to describe the state of the economy—whether inflation, unemployment, the Consumer Price Index (CPI), or wages and profits—all are derivatives of GDP, and all consist of central components defined by GDP.

79. For an excellent introduction, see Robert Heilbroner, *The Economic Transformation of America* (1998); see also Mark A. Martinez, *The Myth of the Free Market: The Role of the State in a Capitalist Economy* (2009); for a fascinating case study of how government investment stimulated growth and created the (white) middle class, see Ira Katznelson, *When Affirmative Action Was White* (2005); for a more comprehensive study, exploring the rise of Keynesian economics, the focus on economic growth, and the radical changes consumerism brought to American culture, see Cohen, ibid. (2003).

80. Ironically, the war also raised the possibility that command economies can actually work, perhaps even more efficiently than market economies.

81. Paul A. Samuelson, *Problems of the American Economy: An Economist's View* (1962), 3.

82. Bernstein, ibid., 89.
83. John Kenneth Galbraith, *Economics in Perspective* (1987), 250. Most economists who wanted to remain relevant had become Keynesian by the late 1940s. Even before the end of hostilities on the battlefields, the impact of Keynes morphed from crisis management in times of depression and war into something different altogether: an exclusive focus on growth as defined by GDP. In this sense, as Bernstein concludes, "The entire wartime experience of American economists would profoundly affect the postwar evolution of the discipline." Bernstein, ibid., 82.
84. As noted in chapter 5, several economists have cast doubt on the originality and revolutionary nature of John Maynard Keynes's central theses. See, for instance, J. Adam Tooze, *Statistics and the German State, 1900–1945* (2001); John Kenneth Galbraith, *A Life in Our Times* (1981) and ibid. (1987); Bernstein, ibid.; Don Patinkin, "Keynes and Econometrics: On the Interaction between the Macroeconomic Revolutions of the Interwar Period" (1976), 1091–123; the early intellectual history of Keynesianism is covered in Peter Clarke, *The Keynesian Revolution in the Making, 1924–1936* (1988).
85. For a wide-ranging discussion on the so-called "Keynesian Revolution," see Thomas Cate, ed. *Keynes's General Theory: Seventy-Five Years Later* (2012).
86. Colin Clark published his first work on national income in 1932, utilizing some of Keynes's concepts and definitions. Clark, *The National Income, 1924–1931* (1932). Reviewing the book, Kuznets stated that "data are strained perilously close to the tolerance point," but nevertheless called Clark's work an "assiduous, and often brilliant, attempt." See Simon Kuznets, "Review of C. Clark (1933), *The National Income, 1924–31*" (1933c), 363–64. In a recent study on national accounting in Britain, Geoff Tily claims that, as "the first to produce an expenditure measure of economic activity, the first to produce quarterly rather than annual estimates, and the first to attempt macroeconomic analysis of his results," Clark's work in many important facets preceded Kuznets's. See Geoff Tily, "John Maynard Keynes and the Development of National Accounts in Britain, 1895–1941" (2009), 331–59.
87. For a brief summary of applications, see Katherine Scrivens and Barbara Iasiello, "Indicators of 'Societal Progress': Lessons from International Experiences" (2010).
88. A point made by Tooze, ibid. (2001), 9–10.
89. Costanza, Hart, et al., ibid. (2009), 9.
90. George W. Bush, *The George Walker Bush Foreign Policy Reader* (2005), 168.

CHAPTER 7

1. The apparatus of measures that generates the overall measure of GDP is called National Income and Product Accounts (NIPA).

2. As formulated by one of the best known economists in the twentieth century, Paul A. Samuelson, in the nineteenth edition of his classic textbook coauthored with William D. Nordhaus, *Economics* ([1948] 2010), 386. To avoid any confusion, his chapter on "Measuring Economic Activity" begins with the sentence, "The single most important concept in macroeconomics is the gross domestic product (GDP);" the second quote is from a European Union position paper, Marcel Canoy and Frédéric Lerais, "Beyond GDP" (2007), 1.

3. The word *final* is used because GDP tries to prevent double counting: it measures, for instance, the car, but not the tires or leather or stereo system that went into the car: the price of the car includes all that.

4. The quotation is a slight alteration from Bruno Latour, *We Have Never Been Modern* (1991), a work that explores the modern condition of artificially separating things, yet also producing "hybrids" that defy such separation; GDP would have to be seen as a kind of über-hybrid in its attempt to capture virtually all aspects of life. Essentially, there are four different kinds of final goods. The most important are (1) consumption goods, comprising almost 70 percent of our economy; they include all things that members of households buy, like cars, clothes, electronics. The second (2) are investment goods bought by businesses, such as material, equipment, buildings. Then there are (3) goods and services that government buys, including everything from roads and bridges to arms and police services. Finally, (4) there is the total value of all the goods and services produced here but sold outside the United States, minus all the goods and services produced elsewhere but bought within its borders.

5. Figures are for 2011.

6. In 2003, McDonalds sold, on average, seventy-five hamburgers every second of every minute, day, and night, year around (Elsa H. Spencer, Erica Frank, and Nicole F. McIntosh, "Potential Effects of the Next 100 Billion Hamburgers Sold by McDonald's" [2005]); surveys suggest that children spent on average 1,700 minutes a week watching TV, while parents spend less than four minutes in meaningful conversations with them (Norman Herr, California State University, Northridge, "Television and Health," http://www.csun.edu/science/health/docs/tv&health.html).

7. As of 2009, about $640 billion for Department of Defense, $17 billion Department of Energy (nuclear weapons and environmental cleanup), $36 billion for Department of State, $96 billion for Department of Veterans Affairs, $52 billion for Department of Homeland Security, $55 for Military Retirement Fund, $9 billion for defense-related expenses of the National Aeronautics and Space Administration, and $126 billion for past debt-financed defense outlays, for a total of about $1.031trillion. Our total combined income and corporate tax revenue in 2012 was about $1.4 trillion.

8. The average annual income of the top 1 percent, meanwhile, exceeds $1 million in the United States; the top .1 percent take home an average annual income of over $21 million. For data, see the World Top Incomes Database (WTID), http://

topincomes.g-mond.parisschoolofeconomics.eu/#Country:United%20States (accessed 15 May 2014).

9. PolitiFact, "Just How Wealthy is the Wal-Mart Walton Family?" 8 Dec. 2013, http://www.politifact.com/wisconsin/statements/2013/dec/08/one-wisconsin -now/just-how-wealthy-wal-mart-walton-family/ (accessed June 2014).

10. For a magisterial compilation of the latest data, see Thomas Piketty, *Capital in the Twenty-First Century* (2014); for wealth statistics, see pp. 343–50. See also compilations by William Domhoff, "Who Rules America?" (2005, 2013).

11. For national economic data, see the Bureau of Economic Analysis (www.bea.gov); CIA Factbook for United States (www.cia.gov/library/publications/the-world -factbook/geos/us.html); all other data can be verified by doing simple Internet searches.

12. Quotation is from their website, www.bea.gov.

13. The idea for this account comes from Libby Rittenberg and Timothy Tregarthen, *Principles of Macroeconomics*. With slight variations, the same procedure plays out in every developed nation. In Germany, for instance, the Statistisches Bundesamt (Federal Agency for Statistics), while dispensing with the theatrics of locked doors, follows the exact timetable: on the last business day of each month, it issues a statement at 9 a.m. with the latest GDP estimates.

14. According to a recent IMF study, average downward revisions within G-20 nations increased significantly during the 2007–9 recession. See Manik Shrestha and Marco Marini, "Quarterly GDP Revisions in G-20 Countries: Evidence from the 2008 Financial Crisis." (2013).

15. In the words of former chairman of the Federal Reserve, Alan Greenspan, "GDP estimates have a profound influence on markets when published and are the basis for Federal budget projections and political rhetoric." J. Steven Landefeld, "GDP: One of the Great Inventions of the 20th Century" (2000), 10.

16. BMI-SB stands for *Bundesministerium des Inneren—Statistisches Bundesamt.* While impressive in range and detail, with a few recent exceptions, the literature on national accounting is almost exclusively a literature on technical developments over time. For international developments, see particularly the magisterial work of Paul Studenski, *The Income of Nations* (1958); Zoltan Kenessy's *The Accounts of Nations* (1994); and André Vanoli's *A History of National Accounting* (2005); for particular developments in the United States, see Carol S. Carson, "The History of the United States National Income and Product Accounts," unpublished diss. (1971); the BEA's "Measuring the Nation's Economy" (2009); and Rosemary Marcuss and Richard E. Kane, "U.S. National Income and Product Statistics" (2007). With the partial exception of Marcuss and Kane, this entire oeuvre is a specialized accounting literature: much of it attempts to relate developments to economic thought at the time, but none of it seriously explores the larger historical context, much less investigates cultural changes based on new economic metrics. Exceptions that couch national accounting developments within specific historical developments are, for instance, Mark

Perlman, "Political Purpose and the National Accounts" (1987), or Jeroen C.J.M. van den Bergh, "The GDP Paradox" (2009); Lorenzo Fioramonti, *Gross Domestic Problem* (2013). For a comprehensive list of works on national accounts, see the bibliography at the end of the book. Still, it was astonishing to find, for instance, that files essential to the history of national accounts in the United States had not been checked out from the Library of Congress and the National Archives since the early 1970s (unlike, say, the thousands of recorded requests each year for topics like the JFK assassination or the Watergate scandal).

17. Quotation is from Herman Daly, "The End of Uneconomic Growth" (2012), 74. SNAs are a UN international standard system of national accounting; the first such system was approved in 1953. Major revisions were made in 1968, 1993, and 2008 to accommodate goals like better data collection, more accurate pricing, and new understandings of what investment and final product entail. According to the UNSNA, "The broad objective of the System of National Accounts (SNA) is to provide a comprehensive conceptual and accounting framework for compiling and reporting macroeconomic statistics for analysing and evaluating the performance of an economy," http://unstats.un.org/unsd/nationalaccount/hsna.asp.

18. What to count, and how to count it, of course, has generated an ongoing debate. Here is an example of early debates among European accountants (from 1963): "Are transfers from the City of Ostende to urban transportation to be considered as subsidies or current transfers to households? Do payments made by the Ministries of Finance to Post Offices on behalf of net deposits on postal cheque accounts deposited with the Treasury represent interest or purchases of services? Are real estate taxes of a direct or an indirect nature? Should pension funds of civil servants in the Netherlands be considered general government or financial institutions?" See Vanoli, ibid., 133.

19. Samuelson and Nordhaus, ibid. (2010), 390; J. W. Kendrick, *The New System of National Accounts* (1996), 1; Michael J. Boskin, as quoted in Landefeld, ibid., 3.

20. All other uses of GDP are far less familiar to the public, yet intensely used by experts. Some examples: at the time of this writing (summer 2014), total annual GDP of the United States stands at roughly $17 trillion—still the largest for any national economy. With little more than 12 percent of the world's population, the combined total of just the United States and the EU accounts for 45 percent of global GDP. National debt is analyzed in relation to GDP. Currently, it is roughly the same as national GDP, or about $17 trillion. In the next ten years or so, the government will spend about 14 percent of its revenue—some $5 trillion—paying interest on the national debt. According to estimates by the World Bank and IMF, the combined total of global GDP in 2014 is about $75 trillion—about sixteen times the $4 to $5 trillion of its 1950 value. To put this into historical perspective: according to such statistics, the United States, all by itself, accomplished more GDP growth in the past sixty years than all of humanity combined did between prehistoric times and the middle of the twen-

tieth century. Imagine: more output during the span of one single lifetime than in some ten thousand years prior. For data, see Bradford De Long, "Estimates of World GDP, One Million B.C. to Present" (1998); CIA World Factbook (2013); Angus Maddison, *The World Economy: Volume 2: Historical Statistics* (2007).

21. Rarely noted is that Americans at the same time rank around twenty-fourth in infant mortality, eighth in life expectancy, yet first in obesity-related illnesses and in the number of citizens in jail. Remarkably, many countries with much lower per capita GDP provide healthier and longer lives for their citizens.

22. Angus Maddison, *Growth and Interaction in the World Economy* (2005), 5.

23. As quoted by Noreena Hertz, *The Silent Takeover: Global Capitalism and the Death of Democracy* (2003), 7.

24. A point well made in the excellent animated presentation "The Story of Stuff" (2007), available at http://storyofstuff.org/.

25. For what is probably still the best and most comprehensive discussion of the many subjective choices accountants and economists have to make when estimating national income or product, see Simon Kuznets, *National Income and Its Composition, 1919–1938* (1941), and particularly Part One, "Concepts, Classifications, and Procedures," pp. 3–60.

26. Examples are virtually endless. As of the day of this writing, two stories showed up in the news: one about how GDP predicts auto sales in every industrialized country around the world, finding that "the logarithm of GDP accounted for nearly 90 percent of the variance in the logarithm of vehicle sales from 2005 to 2011"; the other about "the latest fad in Washington economic policy debates" arguing over "the level at which the government should stabilize the debt-to-GDP ratio."

27. Anwar M. Shaikh and E. Ahmet Tonak, *Measuring the Wealth of Nations* (1994), 1.

28. Daly, ibid. (2012), 74.

29. Economic textbooks sometimes refer to it as the "married maid paradox." The economist who first wrote about it was Arthur Cecil Pigou, who raised the issue prior to the invention of national income accounts in his book *The Economics of Welfare* ([1920] 2013), 32.

30. Except, of course, for things like food, clothes, electricity, and water you need to live at home.

31. For a good brief discussion on mental disorders, see Bruce Levine, "Why the Rise of Mental Illness? Pathologizing Normal, Adverse Drug Effects, and a Peculiar Rebellion," *Mad in America* (31 July 2013), http://www.madinamerica.com/ (accessed Nov. 2014).

32. Mitchell L. Moss and Carson Quing, "The Emergence of the 'Super-Commuter'" (2012).

33. For latest figures, see Bureau of Economic Analysis, http://www.bea.gov/news releases/industry/gdpindustry/2014/pdf/gdpind114.pdf.

34. Researchers from the United States and Europe have put the price tag on "free" ecosystem services we daily receive at roughly twice the amount of global GDP.

This would mean that earth provides us with twice as much "value" as all human labor combined. See Robert Costanza , R. d'Arge, et al., "The Value of the World's Ecosystem Services and Natural Capital" (1997), 256.

35. A brief "official" introduction of what is counted, and how the system of national accounts developed, can be found in Marcuss and Kane, ibid. (2007), 32–46.

36. Simon Kuznets, Discussion section, in M.A. Copeland, "Concepts of National Income," (1937), 1:37.

37. Using the same accounting standards for wages and salaries as we do for profit, we would likely find that the amount of corporate profits (currently about $1.7 trillion) may well exceed the total national amount of wages and salaries (i.e., after deducting Kuznets's "evils necessary," like work clothes, transportation, child care, and so forth).

38. Martin O'Malley, Governor's Address at the Genuine Progress Indicators Conference (2013).

39. According to the Federal Reserve Board, in 2007, the latest year for which figures are available, the richest 1 percent of U.S. households owned 33.8 percent of the nation's private wealth, which is more than the combined wealth of the bottom 90 percent. Arthur B. Kennickell, "Ponds and Streams: Wealth and Income in the U.S., 1989 to 2007" (2009). In 2010, *Forbes* magazine rated Bill Gates second in the world among wealthy people with a net worth of roughly $60 billion, at a time when the median net worth of an American family was about $80,000, while the average net worth for families in the bottom 20 percent is just a little over $8,000.

40. Herman Daly, *Steady-State Economics* (1991), 248.

41. Mark Anielski, *The Economics of Happiness: Building Genuine Wealth* (2007), 32.

42. There is an increasingly voluminous literature on all these points, no longer allowing for summary justice. The bibliography at the end of the book offers a sample of works detailing all seven points made.

43. David Korten, *When Corporations Rule the World* (2001), 44.

44. E. J. Mishan, *The Economic Growth Debate* (1977), 28.

45. Juliet Schor, "The Good Life or the Goods Life" (2007).

46. Steven Stoll, *The Great Delusion* (2008), 161. See Piketty, ibid., which demonstrates that the rate of return on capital exceeds the rate of growth, in other words, benefits increasingly go to the top 1 percent at the expense of the 99 percent.

47. Richard Anderson, Delta Airline CEO, interview, National Public Radio, *With Good Reason*, 31 Oct. 2013.

48. Merely scratching the surface of its significance, a European Union report on GDP simply stated, "GDP is used in a large variety of political and financial arenas. It serves as a criterion to decide who has access to funds at international organisations such as the EU, UN, IMF and World Bank, GDP plays an important part in the Stability and Growth Pact, and it is a lead indicator for forecasts of financial markets and banks, to mention just a few examples. It is also used

for international comparison and rankings and plays a crucial role in political debates." Canoy and Lerais, ibid. (2007).

49. The primary categories we use in order to describe, count, and evaluate economic activity and its consequences are all defined by the System of National Accounting (SNA), which is used to generate National Income and Product Accounts (NIPAs), which, in turn, are combined into the single number that is GDP. As discussed in earlier chapters, we should also note that national income and product accounts ended up closely following the logic of business accounts. Otto Eckstein, "The NIPA Accounts" (1983), 315.

50. It is with some justified pride when the Bureau of Economic Analysis claims that GDP is "one of the most comprehensive and closely watched economic statistics: it is used by the White House and Congress to prepare the Federal budget, by the Federal Reserve to formulate monetary policy, by Wall Street as an indicator of economic activity, and by the business community to prepare forecasts of economic performance that provide the basis for production, investment, and employment planning." McCulla and Smith, *Measuring the Economy* (2007), 1. BEA publishes its findings in the *Survey of Current Business*, which in 2014 was in its ninety-fourth year.

51. Jonathan Rowe and Judith Silverstein, "False Readings—How the GDP Leads Us Astray" (2008).

52. Greenspan, ibid. (2000), 5.

53. Realizing the dangers of GDP growth does not imply a general indictment of economic growth. The particular kind of growth promoted by the logic of GDP—monetized volume over quality, privileging flow over stock, and output over development or sustainability—is not the only conceivable kind of growth. There are many others. As discussed in chapters 9 and 10 of this book, many other kinds of growth are conceivable. An economy that includes externalized costs into the price of products, or that counts the work of a stay-at-home parent, or that subtracts from its final tally the depletion of resources, could still be a growth-centered economy. And yet, under such alternative accounting rules, how companies conduct business would be hardly recognizable by today's standards, as would be the makeup of our neighborhoods and the character of our jobs. The change would happen for one reason: we would follow a different set of indicators. The profit motive would not change. But what people would do in order to make a profit would change dramatically. Quality and good stewardship could be rewarded. Harm, depletion, and exploitation could count against profit. All that would have changed is this: the indicators by which we measure economic success.

54. Researchers at the New Economic Foundation made this very point in their 2006 publication *The (un)Happy Planet Index*, adding that "putting a number on something somehow endows it with greater reality. It can transform a short-term objective into the very definition of success" (p. 19).

CHAPTER 8

1. All figures are from Organization of Economic Cooperation and Development (OECD), *Health at a Glance—2011* (2012).
2. David A. Stockman, "Sundown in America: How Crony-Capitalism Left Us State-Wrecked" (2013).
3. Edmund Burke, referring to how manners operate in modern cultures. See *The Works of the Right Honourable Edmund Burke* ([1815] 2011), 8: 172.
4. Economists in particular appear to have difficulties conceptualizing a growth model that exceeds the planet's ecosystem. In 2004, Nobel Prize–winning economist Kenneth Arrow, in collaboration with ten other prominent scholars, set out to research the question "are we consuming too much?" Their exceedingly careful conclusion: "We find some support for the view that consumption's share of output is likely to be higher than that which is prescribed by the maximize present value criterion." See Arrow, Kenneth, et al. "Are We Consuming Too Much?" (2004), 147–72.
5. A problem discussed in a seminal paper by Martin L. Weitzman, "On the Welfare Significance of National Product in a Dynamic Economy" (1976), 156–62, later critiqued and expanded by Swapan Dasgupta and Tapan Mitra, "On the Welfare Significance of National Product for Economic Growth and Sustainable Development" (1999), 422–42; both work with the concept of "Net National Product" in an attempt to include depreciation of things like natural and social capital in order to come up with a better correlation between national product and welfare.
6. "Let them eat GDP"—as in slight alteration to what Queen Marie Antoinette is commonly believed to have said about starving French peasants: *Qu'ils mangent de la brioche* (Let them eat cake).
7. A point first developed by Herman Daly, *Toward a Steady-State Economy* (1973), 167.
8. For a recent summary of research arguing a "roughly linear-log" relationship between well-being and income, see Betsey Stevenson and Justin Wolfers, "Subjective Well-being and Income: Is There Evidence of Satiation?" (April 2013).
9. In their attempts to show that growing GDP raises standards of living, pundits routinely use very select indicators, some of which are themselves direct or indirect derivatives of GDP, such as per capita income or levels of employment; not usually found in such arguments are broader indicators such as security, job satisfaction, or state of the environment. What we see depends on what we choose to look at.
10. The literature across disciplines disputing the logic that increased GDP translates into higher quality of life is much too vast to cite in a note. Some prominent examples are: Ronald H. Coase, "The Problem of Social Cost" (1960); Rachel Carson, *Silent Spring* (1962); Kenneth Boulding, "The Economics of the Coming

Spaceship Earth" (1966); Nicholas Georgesçu-Roegen, *The Entropy Law and the Economic Process* (1971); Richard A. Easterlin, "Does Money Buy Happiness?" (1973); E.J. Mishan, *The Economic Growth Debate* (1977); Juliet Schor, *The Overworked American: The Unexpected Decline of Leisure* (1992); Manfred Max-Neef, "Economic Growth and Quality Of Life: A Threshold Hypothesis" (1995); Clifford Cobb, Ted Halstead, and Jonathan Rowe, "If the GDP Is Up, Why Is America Down?" (1995b); Herman Daly, *Beyond Growth: The Economics of Sustainable Development* (1997); William Greider, *One World, Ready or Not* (1997); Richard Douthwaite, *The Growth Illusion: How Economic Growth Has Enriched the Few, Impoverished the Many and Endangered the Planet* (1999); Amartya Sen, *Development as Freedom* (2000); Kenneth Arrow, "Are We Consuming Too Much?" (2004); Jared Diamond, *Collapse: How Societies Choose to Fail or Succeed* (2005); Richard Layard, *Happiness: Lessons from a New Science* (2006); Peter Linebaugh, *The Magna Carta Manifesto: Liberties and Commons for All* (2008); Tim Jackson, *Prosperity without Growth: Economics for a Finite Planet* (2009); Derek Bok, *The Politics of Happiness* (2010); Paul Gilding, *The Great Disruption—Why the Climate Crisis Will Bring on the End of Shopping and the Birth of a New World* (2011).

11. See Ross Gittins, "At the Coal Face Economists Are Struggling to Measure Up" (2014), who cites research showing that some 80 percent of trained economists could not answer basic questions about how to figure out opportunity costs.

12. Among the first and most effective to make this point was New Zealand politician, activist, scholar, and feminist Marilyn Waring in her book *If Women Counted* (1988).

13. Muller, Nicholas Z., Robert Mendelsohn, and William Nordhaus, "Environmental Accounting for Pollution in the United States Economy" (2011), 1649–75. Other examples of industries noted in the article that produce more damage than value are sewage treatment, solid waste combustion, stone quarrying, marinas, and petroleum-fired power plants. The study imputed a price on air pollution emissions equal to marginal damages in order to measure the externalities from air pollution. Their estimated total for air pollution related costs for all industries in 2002 was $119.8 billion.

14. For stats and information, see the United States Energy Information Administration, http://www.eia.gov/coal/ (accessed 16 April 2012). Joseph Stiglitz, Nobel laureate in economics, recounts the serious blowback from the coal industry he received when, as chairman of the Council of Economic Advisors to the President, he tried to encourage the United States to account for "the depletion of natural resources and the degradation of the environment; see *The Price of Inequality* (2012), 185.

15. Some economists also refer to such consequences of market transactions as "spillover effects" or "social costs." Modern analysis of "externalities" originated with two economists: Arthur C. Pigou (see his *Economics of Welfare* [1920] 2013) and Ronald H. Coase (see his "Problem of Social Cost" 1960).

16. At least to the extent that government regulations allow this to take place.

17. For an illuminating example, see Donald Shoup, a professor of urban planning, in his recent book *The High Cost of Free Parking* (2011), which effectively argues that free parking is the ultimate Trojan horse, because average citizens end up paying for it—whether they have cars or not—with congestion on our streets as well as increased grocery prices, rents, and pollution levels.

18. Economists like to point out that no form of production generates zero harm or pollution, and it is thus absurd to aim for such a goal. The key, therefore, should be to show that the social benefit of production exceeds the social harm or damage—precisely the topic to which Muller et al. attended.

19. For an introductory overview, see Nathaniel Keohane and Sheila M. Olmstead, *Markets and the Environment* (2007); Michael Sandel, *What Money Can't Buy: The Moral Limits of Markets* (2012); Frank Ackerman and Lisa Heinzerling, *Priceless—On Knowing the Price of Everything and the Value of Nothing* (2004); Jan Tinbergen and Roefie Hueting, "GNP and Market Prices: Wrong Signals for Sustainable Economic Success that Mask Environmental Destruction" (1991).

20. Eric Zenzey, "G.D.P.R.I.P" (2009); the author also noted that this is not "nickel-and-dime stuff," as the roughly $90 billion of damages in New Orleans demonstrate; oil-spill cleanups, Superfund sites, or the prison-industrial complex—there is no shortage of such expenses reaching into the tens of billions of dollars.

21. See, for instance, Douthwaite, ibid. (1999).

22. People living near surface mining sites have a 50 percent greater risk of fatal cancer and a 42 percent greater risk of birth defects than the general population; see Jason Howard, "Appalachia Turns on Itself," (2012), A15.

23. Dutch economist Jeroen C.J.M. van den Bergh has shown how GDP even violates basic principles of bookkeeping by not clearly dividing benefits and costs (GDP adds up both, rather than subtracting the latter from the former), and by counting as a "plus" the depletion of valuable resources (in this case, coal). See his paper "Abolishing GDP" (2007), 6.

24. The claim of "clean coal" is worthy of a "Propaganda Seal of Approval." The idea is that "big lies," if only propagated often enough, will be believed eventually.

25. See Waring, ibid. (1988), for an eloquent early discussion of this failure.

26. A good term to describe this phenomenon is "information failure," first developed by Jerone C.J.M. van den Bergh, "The GDP Paradox" (2009), 125.

27. Report for coal industry, written by economist Roger Bezdek: "Industry Awakens to the Threat of Climate Change" (2014).

28. See George P. Brockway, *The End of Economic Man An Introduction to Humanistic Economics* (2001), 241, 247.

29. Martin Collier, Director of the Glaser Progress Foundation, interview on theREALnews.com (2008). The same point was made by Gus Speth, chairman of the Council on Environmental Quality, and later founder of the World Resource Institute: "we tend to get what we measure, so we should measure what we want." See Gus Speth, "Toward a Post-Growth Society" (2011). For a full discussion of

this point, see his *Bridge at the Edge of the World: Capitalism, the Environment, and Crossing from Crisis to Sustainability* (2008).

30. According to 2009 data from the U.S. Energy Information Administration, both Germany and Denmark emitted about nine tons of carbon dioxide per capita, while the United States emitted almost eighteen tons per capita. For comparison, the world average is under five tons per person. See http://www.eia.gov/ (accessed 17 May 2012); according to World Bank data, the average per capita electricity consumption in the United States was about 13,000 kwh in 2009, versus a little more than 6,000 for Germany and Denmark (the world average was 2,800). On the 2011 UN Human Development Index, however, the United States ranks almost equal to Germany and Denmark (though its per capita GDP is still about 25 percent higher).

31. Worldwide, energy consumption, and with it CO_2 emissions, continues to rise sharply with growing GDP, despite progress in energy efficiency; overall energy consumption has doubled since 1970; see Jan-Erik Lane, "Energy: The Link between GDP and Emissions" (2013), 49–54; World Meteorological Institute, press release (9 Sept. 2014), https://www.wmo.int/pages/mediacentre/press_releases/pr_1002_en.html (accessed 10 Sept. 2014).

32. Jonathan Rowe and Judith Silverstein, "False Readings: How the GDP Leads Us Astray" (2008).

33. This particular quote, one of hundreds with the same meaning one could cite, is taken from Edgar Z. Palmer, *The Meaning and Measurement of the National Income* (1966).

34. Given the prominence of numbers and metrics in the work of both accountants and economists, one would assume this should be cause for great concern.

35. There is a long-standing discussion on how to measure progress, particularly since many parts of a good life are not quantifiable (happiness, security, belonging, etc). Broader, more inclusive measures have been the focus of the social indicators movement that started in the 1960s and 1970s, ongoing work on environmental indicators, and assessments of sustainability and human development measures that emerged in the 1990s. Several high-level international initiatives, such as European Commission's "Beyond GDP," the World Bank's "Moving Beyond GDP" and "Human Development Index," or the "Commission on the Measurement of Economic Performance and Social Progress" that was initiated in France, show that the issue of societal progress is of increasing political and public interest. For a summary evaluation, see Katherine Scrivens and Barbara Iasiello, "Indicators of 'Societal Progress': Lessons From International Experiences," OECD Working Paper no. 33, June 2010.

36. Simon Kuznets, "Concepts of National Income" (1937), 37.

37. One of the earliest to make this argument were William Nordhaus and James Tobin, who argued in 1972 in an essay that pioneered the alternative GDP movement: "GNP is not a measure of economic welfare. Economists all know that." William D. Nordhaus and James Tobin. *Is Growth Obsolete?* (1972).

38. During an event celebrating the accomplishments of GDP, then Chairman of the Federal Reserve, Alan Greenspan, went as far as saying that GDP "is not necessarily a measure of welfare or even a significant measure of standards of living." Greenspan, as quoted in J. Steven Landefeld, "GDP: One of the Great Inventions of the 20th Century" (2000), 9.

39. N. Gregory Mankiw, *Principles of Economics* (2011), 492; Jeroen C.J.M. van den Bergh, "The GDP Paradox" (2009), 117.

40. As explained in the introduction, the "N" in GNP stands for *National*, meaning that it counts all goods and services produced by Americans, whether in the United States or abroad, whereas GDP counts all goods and services produced in the United States, whether by Americans or not. In the United States, the difference between the two is minimal.

41. For a very brief period, the United States attempted to generate its own environmental accounts, or so-called IEESA's (Integrated Economic and Environmental Satellite Accounts). The first results were published in 1994. Adjusting the GDP for pollution expenses and resource depletion, the reduced results for wealth creation in the U.S. economy created such a stir that Congress almost immediately shut down the effort. According to a spokesperson for the Commerce Department at the time, Congress essentially made "thinking about Green GDP a thought crime." See Linda Baker, "Real Wealth" (1999).

42. J. Steven Landefeld, Director of the Bureau of Economic Analysis (agency officially responsible for the GDP accounts in the United States), in "Rethinking the Gross Domestic Product as a Measurement of National Strength" (2008). See also Katharine Abraham, "Expanded Measurement of Economic Activity: Progress and Prospects" (2013); William Daley, "Press Conference Announcing the Commerce Department's Achievements of the Century" (1999).

43. Michael J. Boskin, "GDP—A Debate" (2010).

44. A friend and colleague of Simon Kuznets from their days at the National Bureau of Economic Research and the War Production Board, Abramovitz focused his research on business cycles and long-term economic growth. Moses Abramovitz, "The Welfare Interpretation of Secular Trends in National Income and Output" (1959), 21.

45. In the mid-seventies, he began publishing his concerns. In his book by the same title, Daly defines steady-state economics as "an economy with constant stocks of people and artifacts, maintained at some desired, sufficient levels by low rates of maintenance 'throughput,' that is, by the lowest feasible flows of matter and energy from the first stage of production to the last stage of consumption." Herman Daly, *Steady-State Economics* (1991), 17.

46. According to the Bureau of Economic Analysis, the U.S. economy has grown by an average annual rate of about 3.3 percent in chained dollars since 1947. To figure out how long it takes an economy to double in size of output, you can follow the "rule of 72," which states that a variable's approximate doubling time equals 72 divided by the growth rate. In other words, if the level of output were increasing at a 4 percent rate, for example, its doubling time would be roughly 72/4, or 18 years.

47. For a more extensive discussion of this point, see Van den Berg, ibid. (2007).

48. Professor Layard, however, was not merely talking about any kind of growth. He was, specifically, talking about GDP growth, by the logic of which the more "productive" citizen is the fast-food devouring couch potato addicted to video games and strung out on ADD meds. The well-adjusted citizen, reading a book at home after a long walk, on the other hand, is an economic drain. Richard Layard, "Happiness: New Lessons," 16 June 2011, talk delivered at Renaissance Society of America talk, podcast, http://itunes.apple.com/us/podcast/rsa-events-vision-videos/id325808178. Layard likely borrowed the phrase from economist Kenneth Boulding.

49. Building on work done by Kuznets and Abramovitz, Easterlin became quite well known among experts in the field when he published a piece in 1974 that fundamentally questioned the taken-for-granted correlation between economic growth and human welfare. Richard Easterlin, "Does Economic Growth Improve the Human Lot?" (1974), 89–125. See also his later "Will Raising the Incomes of All Increase the Happiness of All?" (1995), 35–47; and Easterlin, together with L. A. McVey, M. Switek, O. Sawangfa, and J. S. Zweig, "The Happiness Income Paradox Revisited" (2010). Quotations are from Easterlin, "Feeding the Illusion of Growth and Happiness" (2005), 441.

50. "If we are genuinely interested in the welfare, and the character, of society," Mishan concludes, "we should be unwilling to reconcile ourselves to this restriction of our judgment." Mishan, ibid. (1977), 34–35.

51. Marilyn Waring, *If Women Counted* (1988). In his first report to Congress, the father of national accounts, Simon Kuznets, called the volume of such domestic services "imposing indeed," and considered their exclusion from national accounts an "omission [that] lowers the value of national income measurements." See Kuznets, "National Income, 1929–32" (1934), 4.

52. See Amartya Sen, *Choice, Welfare, and Measurement* (1982). Sen was also a developer of the UN Human Development Index (HDI), a composite statistic of life expectancy, education, and income indices used to rank countries (the United States currently ranks fourth, while Norway ranks first; on a new inequality-adjusted IHDI, the United States ranks only twenty-third, with Norway still holding the top spot).

53. An article they published the same year, entitled "If the GDP Is Up, Why Is America Down," revealed some of the absurd consequences of prevailing economic indicators, and likely remains the most widely read full-scale critique of GDP. Clifford Cobb, Ted Halstead, and Jonathan Rowe, ibid. (1995b).

54. Quoted in Ron Colman, "Measuring Genuine Progress" (1999), 7.

55. His thesis, in short, was not just that growth no longer generated more quality —it actually caused more harm than good. His findings independently matched the results of the GPI studies: with slight variations, most rich countries saw their quality of life begin to decline between the mid-1960s and late 1970s, despite ongoing solid GDP growth. See Max-Neef, ibid., 117.

56. Mathis Wackernagel and William Rees, *Our Ecological Footprint: Reducing Human Impact on the Earth* (1996). In order to find out your own ecological footprint, go to http://www.myfootprint.org/.

57. Many have proposed possible alternatives: most either reject the "one-indicator" model and provide a spectrum of social, economic, and environmental measures (such as the Sustainable Development Indicators), or they reconceptualize the one-indicator model to include social and environmental considerations (such as the Genuine Progress Indicator, or the UN's Human Development Index—HDI—which takes GDP, life expectancy, and educational achievements to arrive at a single measure). Another promising single-indicator project, unlike HDI, takes sustainability into account. All of these will be discussed further in chapter 10, along with the New Economic Foundation's "Happy Planet Index," a single figure that is a function of a country's average subjective life satisfaction, its life expectancy at birth, and, importantly, its overall ecological footprint per capita.

58. See, for instance, John Gertner, "The Rise and Fall of the GDP" (2010), 60–71; Andrew Oswald and J. Steve Landefeld, "This House Believes that GDP is a Poor Measure of Improving Living Standards" (2010); Alexander von Jung, "Der Kult ums BIP" (2009).

59. The French effort was led by Nobel laureates Amartya Sen and Joseph Stiglitz. It is based on the realization that no single measure can possibly capture progress or welfare. The idea behind a broader range of metrics, in turn, has led to a host of initiatives around the world to generate more sophisticated indicators, measuring everything from per capita resource-use to job satisfaction, equality, savings and homeownership rates, to the correlation between social security and religiosity.

60. As of 2011 the Australian Bureau of Statistics (ABS) had identified seventy major international projects to create alternative national indicators, and fifty-eight projects in Australia alone.

61. Gertner, ibid.; H.R. 3590, Patient Protection and Affordable Care Act, signed into law by President Obama on 23 March 2010.

62. See *Social Progress Imperative*, http://www.socialprogressimperative.org/ (accessed 6 Jan. 2014).

63. While we can trace how economists and accountants have been very successful in generating ever more sophisticated econometric models over the past seventy years, using terminology and graphs and equations that far surpass most people's comprehension, the basic assumption upon which most of it is built is very simple. And has not changed. And is rarely questioned. That assumption: more is better.

CHAPTER 9

* Title represents last line of the seminal study of New England environmental history, William Cronon, *Changes in the Land* (2008), 170.

1. It is an essentially Keynesian model. As John Maynard Keynes, one of the most influential economic minds of the modern era, famously penned in 1936, "pyramid-building, earthquakes, even wars may serve to increase wealth." And what about jobs for people? Keynes again provides a telling answer: "'To dig holes in the ground,' paid for out of savings, will increase, not only employment, but the real national dividend of useful goods and services." A good definition, it seems to me, of indiscriminate growth. See John Maynard Keynes, *The General Theory of Employment, Interest, and Money* (1965), 129, 220.

2. Janet Abramovitz, "Learning to Value Nature's Free Services" (1997), 39.

3. Maligned and largely dismissed by elite policy circles at the time, the report was based on a computer simulation model of interactions between population, industrial growth, food production, and limits in the ecosystems of the earth; see Donella Meadows et al., *The Limits to Growth—A Report for the Club of Rome's Project on the Predicament of Mankind* (1972). Several recent studies confirm that the 1972 predictions were mostly right on target. See, for instance, Graham Turner, "A Comparison of the Limits to Growth with 30 Years of Reality" (2008), 397–411.

4. See Millenium Ecosystem Assessment (MEA), *Ecosystems and Human Well-Being* (2005), 15, http://www.millenniumassessment.org/documents/document .356.aspx.pdf; Pushpam Kumar, ed., *The Economics of Ecosystems and Bio-diversity Ecological and Economic Foundations* (2010); for an excellent summary of findings, see Tim Jackson, *Prosperity without Growth: Economics for a Finite Planet* (2009).

5. For a good example of this perspective, see Peter Ferrara, "Economic Growth, Not Redistribution, Most Benefits the Poor, the Working People, and the Middle Class" (2012).

6. For a good introductory history of environmentalism, see Michael Egan and Jeff Crane, eds. *Natural Protest* (2009).

7. For extensive updated documentation on this, see Thomas Piketty, *Capital in the Twenty-First Century* (2014).

8. See, in order, Betty Friedan, *The Feminine Mystique* (1963); Rachel Carson, *Silent Spring* (1962); Ira Katznelson, *When Affirmative Action was White* (2005); Lizabeth Cohen, *A Consumers' Republic: The Politics of Mass Consumption in Postwar America* (2003); Robert Putnam, *Bowling Alone: The Collapse and Revival of American Community* (2000).

9. David Riesman, Nathan Glazer, and Reuel Denney, *The Lonely Crowd: A Study of the Changing American Character* (1950).

10. Among the first to generate a comprehensive critique of economic growth was economist E. J. Mishan in his controversial 1967 *The Costs of Economic Growth*. For a study that shows the extent to which oil is necessary for almost everything associated with a modern life (transportation, plastics, pharmaceuticals), see Vaclav Smil, *Oil* (2008); the challenges and conflicts faced by a world economy dependent on oil are judiciously explored in Gavin Bridge and Philippe Le Billon, *Oil* (2013).

11. President Jimmy Carter, televised speech, 15 July 1979, http://www.pbs.org/ wgbh/americanexperience/features/primary-resources/carter-crisis/ (accessed 20 Nov. 2012).

12. Some have even argued that they significantly contributed to his failed reelection attempt in 1980. Carter himself never used the word "malaise;" for an excellent broader discussion of the speech and its consequences, see Kevin Mattson, *"What the Heck Are You Up To, Mr. President?": Jimmy Carter, America's "Malaise," and the Speech That Should Have Changed the Country* (2010); Carter lost his bid for reelection to a candidate, Ronald Reagan, who himself was unimpeded by such delicate considerations.

13. For a nice summary of trash-related questions, see "What a Waste," www.popu lationeducation.org/docs/earthmatters/em2_unit7.pdf (accessed 23 Dec. 2012).

14. Gary Cross, *An All-Consuming Century* (2000), 239.

15. At least among scientists, the fact that the earth is getting warmer, with potentially devastating effects, is no longer in any serious dispute; for a good summary of the findings and challenges, see Bill McKibben, "Global Warming's Terrifying New Math" (2012).

16. Cited in Susan George and Fabrizio Sabelli, *Faith and Credit: The World Bank's Secular Empire* (1994), 109.

17. Joseph E. Stiglitz, "GDP Fetishism," *The Economists' Voice* 6, no. 8 (2009), Article 5. The distinguished economist Richard Layard calls it "the obscenity of the GDP." See Layard, *Business Wellbeing Network 2010 Annual Conference*, http:// www.youtube.com/watch?v=UJP82-BvXSE.

18. Bruno Latour, *We Have Never Been Modern* (1993), 8.

19. Years before the turn of the twenty-first century, a few select key events in the emergence of an environmental awareness in America were the publication of Rachel Carson's seminal book *Silent Spring* (1962); the spontaneous combustion of the Cuyahoga River in Cleveland, Ohio (June 1969); the first major international conference on the environment in Stockholm (1972); and the publication of the internationally commissioned *The Limits to Growth* (1972). Such events were experienced in the context of increasing pollution, oil spills, nuclear accidents, and, significantly, the first full-view picture of earth, taken by Apollo 17 (1972)—an iconic image that brought into dramatic relief how small and finite a planet we inhabit.

20. For a brief summary of findings, see World Resource Forum 2011, http://www .worldresourcesforum.org/the-issue.

21. For two excellent summary explorations, see Paul Hawken, *The Ecology of Commerce* (2010) and Leslie Paul Thiele, *Sustainability* (2013).

22. Carrying capacity includes two central components: (1) the "regenerative" capacity, or the planet's ability to reproduce/regrow the resources humans are depleting; and (2) the "absorptive" capacity, which is the planet's ability to absorb all of our trash and pollution, as well its capacity to clean basic resources such as air, water, and soil. For an excellent and comprehensive review on the ecosystem

services of the planet, see a 2004 report that resulted from the work of some 1,400 international scientists commissioned by the UN: Millenium Ecosystem Assessment (MEA), *Ecosystems and Human Well-Being* (2005).

23. Roger Cohen, "The Narcissus Society," *New York Times*, 23 February 2010.

24. Mark O'Connell, "What a Raw Deal for the Poor Little Guy," *New York Times Magazine*, 3 August 2014, p. 45.

25. Simon Kuznets, in a summary reflection on economic growth, argued in 1973 that "all economic growth" also generates negative effects; see Simon Kuznets, "Modern Economic Growth: Findings and Reflections" (1973), 247–58.

26. Thomas Pogge, "Getting Serious about Ending Poverty," unpublished lecture, Kenan Institute for Ethics, Duke University, 31 March 2014. See also his *Politics as Usual: What Lies behind the Pro-Poor Rhetoric* (2010), which exposes the self-serving nature of many tales of progress.

27. David S. Landes, *The Wealth and Poverty of Nations* (1998), 516; for discussion on the increasingly tenuous linkage between economic growth and social welfare, see Doh C. Shin, "Does Rapid Economic Growth Improve the Human Lot? Some Empirical Evidence," (1980), 199–221; Fred Hirsch, *Social Limits to Growth* (2005); Donella Meadows, Jørgen Randers, and Dennis Meadows, *The Limits to Growth—A 30-Year Update* (2004); Kenneth Arrow, Bert Bolin, et al. "Economic Growth, Carrying Capacity, and the Environment" (1995), 520–21.

28. Douthwaite, ibid. (1999), 5.

29. Jeremy Grantham, "On the Road to Zero Growth," *GMO Quarterly Letter* (Nov. 2012), 15.

30. According to recent polls, for instance, only 23 percent of Britons and 44 percent of Americans thought that today's youth would enjoy a higher quality of life than their parents. See, for instance, "The New Pessimism," *The Guardian* (3 Dec. 2011). In August 2014, a Wall Street Journal/NBC poll found that 76 percent of Americans over 18 were not confident that their children would fare better than themselves; see http://msnbcmedia.msn.com/i/MSNBC/Sections/A_Poli tics/14643%20AUGUST%20NBC-WSJ%20POLL.pdf.

31. An illuminating recent example for how an exclusive economic focus based on GDP data leads to astonishingly narrow results is a collaborative study by leading economists trying to determine the costs of what they considered the ten problems that have most blighted human development, ranging from malnutrition, lack of education, and climate change to trade barriers and armed conflicts. Here is one example of what one finds if one looks only at the current prices of things. Climate change, in the words of the editor, provides "a net benefit." How is that possible? Apparently not consulting future generations or dying species, he explains, "largely because increased carbon dioxide in the atmosphere has boosted agriculture. This contributes a positive impact of 0.8 per cent of GDP. Moderate warming prevents more deaths from the cold than it causes deaths related to the heat. It also reduces the demand for heating more than it increases the cost of cooling. Together these add another 0.4 percent." See Bjorn Lomborg,

ed., *How Much Have Global Problems Cost the World?* (2013). Quotation is from Lomborg, "Is the World Getting Better or Worse?" *The New Scientist* (14 Oct. 2013), available at http://www.newscientist.com/article/mg22029380.200 -is-the-world-getting-better-or-worse.html?full=true#.U-zWlkh602c (accessed August 2014).

32. A typical male worker's income was larger in 1968 than it is today. In the meantime, Americans' most important personal asset, their homes, shrunk in value by some 40 percent between 2007 and 2012. Just over the past twenty years, most remarkably, wealth inequality in America has more than tripled. See Joseph E. Stiglitz, "Inequality Is Holding Back the Recovery," *New York Times* (20 Jan. 2013); and Daniel Altman, "To Reduce Inequality, Tax Wealth, not Income," *New York Times* (18 Nov. 2012).

33. For a good recent summary of research, see Nic Marks, *The Happiness Manifesto: How Nations and People Can Nurture Well-Being Kindle* (2011).

34. For a brief and accessible sample of the most updated and comprehensive findings, see Jackson, ibid. (2009), which summarizes the findings of an official report of the U.K. Sustainable Development Commission; the *Living Planet Report 2010*, published by the World Wildlife Foundation and the Global Footprint Network, www.footprintnetwork.org; Meadows et al., ibid. (2004), an updated version of the famous original report commissioned by the Club of Rome (Meadows et al., ibid. [1972]); the 2010 edition of *State of the World*, published by the Worldwatch Institute; and an excellent introduction to the history of the environmental debate, Paul Gilding's *The Great Disruption* (2011).

35. Juan Luis Arsuaga and Ignacio Martinez, *The Chosen Species* (2006), 267.

36. For a selection of many studies that convincingly make this case, see Richard Heinberg, *The End of Growth* (2011); Gilding, ibid. (2011); Jackson, ibid. (2009). Consolation or not, some scientists think that, even if we continued on the same course, a few million of us might survive to tell the tale in places like northern Canada. See James Lovelock, *The Vanishing Face of Gaia: A Final Warning* (2011).

37. Millennium Ecosystem Assessment, *Ecosystems and Human Well-Being* (2005), 1. Among the wealth of literature on this point, a solid classic introduction is Herman Daly's *Beyond Growth* (1997). For a continuously updated report that includes all the data and methodologies on why and how we consume well above what the planet can sustain, see The Footprint Network, www.footprint network.org. Their data show that the global economy is currently operating at 140 percent of the world's carrying capacity.

38. The first quotation is from Andrew Revkin, "Who Made This Mess of Planet Earth?" *New York Times Book Review*, 15 July 2011. See also James Lovelock, "The Earth Is about to Catch a Morbid Fever that May Last as Long as 100,000 Years" (2006).

39. Barack Obama, speech on "The Coming Storm: Energy Independence and the Safety of Our Planet," Chicago, 3 April 2006. See also Revkin, ibid., 16; Lovelock, ibid. (2006). For a detailed account, see Lovelock, ibid. (2011).

40. United Nations Millennium Declaration, section I, pt. 5, United Nations, Dec. 2000.

41. 2004 Pentagon Report, *Observer* newspaper 22 Feb. 2004, as quoted in Gilding, ibid., 109; see also the military's "Climate Adaptation Roadmap" of 2014 that states "we must be clear-eyed about the security threats presented by climate change, and we must be pro-active in addressing them, DoD 2014 Climate Change Adaptation Roadmap," http://www.acq.osd.mil/ie/download/CCAR print.pdf (accessed October 2014); Nicolas Sarkozy, foreword to Joseph E. Stiglitz et al., *Mismeasuring Our Lives* (2010), viii..

42. See National Public Radio, *All Things Considered*, 5 March 2013; BBC Business News, "Oil Shock Warning to Government from UK Business," 17 November 2010; *New York Times*, "Global Temperatures Highest in 4,000 Years," 8 March 2013.

43. John R.W. Stott, *The Cross of Christ* (2006), 285; Norman Wirzba, "In God's Garden" (2012), 95.

44. John Robert McNeill, *Something New Under the Sun* (2001), 4.

45. This point is further developed by distinguished historian Dipesh Chakrabarty, "The Climate of History: Four Theses" (2009), 197–222. For the first time, he argues, human beings have become "geological agents" who are, based on their numbers and invented technologies, changing the planet itself.

46. Most of the mansions, of course, were merely vacation homes, and were soon rebuild with multimillion- dollar insurance settlements. Those born with the handicap of no wealth fared far worse. For quotation, see Ronald Wright, *A Short History of Progress* (2004), 131.

47. The research of economist Partha Dasgupta leads to the conclusion that growth in GDP that depends on resource depletion leads to the creation of poverty. See "The Welfare Economic Theory of Green Accounts," *Environmental Resource Economics* 42 (2009), 3–38. The first to popularize calculations that show that the ecosystem services of the planet far exceed the value of all human activities combined was ecological economist Robert Costanza; see Costanza, R. d'Arge, et al., "The Value of the World's Ecosystem Services and Natural Capital," (1997), 253–60.

48. Mike Davis, "Who Will Build the Ark?" *New Left Review* (Jan./Feb. 2010, 61), 30; Naomi Oreskes, "The Scientific Consensus on Climate Change: How Do We Know We're Not Wrong?" in Joseph F. C. Dimento and Pamela Doughman, eds., *Climate Change: What It Means for Us, Our Children, and Our Grandchildren* (2007), 73–74. Another large international study found in 2013 a solid consensus (97.2 percent) of scientific papers on climate change believed it was caused by human action, see John Cook et al., "Quantifying the Consensus on Anthropogenic Global Warming in the Scientific Literature," *Environmental Research Letters* (2013, 8/2).

49. James Hansen et al., "Target Atmospheric CO_2: Where Should Humanity Aim?" *The Open Atmospheric Science Journal* 2 (2008), 217–31. The conclusion is supported by virtually all leading climate scientists around the world.

50. See Steven C. Sherwood and Matthew Huber, "An Adaptability Limit to Climate Change Due to Heat Stress," *Proceedings of the National Academy of Sciences* 107, no. 21 (2010), 9552–55. An excellent summary of research findings on the consequences of people's actions on the earth's environment is "Global Change and the Earth System: A Planet under Pressure" (2004), http://www.igbp.net/download/18.1b8ae20512db692f2a680007761/IGBP_ExecSummary_eng.pdf, (accessed June 2014).

51. As quoted by the Center for the Advancement of Steady State Economics (CASSE), "Downsides of Growth" (2012).

52. Gar Alperovitz, *What Then Must We Do?* (2013), 2.

53. "The Economist's Intelligence Unit's Quality of Life Index 2012," *The Economist*, http://www.economist.com/media/pdf/QUALITY_OF_LIFE.pdf (accessed 12 May 13).

54. Christopher DeMuth, "The Real Cliff," *The Weekly Standard* 18, no. 15 (24 Dec. 2012).

55. "Biocapacity" denotes the availability of resources combined with the waste/pollution absorption capacity of a given area (or the total earth).

56. John Pilger, in his speech accepting Australia's human rights award, the Sidney Peace Prize, 5 Nov. 2009.

57. At a conference advocating alternatives to GDP, Governor O'Malley of Maryland, speaking to those unwilling to address the failures of the current system, pointedly raised the question: "Things that get measured are things that get done. The ultimate test of any public policy is whether it works. Spare me your ideology. Does it work for me and my family?" Martin O'Malley, Governor's Address at the Genuine Progress Indicators Conference (2013).

58. Gilding, ibid. (2011), 6.

59. William E. Rees, "The Ecological Crisis and Self-delusion: Implications for the Building Sector," (2009).

60. We should readily admit that predictions about what the future holds are inherently prone to failure. Past attempts have rarely stood the test of time. There were the dire expert warnings of the 1890s that American cities were about to drown in horse manure: horses at the time were essential for transport of goods and people. Their numbers had doubled every ten years or so. Few could readily anticipate that horses would soon be a thing of the past, replaced by cars and trucks. Modern examples include rare commodities like copper being replaced by manufactured (and in some cases superior) alternatives, such as optical fibers, or the dangers of ozone-depleting substances like chlorofluorocarbon (CFC), widely used as refrigerants and aerosol propellants, until they were successfully phased out in the late 1990s. On the other hand, there are the examples of late-twentieth-century worst-case scenarios of glacier and perma-icesheet meltdowns, which experts a mere ten years later regarded as ruefully inadequate: the actual rate of global melting had ominously exceeded predictions of yesterday's greatest doomsayers. See, for instance, David H. Bromwich

et al., "Central West Antartica among the Most Rapidly Warming Regions on Earth," *Nature Geoscience* 6 (Jan 2013), which documents warming rates much greater than anticipated, causing an imminent threat of sea level rises of ten feet or more.

61. For a well-known example of the first type, see economist Julian L. Simon, *The Ultimate Resource 2* (1998); for the latter see former NASA scientist James Lovelock, ibid. (2011). For an excellent recent discussion, see Evgeny Morozov, *To Save Everything, Click Here: The Folly of Technological Solutionism* (2013).

62. Landes, ibid., xx.

63. A point further investigated by Joel Bakan's study *The Corporation—The Pathological Pursuit of Profit and Power* (2005), 56–57.

64. Robert Jensen, "In the Face of This Truth" (2010).

65. For a good sample of recent works that suggest viable alternatives, see Thomas Kostigen, *You Are Here: Exposing the Vital Link Between What We Do and What That Does to Our Planet* (2008); Gilding, ibid. (2011); and Bill McKibben, *Earth—Making a Life on a Tough Planet* (2011).

66. From the Genuine Progress Indicator website; see http://genuineprogress.net/genuine-progress-indicator (accessed July 2014).

67. Chapters 10 and 11 will explore in more detail what such plans might entail, and whether critics may have a point in calling them "unrealistic."

68. Steven Stoll, *The Great Delusion* (2008), 7.

69. Jane Gleeson-White, *Double Entry* (2012), 249

70. If the most antigovernment zealots can suddenly support a full-scale government bailout (and actual takeover) of major corporations during a financial meltdown, as happened in 2008, we can imagine how people's responses might change in the face of a worldwide ecosystem collapse.

71. It requires the kind of "paradigm shift" Thomas Kuhn was discussing in his classic work *The Structure of Scientific Revolutions* (1962).

CHAPTER 10

1. Simon Kuznets, "How to Judge Quality" (1962), 31.

2. Michael Lewis, *Moneyball* (2011), xiii.

3. Daniel Kahneman, *Thinking Fast and Slow* (2013), 211.

4. Paul Hawken, "Commencement: Healing or Stealing," as quoted in Rob Dietz and Dan O'Neill, *Enough Is Enough: Building a Sustainable Economy in a World of Finite Resources* (2013), 193.

5. Brian Eno, "The Big Here and the Long Now." In one of his many essays addressing the combination of unprecedented dangers and opportunities, he goes on to say "We face a future where almost anything could happen. Will we be crippled by global warming, weapons proliferation and species depletion, or liberated by

space travel, world government and molecule-sized computers? We don't even want to start thinking about it. This is our peculiar form of selfishness, a studied disregard of the future. Our astonishing success as a technical civilisation has led us to complacency, to expect that things will probably just keep getting better." The Long Now Foundation, http://longnow.org/essays/big-here-long-now/.

6. For an excellent discussion that builds on the concept of "comprehensive wealth," or wealth that is sustained for future generations, see Kenneth J. Arrow et al., "Sustainability and the Measurement of Wealth" (2012), 317–53.

7. Why and how this happened is brilliantly described in Emanuel Derman, *Models. Behaving. Badly: Why Confusing Illusion with Reality Can Lead to Disaster, on Wall Street and in Life* (2012).

8. According to the *Wall Street Journal* (10 December 2011), right after the Great Recession, the financial sector grew to 8.4 percent (from 2.8 percent in 1950), while its share of corporate profits reached 30 percent. For an interesting set of charts documenting the same trend, and showing that finance never made up more than 5 percent of employment, see Jordan Weissman, "How Wall Street Devoured Corporate America," *The Atlantic* (5 March 2013).

9. In his book *Economyths*, the applied mathematician David Orrell explores in detail how orthodox assumptions about efficiency, stability, and rationality that inform traditional economic models in reality produce an "economy that is unfair, unstable, and unsustainable." See Orrell, *Economyths* (2010), 4.

10. Global Footprint Network. *What Happens When an Infinite Growth Economy Runs Into a Finite Planet?* Annual Report (2011), 36.

11. Ibid., 48.

12. Ronald Wright, *A Short History of Progress* (2004), 131.

13. Ecological creditor nations, those who live below their capacity, are usually poor and/or exporters of natural resources. Those nations require international development funds to achieve a higher standard of living without also, in turn, surpassing their own national biocapacity. See below for further discussion on what sustainability may encompass.

14. The "spaceship earth economy" idea was, to my knowledge, first introduced in 1966 by Kenneth E. Boulding in an article entitled "The Economics of the Coming Spaceship Earth."

15. The literature on sustainability distinguishes between concerns for the current generation from well-being of future generations. As I consider all steps taken to enhance future well-being to be not only of supreme importance, but also directly beneficial to the current generation, I fully subscribe to the latter. An excellent and more comprehensive definition for sustainability is "an adaptive art wedded to science in service to ethical vision. It entails satisfying current needs without sacrificing future well-being through the balanced pursuit of ecological health, economic welfare, social empowerment, and cultural creativity"; see Leslie P. Thiele, *Sustainability* (2013), 4.

16. John Maynard Keynes, "Economic Possibilities for Our Grandchildren" (1930), reprinted in Keynes, *Essays in Persuasion* (1963), 363.

17. Several studies have shown that, above a certain income level (about $15,000), there is little or no correlation between happiness and more money or more stuff. Indeed, in several rich countries general life satisfaction has declined over the past thirty years despite consistent increases in GDP. See Worldwatch Institute, *Vital Signs 1992 to 2008* and *State of the World 2010*, fig. 4.1; Richard Layard, *Happiness: Lessons from a New Science* (2006); and Tim Jackson, *Prosperity without Growth: Economics for a Finite Planet* (2011), 39–44.

18. Quotation comes from Pope John Paul II's address to the UN. The International Bill of Human Rights consists of the Universal Declaration of Human Rights (UDHR—originally signed in 1948 by all nations except Soviet bloc countries and apartheid South Africa), as well as two additional treaties added in 1966: the International Covenant on Civil and Political Rights, and the International Covenant on Economic, Social, and Cultural Rights. The original declaration, while strong on basic human rights, was considerably less strong on economic and social rights. The U.S. Constitution, similar to UDHR, also provides strong protections for civil and political rights, but fails to recognize the economic, social, and cultural rights guaranteed in the International Bill of Human Rights.

19. See http://www.ohchr.org/Documents/Publications/FactSheet2Rev.1en.pdf (accessed June 2012).

20. One of a handful of countries, the United States signed but never ratified ICESCR. For a history of UDHR, see Johannes Morsink, *The University Declaration of Human Rights: Origins, Drafting, and Intent* (2000).

21. Simon Kuznets, Discussion section, in M.A. Copeland, "Concepts of National Income" (1937), 1:37.

22. Thomas Hobbes, *Leviathan*, chap. 13: "Of the Natural Condition of Mankind as Concerning their Felicity, and Misery."

23. The same, by the way, may be said about characteristics like intelligence or knowledge: neither is inherently good or bad. They are merely tools. They may even be necessary tools. Yet it is only what they are used for that defines whether they are good or bad.

24. For a fuller discussion of this point, see Dirk Philipsen, "Uncle Sam's Broken Arm—Historical Reflections on Race, Class, and Government in the Wake of Katrina" (2007), 33–45.

25. This is true even for the most basic guarantees that American ordinarily take for granted, like the right to due process and trial by jury, enshrined in the U.S. Bill of Rights. The 2013 National Defense Appropriations Act (NDAA) contains a section, 1021(b)(2), which permits the government to use the military to detain U.S. citizens, strip them of due process, and hold them indefinitely in military detention centers.

26. See Joel Magnuson, *Mindful Economics* (2008), 74, where he shows that the way businesses are legally set up (limited liability status and such) essentially means no accountability for social or environmental destructiveness.

27. Important to note, not only are profit-seeking businesses in conflict with each other, but also, increasingly, the point of production is no longer the main source of profit—the point of distribution and financial services is. Take Walmart, for instance: immensely profitable as a distributor of goods, the various producers of those same goods tend to make very little money in comparison. The same is true for increasing profit margins of banks and investment companies, who produce nothing but paper and digital numbers on computer screens.

28. Not to mention my frustration with 1/8 or 1/16 of an inch—fractions do not exist when building in meters and centimeters.

29. For three great examples debunking the notion of objectivity, see Thomas S. Kuhn, *The Structure of Scientific Revolutions* (1962); Marilyn Waring, *Counting For Nothing: What Men Value and What Women are Worth* (1999); and Peter Novick, *That Noble Dream: The "Objectivity" Question* (1988). Having looked at the criteria that go into both so-called objective and so-called subjective measures of well-being and quality of life, a multidisciplinary team of researchers concluded that "so-called 'objective' measures are actually proxies for experience identified through 'subjective' associations of decision-makers"; hence the distinction between objective and subjective indicators is somewhat illusory; Robert Costanza, B. Fisher, et al., "Quality of Life: An Approach Integrating Opportunities, Human Needs, and Subjective Wellbeing," (2007), 268.

30. For an excellent summary evaluation of alternatives, see Jeroen C.J.M. van den Bergh and Miklos Antal, "Evaluating Alternatives to GDP as Measures of Social Welfare/Progress, *Welfare/Wealth/Work Europe*, Working Paper no. 56, March 2014.

31. This is generally referred to as "ecosystem valuation," and can be accomplished through a wide range of approaches, from changes in production to survey-based information to so-called "revealed preferences (hedonic pricing), to surrogate market approaches; for a good summary, see, for instance, Katherine Hawkins, "Economic Valuation of Ecosystem Services," University of Minnesota, 2003; for a fuller account, see Shunsuke Managi, *The Economics of Biodiversity and Ecosystem Services* (2012).

32. Emphasis in original. John Talbert, Clifford W. Cobb, and Noah Slattery, *The Genuine Progress Indicator* (2007), 1.

33. For a summary of such developments on a state level, see Lew Daly and John McElwee, "Forget the GDP. Some States Have Found a Better Way to Measure Our Progress" (2014).

34. Perhaps the most famous is Gross National Happiness (GNH), an attempt by the Bhutanese government to generate an alternative measure for national progress. It is not yet, however, a fully developed indicator.

35. An early classic is E. F. Schumacher's *Small Is Beautiful* (1973). For good recent summaries of research, see Robert Skidelsky and Edward Skidelsky, *How Much*

Is Enough: Money and the Good Life (2012), and Tim Jackson, *Prosperity without Growth: Economics for a Finite Planet* (2009). For an introduction to happiness economics, see Bruno S. Frey, *Happiness: A Revolution in Economics* (2010). For happiness studies, see Derek Bok, *The Politics of Happiness* (2010); Richard Layard, *Happiness: Lessons from a New Science* (2006).

36. Mahbub ul Haq, *Reflections on Human Development* (1995). The measure is greatly influenced by Amartya Sen's capabilities approach to human development, defined as the process of enlarging a person's "functionings and capabilities to function, the range of things that a person could do and be in her life."

Intentionally flexible in its method, capabilities include a wide range of things, changing in weight and importance according to circumstances, from poverty reduction and sustainable development to gender equality and democratic governance. As such, HDI, by using only three set measures, is merely a crude attempt to approximate a fuller understanding of human development.

37. See Roberto Patricio Korzeniewicz, Angela Stack, Vrushali Patil, and Timothy Patrick Moran, "Measuring National Income" (2004), 535–86.

38. The BEA created a prototype of Integrated Environmental and Economic Satellite Accounts (IEESA), first published in 1994. In 1995, Congress directed the BEA to suspend work on environmental accounting. Currently, BEA's only fully maintained satellite account is the "Travel and Tourism Satellite Account" (TTSA).

39. See UN Millennium Development Goals Indicators, http://mdgs.un.org/unsd/mdg/Host.aspx?Content=Indicators/About.htm (accessed 28 Dec. 2012). The "one dollar a day" figure, of course, was solely established by GDP criteria. A subsistence farmer working his own land, by such standards, can be as poor as the unemployed urban welfare recipient.

40. United Nations, "Millennium Development Goals: 2012 Progress Chart" (2012). As noted earlier, many of the report's claimed successes are a result not of actual improvements on the ground, but rather alterations of how results were measured. See *Politics as Usual: What lies Behind the Pro-Poor Rhetoric* (2010), for Thomas Pogge's research on this issue.

41. See European Commission, *Beyond GDP*, http://www.beyond-gdp.eu/index.html (accessed 30 Dec. 2012).

42. Economist and scholar of national accounts Katharine Abraham concluded a recent survey of alternative measures by noting that they may well be intellectually interesting, but that it remains unclear whether they will also prove "useful to policy purposes." See her "Expanded Measurement of Economic Activity: Progress and Prospects" (2013).

43. Simon Kuznets, *National Income: A Summary of Findings* (1946), 5. Kuznets also maintained that quantitative data on national income were not even necessarily more reliable than qualitative data: "to analyze the reliability of data and procedures used to derive national income totals and their components is essentially an insoluble task," he argued. Indeed, when it came to Systems of

National Accounts, Kuznets was adamant that everything possible should be done to improve on data and sampling errors and limits of inference, yet he was also clear that, in the end, "the best we can do is to express an opinion in quantitative form." Ibid., 535.

44. Simon Kuznets, Personal Papers, Harvard University, Box 1 of 15, HUG FP-88.10—Miscellaneous Correspondence.
45. Kuznets, ibid. (1962), 31.
46. Kuznets, ibid. (1937), 1:36–37.
47. Simon Kuznets, "National Income: A New Version" (1948), 163.
48. Kuznets, ibid. (1948), 151–53.
49. According to Kuznets's logic, war and national security, for instance, not only *do not* meet the criteria for generating a net service, they actually are the opposite: necessarily they lead to a decline in private and public consumption, as well as a decline in investment. For a detailed discussion, see Kuznets, ibid. (1946), especially chap. 4, "Problems of Interpretation": 111–39; see also "National Income: A New Version" (1948), 56–57.
50. Kuznets, ibid. (1962), 32.
51. "Everything else," he argued, "is intermediate product whose inclusion in the output would constitute duplication." Kuznets, ibid. (1948), 156.
52. Ibid., 156–57.
53. Kuznets, ibid. (1948), 151.
54. It should be emphasized that such an exercise can work only if it includes many voices from a wide range of perspectives and backgrounds. For a single author to propose a path necessarily represents a fool's errand. The task at hand, both complex and vital as it is, requires broad input and discussion—not just narrowly specialized debates.
55. See Thomas Piketty, *Capital* (2014); see also later in this chapter and chapter 11 for further discussion.
56. A point most recently developed in Benjamin H. Mitra-Kahn, "Redefining the Economy: How the 'Economy' Was Invented in 1620" (2011), 287, whose work also demonstrates how often dominant concepts, and thus structural realities, of the economy have changed over time.
57. Which, in my estimation, describes most if not all current leaders from President Xi Jinping to Chancellor Merkel, Prime Minister David Cameron, and President Obama.
58. Piketty, ibid. (2014), 508–39; Thomas Piketty interview with Martin O'Neill and Nick Pearce, *Renewal—A Journal of Social Democracy* (2014); see http://www.renewal.org.uk/articles/interview-inequality-and-what-to-do-about-it (accessed October 2014).
59. Hedrick Smith, *Who Stole the American Dream* (2013), 12.
60. Joseph Stiglitz, *The Price of Inequality* (2012), xvii, 182, 282.
61. Gar Alperovitz, *What Then Must We Do?* (2013), 108.

62. Paul Hawken, *The Ecology of Commerce* (2010), 180–82.
63. David Korten, *Agenda for a New Economy* (2009), 48, 99, 100, 92.

CHAPTER 11

1. These points are well developed in Rob Dietz and Dan O'Neill, *Enough Is Enough: Building a Sustainable Economy in a World of Finite Resources* (2013), 46.
2. For an exploration of the anthropological origins of our desire to cooperate, see Michael Tomasello, *Why We Cooperate* (2009).
3. A ragtag horde of colonists with a taste for freedom defeated the mightiest empire on earth; today we simply call it the American Revolution. The civil rights movement destroyed the tyranny of Jim Crow—few had thought it possible. American policymakers and economists outproduced the enemy and won World War II. After the war, a combination of regulatory government inventions helped produce an unprecedented era of GDP-growth. Throughout the post–World War II era, dissident voices worldwide sparked new conversations about political and economic goals, obliterating tyrannical structures and oppressive cultures. Regimes crumbled, and fresh ideas rejuvenated calcified brains.
4. The very indicators that reveal the limits of GDP growth all take a back seat the minute robust GDP growth rates are endangered. During the Great Recession of 2007–9 and its aftermath, the debate among liberals and conservatives alike again centered on how best to promote growth. Job or food insecurity, droughts or toxins, wealth concentration or species extinction, soil erosion or ocean acidification, industrial-style education or the decline of civil society—all represented but a sideshow to the play on central stage.
5. James Gustave Speth, *The Bridge at the Edge of the World: Capitalism, the Environment, and Crossing from Crisis to Sustainability* (2008); Herman E. Daly and John B. Cobb, *For the Common Good: Redirecting the Economy toward Community, the Environment, and a Sustainable Future* (1994); Leslie Paul Thiele, *Sustainability* (2013); Michael Braungart and William McDonough, *Cradle to Cradle: Remaking the Way We Make Things* (2002); Dietz and O'Neill, ibid. (2013); Tim Jackson, *Prosperity without Growth: Economics for a Finite Planet* (2009).
6. A phrase used by German economist Niko Paech at said conference organized by tazlab in Berlin, "Geld oder Leben" ("Money or Life"), 20 April 2013.
7. For a good explanation of why performance indicators can be no better than the clarity of the defined objectives, see John E. Gibson and William T. Scherer, *How to Do Systems Analysis* (2007). For the past ten years, private organizations are catching on to this logic. In their mission statement on measurements and evaluations, for instance, the Bill and Melinda Gates Foundation states that only "clear and specific outcomes" that are based on "the most critical metrics of progress"

NOTES TO PAGES 248-251

provide blueprints for investments. The purpose: "to define and measure results" rather than merely "inputs and activities." Bill and Melinda Gates Foundation, "Our Approach to Measurement and Evaluation," http://www.gatesfoundation.org/How-We-Work/General-Information/Our-Approach-to-Measurement-and-Evaluation (accessed 3/28/14).

8. See Philip B. Smith and Manfred Max-Neef, *Economics Unmasked* (2011). See also a new working paper by the New Economics Foundation, "A New Social Settlement for People and Planet—Understanding the Links between Social Justice and Sustainability" (2014), http://b.3cdn.net/nefoundation/550bcded7f0b7a8b45_5rm6b17dz.pdf (accessed Aug 2014). Another excellent source of information is ASAP (Alliance for Sustainability and Prosperity), see http://www.asap4all.com/.

9. See Daly and Cobb, ibid., 10.

10. Christopher G. Weeramantry, foreword to Klaus Bosselmann's *The Principle of Sustainability* (2008), vii. What this might look like for production and consumption is explored in the classic study by Braungart and McDonough, ibid.

11. For a recent selection of "Future Histories," see Robert Costanza and Ida Kubiszewski, *Creating a Desirable and Sustainable Future* (2014); two excellent and continuously updated resources of ideas for rebuilding an economy along shared values are The New Economy Coalition (http://neweconomy.net/) and the British-based New Economics Foundation (http://www.neweconomics.org/).

12. For select references, see Daly and Cobb, ibid.; Richard Douthwaite, *The Growth Illusion: How Economic Growth Has Enriched the Few, Impoverished the Many and Endangered the Planet* (1999); Jackson, ibid.(2009); Karl Polanyi, *The Great Transformation* ([1944] 2011).

13. Humans are the only species that tolerates in its midst things like poverty and unemployment, despite an overabundance of wealth. If our species wants to hold on to any legitimate claim to superiority over cockroaches, it would be to allow everyone to rise above the level of a brutish, nasty, and short existence.

14. Practical experiments exist by now. See, for instance, a multiyear experiment in two Canadian cities that provided basic income to residents with no strings attached, coined "Mincome"; it has generated solid evidence that a basic income reduces poverty, increases mobility, furthers health, improves education, and stabilizes communities. For an even-handed discussion of this and other experiments, see Matthew C. Murray and Carole Pateman, *Basic Income Worldwide: Horizons of Reform* (2012).

15. Inequality wreaks havoc on everything from our social fabric to our health and happiness to nature itself. As Rob Dietz, Dan O'Neill, and others have noted, furthermore, financial incentives don't even succeed in making people work more or better—they are, in fact, counterproductive. What matters most to people who have access to the essentials, according to a growing variety of research, is freedom, control over their work, and, above all, meaning and purpose. Not rising incomes. Rob Dietz and Dan O'Neill, ibid., 93.

16. The problem is, as Thomas Piketty has demonstrated, that capitalism, as currently designed, systemically promotes growing inequality. "Wealth accumulated in the past grows more rapidly than output or wages." The result: "the past devours the future;" Thomas Piketty, *Capital in the Twenty-First Century* (2014), 571.

17. Most plans are based on a simple fairness rationale, parts of which find increasing support from economists themselves: a severely progressive consumption tax coupled with high taxes on luxury items, and high taxes/penalties on all activities that harm people or the planet, and, progressively, all incomes beyond the "dignity wage" level. Significant funds could come from heavy taxation of the sale and use of nonrenewable natural resources and stiff penalties on pollution of air, water, and land. The basic principle is simple: the more you use up beyond your fair share, the more you pay; everyone contributes to the healthy maintenance of the commons—of people, communities, civil society, the ecosystem.

18. For a good sample of recent work, see Piketty, ibid. (2014); Joseph E. Stiglitz, *The Price of Inequality* (2012); David C. Johnston, *Divided: The Perils of Our Growing Inequality* (2014); Matt Taibbi, *The Divide: American Injustice in the Age of the Wealth Gap* (2014); and Robert Reich's documentary *Inequality for All* (2013a).

19. Dietz and O'Neill show that a basic income could be paid just from the wealth of the Walton family (heirs to the Walmart fortune). On a more serious note, there is a steadily growing literature on both the political right and left supporting a basic income guarantee. See, for instance, Richard K. Caputo, ed., *Basic Income Guarantee and Politics: International Experiences and Perspectives on the Viability of Income Guarantee* (2012); Erik Olin Wright, "Redesigning Distribution: Basic Income and Stakeholder Grants as Cornerstones of a More Egalitarian Capitalism"; Clive Lord, Miriam Kennet, and Judith Felton, *Citizen's Income and Green Economics* (2011); Allan Sheahen, *Basic Income Guarantee: Your Right to Economic Security* (2012); Charles Murray, *In Our Hands: A Plan to Replace the Welfare State* (2006). For an updated, comprehensive plan, see the original book behind the international movement for the "Economy for the Common Good": *Gemeinwohlökonomie*, by Christian Felber (5th ed, 2012). The growing academic debate on basic income guarantee has resulted in an online journal dedicated to the topic, *Basic Income Studies*, www.bepress.com/bis/.

20. See, for instance, research done by The Equality Trust, https://www.equality trust.org.uk/about-inequality/effects (accessed 30 March 2014).

21. Tim Kasser, *The High Price of Materialism* (2003), especially pp. 76–86.

22. In *Mindful Economics* (2008), economist Joel Magnuson makes the point that it is entirely up to us how we "define the DNA" of a corporation, whether we charter it as a "predatory transnational company," or define it as "a community-based cooperative." He considers this legal transition "arguably the single most important step in evolving an economic system toward a mindful economy" (406).

23. For a good selection informing about the historical, political, and legal dimensions of corporations, see Robert Heilbroner, *The Economic Transformation of*

America (1998); Joel Bakan, *The Corporation: The Pathological Pursuit of Profit and Power* (2004); David Korten, *When Corporations Rule the World* (2001); Thomas Frank, *One Market Under God* (2001); Marjorie Kelly, *The Divine Right of Capital* (2003); Noreena Hertz, *The Silent Takeover: Global Capitalism and the Death of Democracy* (2001); Magnuson, ibid.; and Jeffrey Clements, *Corporations Are Not People* (2014).

24. For select references, see Steven Gorelick, "Small Is Beautiful, Big Is Subsidized" (1998); David Johnston, *Free Lunch: How the Wealthiest Americans Enrich Themselves at Government Expense (And Stick You With the Bill)* (2007); Mark Zepezaurer, and Arthur Naiman, *Take the Rich off Welfare* (2004).

25. The rationales for working much less, and more productively, are long and virtually irrefutable. For a good summary of research indicating that, if organized correctly, twenty hours or less can in most cases produce as much as over forty hours as organized today, see Tony Schwartz, "Relax! You'll be More Productive," *New York Times* (9 February 2013); for a good comprehensive report, see the 2011 New Economics Foundation report, "21 Hours—Why a Shorter Working Week Can Help Us All Flourish in the 21st Century," http://dnwssx4l7gl7s.cloud front.net/nefoundation/default/page/-/files/21_Hours.pdf.

26. In a larger historical context, this is not a radical idea. Rather, it should be considered as authentically conservative. As an early conservative proponent of this idea, see Willford I. King, *The Wealth and Income of the People of the United States* (1915); see also earlier discussion in chapter 4.

27. For select references, see Hans-Werner Sinn, *Casino Capitalism: How the Financial Crisis Came About and What Needs to be Done Now* (2012); Lawrence Goodwyn, *The Populist Moment* (1978); Andrew Jackson and Ben Dyson, *Modernising Money* (2013); Herman Daly, *Steady State Economics* (1991); Matt Taibbi, *Griftopia: A Story of Bankers, Politicians, and the Most Audacious Power Grab in American History* (2011); Carmen Reinhart, Kenneth S. Rogoff. *This Time is Different: Eight Centuries of Financial Folly* (2009).

28. An updated version of this is the WuTang Clan song C.R.E.A.M. ("Cash Rules Everything around Me") from the 1993 album *Enter the Wu-Tang (36 Chambers)*. It is a brilliant reprise of the "old song," and shows just how new and devastating that reality is on young people.

29. Quite simply, values and character are not part of the financial bottom line; they thus get ignored, trampled on, and in many cases obliterated. For an excellent sample of extensive and detailed literature on this, see Korten, ibid. (2001); William Greider, *One World, Ready or Not* (1997); Vandana Shiva, *Making Peace with the Earth* (2013b); Jackson, ibid. (2009); Felber, ibid.; Joel Magnuson, ibid. (2008), and, my favorite, a wide-ranging book, simply called *Sustainability* by Leslie Paul Thiele (2013).

30. For global financial assets, see Bain Report, "A World Awash in Money" (2012); for wealth distribution statistics, see the World Institute for Development Economics Research of the United Nations, "Personal Assets from a Global Perspec-

tive"; on unregulated financial capitalism, see Hans-Werner Sinn, ibid.. See also Anthony Atkinson, Thomas Piketty, and Emmanuel Saez, "Top Incomes in the Long Run of History" (2011), 3–71.

31. For a selection of more detailed accounts, see William Greider, *The Secrets of the Temple;* David Graeber, *Debt: the First 5,000 Years;* Giovanni Arrighi, *The Long Twentieth Century: Money, Power, and Origins of Our Times;* Jackson and Dyson, ibid.

32. This was a key demand of the largest working-class movement in American history, the Populist movement of the 1880s; see Lawrence Goodwyn, *The Populist Moment—A Short History of the Agrarian Revolt in America* (1978).

33. For select references, see Ulrich Grober, *Sustainability: A Cultural History* (2012); Bill McKibben, *Deep Economy* (2007); Magnuson, ibid.; Gar Alperovitz, *What Then Must We Do?* (2013); Rachel Carson, *Silent Spring* (1962); Herman Daly and Joshua Farley. *Ecological Economics: Principles and Applications* (2002); Eric Davidson, *You Can't Eat GNP* (2000); Paul Ekins, *Economic Growth and Environmental Sustainability—The Prospects for Green Growth* (2000); Daniel Goleman, *Ecological Intelligence: How Knowing the Hidden Impacts of What We Buy Can Change Everything* (2010); Hazel Henderson, *Ethical Markets: Growing the Green Economy* (2006); Donella Meadows, Jørgen Randers, and Dennis Meadows. *Limits to Growth: The 30-Year Update* (2004).

34. Two excellent models of how to generate prosperity without GDP growth are Peter A. Victor, *Managing without Growth* (2008), and Jackson, ibid. (2009).

35. In his recent *Happy City—Transforming Our Live Through Urban Design* (2013), Charles Montgomery explored the intersection between happiness and urban design and finds that much is known not only about how to build cities that are sustainable and make sense, but cities that make people happy.

36. For examples of what this might look like, see Richard Daly, *Beyond Growth* (1997); Magnuson, ibid.; Braungart and McDonough, ibid.; James Gustave Speth, *America the Possible* (2008), Shiva, ibid. (2013b).

37. For select references, see John Cavanagh, and Jerry Mander, eds. *Alternatives to Economic Globalization: A Better World is Possible* (2004); Paul Gilding, *The Great Disruption: Why the Climate Crisis Will Bring on the End of Shopping and the Birth of a New World* (2011); William Greider, *One World, Ready or Not: The Manic Logic of Global Capitalism* (1998).

38. Braungart and McDonough use shoes as one of an endless number of examples of industrial products that are designed from cradle to grave, rather than cradle to cradle, see ibid., 99.

39. This passage is from the famous Brundtland Report on sustainability, published by the UN in 1987.

40. Rob Hopkins, *Transition Handbook* (2008); see also www.transitiontowns.org.

41. See Ezra Klein, "Think Gas is Too Pricey? Think Again," *Washington Post*, 13 June 2010.

42. Charles M. Blow, "A Lesson Before Dying," *New York Times*, 7 Dec. 2013.

43. Roberto Mangabeira Unger, "Freedom, Equality and a Future Political Economy: the structural change we need," lecture given at RSA, 13 Nov. 2013.
44. Ibid.
45. David S. Landes, *The Wealth and Poverty of Nations* (1998), 524.

APPENDIX A

1. Historians are very familiar with this problem. Studying—and in some ways measuring the contributions of—prosperous white men in positions of power, as was almost the sole focus of pre-1960s historiography, yields results that are not so much necessarily incorrect as they are ruefully incomplete. A narrow lens necessarily hides complexity—different actors, connections, interactions. It also misses essential context, including an awareness of its own origins and function. Even rich white men's history, though, offers far more complexity than reducing economic reality to volume of output.
2. See Gretchen Morgenson, "The Perils of Feeding a Bloated Industry" (2012); see also, Robin Greenwood and David Scharfstein, "The Growth of Modern Finance" (2012).
3. In the fall of 2012, BP pleaded guilty to fourteen criminal charges, including manslaughter, and agreed to the largest-ever settlement with the federal government of $4 billion over the 20 April 2010, drilling disaster in the Gulf of Mexico. The deal was court approved in January 2013.
4. One could start, instead, with a "multiple bottom line," which is a term used by many local and sustainable businesses; it is more commonly referred to as "triple-bottom-line," *triple* denoting "people, planet, profit," or, more specifically, a viable business that cares about social equity and sound, sustainable environmental practices; see Andrew Savitz, and Karl Weber. *The Triple Bottom Line* (2006). What I have suggested in these pages is a four-sided goalpost (or, if you will, a quadruple bottom line): sustainability, social equity, democratic accountability, and economic viability.
5. Richard Stone, by many considered the intellectual father of modern national accounting, was fully aware that all models of measuring economic output would necessarily be deficient. More importantly, he saw the role of national accountants merely in "collecting and ordering facts. . . . But aims and policies are primarily the concern of the politician, and controls and plans are primarily the concern of the administrator." Stone, in short, advocated the kind of informed and open dialogue about meaning and purpose of national accounts that, to this very day, has never taken place. See Richard Stone, "The Accounts of Society," Nobel Memorial Lecture, given on 8 December 1984, reproduced in *American Economic Review* (Dec. 1997).

6. Annie Lowrey, "The Low Politics of Low Growth (2013).
7. Canadian mathematician David Orrell cites another example: in 2006 "Greece revised its GDP up by 25 percent after deciding to include activities such as prostitution, cigarette smuggling, and money laundering"; see *The Other Side of the Coin* (2008), 77.
8. Clifford Cobb, Ted Halstead, and Jonathan Rowe. "If the GDP Is Up, Why Is America Down?" (1995b), 8.
9. This particular quote comes from a campaign brochure of Christopher Shays, former Republican member of Congress from Connecticut.
10. World Health Organization, "Health, Economic Growth, and Poverty Reduction" (2002); World Bank, Commission on Growth and Development, "The Growth Report" (2008), 1.
11. Elizabeth Dickinson, "One State to Rule Them All: Anthropology of an Idea: GDP" (2011), 37.
12. *New York Times* headline, 23 Feb 2013, of an article about Europe, forecasting zero or negative growth.
13. Mark Blyth in his book *Great Transformations* (2002) explores the phenomenon that ideas "alter people's conception of their own self-interest," and thus become important in the real world independent of whether they are true or useful.

BIBLIOGRAPHY

Abraham, Katharine. "Expanded Measurement of Economic Activity: Progress and Prospects." Unpublished manuscript, June 2013. http://www.nber.org/chapters/c12838.pdf, accessed August 2014.

Abramovitz, Janet. "Learning to Value Nature's Free Services." *The Futurist* (July/August 1997).

Abramovitz, Moses. "The Welfare Interpretation of Secular Trends in National Income and Output." Pp. 1–22 in *The Allocation of Economic Resources*. Stanford Studies in History, Economics, and Political Science. Stanford: Stanford University Press, 1959.

———. "Simon Kuznets, 1901–1985." *Journal of Economic History* 46, no. 1 (1986): 241–46.

———. *Thinking about Growth*. Cambridge: Cambridge University Press, 1989.

Ackerman, Frank. *Can We Afford the Future? The Economics of a Warming World*. New York: Zed Books, 2009.

Ackerman, Frank, and Lisa Heinzerling. *Priceless—On Knowing the Price of Everything and the Value of Nothing*. New York, London: New Press, 2004.

Adams, John C. "Sir William Petty: Scientist, Economist, Inventor, 1623–1687." *Historian* 62 (Summer 1999): 12.

Alchon, Guy. *The Invisible Hand of Planning: Capitalism, Social Science, and the State in the 1920s*. Princeton: Princeton University Press, 1985.

Alesina, Alberto, Edward Glaeser, and Bruce Sacerdote. *Work and Leisure in the U.S. and Europe: Why So Different?* Working Paper no. 11278. Cambridge, Mass.: National Bureau of Economic Research, 2005.

Allen, Robert C. "Pessimism Preserved: Real Wages in the British Industrial Revolution." Working Paper no. 314. Oxford University, Department of Economics, 2007.

———. *The British Industrial Revolution in Global Perspective*. Cambridge: Cambridge University Press, 2009.

Alperovitz, Gar. *America beyond Capitalism: Reclaiming Our Wealth, Our Liberty, and Our Democracy*. Boston: Dollars and Sense, 2011.

———. *What Then Must We Do? Straight Talk about the Next American Revolution*. White River Junction, Vt.: Chelsea Green, 2013.

Alperovitz, Gar, and Lew Daly. *Unjust Deserts—How the Rich Are Taking Our Common Inheritance*. New York: New Press, 2008.

Aly, Götz, and Karl-Heinz Roth. *Die restlose Erfassung: Volkszählen, Identifizieren, Aussondern im Nationalsozialismus*. Berlin: Springer, 1984.

Anderson, Richard. Interview. *With Good Reason*. National Public Radio. 31 October 2013.

Anderson, Victor. *Alternative Economic Indicators*. London: Routledge, 1991.

Anielski, Mark. *The Economics of Happiness: Building Genuine Wealth*. Gabriola, British Columbia: New Society, 2007.

———. *The Alberta GPI Blueprint: The Genuine Progress Indicator (GPI) Sustainable Well-Being Accounting System*. Drayton Valley, Alberta: Pembina Institute for Appropriate Development, 2001.

Anielski, Mark, D. Pollock, M. Griffiths, A. Taylor, J. Wilson, and S. Wilson. *Alberta Sustainability Trends 2000: Genuine Progress Indicators Report 1961 to 1999*. Drayton Valley, Alberta: Pembina Institute for Appropriate Development, 2001.

Anielski, Mark, and C. Soskolne. 2001. "Genuine Progress Indicator (GPI) Accounting: Relating Ecological Integrity to Human Health and Well-Being." In Peter Miller and Laura Westra, eds., *Just Ecological Integrity: The Ethics of Maintaining Planetary Life*. Lanham, Md.: Rowman and Littlefield, 2001.

Ariely, Dan. *Predictably Irrational—The Hidden Forces That Shape Our Decisions*. New York: HarperCollins, 2010.

Aristotle. *Politics*. Trans. Ernest Barker. New York: Oxford University Press, 1961.

Arndt, H. W. *The Rise and Fall of Economic Growth*. Chicago: University of Chicago Press, 1984.

Arrighi, Giovanni. *Adam Smith in Beijing: Lineages of the Twenty-First Century*. London: Verso, 2007.

——. *The Long Twentieth Century: Money, Power, and Origins of Our Times*. London, New York: Verso, 1994.

Arrow, Kenneth, Bert Bolin, Robert Costanza, Partha Dasgupta, Carl Folke, C. S. Holling, Bengt-Owe Jansson, et al. "Economic Growth, Carrying Capacity, and the Environment." *Science (Washington)* 268, no. 5210 (1995).

Arrow, Kenneth, et al. "Are We Consuming Too Much?" *Journal of Economic Perspectives* 18, no. 3 (Summer 2004): 147–72.

Arrow, Kenneth J., et al. "Sustainability and the Measurement of Wealth. *Environment and Development Economics* 17, no. 3 (June 2012): 317–53

Arsuaga, Juan Luis, Ignacio Martinez, et al. *The Chosen Species: The Long March of Human Evolution*. Malden, Mass.: Blackwell, 2006.

Aspromourgos, Tony, "New Light on the Economics of William Petty (1623–1687)." *Contributions to Political Economy* 19, no. 1 (2000): 54.

Atkinson, G., R. Dubourg, K. Hamilton, M. Munasinghe, D. Pearce, and C. Young. *Measuring Sustainable Development: Macroeconomics and the Environment*. Cheltenham, England: Edward Elgar, 1997.

Atkinson, Anthony B., Thomas Piketty, and Emmanuel Saez. "Top Incomes in the Long Run of History." *Journal of Economic Literature* 49, no. 1 (2011).

Aune, James Arnt. *Selling the Free Market: The Rhetoric of Economic Correctness*. New York: Guilford Press, 2001.

Bacevich, Andrew J. *The Limits of Power: The End of American Exceptionalism*. New York: Metropolitan, 2008.

Bagchi, Amiya Kumar. *Perilous Passage: Mankind and the Global Ascendancy of Capital*. New York: Rowman and Littlefied, 2008

Bailey, Stephen Kemp. *Congress Makes a Law: The Story Behind the Employment Act of 1946*. New York: Columbia University Press, 1950.

Bain Report. "A World Awash in Money" (14 November 2012). http://www.bain.com/publications/articles/a-world-awash-in-money.aspx, accessed 23 December 2014.

Bakan, Joel. *The Corporation: The Pathological Pursuit of Profit and Power*. New York: Free Press, 2004.

Baker, Dean. *The Conservative Nanny State*. Washington, D.C.: Center for Economic and Policy Research, 2006.

———. *Plunder and Blunder: The Rise and Fall of the Bubble Economy*. San Francisco.: Berrett-Koehler, 2010.

Baker, Linda. "Real Wealth." *E Magazine*, 30 April 1999.

Banaian, King, and Bryan Roberts. *The Design and Use of Political Economy Indicators: Challenges of Definition, Aggregation, and Application*. New York: Palgrave Macmillan, 2008.

Barber, William J. *From New Era to New Deal. Herbert Hoover, the Economist, and American Economic Policy, 1921–1933*. New York: Columbia University Press, 1988.

Barker, Terry. "Equilibrium Economics." Cambridge Trust for New Thinking in Economics. http://www.neweconomicthinking.org/, accessed 20 February, 2013.

Barlow, Maude. *Blue Gold: The Global Water Crisis and the Commodification of the World's Water Supply*. San Francisco: International Forum on Globalization, 2001.

Barro, Robert J. *Macroeconomics: A Modern Approach*. Mason, Ohio: Thomson South-Western, 2008.

Baumol, William J., Sue Anne Batey Blackman, and Edward N. Wolff. *Productivity and American Leadership: The Long View*. Cambridge: MIT Press, 1989.

———. *Profit Is Not the Cure*. Toronto: McClelland and Stewart, 2002.

Beddoe, Rachel, et al. "Overcoming Systemic Roadblocks to Sustainability: The Evolutionary Redesign of Worldviews, Institutions, and Technologies." *Proceedings of the National Academy of Sciences* 106, no. 8 (2009): 2483–89.

Bekoff, M. "Wild Justice and Fair Play: Cooperation, Forgiveness, and Morality in Animals." *Biology and Philosophy* 19, no. 4 (2004): 489–520.

Bell, Simon. *Sustainability Indicators: Measuring The Immeasurable?* London and Sterling, Va.: Earthscan, 2008.

Berkowitz, Edward D., and Kim McQuaid. *Creating the Welfare State: The Political Economy of Twentieth-Century Reform*. New York: Praeger, 1980.

Berman, Greg. *The Most Noble Adventure: The Marshall Plan and the Time When America Helped Save Europe*. New York: Free Press, 2008.

Bernanke, Ben S. "Nonmonetary Effects of the Financial Crisis in the Propagation of the Great Depression." *American Economic Review* 73 (June 1983): 257–76.

Bernstein, Michael. *A Perilous Progress*. Princeton: Princeton University Press, 2001.

Berry, Wendell. *The Way of Ignorance*. Washington, D.C.: Shoemaker and Hoard, 2005.

Bevan, Wilson Lloyd. "Sir William Petty: A Study in English Economic Literature." *Publications of the American Economic Association* 9, no. 4 (1894): 370.

Bezdek, Roger. "Industry Awakens to the Threat of Climate Change." *New York Times*, 24 January 2014.

Binswanger, Hans. *Money and Magic: A Critique of the Modern Economy in the Light of Goethe's "Faust."* Translated by J. E. Harrison. Chicago: University of Chicago Press, 1994.

Bleys, B. *The Index of Sustainable Economic Welfare: Case Study for Belgium—First Attempt and Preliminary Results.* Belgium: Vrije Universiteit Brussel, 2006.

Blyth, Mark. *Great Transformations: Economic Ideas and Institutional Change in the 20th Century.* New York: Cambridge University Press, 2002.

———. *Austerity: The History of a Dangerous Idea.* New York: Oxford University Press, 2013.

Bok, Derek. *The Politics of Happiness: What Government Can Learn from the New Research on Well-Being.* Princeton: Princeton University Press, 2010.

Boo, Katherine. *Behind the Beautiful Forevers.* New York: Random House: 2012.

Bos, Frits. *The National Accounts as a Tool for Analysis and Policy: In View of History, Economic Theory and Data Compilation Issues.* Saarbrücken: Verlag Dr. Müller (VDM), 2009.

Boskin, Michael J. "GDP—A Debate." *The Economist*, 26 April 2010.

Bosselmann, Klaus. *The Principle of Sustainability.* Burlington, Vt.: Ashgate, 2008:

Boulding, Kenneth. "The Economics of the Coming Spaceship Earth." Pp. 3–14 in H. Jarrett, ed., *Environmental Quality in a Growing Economy.* Baltimore: Resources for the Future/Johns Hopkins University Press, 1966.

Bouton, Terry. *Taming Democracy—"The People," the Founders, and the Troubled Ending of the American Revolution.* New York: Oxford University Press, 2007.

Bowles, Samuel, and Herbert Gintis. *Democracy and Capitalism: Property, Community and the Contradictions of Modern Social Thought.* New York: Basic Books, 1986.

Bramall, Chris. "Sources of Chinese Economic Growth, 1978–1996." *OUP Catalogue,* 2011.

Brand, Stewart. *The Clock of the Long Now: Time and Responsibility.* London: Phoenix, 1999.

Braudel, Fernard. *Civilization and Capitalism, 15th–18th Century.* Berkeley: University of California Press, 1992.

Bridge, Gavin, and Philippe Le Billon. *Oil.* New York: John Wiley, 2013.

Braungart, Michael, and William McDonough. *Cradle to Cradle—Remaking the Way We Make Things* New York: North Point, 2002.

Braverman, Harry. *Labor and Monopoly Capitalism.* New York: Monthly Review Press, 1974.

Brazelton, W. Robert. *Designing U.S. Economic Policy—An Analytical Biography of Leon H. Keyserling.* New York: Palgrave, 2001.

Bremner, Robert H. *American Philanthropy.* 2nd edition. Chicago: University of Chicago Press, 1988.

Breslau, Daniel. "Economics Invents the Economy: Mathematics, Statistics, and Models in the Works of Irving Fisher and Wesley Mitchell." *Theory and Society* 32 (2003): 379–411.

Brigante, John. *The Feasibility Dispute: Determination of War Production Objectives for 1942–1943.* Washington, D.C.: Committee on Public Administration Cases, 1950.

Brinkley, Alan. *The End of Reform: New Deal Liberalism in Recession and War.* New York: Vintage, 1989.

Brockway, George P. *The End of Economic Man: An Introduction to Humanist Economics.* 4th edition. New York: W.W. Norton, 2001.

Bromley, Daniel. "Resources and Economic Development: An Institutionalist Perspective." *Journal of Economic Issues* (1985): 779–96.

Brown, Lester. *Eco-Economy: Building an Economy for the Earth.* New York: W.W. Norton, 2001.

Brownlee, W. Elliot. *Federal Taxation in America.* 2nd edition. Washington, D.C.: Woodrow Wilson Center Press, 2004.

Bryer, R. A. "The History of Accounting and the Transition to Capitalism in England. Part One: Theory." *Accounting, Organizations and Society* 25, no. 2 (2000a): 131–62.

———. "The History of Accounting and the Transition to Capitalism in England. Part Two: Evidence." *Accounting, Organizations and Society* 25, no. 4 (2000b): 327–81.

Bureau of Demobilization, Civilian Production Administration. *Industrial Mobilization for War: History of the War Production Board and Predecessor Agencies, 1940–1945.* Vol. 1: *Program and Administration.* Washingtion, D.C.: U.S. Government Printing Office, 1947.

Bureau of Economic Analysis. *Readings in Concepts and Methods of National Income Statistics.* Washington, D.C.: BEA, 1976.

———. *National Income and Product Accounts.* Tables 1.1, 1.2, and 3.2. Washington, D.C.: BEA, 1997.

Burke, Edmund. *The Works of the Right Honourable Edmund Burke* Google ebooks ([1815] 2011): 8: 172.

Burns, Arthur F. *Wesley Mitchell and the National Bureau.* New York: National Bureau of Economic Research, 1949.

Bynum, Cornelius A. *Philip Randolph and the Struggle for Civil Rights.* Chicago: University of Illinois Press, 2010.

Camerer, Colin, et al. "Neuroeconomics: How Neuroscience Can Inform Economics." *Journal of Economic Literature* 43, no. 1 (2005).

Cameron, Rondo, and Larry Neal. *A Concise Economic History of the World from Paleolithic Times to the Present.* Oxford: Oxford University Press, 2003.

Canoy, Marcel, and Frédéric Lerais. "Beyond GDP." *European Union* (2007): 1.

Caputo, Richard K., ed. *Basic Income Guarantee and Politics: International Experiences and Perspectives on the Viability of Income Guarantee.* New York: Palgrave MacMillan, 2012.

Carruthers, Bruce G, and Wendy Nelson Espeland, "Accounting for Rationality: Double-Entry Bookkeeping and the Rhetoric of Economic Rationality." *American Journal of Sociology* 97, no. 1 (July 1991): 31–69.

Carson, Carol S. "The History of the United States National Income and Product Accounts." Unpublished diss. The George Washington University, 1971.

———. "The History of the United States National Income and Product Accounts: The Development of an Analytical Tool," *Review of Income and Wealth: Journal of the International Association for Research in Income and Wealth* 25 (1975): 153–81.

————, "In Memoriam: George Jaszi," *Review of Income and Wealth* 39, no. 3 (June 1993): 225.

Carson, Rachel. *Silent Spring.* New York: Fawcett, 1962.

Carter, Connie, and Andrew Harding, eds. *Special Economic Zones in Asian Market Economies.* New York: Routledge, 2010.

Carter, Susan, Scott Sigmund Gartner, et al., eds. *Historical Statistics of the United States, Earliest Times to the Present, Millennial Edition.* New York: Cambridge University Press, 2006.

Cate, Thomas, ed. *Keynes's General Theory: Seventy-Five years Later.* Vol. I. Cheltenham, England: Edward Elgar, 2012.

Cato, Molly Scott. *Green Economics: An Introduction to Theory, Policy, and Practice.* London and Sterling, Va.: Earthscan, 2009.

Cavanagh, John, and Jerry Mander, eds. *Alternatives to Economic Globalization—A Better World Is Possible.* San Francisco: Berrett-Koehler, 2004.

Center for the Advancement of Steady State Economics (CASSE). "Downsides of Growth." http://steadystate.org/discover/downsides-of-economic-growth/, accessed 4 February 2012.

Chakrabarty, Dipesh. "The Climate of History: Four Theses." *Critical Inquiry* 35 (Winter 2009): 197–222.

Chambers, Nicky, Craig Simmons, and Mathis Wackernagel. *Sharing Nature's Interest: Ecological Footprints as an Indicator of Sustainability.* London: Earthscan, 2000.

Chang, Ha-Joon. *Bad Samaritans–The Myth of Free Trade and the Secret History of Capitalism.* Bloomsbury Press, 2008.

————. *23 Things They Don't Tell You about Capitalism.* New York: Bloomsbury, 2011.

Chiapello, Eve. "Accounting and the Birth of the Notion of Capitalism." *Critical Perspectives on Accounting* 18 (2007): 263–96.

Childe, Vere Gordon. *What Happened in History.* Baltimore: Penguin, 1946.

Chomsky, Noam. *Profit over People: Neoliberalism and Global Order.* New York: Seven Stories Press, 1999.

Chossudovsky, Michel. *The Globalization of Poverty and the New World Order.* Pincourt, Quebec: Center for Research on Globalization, 2003.

CIA World Factbook. Washington, D.C.: Central Intelligence Agency, 2013.

Clark, Colin. *The National Income, 1924–1931.* London: MacMillan, 1932.

————. *The Conditions of Economic Progress.* London: MacMillan, 1951.

Clarke, Kamari Maxine, "Treat Greed in Africa as a War Crime." *New York Times,* 13 January 2013.

Clarke, Peter. *The Keynesian Revolution in the Making, 1924–1936.* Oxford: Clarendon, 1988.

Clements, Jeffrey. *Corporations Are Not People.* San Francisco: Berrett and Koehler, 2014.

Coase, Ronald H. "The Problem of Social Cost." *Journal of Law and Economics* 3 (October 1960): 1–44.

Cobb, Clifford, Mark Glickman, and Craig Cheslog. "The Genuine Progress Indicator 2000 Update." *Redefining Progress Issue Brief* (2001).

Cobb, Clifford, Ted Halstead, and Jonathan Rowe. "Gross Production vs. Genuine Progress." Excerpt from *The Genuine Progress Indicator: Summary of Data and Methodology*. San Francisco: Redefining Progress, 1995a.

———. "If the GDP Is Up, Why Is America Down?" *Atlantic Monthly*, October 1995b.

Cobb, John B. *The Green National Product: An Alternative to Gross National Product to Measure Well-Being*. Tucson: University Press of America, 1994.

Cohen, Lizabeth. *A Consumers' Republic: The Politics of Mass Consumption in Postwar America*. New York: Knopf, 2003.

Cole, Harold L., and Lee E. Ohanian. "The Great Depression in the United States from a Neoclassical Perspective." *Federal Reserve Bank of Minneapolis Quarterly Review* 23, no. 1 (Winter 1999): 2–24.

Colm, Gerald. "Experiences in the Use of Social Accounting in Public Policy in the United States." *Income and Wealth*, Series I (1951): 75–111.

Colman, Ron. "Measuring Genuine Progress." Presentation at "Made to Measure: Designing Research, Policy, and Action Approaches to Eliminate Gender Inequality." Dalhousie University, Halifax, Nova Scotia, 3–6 October 1999.

Collier, Martin, Director of the Glaser Progress Foundation. Interview on theREALnews.com, 19 March 2008. http://www.youtube.com/watch?v=_yJ_ZkVvrYw, accessed 11 February 2012).

Collins, Chuck, and Mary Wright. *The Moral Measure of the Economy*. Maryknoll, N.Y.: Orbis, 2007.

Collins, Robert M. "Positive Business Responses to the New Deal: The Roots of the Committee for Economic Development, 1933–1942." *Business History Review* 52, no. 3 (Autumn 1978): 369–91.

———. *More: The Politics of Economic Growth in Postwar America*. Oxford: Oxford University Press, 2000.

Commission of the European Communities, International Monetary Fund, Organisation for Economic Co-operation and Development, United Nations, and the World Bank. *System of National Accounts 1993*. Brussels/Luxembourg, New York, Paris, and Washington, D.C., 1993.

Commission on Growth and Development. *The Growth Report: Strategies for Sustained Growth and Inclusive Development*. Washington, D.C.: World Bank, 2008.

Committee on Manufacturers, Index to Congressional Committees. Library of Congress.

Committee on Finance, Index to Congressional Committees. Library of Congress. Congressional Records, 71st Congress. 4 March 1929 to 4 March 1931.

———. 72nd Congress. 4 March 1931 to March 4, 1933.

———. 73rd Congress. 4 March 1933 to January 3, 1935.

Cone, Frederick M. "Revised Estimates of Monthly Income Payments in the United States, 1929–38." *Survey of Current Business* 18 (September 1939): 15–18. library.bea.gov/u?/SCB,3059.

Cook, John, et al. "Quantifying the Consensus on Anthropogenic Global Warming in the Scientific Literature." *Environmental Research Letters* 8, no. 2 (2013).

Copeland, Morris A. "National Wealth and Income—an Interpretation," *Journal of the American Statistical Association* 30, no. 190 (1935): 377–86.

Costanza, Robert, R. d'Arge, et al. "The Value of the World's Ecosystem Services and Natural Capital." *Nature* 387 (1997): 253–60.

Costanza, Robert, B. Fisher, et al. 2007. "Quality of Life: An Approach Integrating Opportunities, Human Needs, and Subjective Well-Being." *Ecological Economics* 61 (2007): 267–76.

Costanza, Robert, Maureen Hart, Stephen Posner, and John Tall. "Beyond GDP: The Need for New Measures of Progress." *The Pardee Papers* (January 2009, 4).

Costanza, Robert, and Ida Kubiszewski. *Creating a Desirable and Sustainable Future: Insights from 45 Global Thought Leaders*. Hackensack, N.J.: World Scientific, 2014.

Coyle, Diane. *The Economics of Enough—How to Run the Economy as if the Future Matters*. Princeton: Princeton University Press, 2011.

———. *GDP: A Brief but Affectionate History.* Princeton: Princeton University Press, 2014.

Crafts, Nicholas, and Peter Fearon, eds. *The Great Depression of the 1930s: Lessons for Today*. Oxford: Oxford University Press, 2013.

Crawford, Matthew B. "Shop Class as Soulcraft," *The New Atlantis* (Summer 2006).

———. *Shop Class as Soulcraft: An Inquiry into the Value of Work*. New York: Penguin, 2009.

Crist, Eileen. "Beyond the Climate Crisis: A Critique of Climate Change Discourse." *Telos* 141 (2007): 29–55.

Cronon, William. *Changes in the Land: Indians, Colonists, and the Ecology of New England*. New York: Macmillan, 2011.

Cross, Gary, *An All-Consuming Century: Why Commercialism Won in Modern America*. New York: Columbia University Press, 2000.

Crouch, Colin. *Post-Democracy*. London: Polity Press, 2004.

Czech, Brian. *Shoveling Fuel on a Runaway Train*. Berkeley: University of California Press, 2000.

D'Acci, Lucca. "Measuring Well-Being and Progress." *Social Indicators Research* 104, no. 1 (2011): 47–65.

Daley, William M. "Press Conference Announcing the Commerce Department's Achievements of the Century." Secretary, U.S. Department of Commerce, 7 December 1999.

Daly, Herman E. *Toward a Steady-State Economy*. San Francisco: W.H. Freeman, 1973.

———. *Steady-State Economics.* 1st edition. Washington, D.C.: Island Press, 1991.

———. *Beyond Growth: The Economics of Sustainable Development*. Boston: Beacon Press, 1997.

———. *Ecological Economics and Sustainable Development*. Cheltenham, England, Northampton, Mass.: Edward Elgar, 2008.

———. "The End of Uneconomic Growth." In J. Randers, ed., *2052—A Global Forecast for the Next Forty Years*. White River Junction, Vt.: Chelsea Green, 2012.

Daly, Herman E., and John B. Cobb. *For the Common Good: Redirecting the Economy toward Community, the Environment, and a Sustainable Future.* Boston: Beacon Press, 1994.

Daly, Herman E., and Joshua Farley. *Ecological Economics: Principles and Applications.* Washington, D.C.: Island Press, 2002.

Daly, Herman E., and K. N. Townsend, eds. *Valuing the Earth: Economics, Ecology, Ethics.* Cambridge: MIT Press, 1993.

Daly, Lew, and John McElwee. "Forget the GDP. Some States Have Found a Better Way to Measure Our Progress." *The New Republic*, 3 February 2014.

Dartnell, Lewis. "Civilization's Starter Kit." *New York Times*, 30 March 2014.

Dasgupta, Swapan, and Tapan Mitra. "On the Welfare Significance of National Product for Economic Growth and Sustainable Development." *Japanese Economic Review* 50, no. 4 (1999): 422–42.

Davidson, Eric A. *You Can't Eat GNP: Economics as if Ecology Mattered.* Cambridge, Mass. Perseus, 2000.

De Angelis, Massimo. *The Beginning of History: Value Struggles and Global Capital.* London: Pluto, 2007.

Degler, Carl N., "The Ordeal of Herbert Hoover." Bobbs-Merrill reprint series, History, No. H-52. Reprinted from the *Yale Review* 52, no.4 (Summer 1963): 563–83.

De Graaf, John. *Affluenza: The All-Consuming Epidemic.* San Francisco: Berrett-Koehler, 2005.

De Haan, Mark. "On the International Harmonisation of Environmental Accounting: Comparing the National Accounting Matrix including Environmental Accounts of Sweden, Germany, the UK, Japan and the Netherlands." *Structural Change and Economic Dynamics* 10, no. 1 (1999): 151–60.

De Long, J. Bradford. "Estimates of World GDP, One Million B.C. to Present." Working Paper. University of California, Berkeley, Department of Economics, 1998. http:// delong.typepad.com/print/20061012_LRWGDP.pdf, accessed June 2012.

De Long, J. Bradford, and Martha L. Olney. *Macroeconomics.* Chapter 5. Boston: McGraw-Hill, 2009.

Demos. "Beyond GDP—New Measures for a New Economy" (2011): 7–9. http://www .demos.org/sites/default/files/publications/BeyondGDP_0.pdf.

Denison, Edward F. "Report on Tripartite Discussions of National Income Measurement." *Studies in Income and Wealth*, vol. 10. National Bureau of Economic Research. 1947, pp. 3–22.

———. "Welfare Measurement and the GNP." *Survey of Current Business.* U.S. Department of Commerce. Washington, D.C. January 1971, pp. 13–16.

Dennis, Kingsley, and John Urry. *After the Car.* Cambridge, England: Polity Press, 2009.

Derman, Emanuel. *Models. Behaving. Badly: Why Confusing Illusion with Reality Can Lead to Disaster, on Wall Street and in Life.* New York: Free Press, 2012.

Desrosières, Alain. *The Politics of Large Numbers: A History of Statistical Reasoning.* Cambridge: Harvard University Press, 2002.

Diamond, Jared. *Guns, Germs, and Steel*. New York: W.W. Norton, 1999.

———. *Collapse: How Societies Choose to Fail or Succeed*. New York: Penguin, 2005. 2005.

Dickinson, Elizabeth. "One State to Rule Them All: Anthropology of an Idea: GDP," *Foreign Policy* (January–February 2011).

Dietz, Rob, and Dan O'Neill. *Enough Is Enough: Building a Sustainable Economy in a World of Finite Resources*. San Francisco: Berrett and Koehler, 2013.

Doan, Edward Newell. *The La Follettes and the Wisconsin Idea*. New York: Rinehart, 1947.

Domhoff, William. "Who Rules America? Wealth, Income, and Power." Department of Sociology, University of California-Santa Cruz. Originally posted September 2005, updated February 2013. http://www2.ucsc.edu/whorulesamerica/power/wealth.html, accessed 15 May 2014.

Dorfman, Joseph. *The Economic Mind in American Civilization*. Vols. 4 and 5: 1918–1933. New York: Viking Press, 1959.

Douthwaite, Richard. *The Growth Illusion: How Economic Growth Has Enriched the Few, Impoverished the Many and Endangered the Planet*. London: Green Books, 1999.

———. *The Ecology of Money*. Schumacher Briefings no.4. Totnes, Devon, England: Green Books, 2000.

Dowd, Douglas. *Capitalism and Its Economics—A Critical History*. London: Pluto, 2000.

Dryzek, J. S. "Global Ecological Democracy." Pp. 264–82 in N. Low, ed., *Global Ethics and the Environment*. London and New York: Routledge, 1999.

Duncan, Joseph W., and William C. Shelton. *Revolution in United States Government Statistics, 1926–1976*. Washington, D.C.: U.S. Government Printing Office, 1978.

Dunne, Nancy. "Why a Hamburger Should Cost 200 Dollars: The Call for Prices to Reflect Ecological Factors." *Financial Times*, 12 January 1994.

Durning, Alan. *How Much Is Enough? The Consumer Society and the Future of the Earth*. New York: W.W. Norton, 1992.

Easterlin, Richard A. "Does Money Buy Happiness?" *The Public Interest* 30 (1973): 3–10.

———. "Does Economic Growth Improve the Human Lot? Some Empirical Evidence." Pp. 89–125 in P. A. David and M. W. Reder, eds., *Nations and Households in Economic Growth: Essays in Honor of Moses Abramowitz*. New York: Academic Press, 1974.

———. "Will Raising the Incomes of All Increase the Happiness of All?" *Journal of Economic Behavior and Organization* 27 (1995): 35–47.

———. "Income and Happiness: Toward a Unified Theory." *Economic Journal* 111 (2001): 465–84.

———. "Feeding the Illusion of Growth and Happiness." *Social Indicators Research* no. 74 (2005): 429–43.

Easterlin, Richard A., and L. A. McVey, M. Switek, O. Sawangfa, and J. S. Zweig, "The Happiness Income Paradox Revisited." *Journal Proceedings of the National Academy of Sciences* 107, no. 52 (28 December 2010).

Easterly, William. "Life during Economic Growth." *Journal of Economic Growth* (4/1999): 239–76.

Easterly, William, and Luis Serven, eds. *The Limits of Stabilization: Infrastructure, Public Deficits and Growth in Latin America*. Washington, D.C.: World Bank Publications, 2003.

Eckstein, Otto. "The NIPA Accounts." In Murray F. Foss, ed., *The U.S. National Income and Product Accounts*. Chicago: University of Chicago Press, 1983.

Edelstein, Michael. "The Size of the U.S. Armed Forces during World War II: Feasibility and War Planning." *Research in Economic History* 20 (2001).

Edwards, Andres R. *The Sustainability Revolution: Portraits of a Paradigm Shift*. Gabriola Island, British Columbia: New Society, 2005.

Egan, Michael, and Jeff Crane, eds. *Natural Protest: Essays on the History of American Environmentalism*. New York: Routledge, 2009.

Eichengreen, Barry. "Hegemonic Stability Theories of the International Monetary System." In Richard N. Cooper, ed., *Can Nations Agree: Issues in International Economic Cooperation*. Washington, D.C.: Brookings Institution Press, 2001.

———. *Globalizing Capital: A History of the International Monetary System*. Princeton: Princeton University Press, 2008.

Eid, Michael, and Randy J. Larsen, eds. *The Science of Subjective Well-Being*. New York and London: Guilford, 2008.

Eisner, Robert. "The Total Incomes System of Accounts." *Survey of Current Business* 1, no. 65 (1985): 24–48.

———. *The Misunderstood Economy: What Counts and How to Count It*. Boston: Harvard Business School Press, 1994.

Ekins, Paul. *Economic Growth and Environmental Sustainability: The Prospects for Green Growth*. London and New York: Routledge, 2000.

Ekins, Paul, and Manfred Max-Neef, eds. *Real-Life Economics: Understanding Wealth Creation*. London and New York: Routledge, 1992.

Eltis, Walter. *The Classical Theory of Economic Growth*. New York: St. Martin's, 1984.

Engerman, David C. "American Knowledge and Global Power." *Diplomatic History* 31, no. 4 (September 2007): 599–622.

Engerman, David C., Nils Gilman, Mark H. Haefele, and Michael Latham, eds. *Staging Growth: Modernization, Development, and the Cold War*. Amherst, Mass.: University of Massachusetts Press, 2003.

Fabricant, Solomon. *Toward a Firmer Basis of Economic Policy: The Founding of the National Bureau of Economic Research*. Cambridge, Mass: NBER, 1984.

Federal Trade Commission. "National Income and Wealth: Response to Senate Resolution No. 451." 67th Congress, 4th Session. Senate Document no. 126, 1926.

Federici, Silvia. *Caliban and the Witch*. New York: Autonomedia, 2004.

Felber, Christian. *Gemeinwohlökonomie*. 5th ed. Vienna: Deuticke, 2012.

Felkerson, James, et al. "$29,000,000,000,000: A Detailed Look at the Fed's Bailout by Funding Facility and Recipient," Levi Economics Institute, Working Paper no. 698, December 2011.

Ferrara, Peter. "Economic Growth, Not Redistribution, Most Benefits the Poor, the Working People, and the Middle Class." *Forbes*, 15 November 2012.

Fioramonti, Lorenzo. *Gross Domestic Problem—The Politics behind the World's Most Powerful Number*. New York: Zed Books, 2013.

Fisher, Irving. *The Making of Index Numbers: A Study of their Varieties, Tests and Reliability*. Boston: Houghton Mifflin, 1922.

———. *Nature of Capital and Income*. New York: A.M. Kelly, 1936.

Fleurbaey, Marc. "Beyond GDP: The Quest for a Measure of Social Welfare." *Journal of Economic Literature* 47, no. 4 (2009): 1029–75.

Fogel, Robert William. "Some Notes on the Scientific Methods of Simon Kuznets." NBER Working Paper no. W2461. Cambridge, Mass: NBER, 1987.

———. "Simon S. Kuznets: April 30, 1901–July 9, 1985." NBER Working Paper no. 7787. Cambridge, Mass., 2000.

Fox, Justin. "Don't Ditch the GDP." *Time* magazine, 10 April 2008.

———. *The Myth of the Rational Market: A History of Risk, Reward, and Delusion on Wall Street*. New York: HarperBusiness, 2009.

Francis. "Apostolic Exhortation Evangelli Gaudium of the Holy Father Francis to the Bishops, Clergy, Consecrated Persons and the Lay Faithful on the Proclamation of the Gospel in Today's World." November 2013.

Franks, Oliver. "The Evolution of Twentieth-Century Capitalism." In National Industrial Conference Board, ed., *The Future of Capitalism*. New York: Macmillan, 1967. A symposium of distinguished commentary by internationally known leaders of industry, science, government, education, religion, and the arts delivered at the world convocation in New York City, September 19–21, 1966, on the occasion of the fiftieth anniversary of the National Industrial Conference Board.

Frank, Thomas. *One Market Under God*. New York: Random House, 2001.

Fraser, Steve, and Gary Gerstle, eds. *The Rise and Fall of the New Deal Order, 1930–1980*. Princeton: Princeton University Press, 1989.

Frey, Bruno S., et al. *Happiness: A Revolution in Economics*. Cambridge: MIT Press, 2010.

Friedan, Betty. *The Feminine Mystique*. New York: W.W. Norton, 1963.

Friedman, Benjamin. *The Moral Consequences of Economic Growth*. New York: Knopf, 2005.

Friedman, Milton. "The Inflationary Gap: II Discussion of the Inflationary Gap." *American Economic Review* 32 (February 1942): 314–20.

Friedman, Thomas. *Hot, Flat, and Crowded: Why We Need a Green Revolution—and How It Can Renew America*. New York: Farrar, Straus and Giroux, 2008.

Frumkin, Norman. *Guide to Economic Indicators*. Armonk, N.Y.: M.E. Sharpe, 1990.

Furner, Mary O., and Barry Supple, eds. *The State and Economic Knowledge: The American and British Experience*. Woodrow Wilson Center Series. Cambridge: Cambridge University Press, 2002.

Galbraith, James K. *The Predator State: How Conservatives Abandoned the Free Market and Why Liberals Should Too*. New York: Free Press, 2008.

――――. *Inequality and Instability: A Study of the World Economy Just Before the Great Crisis*. New York: Oxford University Press, 2012.

Galbraith, John Kenneth. "The Job before Us." *Fortune,* January 1943, p. 65.

――――. *The Affluent Society*. New York: Mentor, 1958.

――――. "The National Accounts: Arrival and Impact." In Norman Cousins, ed., *Reflections of America—Commemorating the Statistical Abstract Centennial*. Washington, D.C.: U.S. Department of Commerce, 1980.

――――. *A Life in Our Times: Memoirs*. Boston: Houghton Mifflin, 1981.

――――. "Economics in Perspective." *A Critical History* (1987): 245.

Gates, Jeff. *The Ownership Solution: Toward a Shared Capitalism for the Twenty-First Century*. Cambridge, Mass.: Perseus, 1999.

――――. *Democracy at Risk: Rescuing Main Street from Wall Street*. Cambridge, Mass.: Perseus, 2000.

Geithner, Timothy. Interview with Jon Stewart, *Daily Show*. 21 May 2014.

George, Susan, and Fabrizio Sabelli. *Faith and Credit: The World Bank's Secular Empire*. Boulder, Colo.: Westview, 1994.

Georgesçu-Roegen, Nicholas. *The Entropy Law and the Economic Process*. Cambridge: Harvard University Press, 1971.

Gertner, John. "The Rise and Fall of the GDP." *New York Times*, 13 May 2010.

Gibson, John E., and William T. Scherer. *How to Do Systems Analysis*. Hoboken, N.J.: Wiley, 2007.

Gilbert, Daniel T. *Stumbling on Happiness*. New York: Knopf, 2006.

Gilbert, Milton. "Measuring National Income as Affected by the War." *Journal of the American Statistical Association*, 37, no. 218 (June 1942a): 186–98.

――――. "War Expenditures and National Production." *Survey of Current Business*. 22, no. 3 (1942b): 9–16.

――――. "National Income: Concepts and Measurement." *Measuring and Projecting National Income*. Studies in Business Policy, no. 5. New York: National Industrial Conference Board, 1945.

Gilding, Paul. *The Great Disruption—Why the Climate Crisis Will Bring on the End of Shopping and the Birth of a New World*. New York: Bloomsbury, 2011.

Gittins, Ross. "At the Coal Face Economists Are Struggling to Measure Up." *The Sydney Morning Herald, Business Day*, 19 April 2014.

Gleeson-White, Jane. *Double Entry: How the Merchants of Venice Created Modern Finance*. New York: W.W. Norton, 2012.

Global Footprint Network. *What Happens When an Infinite Growth Economy Runs Into a Finite Planet? Annual Report*. Oakland, Calif.: Global Footprint Network, 2011.

Goleman, Daniel. *Ecological Intelligence: How Knowing the Hidden Impacts of What We Buy Can Change Everything*. New York: Broadway Books, 2010.

Goodwin, Neva R., ed. *Human Well-Being and Economic Goals*. Covelo, Calif.: Island Press, 1997.

Goodwyn, Lawrence. *The Populist Moment: A Short History of the Agrarian Revolt in America.* New York: Oxford University Press, 1978.

———. *Breaking the Barrier.* New York: Oxford University Press, 1991.

Goossens, Y., A. Mäkipää, et al. *Alternative Progress Indicators to Gross Domestic Product (GDP) as a Means Towards Sustainable Development.* Brussels: European Parliament, Policy Department A: Economic and Scientific Policy, 2007.

Gorelick, Steven. "Small Is Beautiful, Big Is Subsidized." *International Society of Ecology and Culture* (October 1998).

Graeber, David. *Debt: The First 5,000 Years.* New York: Melville House, 2011

Gray, John. *False Dawn: The Delusions of Global Capitalism.* London: Granta, 2002.

———. "The End of the World as We Know It." *The Guardian,* 14 September 2007.

Green, Francis, and N. Tsitsianis. "An Investigation of National Trends in Job Satisfaction in Britain and Germany." *British Journal of Industrial Relations* 43, no. 3 (2005): 401–29.

Greenspan, Alan. "Testimony of Dr. Alan Greenspan to the Committee of Government Oversight and Reform, October 23, 2008." http://oversight.house.gov/images/stories/documents/20081024163819.pdf, accessed 10 March 2010.

Greenwood, Robin, and David Scharfstein. "The Growth of Modern Finance." NBER Working Paper, July 2012.

Gregory, Paul, Robert C. Stuart, and Steven L. Husted. *Russian and Soviet Economic Performance and Structure.* Englewood Cliffs, N.J.: Prentice Hall, 2000.

Greider, William. *The Secrets of the Temple.* New York: Simon and Schuster, 1987.

———. *One World, Ready or Not: The Manic Logic of Global Capitalism.* New York: Simon and Schuster, 1997.

———. *The Soul of Capitalism.* New York: Simon and Schuster, 2003.

Griliches, Zvi. Papers. HUGFP 153. Harvard University Archives. Cambridge, Mass.

Grober, Ulrich. *Sustainability—A Cultural History.* Totnes, Devon, England: Green Books, 2012.

Gruber, Lloyd. *Ruling the World: Power Politics and the Rise of Supranational Institutions.* Princeton: Princeton University Press, 2000.

Gurven, Michael and Hillard Kaplan, "Longevity among Hunter-Gatherers." *Population and Development Review* 33, no. 2 (June 2007): 321–65.

Hacker, Jacob S. *The Great Risk Shift: The Assault on American Jobs, Families, Health Care, and Retirement, and How You Can Fight Back.* New York: Oxford University Press, 2006.

Haig, B. P., and S. S. McBurney. *The Interpretation of National Income Estimates.* Canberra: Australian National University Press, 1968.

Hák, Tomáš, and Svatava Janoušková. "Review Report on Beyond GDP Indicators: Categorisation, Intentions and Impacts." *Brainpool* (2012). http://www.brainpoolproject.eu/wp-content/uploads/2012/12/D1.1_BRAINPOoL_Review_report_Beyond-GDP_indicators.pdf, accessed November 2013.

Hamilton, Alexander. *Report on Manufactures*, 5 December 1791, Article 1, Section 8, Clause 1, Papers 10:302–4. http://press-pubs.uchicago.edu/founders/documents/a1_8_1s21.html, accessed 30 May 2012.

Hamilton, Clive. *Growth Fetish*. Crows Nest, Australia: Allen and Unwin, 2003.

Hamilton, Clive, and Richard Denniss. *Affluenza: When Too Much Is Never Enough.* Crow's Nest, Australia: Allen and Unwin, 2006.

Hamilton, Kirk, ed. *Where Is the Wealth of Nations? Measuring Capital for the 21st Century.* Washington, D.C.: World Bank, 2006.

Hansen, Alvin H. *Business Cycles and National Income.* Expanded edition. New York: W.W. Norton, 1964.

Hansen, James. *Storms of My Grandchildren: The Truth about the Coming Climate Catastrophe and Our Last Chance to Save Humanity.* New York: Bloomsbury, 2009.

Hardin, Garrett, "The Tragedy of the Commons," *Science* 162, no. 13 (December 1968): 1243–48.

Harman, Chris. *A People's History of the World.* London: Verso, 2008.

Hartwig, Jochen. "Petty—oder: Die Geburt der Arbeitswertlehre aus ökonomischen Problemen des Frühkapitalismus." *Historical Social Research* 26 no. 4 (2001): 88–124.

Harvey, David. *A Brief History of Neoliberalism.* Oxford: Oxford University Press, 2005.

Hawken, Paul. *The Ecology of Commerce.* New York: HarperCollins, 2010.

Hawken, Paul, Amory B. Lovins, and L. Hunter Lovins. *Natural Capitalism: Creating the Next Industrial Revolution.* Boston: Little, Brown, 1999.

Hedges, Chris. *Empire of Illusion: The End of Literacy and the Triumph of Spectacle.* New York: Nation Books, 2009.

Heilbroner, Robert. *21st Century Capitalism.* New York: W.W. Norton, 1993.

———. *The Nature and Logic of Capitalism.* New York: W.W. Norton, 1985.

———. *The Economic Transformation of America.* 4th edition. Fort Worth, Texas: Harcourt Brace; Boston: Cengage Learning, 1998.

———. *The Worldly Philosophers: The Lives, Times, and Ideas of the Great Economic Thinkers.* New York: Touchstone, 1999.

Heinberg, Richard. *The End of Economic Growth: Adapting to Our New Economic Reality.* Gabriola, British Columbia: New Society, 2011.

Held, D., A. McGrew, D. Goldblaatt, and J. Perraton. *Global Transformations: Politics, Economics, and Culture.* Stanford: Stanford University Press, 1999.

Helpman, Elhanan, *The Mystery of Economic Growth*, Cambridge, Mass., and London: Belknap Press / Harvard University Press, 2010.

Henderson, Hazel. *The Politics of the Solar Age: Alternatives to Economics.* Garden City, N.Y.: Anchor Press, 1981.

———. *Ethical Markets: Growing the Green Economy.* With Simran Sethi. White River Junction, Vt.: Chelsea Green, 2006.

Henderson, Hazel, Jon Lickerman, et al. *Calvert-Henderson Quality of Life Indicators: A New Tool for Assessing National Trends.* Bethesda, Md.: Calvert Group, 2000.

Herman, Arthur. *Freedom's Forge: How American Business Produced Victory in World War II*. New York: Random House, 2012.

Herr, Norman. "Television and Health." California State University, Northridge, http://www.csun.edu/science/health/docs/tv&health.html.

Hertz, Noreena. *The Silent Takeover: Global Capitalism and the Death of Democracy*. New York: Harper Collins, 2003.

Hicks, J. R. "Valuation of the Social Income." *Economica*, New Series, 7, no. 26 (May 1940): 105–24.

——. *Value and Capital: An Inquiry into Some Fundamental Principles of Economic Theory*. 2nd edition. London: Oxford University Press, 1975.

Higgs, Robert. "Wartime Prosperity? A Reassessment of the U.S. Economy in the 1940s." *Journal of Economic History* 51, no. 1 (March 1992).

——. "Military Spending / GDP = Nonsense for Budget Policy Making," *The Independent Institute* (5 March 2008). http://www.independent.org/newsroom/article.asp?id=2143, accessed 2 April 2013.

Hill, Christopher. *The World Turned Upside Down: Radical Ideas During the English Revolution*. London, New York: Penguin Books, 1975.

Hirsch, Fred. *Social Limits to Growth*. New York; Routledge, 2005.

Hirschman, Albert O. *National Power and the Structure of Foreign Trade*. Berkeley: University of California Press, 1945.

Hirschman, Daniel. "Inventing the Economy: Or, How We Learned to Stop Worrying and Love the GDP." Ph.D. diss., University of Michigan, forthcoming.

Hobsbawm, Eric J. *Industry and Empire: The Birth of the Industrial Revolution*. New York: New Press, 1999.

Hogan, Michael J. *The Marshall Plan: America, Britain, and the Reconstruction of Western Europe, 1947–1952*. Cambridge: Cambridge University Press, 1987.

Hogan, Wesley. *Many Minds, One Heart: SNCC's Dream for a New America*. Chapel Hill: University of North Carolina Press, 2007.

Homer-Dixon, Thomas. *A Century of Revolution, 1603–1714*. New York: W.W. Norton, 1982.

——. *The Upside of Down: Catastrophe, Creativity, and the Renewal of Civilization*. Washington, D.C.: Island Press, 2008.

Hoover, Herbert. *The Memoirs of Herbert Hoover*. New York: Macmillan, 1952.

Hoover, Kevin. "Applied Intermediate Macroeconomics." Unpublished manuscript, 2010.

Hopkins, Rob. *Transition Handbook*. White River Junction, Vt.: Chelsea Green, 2008.

Horrigan, Leo, Robert S. Lawrence, and Polly Walker. "How Sustainable Agriculture Can Address the Environmental and Human Health Harms of Industrial Agriculture." *Environmental Health Perspectives* 110, no. 5 (2002): 445–56.

Hoskyns, Catherine, and Shirin M. Rai. "Recasting the Global Political Economy: Counting Women's Unpaid Work." *New Political Economy* 12, no. 3 (2007): 297–317.

Howard, Jason. "Appalachia Turns on Itself." *New York Times*, 9 July 2012, p. A15.

Hsing, Yu. "Economic Growth and Income Inequality: The Case of the U.S." *International Journal of Social Economics* 32, no. 7 (2005): 639–47.

Hughes, Jonathan, and Louis Cain, eds. *American Economic History*. 6th edition. Boston: Addison Wesley, 2003.

Hunger Notes. "2013 World Hunger and Poverty Statistics." http://www.worldhunger.org/articles/Learn/world%20hunger%20facts%202002.htm.

Hutchinson, Frances. *What Everybody Really Wants to Know about Money*. Charlbury, Oxfordshire, England: Jon Carpenter, 1998.

Hylton, Wil S. "Broken Heartland: The Looming Collapse of Agriculture on the Great Plains." *Harper's Magazine*, July 2012.

Ikerd, John. *Sustainable Capitalism: A Matter of Common Sense*. West Hartford, Conn.: Kumarian Press, 2005.

Jackson, Andrew, and Ben Dyson. *Modernising Money*. London: Positive Money, 2013

Jackson, Tim. *Chasing Progress: Beyond Measuring Economic Growth*. London: New Economics Foundation, 2002.

———. *Prosperity without Growth: Economics for a Finite Planet*. London: Earthscan, 2009.

———. "Let's Be Less Productive." *New York Times*, 26 May 2012

Jaszi, George. "The Concept of National Income and National Product with Special Reference to Government Transactions," Unpublished Ph.D. diss., Harvard University, 1946.

———. "The Conceptual Basis of the Accounts: A Re-examination." Pages 13–148 in NBER, *A Critique of the United States Income and Product Accounts*. Princeton: Princeton University Press, 1958.

———. "The Quarterly National Income and Product Account of the United States, 1942–62." In Simon Goldberg and Phyllis Deane, eds., *Income and Wealth*. Series 11: Studies in Short-term National Accounts and Long-term Economic Growth. New Haven, Conn.: International Association for Research in Income and Wealth, 1965.

———. "An Economic Accountant's Audit." *American Economic Review* 76, no. 2 (1986): 411–18.

Jensen, Robert. "In the Face of this Truth." *YES Magazine*, 17 September 2010.

Johnston, David C. *Free Lunch: How the Wealthiest Americans Enrich Themselves at Government Expense (And Stick You With the Bill)*. New York: Portfolio, 2007.

———. *Divided: The Perils of Our Growing Inequality*. New York: New Press, 2014

Jordan, Chris, *Running the Numbers: An American Self-Portrait*. Pullman, Wash., and Munich: Museum of Fine Art / Washington State University, 2009.

Jorgensen, Dale W., J. Steven Landefeld, and William D. Nordhaus. *A New Architecture for the U.S. National Accounts*. Conference on Studies in Income and Wealth, vol. 66. Chicago: Chicago University Press, 2006. The document from the conference was published as an e-book also in 2006.

Judge, William, Shaomin Li, and Robert Pinsker. "National adoption of international accounting standards: an institutional perspective." *Corporate Governance: An International Review* 18, no. 3 (2010): 161–74.

Judkins, Calvert. Memorandum dated 24 February 1932. National Archives, record group 151, Frederick M. Feiker File.

Kahn, Joseph, and Jim Yardley. "As China Roars, Pollution Reaches Deadly Extremes." *New York Times*, 26 August 2007.

Kahnemann, Daniel. *Thinking Fast and Slow.* New York: Farrar, Straus and Giroux, 2013.

Kahnemann, Daniel, and Alan B. Krueger. "Developments in the Measurement of Subjective Well-Being." *Journal of Economic Perspectives*, 20, no 1 (Winter 2006): 3–24.

Kanter, James. "Dismal Data and Gloomy Forecasts from Europe." *New York Times*, 22 February 2013.

Kapuria-Foreman, Vibha, and Mark Perlman. "An Economic Historian's Economist: Remembering Simon Kuznets." *Economic Journal* 105, no. 433 (November1995).

Karacuka, Mehmet, and Asad Zaman. "The Empirical Evidence against Neoclassical Utility Theory." *International Journal of Pluralism and Economics Education* 3, no. 4 (2012): 366–414.

Kars, Marjoleine. *Breaking Loose Together: The Regulator Rebellion in Pre-Revolutionary North Carolina.* Chapel Hill: University of North Carolina Press, 2002.

Kasser, Tim. *The High Price of Materialism.* New York: Bradford, 2003.

Katz, Arnold J. "A Tribute for Robert R. Nathan." *Survey of Current Business* 82, no. 2 (February 2002): 8.

Katznelson, Ira. *When Affirmative Action Was White.* New York: W.W. Norton, 2005.

Kelly, Marjorie. *The Divine Right of Capital.* San Francisco: Berrett and Koehler, 2003.

Kendrick, John W. "The Historical Development of National-Income Accounts." *History of Political Economy* 2, no. 2 (Fall 1970): 284–315.

———. *The New System of National Accounts.* London: Kluwer Academic Publishers, 1996.

Kenessey, Zoltan, ed. *The Accounts of Nations.* Washington, D.C.: IOS Press, 1994.

Kennedy, David M. *Freedom from Fear: The American People in Depression and War, 1929–1945.* New York: Oxford University Press, 1999.

———. *Over Here: The First World War and American Society.* New York: Oxford University Press, 2004.

Kennedy, Robert F. "Remarks of Robert F. Kennedy at the University of Kansas." 18 March 1968.

Kennickell, Arthur B. "Ponds and Streams: Wealth and Income in the U.S., 1989 to 2007." Federal Reserve Board Working Paper, 7 January 2009.

Kenyon, John, Jane Ohlmeyer, and J. S. Morrill. *The Civil Wars: A Military History of England, Scotland, and Ireland, 1638–1660.* Oxford and New York: Oxford University Press, 1998.

Keohane, Nathaniel O., and Sheila M. Olmstead. *Markets and the Environment.* Washington, D.C.: Island Press, 2007.

Keynes, John Maynard. "The British Balance of Trade, 1925–27." *Economic Journal* 37, no. 148 (1927): 551–65.

———. *How to Pay for War.* New York: Harcourt, Brace, 1940.

———. *Essays in Persuasion.* New York: W.W. Norton, 1963.

———. *The General Theory of Employment, Interest and Money* [1936]. New York: Harcourt, Brace and World, 1965.

———. *The Collected Writings of John Maynard Keynes.* Vols. 1–29. London: Macmillan, 1973–79.

King, Willford I. *The Wealth and Income of the People of the United States.* New York and London: Macmillan, 1915.

———. "Income and Wealth." *The American Economic Review* 15, no. 3 (September 1925).

Kirdar, Uener, and Leonard Silk. *A World Fit For People: Thinkers From Many Countries Address The Political, Economic, And Social Problems Of Our Time.* New York: New York University Press, 1994.

Klein, Judy L., and Mary Morgan. *The Age of Economic Measurement.* Annual Supplement to "History of Political Economy." Durham, N.C.: Duke University Press, 2001.

Klein, Naomi. *The Shock Doctrine: The Rise of Disaster Capitalism.* New York: Macmillan, 2007.

Koistinen, Paul A. C. *Arsenal of World War II: The Political Economy of American Warfare, 1940–1945.* Lawrence: University Press of Kansas, 2004.

Kolbert, Elizabeth. "Head Count." *The New Yorker,* 21 October 2013.

Konow, James, and Joseph Earley. "The Hedonistic Paradox: Is Homo Economicus Happier?" *Journal of Public Economics* 92, no. 1 (2008): 1–33.

Korten, David C. *When Corporations Rule the World.* San Francisco: Berrett-Koehler, 2001.

———. *The Post-Corporate World: Life after Capitalism.* San Francisco: Berrett-Koehler, 1999.

———. *Agenda for a New Economy: From Phantom Wealth to Real Wealth.* San Francisco: Berrett-Koehler, 2009

Korzeniewicz, Roberto Patricio, Angela Stack, Vrushali Patil, and Timothy Patrick Moran. "Measuring National Income: A Critical Assessment." *Comparative Studies in Society and History* 46, no. 3 (July 2004): 535–86.

Kostigen, Thomas. *You Are Here: Exposing the Vital Link Between What We Do and What That Does to Our Planet.* New York: HarperCollins, 2008.

Kragh, Martin. "The Soviet Enterprise." *Enterprise and Society* 14, no. 2 (2013): 360–94.

Kuhn, Thomas S. *The Structure of Scientific Revolutions.* Chicago: University of Chicago Press, 1962.

Kula, Withold. *Measures and Men.* Princeton: Princeton University Press, 1986.

Kumar, Pushpam, ed. *The Economics of Ecosystems and Biodiversity: Ecological and Economic Foundations.* New York: Routledge, 2010.

Kuznets, Simon. Papers. Harvard University Archives, Cambridge, Mass.

———. *Secular Movements in Production and Prices, Their Nature and Their Bearing upon Cyclical Fluctuations.* Boston: Houghton Mifflin, 1930.

————. "Memorandum on the History and Progress of the Study of National Income for 1929–32." Attached to a letter from Simon Kuznets to Dr. Willard L. Thorp, 7 September 1933a. National Archives, Record Group 151, Willard L. Thorp File.

————. "National Income." In E.R.A. Seligman and A. Johnson, eds., *Encyclopedia of the Social Sciences*, 11: 205–24. New York: Macmillan, 1933b.

————. "Review of C. Clark (1933), *The National Income, 1924–31.*" *Journal of the American Statistical Association*, 28, no. 183 (1933c): 363–64.

————. "National Income, 1929–1932." Senate Report to 73rd U.S. Congress, 2d session, 1934, Senate document no. 124, p. 7. 1934. http://library.bea.gov/u?/NI_reports,539.

————. Discussion section in M. A. Copeland, "Concepts of National Income," *Studies in Income and Wealth* 1 (1937).

————. *National Income and Its Composition 1919–1938*. New York: National Bureau of Economic Research, 1941.

————. *National Income: A Summary of Findings*. New York: National Bureau of Economic Research, 1946.

————. "National Income: A New Version." *Review of Economics and Statistics* 30, no. 3 (August 1948): 151–79.

————. *National Income and Industrial Structure*. London: Economic Change, 1954.

————. *Capital in the American Economy: Its Formation and Financing*. Princeton: Princeton University Press, 1961.

————. "How to Judge Quality." *The New Republic*, 147, no. 16 (October 1962).

————. *Toward a Theory of Economic Growth*. New York: W.W. Norton, 1968.

————. "Modern Economic Growth: Findings and Reflections." *American Economic Review* 63, no. 3 (June 1973).

Lacey, James G. *Keep from All Thoughtful Men: How U.S. Economists Won World War II*. Annapolis, Md.: Naval Institute Press, 2011.

La Follette, Robert M. Jr. Papers. Library of Congress, Washington, D.C.

————. *New York Times*, 27 April 1931.

Lampton, David. *The Three Faces of Chinese Power*. Berkeley: University of California Press, 2008.

Landefeld, J. Steven. "GDP: One of the Great Inventions of the 20th Century." *Survey of Current Business* 80, no. 1 (2000): 6–14

————. "Rethinking the Gross Domestic Product as a Measurement of National Strength." Testimony before the Interstate Commerce, Trade, and Tourism Subcommittee of the Senate Committee on Commerce, Science, and Transportation, Sen. Byron Dorgan presiding. 12 March 2008.

Landefeld, J. Steven, Eugene P. Seskin, and Barbara M. Fraumeni. "Taking the Pulse of the Economy: Measuring GDP." *Journal of Economic Perspectives* 22, no. 2 (Spring 2008): 193–216.

Landes, David S. *The Wealth and Poverty of Nations: Why Some Are so Rich, and Some so Poor*. New York: Norton, 1998.

Lane, Jan-Erik. "Energy: The Link between GDP and Emissions." *Research in World Economy* 4, no. 1 (2013): 49–54.

Lane, Robert E. *The Loss of Happiness in Market Democracies*. New Haven: Yale University Press, 2001.

Lardner, James, and David A. Smith, eds. *Inequality Matters*. New York: 2005.

Latour, Bruno. *We Have Never Been Modern*. Translated by Catherine Porter. Cambridge: Harvard University Press, 1993.

Lawn, Philip A. "A Theoretical Foundation to Support the Index of Sustainable Economic Welfare (ISEW), Genuine Progress Indicator (GPI), and Other Related Indexes." *Ecological Economics* 44 (2003): 105–18.

———. *Sustainable Development Indicators in Ecological Economics*. Current Issues in Ecological Economics Series. Northhampton, Mass.: Edward Elgar, 2006.

Layard, Richard. *Happiness: Lessons from a New Science*. New York: Penguin, 2006.

Lebow, Victor. "What Makes the Consumer Buy?" *Challenge* 6, no. 6 (1958): 28.

Leete-Guy, Laura, and Juliet B. Schor. *The Great American Time Squeeze: Trends in Work and Leisure, 1969–1989*. Washington, D.C.: Economic Policy Institute, 1992.

Leipert, Christian. "A Critical Appraisal of Gross National Product: The Measurement of Net National Welfare and the Environmental Accounting." *Journal of Economic Issues* 21, no. 1 (1987): 362.

Leuchtenberg, William E. *The Perils of Prosperity, 1914–1932*. Chicago: University of Chicago Press, 1993.

———. *The FDR Years: On Roosevelt and His Legacy*. New York: Columbia University Press, 1995.

———. *Franklin D. Roosevelt and the New Deal, 1932–1940*. New York: Harper Perennial, 2009.

Lewis, John P., and Robert C. Turner. *Business Conditions Analysis*. 2nd edition. New York: McGraw Hill, 1967.

Lewis, Michael. *Moneyball: The Art of Winning an Unfair Game*. New York: Random House Audio, 2011. Originally published in 2003 by W.W. Norton, New York.

Linebaugh, Peter. *The Magna Carta Manifesto: Liberties and Commons for All*. Berkeley: University of California Press, 2008.

Ling, L.H.M. "Hegemony and the Internationalizing State: A Post-Colonial Analysis of China's Integration into Asian Corporatism." *Review of International Political Economy* 3, no. 1 (1996): 1–26

Linklater, Andro. *Measuring America: How the United States Was Shaped by the Greatest Land Sale in History*. New York: Plume, 2003.

Liu, Jianguo, and Jared Diamond, "Revolutionizing China's Environmental Protection." *Science* 319, no. 5859 (4 January 2008).

Livingston, S. Morris. *Markets after the War: An Approach to Their Analysis*. Washington, D.C.: U. S. Department of Commerce, 1943.

Lomborg, Bjørn, ed. *How Much Have Global Problems Cost the World?* New York: Cambridge University Press, 2013.

Lord, Clive, Miriam Kennet, and Judith Felton. *Citizen's Income and Green Economics.* Oxford: The Green Economics Institute, 2011.

Lovelock, James. "The Earth Is about to Catch a Morbid Fever that May Last as Long as 100,000 Years." *The Independent,* 16 January 2006.

———. *The Revenge of Gaia: Earth's Climate Crisis and the Fate of Humanity.* New York: Basic Books, 2007.

———. *The Vanishing Face of Gaia: A Final Warning.* New York: Basic Books, 2011.

Lowrey, Annie. "The Low Politics of Low Growth. *New York Times,* 13 January 2013.

MacKenzie, Donald A., Fabian Muniesa, and Lucia Siu. *Do Economists Make Markets? On the Performativity of Economics.* Princeton: Princeton University Press, 2007.

MacNeill, Jim, et al. *Beyond Interdependence: The Meshing of the World's Economy and the Earth's Ecology.* New York: Oxford University Press, 1991.

Maddison, Angus. *Economic Growth in the West: Comparative Experience in Europe and North America.* New York: Twentieth Century Fund, 1964.

———. *Growth and Interaction in the World Economy: The Roots of Modernity,* Washington, D.C.: AEI Press, 2005.

———. *Asia: Economic Growth in Japan and the USSR.* New York: Routledge, 2006.

———. *The World Economy: Volume 2: Historical Statistics.* Paris: OECD Publishing, 2007.

Madison, James. "Republican Distribution of Citizens." *National Gazette,* 3 March 1792. In *The Papers of James Madison.* Vol. 14, edited by Robert A. Rutland et al. Charlottesville: University Press of Virginia, 1983.

Magnuson, Joel. *Mindful Economics.* New York: Seven Stories, 2008.

Malthus, Thomas R. *An Essay on the Principle of Population* [1798], edited by Geoffrey Gilbert. Oxford World's Classics. Oxford: Oxford University Press, 2004.

Managi, Shunsuke. *The Economics of Biodiversity and Ecosystem Services.* New York: Routledge, 2012.

Maney, Patrick J. *"Young Bob"—A Biography of Robert M. La Follette, Jr., 1895–1953.* Columbia and London: University of Missouri Press, 1978.

Mankiw, N. Gregory. *Principles of Economics.* Mason, Ohio: Cengage Learning, 2011.

Marcuse, Herbert. *One-Dimensional Man: Studies in the Ideology of Advanced Industrial Society.* Boston: Beacon, 1964.

Marcuss, Rosemary D., and Richard E. Kane. "U.S. National Income and Product Statistics: Born of the Great Depression and World War II." *Bureau of Economic Analysis: Survey of Current Business* 87, no. 2, (2007): 32–46.

Marglin, Stephen, *The Dismal Science: How Thinking Like an Economist Undermines Community.* Cambridge: Harvard University Press, 2008.

Marks, Nic. *The Happiness Manifesto: How Nations and People Can Nurture Well-Being.* New York: TED Books, 2011.

Marks, Nic, and Samaah Abdallah, et al. *The (un)Happy Planet Index: An Index of Human Well-Being and Environmental Impact.* London: New Economics Foundation, 2006.

Marshall, Alfred. *Principles of Economics.* Unabridged 8th edition. New York: Cosimo Classics, 2009.

Marshall, Katherine. *The World Bank: From Reconstruction to Development to Equity.* New York: Routledge, 2008.

Martinez, Mark Anthony. *The Myth of the Free Market: The Role of the State in a Capitalist Economy.* Sterling, Va.: Kumarian Press, 2009.

Martinez-Alier, Juan. *The Environmentalism of the Poor: A Study of Ecological Conflicts and Valuation.* Cheltenham, England: Edward Elgar, 2002.

Marwell, Gerald, and Ruth E. Ames. "Economists Free Ride, Does Anyone Else? Experiments on the Provision of Public Goods, IV." *Journal of Public Economics* 15 no. 3 (1981): 295–310.

Marx, Karl. *Capital: A Critique of Political Economy.* Vol. 3. New York: Penguin, 1993.

———. *The Communist Manifesto* [1848]. New York: Pathfinder, 2008.

Marx, Karl, and Friedrich Engels. "Communist Manifesto" [1848]. In Robert C. Tucker, ed., *The Marx-Engels Reader.* New York: W.W. Norton, 1978.

Mattson, Kevin. *"What the Heck Are You Up To, Mr. President?" Jimmy Carter, America's "Malaise," and the Speech That Should Have Changed the Country.* New York: Bloomsbury, 2010.

Max-Neef, Manfred. "Economic Growth and Quality Of Life: A Threshold Hypothesis." *Ecological Economics* (15 November 1995): 115–18.

McAllister, Judy, Erik van Praag, and Jan Paul van Soest. *Earth Fever: Living Consciously with Climate Change.* New York: Cosimo Books, 2010.

McCormick, Ted. *William Petty and the Ambitions of Political Arithmetic.* Oxford: Oxford Universiy Press, 2010.

McCready, Stuart, ed., *The Discovery of Happiness.* Naperville, Ill.: SourceBooks, 2001.

McCulla, Stephanie H., and Shelly Smith. *Measuring the Economy: A Primer on GDP and the National Income and Product Accounts.* Washington, D.C.: Bureau of Economic Analysis, U.S. Department of Commerce, 2007.

McElvaine, Robert S. *The Great Depression: America, 1929–1941.* New York: Three Rivers, 1993.

McKenzie, Richard B. *Why Popcorn Costs So Much at the Movies: And Other Pricing Puzzles.* New York: Copernicus Books, 2008.

McKibben, Bill. *Deep Economy: The Wealth of Communities and the Durable Future.* New York: Times Books, 2007.

———. *Earth: Making a Life on a Tough Planet.* New York: St. Martin's Griffin, 2011.

———. "Global Warming's Terrifying New Math." *Rolling Stone,* 19 July 2012.

McNeely, Connie L. *Constructing the Nation State.* London: Greenwood, 1995.

McNeill, John R. *Something New Under the Sun: An Environmental History of the Twentieth-Century World.* Global Century Series. New York: W.W. Norton, 2001.

Meadows, Donella. *Leverage Points: Places to Intervene in a System.* Hartland, Vt.: Sustainability Institute, 1999.

Meadows, Donella, Jørgen Randers, and Dennis Meadows. *The Limits to Growth: The 30-Year Update*. White River Junction, Vt.: Chelsea Green, 2004.

Meadows, Donella, Jørgen Randers, Dennis L. Meadows, and William W. Behrens. *The Limits to Growth: A Report for the Club of Rome's Project on the Predicament of Mankind*. New York: Universe Books, 1972.

Mellman, Seymour. *The Permanent War Economy: American Capitalism in Decline*. New York: Simon and Schuster, 1985.

Mill, John Stuart. *Principles of Political Economy: With Some of Their Applications to Social Philosophy* [1848]. Google eBooks. London: Routledge 1891.

———. "Of the Stationary State." Book 4, chapter 6 in *Principles of Political Economy: With Some of Their Applications to Social Philosophy*. London: J.W. Parker, 1848.

———. *On Liberty* [1859]. London: Paragon Books, 2013.

Millen, Joyce V., Alec Irwin, and John Gershman, eds. *Dying for Growth: Global Inequality and the Health of the Poor*. Vol. 8. Monroe, Maine: Common Courage Press, 2000.

Millennium Ecosystem Assessment [MEA]. *Ecosystems and Human Well-Being: Synthesis*. Washington, D.C.: Island Press, 2005.

Mills, C. Wright. *The Power Elite*. New York: Oxford University Press, 1956.

Mills, Nicolaus. *Winning the Peace: The Marshall Plan and America's Coming of Age as a Superpower*. Hoboken, N.J.: Wiley, 2008.

Milward, Alan S. *War, Economy, and Society, 1939–1945*. Berkeley: University of California Press, 1979.

Miringoff, Marc L. *The Social Health of the Nation*. New York: Oxford University Press, 1999.

Mirowski, Philip. *Against Mechanism: Why Economics Needs Protection from Science*. Totowa: Rowman and Littlefield, 1988.

———. *More Heat Than Light: Economics as Social Physics, Physics as Nature's Economics*. Cambridge: Cambridge University Press, 1989.

Mishan, E.J. *The Costs of Economic Growth*. London: Staples, 1967.

———. *The Economic Growth Debate: An Assessment*. London: George Allen and Unwin, 1977.

Mishel, Lawrence, and Jared Bernstein. *Economy's Gains Fail to Reach Most Workers' Paychecks*. Washington, D.C.: Economic Policy Institute, 2007.

Mitchell, Wesley C. "Statistics and Government." *Publications of the American Statistical Association*, 16, no. 125 (March 1919): 223–35.

Mitchell, Wesley Clair, Willford Isbell King, and Frederick R. Macaulay. *Income in the United States: Its Amount and Distribution, 1909–1919*. Vol. 1: *Summary*. New York: NBER, 1921.

Mitra-Kahn, Benjamin H. "Redefining the Economy: How the 'Economy' Was Invented in 1620—And Has Been Redefined Ever Since." Ph.D. diss., Department of Economics, City University London, 2011.

Mokyr, Joel, *The Gifts of Athena: Historical Origins of the Knowledge Economy*. Princeton: Princeton University Press, 2004.

——. "The Intellectual Origins of Modern Economic Growth." *Journal of Economic History* 65, no. 2 (June 2005).

Montenegro, Maywa. "Herman Daly Applies a Biophysical Lens to the Economy and Finds that Bigger Isn't Necessarily Better." *SEED Magazine*, 26 April 2009. http://seedmaga zine.com/content/print/rethinking_growth/, accessed 3 February 2014.

Montgomery, Charles. *Happy City: Transforming Our Lives Through Urban Design.* New York: Farrar, Straus and Giroux (2013).

Morgenson, Gretchen. "The Perils of Feeding a Bloated Industry." *New York Times,* 27 October 2012.

Morgenstern, Oskar. "Does GNP Measure Growth and Welfare." *Business and Society Review* 15 (1974): 23.

Morley, Henry. Introduction to William Petty, *Essays on Mankind and Political Arithmetic* [1888]. Gloucestershire, England: Paperbackshop / Echo Library, 2006.

Morozov, Evgeny. *To Save Everything, Click Here: The Folly of Technological Solutionism.* New York: PublicAffairs, 2013.

Morsink, Johannes. *The University Declaration of Human Rights: Origins, Drafting, and Intent.* Philadelphia: University of Pennsylvania, 2000.

Moss, Mitchell L., and Carson Quing. "The Emergence of the 'Super-Commuter.'" Rudin Center for Transportation, New York University, 2012.

Muller, Nicholas Z., Robert Mendelsohn, and William Nordhaus. 2011. "Environmental Accounting for Pollution in the United States Economy." *American Economic Review,* 101, no. 5 (2011): 1649–75.

Murray, Charles. *In Our Hands: A Plan to Replace the Welfare State.* Washington, D.C.: American Enterprise Institute for Public Policy Research, 2006.

Murray, Matthew C., and Carole Pateman. *Basic Income Worldwide: Horizons of Reform.* New York: Palgrave MacMillan, 2012.

Nathan, Robert R. *Mobilizing for Abundance.* New York: McGraw Hill, 1944.

——. "National Income and Product of the United States, 1929–1950." National Income Division, U. S. Department of Commerce. Washington, D.C., 1951. Supplement to *Survey of Current Business.*

——. "GNP and Military Mobilization." *Journal of Evolutionary Economics* 4, no. 3 (1994): 3

National Bureau of Economic Research [NBER]. http://www.nber.org/cycles/recessions.html.

Nelson, Donald M. *Arsenal of Democracy: The Story of American War Production.* New York: Harcourt, Brace, 1946.

Nelson, Richard R. *The Sources of Economic Growth.* Cambridge: Harvard University Press, 1996.

Ng, Yew Kwang. "From Preference to Happiness: Towards a More Complete Welfare Economics." *Social Choice and Welfare* 20 (2003): 307–50.

——. "Environmentally Responsible Happy Nation Index: Towards and Internationally Acceptable National Success Indicator." *Social Indicators Research* 85 (2008): 425–46.

Nickerson, Mike. *Life, Money and Illusion: Living on Earth as If We Want to Stay.* Gabriola, British Columbia: New Society, 2009.

Noble, David F. *America by Design: Science, Technology, and the Rise of Corporate Capitalism.* No. 588. Oxford University Press, 1979.

Nordhaus, William D., and James Tobin. *Is Growth Obsolete?* New York: Columbia University Press, 1972.

Norton, Hugh S. *The Employment Act and the Council of Economic Advisors, 1946–1976.* Columbia: University of South Carolina Press, 1977.

Novick, Peter. *That Noble Dream: The "Objectivity" Question and the American Historical Profession.* Cambridge: Cambridge University Press, 1988.

O'Brien, Ellen S. "Contested Accounts: The Evolution of the Meaning and Measurement of National Accounts." Unpublished Ph.D. diss., Department of Economics, Notre Dame University, 1998.

O'Connor, Martin, ed. *Is Capitalism Sustainable? Political Economy and the Politics of Ecology.* New York: Guilford, 1994.

Ofer, Gur. "Soviet Economic Growth: 1928–1985." *Journal of Economic Literature* 25, no. 4 (1987).

Olson, James S. *Saving Capitalism: The Reconstruction Finance Corporation and the New Deal, 1933–1940.* Princeton: Princeton University Press, 1988.

Olson, Mancur. "Big Bills Left on the Sidewalk: Why Some Nations Are Rich, and Others Poor." *Journal of Economic Perspectives* 10, no. 2 (1996): 3–24.

O'Malley, Martin. Governor's Address at the Genuine Progress Indicators Conference. Baltimore, 14 June 2013.

Oreskes, Naomi. "The Scientific Consensus on Climate Change." *Science* 306, no. 5702 (December 2004): 1986.

Oreskes, Naomi, and Erik Conway. *Merchants of Doubt: How a Handful of Scientists Obscured the Truth on Issues from Tobacco Smoke to Global Warming.* New York: Bloomsbury, 2010.

Organization of Economic Cooperation and Development [OECD]. *Health at a Glance: 2011.* Paris: OECD, 2012.

Orrell, David. *The Other Side of the Coin.* Toronto: Key Porter Books, 2008.

———. *Economyths: Ten Ways Economics Gets It Wrong.* Mississauga, Canada: Wiley, 2010.

Oswald, Andrew, and Steve Landefeld. "This House Believes that GDP Is a Poor Measure of Improving Living Standards." Debate. *The Economist.com*, 20–30 April 2010.

Overy, Richard J. *Why the Allies Won.* New York: W.W. Norton, 1995.

Palley, Thomas. *Plenty of Nothing: The Downsizing of the American Dream and the Case for Structural Keynesianism.* Princeton: Princeton University Press, 1998.

Palmer, Edgar Z. *The Meaning and Measurement of the National Income and of Other Social Accounting Aggregates.* Lincoln: University of Nebraska, 1966.

Patel, Raj. *The Value of Nothing: How to Reshape Market Society and Redefine Democracy.* New York: Picador Books, 2010.

Patinkin, Don. "Keynes and Econometrics: On the Interaction between the Macroeconomic Revolutions of the Interwar Period." *Econometrica*, 44, no. 6 (November 1976): 1091–123.

Paxton, John. "Myth vs. Reality: The Question of Mass Production in World War II." *Economics and Business Journal* 1, no. 1 (2008): 91–104.

Peet, Richard. *Unholy Trinity: The IMF, World Bank, and WTO*. New York: Zedbooks, 2009.

Pei, Minxin. "The Dark Side of China's Rise." *Foreign Policy* 153 (March/April 2006): 32–40.

Perlman, Mark. "Political Purpose and the National Accounts." In W. Alonso and P. Starr, eds., *The Politics of Numbers*. New York: Russell Sage, 1987.

———. *The Character of Economic Thought, Economic Characters, and Economic Institutions*. Ann Arbor: University of Michigan Press, 1996.

———. Mark. Speech reprinted in *European Society for the History of Economic Thought Newsletter*, no. 8 (Summer 2003).

Perlman, Mark, and Morgan Marietta. "The Politics of Social Accounting: Public Goals and the Evolution of the National Accounts in Germany, the United Kingdom and the United States." *Review of Political Economy* 17, no. 2 (April 2005): 211–30.

Perlman, Mark, and Charles McCann, Jr. *The Pillars of Economic Understanding.* Vol. I. Ann Arbor: University of Michigan Press, 1998.

Petty, Sir William. *Political Survey of Ireland*. 2nd edition. 1719.

Philipsen, Dirk. *We Were the People: Voices from East Germany's Revolutionary Autumn of 1989*. Durham, N.C.: Duke University Press, 1993.

———. "Uncle Sam's Broken Arm: Historical Reflections on Race, Class, and Government in the Wake of Katrina." *Journal of Race and Policy*, Special Issue, 3, no.1 (Fall 2007): 33–45.

Philipsen, Dirk, and Nevin Cohen, eds. *Green Business*. Thousand Oaks, Calif.: Sage, 2011.

Phillips, Kevin. *Bad Money: Reckless Finance, Failed Politics, and the Global Crisis of American Capitalism*. New York: Penguin, 2008.

Pigou, A. C. *The Economics of Welfare* [1920]. 4th edition. London: Macmillan, 2013.

Piketty, Thomas. *Capital in the Twenty-First Century.* Translated from the French by Arthur Goldhammer. Cambridge: Belknap Press / Harvard University Press, 2014. Originally published in French in 2013 by Éditions du Seuil, Paris.

Pizzigati, Sam. *Greed and Good: Understanding and Overcoming the Inequality That Limits Our Lives*. New York: Apex Press, 2004.

Pogge, Thomas W. *Politics as Usual: What Lies Behind the Pro-Poor Rhetoric*. Malden, Mass.: Polity, 2010.

Polanyi, Karl. *Primitive, Archaic, and Modern Economies*. Boston: Beacon, 1968.

———. *The Great Transformation: The Political and Economic Origins of Our Time* [1944]. Boston: Beacon Press, 2001.

Pollan, Michael. *The Omnivore's Dilemma: A Natural History of Four Meals*. New York: Penguin, 2006.

Porritt, Jonathan. *Capitalism as If the World Matters*. Revised paperback edition. Sterling, Va.: Earthscan, 2007.

Postman, Neil. *Conscientious Objections*. New York: Vintage, 1992.

———. *Technopoly: The Surrender of Culture to Technology*. New York: Vintage, 1992.

Putnam, Robert D. *Bowling Alone: The Collapse and Revival of American Community*. New York: Simon and Schuster, 2000.

Rancière, Jacques, and Steve Corcoran. *Hatred of Democracy*. London: Verso, 2006.

Rautenstrauch, Walter. Letter to Senator Robert J. Bulkley, Chairman, Committee of Manufacturers, 10 May 1938, on the occasion of hearings, 75th Congress, pursuant of S.Res.114, to investigate the desirability of establishing a National Economic Council. Washington, D.C.: U.S. Government Printing Office, 1938.

Records of the Bureau of Foreign and Domestic Commerce (BFDC). Record Group 151. National Archives, College Park, Md.

Rees, William E. "The Ecological Crisis and Self-delusion: Implications for the Building Sector." *Building Research & Information* 37, no. 3 (2009).

Reich, Robert. *Inequality for All*. Documentary. Radius, 2013a.

———. "The Myth of Free Markets." Reader Supported News. 16 September 2013b. http://readersupportednews.org/opinion2/279–82/19437-the-myth-of-the-qfree-marketq, accessed 18 September 2013.

Reinhart, Carmen M., and Kenneth S. Rogoff. *This Time Is Different: Eight Centuries of Financial Folly*. Princeton and Oxford: Princeton University Press, 2009.

Repetto, Robert, William Magrath, Michael Wells, Christine Beer, and Fabrizio Rossini. *Wasting Assets: Natural Resources in the National Income Accounts*. Washington, D.C.: World Resources Institute, 1989.

Revkin, Andrew. "Who Made This Mess of Planet Earth?" *New York Times Book Review*, 15 July 2011.

Ridley, Matt. *The Rational Optimist: How Prosperity Evolves*. New York: Harper, 2011.

Riesman, David. Nathan Glazer, and Reuel Denney. *The Lonely Crowd: A Study of the Changing American Character*. Vol. 16. New York: Doubleday, 1950.

Rifkin, Jeremy. *The Empathetic Civilization: The Race to Global Consciousness in a World in Crisis*. New York: Penguin, 2009.

Rittenberg, Libby, and Timothy Tregarthen. *Principles of Macroeconomics*. http://www.web-books.com/eLibrary/NC/B0/B62/TOC.html, accessed 25 November 2011.

Robertson, James. *Future Wealth: New Economics for the 21st Century*. London: Cassell, 1989.

Rogall, Holger. *Neue Umweltökonomie—Ökologische Ökonomie*. Opladen, Germany: Leske and Budrich, 2002.

Romasco, Albert U. *The Poverty of Abundance: Hoover, the Nation, the Depression*. New York: Oxford University Press, 1965.

———. *The Politics of Recovery: Roosevelt's New Deal*. New York: Oxford University Press, 1983.

Roosevelt, Franklin D. *The Public Papers and Addresses of Franklin D. Roosevelt.* 13 vols. Compiled by Samuel I. Rosenman. New York: Random House, 1938–50.

Rosenberg, Alex. "From Rational Choice to Reflexivity: Learning from Sen, Hayek, Soros, and Most of all, from Darwin." *Economic Thought* 3 (2014): 21–41.

Rothermund, Dietmar. *The Global Impact of the Great Depression.* London: Routledge, 1996.

Rowe, Jonathan. "Our Phony Economy." Testimony delivered 12 March before the Senate Committee on Commerce, Science, and Transportation, Subcommittee on Interstate Commerce. *Harper's Magazine,* June 2008.

Rowe, Jonathan, and Judith Silverstein. "The GDP Myth: Why 'Growth' Isn't Always a Good Thing." *Washington Monthly*, March 1999, pp. 17–21.

———. "False Readings: How the GDP Leads Us Astray." *Columbia Journalism Review* (November / December 2008).

Ruggles, Nancy. "Social Accounting." In *The New Palgrave.* Vol. 4. New York: Macmillan, 1987.

Ruggles, Nancy, and Richard Ruggles. *National Accounting and Economic Policy: The United States and the UN Systems.* Cheltenham, England: Edward Elgar, 1999.

Ruggles, Richard. "The United States National Income Accounts, 1947–1977: Their Conceptual Basis and Evolution." In Murray F. Foss, ed., *National Income and Product Accounts.* Chicago: Chicago University Press, 1983.

———. *National Income Accounting and Its Relation to Economic Policy.* 1949. Paris: Economic Cooperation Administration.

Rutherford, Malcolm. *Institutions in Economics: The Old and New Institutionalism.* Cambridge: Cambridge University Press, 1996.

Ryssdal, Kai. *Market Place.* National Public Radio. 5 March 2013.

Sachs, Jeffrey. *The End of Poverty: Economic Possibilities of Our Time.* New York: Penguin, 2005.

Sachs, Jeffrey, Wing Thye Woo, Stanley Fischer, and Gordon Hughes. "Structural Factors in the Economic Reforms of China, Eastern Europe, and the Former Soviet Union." *Economic Policy* (1994).

Sagoff, Mark. "On the Economic Value of Ecosystem Services." *Environmental Values* 17 (2008).

Sahin, Kemal, *Measuring the Economy: GDP and NIPAs.* Monetary, Fiscal and Trade Policies Series. Hauppauge, N.Y.: Nova Science, 2009.

Samuels, Warren, Marianne F. Johnson, and William H. Perry. *Erasing the Invisible Hand: Essays on an Elusive and Misused Concept in Economics.* Cambridge: Cambridge University Press, 2014.

Samuelson, Paul A. "Unemployment Ahead." *New Republic* 111 (11 September 1944).

———. *Problems of the American Economy: An Economist's View.* Stamp Memorial Lecture at the University of London. London: Athlone, 1962.

Samuelson, Paul A., and William D. Nordhaus. *Economics.* 12th edition. New York: McGraw Hill, 1985. First edition published by Samuelson and Nordhaus as *Economics: An Introductory Analysis,* 1948.

——. *Economics*. 15th edition. New York: McGraw Hill, 1995.

——. *Economics*. 16th edition. New York: McGraw Hill, 1998.

——. *Economics*. 19th edition. New York: McGraw-Hill, 2010.

Sandel, Michael J. *What Money Can't Buy: The Moral Limits of Markets*. New York: Farrar, Straus and Giroux, 2012.

Sanfey, A. G. "Social Decision-Making: Insights from Game Theory and Neuroscience." *Science* (2007).

Santos, Boaventura de Sousa. *Democratizing Democracy: Beyond the Liberal Democratic Canon*. Vol. 1: *Reinventing Social Emancipation*. London: Verso, 2005.

SAPRIN [Organization]. *Structural Adjustment: The SAPRI Report: The Policy Roots of Economic Crisis, Poverty, and Inequality*. Boston: Zed Books, 2004.

Saul, John R. *Voltaire's Bastards: The Dictatorship of Reason in the West*. New York: Vintage, 1992.

——. *The Unconscious Civilization*. New York: Free Press, 2002.

Savitz, Andrew, and Karl Weber. *The Triple Bottom Line*. San Francisco: John Wiley, 2006.

Schlesinger, Arthur M. *The Crisis of the Old Order*. Vol. 1 of *The Age of Roosevelt*. Boston: Houghton Mifflin, 2002. Originally published in 1957 by Houghton Mifflin.

——. *The Coming of the New Deal*. Vol. 2 of *The Age of Roosevelt*. Boston: Houghton Mifflin, 2003. Originally published in 1957 by Houghton Mifflin.

Schor, Juliet. *The Overworked American: The Unexpected Decline of Leisure*. New York: Basic Books, 1992.

——. "The Good Life or the Goods Life." Keynote for national conference "What's the Economy for, Anyway?" Washington, D.C., 5–7 October, 2007.

Schumacher, E. F. *Small Is Beautiful: Economics as If People Mattered*. New York: Harper and Row, 1973.

Schumpeter, Joseph A. *Capitalism, Socialism, and Democracy*. New York: Harper, 1942.

——. *History of Economic Analysis*. New York: Oxford University Press, 1959.

Schwarz, Jordan A. *The Interregnum of Despair: Hoover, Congress, and the Depression*. Urbana: University of Illinois Press, 1970.

Schweickart, David. *After Capitalism*. Oxford: Rowman and Littlefield, 2002.

Scott, James C. *Seeing Like a State: How Certain Schemes to Improve the Human Condition Have Failed*. New Haven: Yale University Press, 1998.

Scott-Cato, Molly. *Green Economics: An Introduction to Theory, Policy, and Practice*. London and Sterling, Va.: Earthscan, 2009.

Scrivens, Katherine, and Barbara Iasiello. "Indicators of 'Societal Progress': Lessons from International Experiences." OECD Working Paper no. 33, June 2010.

Segal, Jerome M. "Alternative Conceptions of the Economic Realm." In Richard M Coughlin, ed., *Morality, Rationality, and Efficiency*. Armonk, N.Y.: M.E. Sharpe, 1991.

——. *Graceful Simplicity: The Philosophy and Politics of the Alternative American Dream*. Berkeley: University of California Press, 2003.

Seligman, Martin. *Authentic Happiness:Using the New Positive Psychology to Realize Your Potential for Lasting Fulfillment.* New York: Free Press, 2002.

Sen, Amartya. "Rational Fools: A Critique of the Behavioral Foundations of Economic Theory." *Philosophy and Public Affairs* 6, no. 4 (Summer 1977): 317–44.

———. *Choice, Welfare, and Measurement.* Oxford: Blackwell, 1982.

———. *Development as Freedom.* New York: Anchor, 2000.

Shaikh, Anwar M., and E. Ahmet Tonak. *Measuring the Wealth of Nations: The Political Economy of National Accounts.* New York: Cambridge University Press, 1994.

Sheahen, Allan. *Basic Income Guarantee: Your Right to Economic Security.* New York: Palgrave MacMillan, 2012.

Shin, Doh C. "Does Rapid Economic Growth Improve the Human Lot? Some Empirical Evidence." *Social Indicators Research* 8, no. 2 (1980).

Shiva, Vandana. *Biopiracy: The Plunder of Nature and Knowledge.* Dartington, England: Green Books, 1998.

———. *Earth Democracy: Justice, Sustainability, and Peace.* Boston: South End Press, 2005.

———. *Soil Not Oil: Environmental Justice in an Age of Climate Crisis.* Boston: South End Press, 2008.

———. "How Economic Growth has Become Anti-Life." *The Guardian*, 1 November 2013a.

———. *Making Peace with the Earth.* New York: Palgrave MacMillan, 2013b.

Shoup, Donald C. *The High Cost of Free Parking.* Chicago: American Planning Association, 2011.

Shrestha, Manik, and Marco Marini. "Quarterly GDP Revisions in G-20 Countries: Evidence from the 2008 Financial Crisis." IMF Working Paper no. 13/60, March 2013.

Simms, Andrew. *Ecological Debt: Global Warming and the Wealth of Nations.* New York: Pluto, 2009.

Simon, Arthur R. *How Much Is Enough? Hungering for God in an Affluent Culture.* Grand Rapids, Mich.: Baker Books, 2003.

Simon, Julian L. *The Ultimate Resource 2.* Princeton: Princeton University Press, 1998.

Sinn, Hans-Werner. *Casino Capitalism: How the Financial Crisis Came About and What Needs to Be Done Now.* New York: Oxford University Press, 2012.

Sitkoff, Harvey, ed. *Fifty Years Later: The New Deal Evaluated.* New York: Knopf, 1985.

Skidelsky, Robert and Edward Skidelsky. *How Much Is Enough: Money and the Good Life.* New York: Other Press, 2012.

Smil, Vaclav. *Oil.* Oxford: One World Book, 2008.

Smiley, Gene. *Rethinking the Great Depression.* Chicago: Ivan R. Dee, 2002.

Smith, Adam. *The Theory of Moral Sentiments* [1759]. Reprint. Oxford: Clarendon, 1976.

———. *An Inquiry into the Nature and Causes of the Wealth of Nations* [1776]. Google ebook, Digireads.com, 2009.

Smith, Hedrick, *Who Stole the American Dream?* New York: Random House, 2013.

Smith, J. W. *Economic Democracy: The Political Struggle of the Twenty-First Century.* Armonk, N.Y.: M.E. Sharpe, 2000.

Smith, Philip G., and M. Max-Neef. *Economics Unmasked.* Foxhole, England: Green Books, 2011.

Smith, Yves. *ECONned: How Unenlightened Self-Interest Undermined Democracy and Corrupted Capitalism.* New York: Palgrave, 2011.

Snell, Ron. "The Great Recession." *State Legislatures* (June 2009).

The Social Progress Imperative. http://www.socialprogressimperative.org/, accessed 6 January 2014.

Solow, Robert M. "A Contribution to the Theory of Economic Growth." *Quarterly Journal of Economics* 70, no. 1 (1956): 65–94.

Sombart, Werner. "Medieval and Modern Commercial Enterprise." Pp. 25–40 in Frederic C. Lane and Jelle Riemersma, eds., *Enterprise and Secular Change.* Homewood, Ill.: Irwin, 1953.

Someya, Kyrojiro. "Accounting 'Revolutions' in Japan." *The Accounting Historians Journal* (1989): 75–86.

Soros, George. *The Crisis of Global Capitalism: Open Society Endangered.* New York: Public Affairs, 1998.

Speth, James Gustave. *On Globalization.* New York: Public Affairs, 2002.

———. *The Bridge at the Edge of the World: Capitalism, the Environment, and Crossing from Crisis to Sustainability.* New Haven: Yale University Press, 2008.

———. "Toward a Post-Growth Society." *YES Magazine*, July 2011.

Spencer, Elsa, H., Erica Frank, and Nicole F. McIntosh. "Potential Effects of the Next 100 Billion Hamburgers Sold by McDonald's." *American Journal of Preventive Medicine* 28, no. 4 (2005). http://www.scribd.com/doc/2606654/mcdonalds-burgers.

Srivastava, Abhishek, Edwin Al. Locke, and Kathryn M. Bartol. "Money and Subjective Well-Being: It's Not the Money, It's the Motives." *Journal of Personality and Social Psychology* 80, no. 6 (2008): 1768–73.

Stannard, David E. *American Holocaust: The Conquest of the New World.* New York: Oxford University Press, 1993.

Stearns, Peter N. *The Industrial Revolution in World History.* Boulder, Colo.: Westview, 2012.

Steil, Benn. *The Battle of Bretton Woods.* Princeton: Princeton University Press, 2014.

Stein, Herbert. *The Fiscal Revolution in America: Policy in Pursuit of Reality.* Washington, D.C.: AEI Press, 1996.

Stevenson, Betsey, and Justin Wolfers. "Subjective Well-Being and Income: Is There Evidence of Satiation?" NBER Working Paper Series 19882, April 2013.

Stewart, Hale. "Consumer Spending and the Economy." *New York Times*, 19 September 2010.

Stiglitz, Joseph E. "Development Policies in an Age of Globalization." Paper presented at the seminar "New International Trends for Economic Development" on the occasion of the fiftieth anniversary of the Brazilian Economic and Social Development Bank (BNDES). Rio Janeiro, 12–13 September, 2002. https://www0.gsb.columbia.edu/faculty/jstiglitz/download/DevelopmentGlobalization.pdf

———. *Globalization and Its Discontents*. New York: W.W. Norton, 2003.

———. "Bleakonomics." *New York Times*, 30 September 2007.

———. *Freefall: America, Free Markets, and the Sinking of the World Economy*. New York: W.W. Norton, 2010.

———. *The Price of Inequality: How Today's Divided Society Endangers Our Future*. New York: W.W. Norton, 2012.

Stiglitz, Joseph E., Amartya Sen, and Jean-Paul Fitoussi. *Mismeasuring Our Lives: Why GDP Doesn't Add Up*. New York: New Press, 2010.

Stockman, David A. "Sundown in America: How Crony-Capitalism Left Us State-Wrecked." *New York Times*, 31 March 2013.

Stoll, Steven. *The Great Delusion*. New York: Hill and Wang, 2008.

Stone, Nahum I. "The Beginnings of the National Bureau of Economic Research." In Wesley C. Mitchell, ed., *The National Bureau's First Quarter-Century*. New York: NBER, 1945.

Stone, Richard. "Definitions and Measurement of National Income and Related Totals." Memorandum in League of Nations, Committee of Statistical Experts. Measurement of National Income and the Construction of Social Accounts. Report of the Subcommittee on National Income Statistics. Geneva: United Nations, 1947.

———. "The Accounts of Society." Nobel Memorial Lecture, given on 8 December 1984. Reproduced in *American Economic Review* 87, no. 6 (December 1997): 17–29.

Stone, Richard, and James Meade. *National Income and Expenditure*. Oxford: Oxford University Press, 1944.

Story of Stuff Project. "The Story of Stuff." 2007. http://storyofstuff.org/.

Stott, John R.W. *The Cross of Christ*. Nottingham, England: InterVarsity Press, 2006.

Street, James H. "The Contribution of Simon S. Kuznets to Institutionalist Development Theory." *Journal of Economic Issues* 22, no. 2 (June 1988): 501.

Studenski, Paul. *The Income of Nations*. New York: New York University Press, 1958.

Surface, F. M. Letter to E. A. Tupper. 19 November 1932. National Archives, Record Group 151, Frederick M. Feiker files.

Sutch, Richard. "Gross Domestic Product: 1790–2002." In Richard Sutch, ed., *Historical Statistics of the United States: Earliest Times to the Present, Millennial Edition*. New York: Cambridge University Press, 2006.

Sutter, Andrew J. "Unlimited Growth and Innovation: Paradise or Paradox?" Working Paper 2010, Social Science Research Network rev1.4 20101117.

Taibbi, Matt. "The Great American Bubble Machine." *Rolling Stone* (July 2009): 52–101.

———. *Griftopia: A Story of Bankers, Politicians, and the Most Audacious Power Grab in American History*. New York: Spiegel & Grau, 2011.

———. *The Divide: American Injustice in the Age of the Wealth Gap*. New York: Spiegel and Grau, 2014.

Talberth, John. "A New Bottom Line for Progress." In Gary T. Gardner et al., *2008 State of the World: Innovations for a Sustainable Economy*. New York: W.W. Norton, 2008.

Talberth, John, Clifford W. Cobb, and Noah Slattery. *The Genuine Progress Indicator, 2006: A Tool for Sustainable Development*. Oakland, Calif.: Redefining Progress, 2007.

Tarasofsky, Abe. "GDP and Its Derivatives as Welfare Measure: A Selective Look at the Literature." Paper presented at the CSLS Conference on the State of Living Standards and the Quality of Life in Canada, Ottawa, 1998.

Tawney, R. H. *Religion and the Rise of Capitalism* [1926]. New York and London: Harcourt Brace, 1958.

Tegtmeier, Erin M., and Michael D. Duffy. "External Costs of Agricultural Production in the United States." *International Journal of Agricultural Sustainability* 2 (2004): 1–20.

Terkel, Studs. *Hard Times: An Oral History of the Great Depression*. New York: New Press, 2000.

Thiele, Leslie Paul. *Sustainability*. Malden, Mass.: Polity, 2013.

Thompson, E. P. *The Making of the English Working Class*. London: Peter Smith, 1966.

Thurow, Lester C. *Dangerous Currents: The State of Economics*. New York: Random House, 1983.

Tilly, Charles. *Coercion, Capital, and European States—AD 990–1992*. Malden Mass.: Blackwell, 1992.

Tily, Geoff. "John Maynard Keynes and the Development of National Accounts in Britain, 1895–1941." *Review of Income and Wealth* 55, no. 2 (2009): 331–59.

Tinbergen, Jan, and Roefie Hueting. "GNP and Market Prices: Wrong Signals for Sustainable Economic Success that Mask Environmental Destruction." *Environmentally Sustainable Economic Development: Building on Brundtland* (1991): 51–57.

Tomasello, Michael. *Why We Cooperate*. Boston: MIT Press, 2009.

Tooze, J. Adam. *Statistics and the German State, 1900–1945: The Making of Modern Economic Knowledge*. Cambridge: Cambridge University Press, 2001.

———. *Wages of Destruction*. New York: Viking, 2006.

Toussaint, Eric, and Damien Millet. *Debt, the IMF, and the World Bank: Sixty Questions, Sixty Answers*. New York: Monthly Review Press, 2010.

Tremayne, Wendy Jehanara. *The Good Life Lab: Radical Experiments in Hands-On Living*. North Adams, Mass.: Storey, 2013.

Tsai, Ming-Chang. "If GDP Is Not the Answer, What Is the Question? The Juncture of Capabilities, Institutions and Measurement in the Stiglitz-Sen-Fitoussi Report." *Social Indicators Research* 102, no. 3 (2011): 363–72.

Tucker, Robert C., ed. *The Marx-Engels Reader*. New York: W.W. Norton, 1978.

Turner, Graham. "A Comparison of the Limits to Growth with 30 Years of Reality." *Global Environmental Change* 18, no. 3 (2008).

Turse, Nick. *The Complex: How the Military Invades Our Everyday Lives*. New York: Metropolitan Books, 2008.

Ul Haq, Mahbub. *Reflections on Human Development*. New York: Oxford University Press, 1996.

UN Human Development Index, 2011.

U.S. Bureau of the Census. *Historical Statistics of the United States: Colonial Times to 1970.* Washington, D.C.: Department of Commerce, 1975. Table V 20–30, p. 912.

U.S. Department of Commerce. *Planning and Control of Public Works.* Washington, D.C.: U.S. Government Printing Office, 1930.

U.S. Energy Information Administration. http://www.eia.gov/coal/, accessed 16 April 2012.

———. http://www.eia.gov/, accessed 17 May 2012.

U. S. Senate. *National Income, 1929–32.* Senate Document 124, 73rd Congress, 2nd session, 1934.

Vallance, Edward. *A Radical History of Britain: Visionaries, Rebels and Revolutionaries— the Men and Women Who Fought for Our Freedoms.* London: Little, Brown, 2009.

Van den Bergh, Jeroen C.J.M. "Abolishing GDP." Tinbergen Institute Discussion Paper, no. 2, 2007.

———. "The GDP Paradox." *Journal of Economic Psychology* 30 (2009): 117–35.

Van der Zwaan, Bob, and Arthur Petersen. *Sharing the Planet: Population-Consumption-Species: Science and Ethics for a Sustainable and Equitable World.* Delft, Netherlands: Eburon, 2003.

Vanoli, André. *A History of National Accounting.* Amsterdam: IOS Press, 2005.

Vartanian, Oshin, ed. *Neuroscience of Decision Making.* Contemporary Topics in Cognitive Neuroscience. London: Psychology Press, 2011.

Vaury, Olivier. "Is GDP a Good Measure of Economic Progress?" *post-autistic economics review,* no. 20 (3 June 2003): article 3. http://www.paecon.net/PAEReview/issue20/Vaury20.htm.

Vernon, Raymond. "The Politics of Comparative Economic Statistics: Three Cultures and Three Cases." In W. Alonso and P. Starr, eds., *The Politics of Numbers.* New York: Russell Sage, 1987.

Victor, Peter A. *Managing without Growth: Slower by Design, Not Disaster.* Cheltenham, England: Edward Elgar, 2008.

Von Jung, Alexander. "Der Kult ums BIP." *Der Spiegel,* 21 September 2009.

Wackernagel, Mathis, and Williams E. Rees. *Our Ecological Footprint: Reducing Human Impact on the Earth.* Gabriola Island, British Columbia: New Society, 1996.

Wagemann, Ernst. *Economic Rhythm: A Theory of Business Cycles.* Translated by D. H. Blelloch, with a prefatory note by Wesley Clair Mitchell. New York: McGraw-Hill, 1930.

Wagner, Robert. Quoted in "Conflict in Senate on Unemployment Delays Tariff Bill." *New York Times,* 9 February 1930.

Wagner, Robert. Quoted in "Senators Demand Action to Check Unemployed." *New York Times,* 4 March 1930, p. 1.

Walker, Frank C. Letter to the Secretary of Commerce, 8 November 1933, NARA, National Income Collection, Thorp Files, Box 162.

Wallach, Lori, and Patrick Woodall, eds. *Whose Trade Organization? The Comprehensive Guide to the WTO.* Vol. 1. New York: Free Press, 2004.

Wallerstein, Immanuel. *World-Systems Analysis*. Durham, N.C.: Duke University Press: 2004.

Wang, Yan, and Yudong Yao. "Sources of China's Economic Growth 1952–1999: Incorporating Human Capital Accumulation." *China Economic Review* 14, no. 1 (2003): 32–52

Warburton, Clark. "Monetary Policy in the United States in World War II." *American Journal of Economics and Sociology* 4, no. 3 (April 1945).

———. "Value of the Gross National Product and Its Components, 1919–1929." *Journal of the American Statistical Association* 29, no. 188 (December 1934): 383–88.

Waring, Marilyn. *If Women Counted*. New York: Harper Collins, 1988.

———. *Counting for Nothing: What Men Value and What Women Are Worth*. 2nd edition. Toronto and Buffalo, N.Y.: University of Toronto Press, 1999.

Warren, Elizabeth. Campaign speech for U.S. Senate in Andover, Mass., August 2011.

Weaver, Frederick S. *The United States and the Global Economy: From Bretton Woods to the Current Crisis*. New York: Rowman and Littlefield, 2011.

Weigley, Russell. *The American Way of War*. Bloomington: Indiana University Press, 1973.

Weintraub, E. Roy. *How Economics Became a Mathematical Science*: Durham, N.C.: Duke University Press, 2002.

Weisberger, Bernard A. *The La Follettes of Wisconsin. Love and Politics in Progressive America*. Madison: University of Wisconsin Press, 1994.

Weitzman, Martin L. "On the Welfare Significance of National Product in a Dynamic Economy." *Quarterly Journal of Economics* 90, no. 1 (February 1976): 156–62.

Whyte, Martin King. "Paradoxes of China's Economic Boom." *Annual Review of Sociology* 35 (2009).

Wilson, Edmund. *The American Jitters: A Year of the Slump* [1932]. Freeport, N.Y.: Books for Libraries Press, 1968.

———. *To the Finland Station: A Study in the Writing and Acting of History* [1940]. New York: Farrar, Straus and Giroux, 1972.

Wing-Chan, Kam. "Economic Growth Strategy and Urbanization Policies in China, 1949–1982." *International Journal of Urban and Regional Research* 16, no. 2 (2009).

Wirzba, Norman. "In God's Garden." In Mallory McDuff, ed., *Sacred Acts: How Churches Are Working to Protect Earth's Climate*. Gabriola, British Columbia: New Society, 2012.

Wolfe, Alan. *America's Impasse: The Rise and Fall of the Politics of Growth*. Boston: South End, 1981.

Wolin, Sheldon S. *Democracy Incorporated: Managed Democracy and the Specter of Inverted Totalitarianism*. Princeton: Princeton University Press, 2008.

Wood, Ellen Meiksins. *The Origin of Capitalism*. New York: Monthly Review Press, 1999.

Woods, Ngaire. *The Globalizers: The IMF, the World Bank, and their Borrowers*. Ithaca: Cornell University Press, 2006.

World Bank. *World Development Indicators 2007*. Washington, D.C., 2007.

World Bank, Commission on Growth and Development. "The Growth Report," 2008, p. 1.

World Commission on Environment and Development. *Our Common Future (The Brundt-land Commission Report)*. Oxford and New York: Oxford University Press, 1987.

World Health Organization. "Health, Economic Growth, and Poverty Reduction." The Report of Working Group 1 of the Commission on Macroeconomics and Health, 2002.

World Institute for Development Economics Research of the United Nations. "Personal Assets from a Global Perspective." 2005.

Worldwatch Institute. *Vital Signs 1992 to 2008: The Trends that are Shaping Our Future.* New York: W.W. Norton, 1993–2007.

———. *State of the World 2010: Transforming Cultures: From Consumerism to Sustainability.* New York: W.W. Norton, 2010.

World Top Incomes Database. *United States.* http://topincomes.g-mond.parisschoolof economics.eu/#Country:United%20States, accessed 15 May 2014.

Wright, Eric Olin. "Redesigning Distribution: Basic Income and Stakeholder Grants as Cornerstones of a More Egalitarian Capitalism." *Politics & Society*, special issue, 32 (2004).

Wright, Ronald. *A Short History of Progess.* Philadelphia: Da Capo, 2004.

Wrightson, Keith. *Earthly Necessities: Economic Lives in Early Modern Britain.* New Haven and London: Yale University Press, 2000.

Xiaoming, Huang. *The Rise and Fall of the East Asian Growth System, 1951–2000: Institutional Competitiveness and Rapid Economic Growth.* London and New York: RoutledgeCurzon, 2013.

Yarrow, Andrew L. 2010. *Measuring America: How Economic Growth Came to Define American Greatness in the Late Twentieth Century.* Amherst: University of Massachusetts Press.

Zak, Paul J., ed. *Moral Markets: The Critical Role of Values in the Economy.* Princeton: Princeton University Press, 2008.

Zenzey, Eric. "G.D.P.R.I.P." *New York Times*, 10 August 2009.

Zepezaurer, Mark, and Arthur Naiman. *Take the Rich off Welfare.* Cambridge, Mass.: South End, 2004.

INDEX

Abramovitz, Moses, 178
abundance, 20, 344n13
accounting. *See* national accounting
advertising, 160–61, 176, 179, 187, 234
Africa, 21, 113, 137, 194
agriculture, 32–35, 60, 84–85, 100, 145, 166, 190
air pollution, 166–68, 176, 264
Alaska, 197
Alperovitz, Gar, 200, 241, 287n21
American century, 85
American Revolution, 42, 245
Apollo 17, 216
Aristotle, 28, 35–36, 230
Army Service Forces (ASF), 113
Arndt, H.W., 127
aspirations, stifled, 208
assumptions: dangers of, 95, 123, 165, 174, 213; dominant, 2, 7–8, 49, 51, 53, 224, 249; faulty, 9, 13, 31, 46, 54, 213, 225, 247
austerity, 84, 127, 275; as function of GDP growth imperative, 17, 158, 136–37
automobiles. *See* cars

Bahro, Rudolph, 265
basic income guarantee (BIG), 251–55
Baudrillart, Henri, 39
behavioral loop, 212–14, 269
Bentham, Jeremy, 40, 230
Beyond GDP (initiative of the European Union), 228
Bhutan, 340n34
biodiversity, 6, 193, 198
BIP (Bruttoinlandsprodukt), 11
Blue Marble, 216
Boskin, Michael J., 149, 177
bottom line: as goal, 7, 27, 117, 213, 238; as measure, 14, 39, 57, 70, 153, 158, 200, 252–59, 271–74
Bouton, Terry, 42
Brazil, 11, 135, 192
Bretton Woods, 88, 128, 131–33, 313n50
Brockway, George, 46, 284n30

Brower, David, 261
Bureau of Economic Analysis (BEA), 126, 147–48, 162, 273–74
Bureau of Foreign and Domestic Commerce (BFDC), 79, 82, 93, 103
Bush, George W., 142, 151

Canada, 181, 197
capital: as defining component of capitalism, 14, 21–26, 30, 33–37, 42–44; 48, 56–57, 104, 112, 114, 121, 214, 239, 255, 259; human, 163, 208; as ignored by GDP, 34, 42, 95, 137, 142, 156–57, 163, 214; natural/environmental, 95, 137–38, 163, 193, 204, 208, 223–24; social, 95, 137–38, 142, 163, 223–24
capitalism, 5, 11, 14–15, 55–57, 75, 119, 127, 140, 146, 189, 193, 200, 247, 250–51, 255, 258, 264; alternatives to, 239–42, 250–65; and government, 44, 57–58, 65, 88, 119, 123–24, 131–33; history of, 22–51; laissez-faire, 67, 72–73
carbon: emissions, 5, 161, 172–73, 255, 264; measured as footprint, 182; taxes of, 237; as world's problem, 195
carrying capacity, 181, 188, 190, 332n23
cars, 83, 115, 159, 173, 179, 192, 202, 235, 244; as boon to GDP, 85, 144, 153–56, 165, 168, 188, 229, 260
Carson, Rachel, 16, 186
Carter, Jimmy, 184, 187–88
CBS, 150
certainties, reasonable list of, 203
change. *See* historical change
China, 7, 11, 16, 134–35, 149, 163, 178, 192–93, 247, 261, 273
choice: consequences of, 5, 95, 192; deliberate, 17, 65, 71, 169, 211, 222, 229, 259; limited, 37, 42, 164–66, 212; within the logic of GDP, 11–12, 31, 63, 159, 163–65, 171–72
civil rights, 245, 266
Civilian Conservation Corps, 108

252, 271–72; history of, 20–39, 40–64, 65–82, 83–106; need for (political, military), 6, 9–11, 14, 27, 50, 52, 121–22, 128, 208, 237; per capita GDP metric (*see* GDP); quantitative vs. qualitative, 97, 120, 122, 152–57, 175, 181, 189, 222, 230, 271–72; and resistance to change, 135, 176–78, 208; subjective (political) nature of, 19, 26–29, 47, 94, 97–98, 110, 123, 222, 271–77; turning into goals. 4, 7, 13, 17, 24, 28, 48, 73, 117, 159, 212–13, 220
media, portrayal of GDP, 50, 143, 147–48, 150, 158, 162–63
Mellon, Andrew, 74
Mencken, H.L., 139
metrics. *See* measures
middle class, as defined by GDP, 138
military industrial complex, 124
Mill, John Stuart, 34–35, 38–39, 55
Millennium Ecosystem Assessment, 194
minimum wage, 124–25,
Mishan, E.J., 179–80
Mississippi, 85
Mitchell, Wesley C, 61–64, 90–91, 97–98
money: as defining metric in GDP, 38, 63, 94–95, 97, 145–47, 150, 155, 163, 171; function of, 23–28, 40, 43, 46–48, 53, 57, 132–33, 147, 179, 215, 222–25, 271, 274, 284n30; future use of, 206, 223–24, 241–42, 257–59
Moorehead, Bob, 254
Morrow, Dwight, 74
Murray, James E., 125
Mussolini, Benito, 78

Nagasaki, 120
Nasheed, Mohamed, 238
Nathan, Robert R., 93, 95, 103, 106, 108–9, 113–15, 127
National Bureau of Economic Research (NBER), 10, 59–64, 71, 85, 90–93, 97, 103
NBER. *See* National Bureau of Economic Research
national accounting: alternatives to, 180–83, 224–30, 258, 263–65; nature of, 24,

51–64, 109, 143–59, 194, 230–36; origins of, 10–12, 25–39, 65–102; policy makers' use of, 107–42, 160–83
national economic council, 78
national income: as central category of GDP, 10–12, 24, 26, 60–62, 78, 83–85, 94, 105, 107–16, 126–47; demand for, 55, 87, 103, 117–22; history of (*see* GDP, history of)
National Income and Product Accounts (NIPA), 143–44
National Resources Planning Board, 117
natural capital, 37, 95, 137–38, 142, 184–85, 204, 208, 223–24
nature. *See* natural capital
Nelson, Donald, 110, 113–15
neoclassical economics, 39, 52–58, 102, 123, 140, 166
Nepal, 149
New Deal, 10, 73, 82, 88, 102–8
New Economic Foundation (nef), 226–27, 344n11
New Economy Coalition, 343n11
New Jersey, shore, 196
New Orleans, 219–20
New York Times, 78, 84, 102, 105, 153, 184
no-growth economy. *See* steady-state economy
Norris, George, 70

Obama, Barack, 184, 188, 195
Obamacare. *See* Patient Protection and Affordable Care Act
objectivity, 51, 60–63, 122, 130, 147, 159, 222–27; challenges to, 71, 95, 122, 222, 236, 273
O'Brien, Ellen, 123
Occupy Wall Street, 191, 256
O'Connell, Mark, 191
OECD. *See* Organization of Economic Cooperation and Development (OECD)
oil: basis for wealth, 53, 125, 154–56, 164,187, 241, 264; consumption, 2, 170,187–88, 237, 244; companies, 5, 271; and environmental degradation, 166–69, 190, 195–96, 201, 265